Axel Munthe

BENGT JANGFELDT

AXEL MUNTHE
The Road to San Michele

I.B. TAURIS
LONDON · NEW YORK

Published in 2008 by I.B.Tauris & Co Ltd
6 Salem Road, London W2 4BU
175 Fifth Avenue, New York NY 10010
www.ibtauris.com

In the United States of America and Canada
distributed by Palgrave Macmillan, a division of St Martin's Press
175 Fifth Avenue, New York NY 10010

ISBN 978 1 84511 720 7

A full CIP record for this book is available from the British Library
A full CIP record is available from the Library of Congress

Library of Congress Catalog Card Number: available

Typeset by JCS Publishing Services Ltd, www.jcs-publishing.co.uk
Printed in the Czech Republic by FINIDR, s.r.o.

~

To Adam and Katriona Munthe,
FOR THEIR GENEROSITY AND UNCONDITIONAL TRUST

~

CONTENTS

〜

ILLUSTRATIONS

~

The Dream
1857–1889

~

Empewow of Sina

I have to be dolled up like a bride here, from morning till night, and I'm never allowed any freedom!

Axel Munthe

In March 1930 Queen Victoria of Sweden lay dying in the Villa Svezia in Rome. A young Swedish journalist tried to gain access to the house, but the footman stopped him and directed him to the queen's doctor, who happened to be passing. The doctor ticked off this journalist who dared to come and disturb the terminally ill queen. But when the reporter opened his mouth to say a few words in his own defence, a smile spread over the doctor's face. The journalist spoke the same dialect as the doctor, who promised to get in touch if there was any change in the queen's condition. Shortly afterwards the journalist received a phone call at his boarding house: 'I promised to phone. Queen Victoria is dead. You're getting the news before the legation.'

The doctor's name was Axel Munthe, a 72-year-old Swede with an astonishing career behind him and an equally remarkable future before him.

Axel Munthe belonged to a family who had fled Flanders in the mid-sixteenth century to escape the Spanish Duke of Alba's bloody rule. The family's first representative in Scandinavia appeared in Sweden during the final years of the sixteenth century. Axel's grandfather Ludvig Munthe, born in 1770, and his grandmother Elisabeth Catharina, a clergyman's daughter, had ten children, five of whom survived into adulthood. Axel's father, Fredrik, was born in 1816 at a country freehold in the vicinity of the town of Vimmerby. This is the soil in which Axel Munthe was rooted: Småland in southern Sweden in the mid-nineteenth century, or, to be more exact, the trading town of Vimmerby, a churchgoing and strongly religious environment, which would leave deep traces in Axel's character and philosophical system.

Fredrik Munthe lost his father when he was 6. His mother was short of money, and to earn an extra crust Fredrik took it upon himself to light the school fire in the mornings. This meant being up very early, he later told his children, and when he had to pass the churchyard in the winter darkness he was so frightened that he ran for all he was worth.

In 1832, when he was barely 15 years old, Fredrik was taken on as an apprentice in a pharmacy in the county town of Linköping, where he slept in a partitioned-off area under the counter along with the other apprentices. Although conditions for study were far from ideal, it was only two years later that Fredrik Munthe took his initial pharmacy examination, and in 1840 he took his pharmacy degree under the aegis of the famous chemist Jacob Berzelius. Fredrik had actually wanted to study medicine, but his mother could not afford to support him. His restlessly wandering existence continued even after he had taken his degree, but 10 years later, in 1850, he had made enough money to afford his own chemist's shop in the coastal village of Döderhultsvik, later renamed Oscarshamn after King Oscar I.

In 1853 Munthe married Aurora Ugarph, the daughter of an attorney. They were not youngsters; he was 37 years old, she was 34. The wedding night appears to have been passed in the prescribed way, as nine months later to the day, a daughter, Anna, was born to them. A year and a half later, their first son Arnold arrived, and on 31 October 1857 Axel Martin Fredrik, the hero of this tale, made his appearance. In 1860 the family moved to Vimmerby, where Fredrik bought the chemist's shop in the town; the circle was closed, Fredrik Munthe was back in his childhood town.

VIMMERBY

Vimmerby in the 1860s was a small town with about 1,800 inhabitants, and Fredrik Munthe soon attained a leading role in society. In 1861 he obtained the monopoly to practise as a chemist there, and two years later he was one of twenty men elected to the town's first council. As far as we can judge, Fredrik Munthe was a good chemist. Axel remembered with pride, 'Father was far more than the usual pill-pusher in Vimmerby', he had 'considerable knowledge of chemistry and knew more than was needed to become a professor, and [. . .] he had read as much medicine as any doctor you like [. . .] and also occupied himself a great deal with medical studies – for himself.'

A good deal of reading was done in the Munthes' home, both of secular and religious literature. On Sundays Fredrik Munthe read sermons and sang hymns to his family. And when theatrical performances for charity were given, the Munthe family simply had to take part, 'since they acted so well'. Fredrik Munthe had a pronounced musical side – as a performer as well as a listener. He is also said to have been an excellent storyteller. Aurora also sang, but her repertoire was more staid and largely consisted of hymns and spiritual songs. This musicality was inherited by Anna and Axel, who both took singing and piano lessons.

The Munthe children received their early education in Vimmerby's schools. Anna went to a girls' school, but needlework, ironing, mangling, scouring, cleaning, and so on, were things she detested, so instead she was allowed to devote herself to drawing, an interest that she would later come to practise on a professional basis.

The boys Arnold and Axel were sent to the grammar school, where Axel began in the autumn term of 1866, with a special dispensation for his young age. He showed more application than Arnold but did best in the same subjects: his marks for mathematics oscillated between acceptable and unacceptable but in history and geography and Swedish he earned good marks, like his brother. During his first years at school, there were no traces of the rich and versatile talent that Axel would later demonstrate.

A Fair-Haired, Chubby Little Chap

Axel's cousins Sofia and Fredrik Lund, who were neighbours of the Munthe family in Vimmerby, remember him as a 'fair-haired, chubby little chap' with 'a flaxen fringe and clear eyes full of wonder, which noticed everything that was going on around him and had something to say about it too'. On being asked what he was going to be when he grew up, Axel answered: 'Pweest and pweecher' or 'Empewow of Sina' – he spoke with a pronounced lisp until his teenage years. The dream of becoming emperor gradually dwindled to the more modest ambition of being a drummer.

Axel was an 'interesting object of study', not least because of his 'changeable moods' and his 'ever-changing whims'. With his sparkling good humour and his 'hilarious witticisms' he was a constant source of fun. He collected 'bones and skulls, stuffed birds and was on intimate terms with every horse, dog, ram and other tame four-footed creature'. His concern encompassed not only pets but also less domesticated species such as snakes, lizards and beetles, which 'were collected, dead or alive, in forest or field, taken home and looked after in not always very suitable places, where they sometimes came into conflict with his father's pronounced sense of tidiness'.

Axel was particularly delighted with 'ugly beasts of every kind'. Fredrik Lund remembers that his 'four- or multi-legged, flying or crawling favourites' were either 'uncommonly ugly or even displayed abnormalities that other people would have found repulsive, but which seemed to attract his particular attention'.

During a forest walk Axel found a parched animal skull. This aroused great admiration among the other boys and gave him an opportunity to demonstrate his rather bizarre sense of humour. His cousins included an engaged couple who liked to sit billing and cooing in the moonlight, and Axel had long been planning to ambush them. On the same day that the skull was found, the couple were sitting by an open window in the salon having a cuddle. As the moonlight streamed in, a wild Indian war-cry arose from the other small boys in the garden below – they had been initiated into the plan of attack on swearing the most hair-raising oath of silence – at the same time as Axel poked a long pole, with the skull on the end, in through the window and let it dangle between the lovers' own heads. His delight at the broken spell knew no limits, but was dampened when his parents and cousins heard of the prank and took him to task for it.

Axel, as we can see, had considerable talents as a young rascal. But he was also a child of great integrity with a strong need to mark out his territory. He hated 'any kind of compulsion', Sofia remembers, even as regards his clothes. On one occasion they were due to visit the vicar. When his mother insisted on a more 'gentlemanly dress', he cried out, with tragic gestures: 'I have to be dolled up like a bride here, from morning till night, and I'm never allowed any freedom!'

Axel's protest should not come as a surprise. Despite his father's musical talents, the atmosphere at home was strictly religious and no doubt quite stifling. Their acquaintances were mostly drawn from clerical families, and social life consisted mainly of innumerable coffee mornings and dinners. On at least one occasion Axel's longing for freedom led to a genuine attempt to run away. In the summer of 1865 the family were staying at a spa outside Vimmerby. Every day was characterised by unchanging routines. The boys decided to run away back home to Vimmerby and hoped their aunt would put them up. But their father caught up with the fugitives before they got away and drove them back to the spa.

Protests about clothes and attempts to run away were part of a young person's perfectly normal struggle for freedom and independence, but in Axel's case it also involved something different and deeper: a strong feeling of existential captivity that he would – unsuccessfully – try all his life to overcome.

Fredrik Munthe had had his eyes trained on Stockholm for many years, most of all because he wanted to give the boys a good education. The decision to move, however, was only taken after he discovered that they were not doing too well at school. As Vimmerby could not offer any instruction beyond the fourth class, the question of moving house was in any case an urgent one.

In October 1868 the Munthe family moved to Stockholm.

STOCKHOLM

The capital city that the Munthe family landed in was seventy times larger than Vimmerby, but still had only 130,000 inhabitants. Stockholm was a very small town compared to London, for example, where the population was over 3,500,000; it was a combination of a small town with a lingering flavour of the eighteenth century and a nascent large city with broad esplanades opening into a new century.

During this period of transition from the old to the new, grand townhouses and hovels stood side by side, and the tenants represented the various layers of society. The building in which the Munthes lived housed a motley crew of inhabitants: master mechanics and journeymen builders, washerwomen, seamen, gas-workers, cleaners, seamstresses, caretakers, stock-makers, journeymen carpenters, and so on.

Anna and Axel had plenty of opportunities to cultivate their musical talents, thanks to the Stockholm branch of the family, with whom they now had closer contact. Beateberg, the family manor outside Stockholm, was for several decades a meeting place for many of the most prominent musicians of the age, with the world-renowned singer Jenny Lind a frequent guest. In his later years, Axel Munthe reminisced in joyful tones about his childhood visits to Beateberg, where he found rich stimuli for his three main interests in life: music, sailing and animals.

In the autumn of 1868 Axel and Arnold began their studies at the Stockholm Lyceum, a private grammar school highly regarded for its humane teaching methods. Here, the cane was used far less than in the state-run educational institutions. According to a pupil who attended the school a few years before Axel, August Strindberg, it was 'a sanctuary [. . .] where human worth was assigned even to the unconfirmed, where it was not a crime to be poorly gifted, where teachers were not the deadly enemies of the young, where the headteacher was not a royal executioner, but a patriarch'. Axel's reports from his first term at school have not survived, but in the spring term of 1869 he was fourth out of eleven pupils, a good position in the upper half of the class.

The first year in Stockholm was over. Arnold had repeated both the second and third classes, and his parents now saw fit to take him out of school. He loved the sea, and in the summer of 1869 he was allowed to undertake a trial voyage to see if he was up to seafaring. While Arnold was at sea,

Axel spent his summer at a little village called Malma, studying Latin and mathematics, and hunting and stuffing birds. But he longed for his home; a letter to his parents signed 'your obedient son from henceforth' suggests that the summer school had been some kind of punishment. Worthy of note is Axel's unsentimental attitude to hunting birds, an amusement he devoted himself to wholeheartedly, and he kept tame birds in a cage at home. In later years he would not only regret this practice but thoroughly revise his views.

Whatever Axel thought of the punishment detail in Malma, it seems to have had the desired effect, as during the autumn of 1869 he moved from fourth place to top of the class. His marks were the best he received during the whole of his school career. The autumn also brought major changes for Arnold. His trial voyage had passed off successfully, and in September he started his studies at naval college.

THE WHITE BEAR

Whether it was economic necessity or boredom that made Fredrik Munthe resume his profession again is unclear, but in February 1870 he took over the White Bear Pharmacy at Nybrogatan, in a new and fashionable part of Stockholm. Socially, the move was a definite step up for the Munthe family. Only a few doors down from the Munthes, for example, lived the justice minister Baron Louis de Geer.

When, in the autumn of 1871, Axel started his first year at grammar school, it was at Stockholm's 'gymnasium' – the high school. He was only 13 years old and would celebrate his fourteenth birthday that October. As we have seen, Axel had been allowed to start school in Vimmerby at a younger age than the norm, and he was considerably younger than his classmates at the gymnasium, who were between 15 and 16. This is something one has to keep in mind when assessing his rather lacklustre school career.

After a decent performance at the end of his second year, in the spring term of 1873 the graph of his school marks pointed steeply downwards. The end of the autumn term of 1873 saw him finish with the lowest possible marks in all subjects. The situation was alarming, and at the start of 1874 Fredrik Munthe was warned that his son might have to repeat the year. With this prospect looming, Axel promised that if his father gave him 200 kronor he would try to finish high school by the summer, skipping one year of study. Fredrik took the promise seriously and gave his son the required sum, which Axel spent on private lessons. During the spring he studied so intensively that in June 1874 he was able to finish high school as a private student.

Axel completed high school one year early, in three years instead of four, and he was only 16, two years younger than the average student. His marks were not exceptional, but if school was no success story for Axel it was not lack of talent but lack of motivation that was the problem. When he wanted to, he could quickly and easily acquire the knowledge he needed. There are many indications that the institution of school in itself, with its hierarchy and regularity, provoked his instinctive disgust. There is, however, a pattern in his school career and his attitude to the different school subjects. He obtained good marks in Christianity and science, as well as in philosophy, a subject that he only studied for his high school certificate. These were interests that would persist throughout his life. Science was the basis of his future profession and philosophical and religious questions would always occupy his thoughts. Axel's interest in science was also bolstered by his father's occupation.

UPPSALA

In the autumn of 1874 Axel enrolled in the faculty of arts and sciences at Uppsala University with a view to taking a 'medico-philosophical' (pre-medical) degree. This course, which was intended to prepare the student for further medical studies, consisted of four subjects: zoology, botany, chemistry and physics.

While Axel was in Uppsala, major changes occurred within the family in Stockholm. In 1875 Munthe senior disposed of the White Bear. He must have got a good price for the chemist's shop, as later in the year he began dealing in real estate. Fredrik Munthe was thus by now a prosperous man who could afford a decent wedding for Anna, who in June 1875 married Reinhold Norstedt, an artistically gifted person, as talented a singer as he was a painter. In Anna Munthe he met a soulmate, someone just as talented as himself and just as unsure of her artistic identity.

At the beginning of July Axel travelled with his parents to a bathing spa on the south-western coast of Sweden. His cousin Ludvig recalled that uncle Fredrik and Axel kept to themselves most of the time – to 'look after themselves', for 'both of them were poorly'. This is an interesting piece of information, as it is the first indication that Axel's health was not all it should have been. Equally interesting is another glimpse of Axel that Ludvig gives in his memoirs. Among the visitors to the baths were a Mr and Mrs Robertson with their two daughters. The elder was very good-looking but not particularly gifted; the younger, by contrast, was 'ugly and wore a pince-nez, but she was intelligent and quick-witted, so that she attracted a lot of attention from cousin Axel'. Axel was drawn to whatever was odd and distinctive. Another of Axel's cousins, Fredrik Lund, noted a similar tendency during his years in Uppsala too:

> The same predilection for abnormalities and more or less unfortunate cases that he manifested during his childhood animal studies also soon emerged in his choice of companions. Many were the attempts he made to wrench distorted existences into order in one way or another, but I hardly remember a single instance where he succeeded. Nor was this perhaps his ultimate motive. He was drawn to these human curiosities – most of them the butts of his friends' practical jokes and pranks – more from natural, spontaneous fellow-feeling and, above all, an instinctive feel for psychological analysis, than from any hope of being able to set them on the right track.

Student life in Uppsala in the 1870s was admittedly unruly, with celebrations that often degenerated into orgies of drinking. Little is known about Axel's student days, but Fredrik Lund commented that Axel attracted attention with his speeches. According to cousin Fredrik, they gave evidence of his 'mastery of form' but also of his ability to 'call forth out of a momentary mood the best and finest that existed in the depths of young people's sentiments'. When reports of Axel's oratorical achievements reached his parents they were as surprised as they had been by his school-leaving certificate. Axel was 'soon in demand', Fredrik Lund explained:

> A large component of this was an unusually agreeable sociability, sensible without pretensions to dazzle, naïve and often quick witted, but most of all he gained popularity within his circle of friends through the absolutely uncalculated practical communism which he constantly practised. His purse, like his heart, stood open for every needy friend, and his good offices were wasted on not always worthy objects.

The portrait may be idealised, but one conclusion can nevertheless be drawn: that Axel must have undergone a metamorphosis since he had left home. Freed from the dominant figure of his father and from his mother's admonitions, he blossomed and revealed sides of his personality that had remained hidden until now.

One example of the tensions between Axel and his father is the dispute about the dog that Axel was so keen to have but which his father refused him. During a visit to Uppsala, Fredrik Munthe reported in a letter to his wife that Axel nagged 'night and day' about 'that blessed dog'. Considering all the coach travel between Uppsala and Stockholm, Axel's father thought that a dog would only be a nuisance: 'I have promised that when he has taken his degree he can have a dog, for God's sake, but he wants it now, and this is causing a great deal of bother.'

In June 1876 Axel's sister Anna gave birth to a daughter at the Norstedt family's mansion of Lunda. Axel and his parents travelled there in order to be godparents at the christening. The other godparents included Baron Axel von Mecklenburg and his wife Sigrid, with whom Axel now became acquainted; the meeting with the latter would prove to have unexpected and far-reaching consequences for Axel's private life.

Axel passed his pre-med. examinations on 15 September 1876, with mediocre marks. The following day he telegraphed his parents to tell them he had passed his exams, and three days later his brother-in-law Reinhold noted in his diary: 'Axel came up a.m. Had a handsome Lapland puppy with him which he calls Rick, and which he has just got for himself since he passed his degree.' Not many hours had passed after Axel's exam before he acquired the 'blessed dog' that his father had promised him!

Axel planned to undertake further studies in the medical faculty, but he was not well. After his degree examinations he moved back to Stockholm, where he stayed with his parents. He saw quite a lot of Anna and Reinhold. On 30 September Reinhold noted in his diary: 'We spent some time with my parents-in-law p.m. Axel was poorly, he had coughed up blood and is worried about his chest.' And the following day: 'Axel coughed up blood again yesterday evening, but less than before.'

At this time everyone knew what this meant: possible tuberculosis. The situation was serious and something had to be done; it was decided that Axel should spend the coming winter in a milder climate. On 30 October Reinhold noted in his diary: 'Anna at my in-laws between 7 and 8 in the morning to say goodbye to Axel. I went with them to the station to meet the morning express, where I took my leave of him.'

Here begins the story of Axel Munthe, a weak-chested young man who on the 30 October 1876 – the day before his nineteenth birthday – boarded the morning express train at Stockholm's Central Station to set out on his journey to the south.

The journey back would take sixty-seven years.

A Ruin Struck by an Earthquake

What was Axel thinking when he left Stockholm and Sweden behind him? How did he regard his childhood, his parents? As a source-book, *The Story of San Michele* is a quagmire, but as far as the depiction of his father is concerned there is good cause to take the author seriously, especially as this is backed up by other material. In the chapter 'Lapland', Axel, in a dream, asks a goblin to tell him about his father, as he remembers so little about him: 'Your father was a strange man,' the goblin explains, 'sombre and silent. He was kind to all the poor and to all animals, but seemed often hard to those around him.'

Axel often got a thrashing, but he was 'a difficult child'. He obeyed nobody and seemed not to care about his father, his mother, his sister or brother or anyone else for that matter. The only person he was fond of was his nurse Lena. 'Most of your troubles', the goblin continued, 'had to do with your animals':

> Your room was full of all sorts of animals, you even slept with them in your bed. Don't you remember how mercilessly you were flogged for lying on eggs? Every bird's egg you could get hold of you used to try to hatch out in your bed. Of course a small child cannot keep awake, every morning your bed was all in a mess with smashed eggs and every morning you were flogged for it but nothing helped. Don't you remember the evening your parents came home late from a house-party and found your sister in her nightgown sitting on the table under an umbrella screaming with terror? All your animals had escaped from your room, a bat had caught her claw in your sister's hair, all your snakes, toads and rats were crawling about on the floor and in your own bed they found a whole litter of mice. Your father gave you a tremendous thrashing, you flew at him and bit your own father in the hand. The next day you stole out of the house at daybreak after breaking into the pantry in the night to fill your knapsack with what eatables you could lay hands on, and smashing your sister's money-box and stealing all her savings – you never had any savings of your own. The whole day and the whole night all the servants were hunting for you in vain. At last your father who had galloped off to the village to speak to the police found you fast asleep in the snow by the roadside, your dog had barked as he rode past. I overheard your father's hunter telling the other horses in the stable how your father lifted you up in the saddle without saying a word and rode home with you and locked you up in a dark room on bread and water for two days and nights. On the third day you were taken to your father's room, he asked you why you had stolen out of the house. You said you were misunderstood by everybody in the house and wanted to emigrate to America.

Then there follows a distressing account that testifies to a total lack of understanding between parents and child:

> But the worst of all happened during your summer holidays when the housemaid found a human skull under your bed, a skull with a tuft of red hair still hanging onto the back of the head. The whole house was in commotion. Your mother fainted and your father gave you the severest thrashing you had ever had so far and you were again locked up in a

dark room on water and bread. It was discovered that the night before you had ridden on your pony to the village churchyard, had broken into the charnel house and stolen the skull from a heap of bones deposited in the cellar. The parson who had been the headmaster of a boys' school told your father that it was an unheard-of thing that a boy of ten should have committed such an atrocious sin against God and man. Your mother, who was a very pious woman, never got over it. She seemed almost afraid of you, and she was not the only one. She said she could not understand that she could have given birth to such a monster. Your father said that surely you had not been begotten by him but by the devil himself.

'But is all this really true what you have told me about my childhood?' Axel asks the goblin, and exclaims: 'I must have been a strange child!'

Although this account contains obvious elements of fiction, everything points to the fact that the dark description of his father and his own childhood reflected actual conditions. In a conversation with a woman friend as early as 1887, he complained that his home had been 'a ruin struck by an earthquake'.

We can only guess what kind of an 'earthquake' Axel was referring to, but there is no reason to believe that the choice of words was just an empty rhetorical figure. He wrote in a letter that his father cast 'a shadow' over the whole of his childhood and youth as a result of his 'despondency' and his 'love for solitude'. Axel added, he had 'nothing to do with his mother, and it was all the worse for me'.

Fredrik Munthe had a rich and complex personality. On the one hand he was a 'great humorist with a keen eye for the changing times', who enjoyed making music and singing. On the other hand he was an enterprising, practical handyman who at the drop of a hat would change the lock on the hall door, mend leaking windows, speculate in property, and much more besides. Photographs of him convey the impression of a man of decision, an impression that is borne out by those who knew him. 'From having been, in his young days, decidedly lively, and, as a not uncommon consequence of this, occasionally impetuous, in later years his mood seemed somewhat irascible.'

Given that this assessment comes from a nephew, it should be regarded rather as a euphemism. Fredrik Munthe was a self-made man, and saw this as a virtue. He was also relatively advanced in years – 41 years old – when Axel was born, and his health was poor. He suffered from a hernia and a kidney ailment that he tried to treat with repeated visits to health spas. This undoubtedly added to his intolerance, not least as regards his youngest son's dreamy and imaginative disposition.

Axel, in his turn, was an over-sensitive child who felt himself to be strange and odd, and his father to be unreasonably strict. His father reacted as one might have expected to Axel's attempts to break free – with verbal and physical abuse. Although Axel's deeply pious mother is described as 'a humorous personality', she was also a woman 'of a prosaic disposition' who failed to understand her creative son. In the give and take of married life she was undoubtedly the weaker party and had little to set against her harsh and domineering husband. The result was that Axel took refuge in his own world. He recalled later that as a boy he had been 'uncommunicative, odd and not well liked'. A common factor in all his interests – music, sailing, nature and animals – is that they all made possible a flight into a world where he was not dependent on others.

When, in adult life, Axel wished to describe people in his immediate surroundings in a positive way, he always did this with exactly the same phrase: 'They are so kind to me' – which suggests that 'kindness' was in rather short supply in his childhood home. This sensitivity to signs of goodwill no doubt originated in his father's strictness and lack of understanding for his talent. One result of this was Axel's lifelong endeavour to be seen and acknowledged.

Despite the differences between father and son there were also traits – both positive and negative – which they shared, and which in Axel's case would be accentuated with the passing years: on the one side humour, musicality and a lively temperament; on the other, restlessness, nervousness, volatility and impetuousness, melancholy and insomnia. When Axel says to the goblin that he has no peace, that he cannot stay anywhere, cannot forget and cannot sleep, the latter replies: 'That is just like your father. How often have I watched him wandering up and down in his room the whole night!'

Doctor Munthe

Are you mad? You owe me nothing!
Axel Munthe to Ville Vallgren

AXEL LEFT SWEDEN just in time for the spa season, which began on 1 November. The destination was Menton by the French–Italian border, a popular health resort for tubercular north Europeans. During his stay there Axel became acquainted with Amadée Courty, a gynaecology professor who took him under his wing. Courty was director of the surgical clinic at the Hôtel-Dieu Saint-Eloi in Montpellier and editor of the journal *Annales de Gynécologie*. He persuaded Axel to enrol in the medical faculty at Montpellier, one of the oldest and best in France, with origins in the twelfth century; Rabelais, among others, had studied there. Like Menton, Montpellier had a favourable climate.

Axel was extremely reticent about his years of study in Montpellier. When in 1883 his cousin Ludvig asked him for information to be included in his history of the family, Axel dictated the details to him: 'I earnestly beg you that, as far as my professors at Montpellier are concerned, you write only "Studied physiology under Prof. Rouget (now Claude Bernard's successor in Paris), surgery under Prof. Dubrueil and gynaecology under Prof. Courty." Not a word more! *S'il vous plaît.*' One has to ask oneself why Axel was so concerned to present his studies in exactly these words. Did he have something to hide? Was he involved in a dispute with someone? It is not improbable. As we shall see, Axel's relations with his medical colleagues were often filled with conflict.

However little we know about Axel's first time abroad, one thing is certain: some time before the New Year of 1877 he visited Capri for the first time. Why, and in what circumstances, is unknown, but in a letter of December 1888 he stated that his first visit to the island had taken place twelve years earlier. There is a picture of Axel taken in a photographer's studio in Naples, perhaps during his first stay in those parts: a young boy in pince-nez and a slouch hat. It is as if he had wanted to immortalise the moment – his first encounter with the Bay of Naples.

The Mediterranean culture was no doubt a revelation to Axel, unexpected and shocking – as for most northerners when they are first confronted with the south. The last hundred years had seen a veritable cult of Italy emerge in northern Europe, thanks to Goethe's *Italian Journey* and *Roman Elegies* and travelogues like Ferdinand Gregorovius's *Wanderjahre in Italien*. In Axel's case the first acquaintance would ripen into a love affair that he celebrated from his first published line to his last.

Axel's first period of study at Montpellier was over by the beginning of June 1877, when he travelled home to Sweden for the summer. He was said to be looking 'pretty healthy' – as opposed to his father, who after Axel's departure for France had been afflicted by stomach cancer, and in addition was ill with rheumatic fever during the winter. Axel remained in Sweden during the first part of September, but on the 17th Reinhold and Anna received an ominous message from her parents: 'Axel returning to Montpellier. Has not been feeling well.' The illness still had its claws in him.

On 6 November Fredrik Munthe died. There is no evidence that Axel was told in time to get to Stockholm for the funeral on the 14th. His father was 61 at the time of his death, but judging from photographs he was prematurely aged. He left a considerable fortune, corresponding to about 4.5 million kronor in today's money (£330,000). His widow remained in undisturbed possession of the estate, but Axel borrowed money from it to finance his stay abroad and his studies.

SWEDISH PRUSSIANS

Axel's stay in France coincided with the great migration of Swedish artists to Paris in the 1870s. The young painters were stifled by the stale atmosphere in Sweden, where artistic life was dominated by historical painting and a generally conservative academic taste. They made their way abroad, to the leading contemporary art centres of Düsseldorf and – above all – Paris. It was in France that landscape painting developed, it was there that the battle over the new art was taking place. By 1878 no fewer than thirty-one Swedish artists were earning their living in Paris, among them painters who were later to become famous, like Carl Larsson and Ernst Josephson. That same year, Reinhold and Anna joined the Paris Swedes. Reinhold studied painting and also taught himself etching. Anna took lessons in painting too. Now the singer Reinhold Norstedt and his wife Anna became painters in earnest.

Less than a decade had passed since the Franco-Prussian War and Paris was still scarred by the conflict. The Tuileries and the Hôtel-de-Ville lay in ruins and a widespread hatred of the Germans pervaded the country. To a French ear the Scandinavian languages sounded suspiciously like German, and Scandinavians were careful not to say *ja* or other words with a Germanic tinge. *Prussiens* – Prussians – was a term of abuse that was often hurled at them nevertheless, a fact that Axel would later enshrine in literary terms in 'The Giant', one of the most hilarious chapters in *The Story of San Michele*, where drunken Swedes are thrown out of a pub, accused of being 'German savages'.

Most of the artists lived in Montmartre, where they also had their favourite haunts. The Café de l'Ermitage was situated on Boulevard de Clichy, and on the other side of the boulevard, on the corner with Rue des Martyrs, was the Restaurant des Lilas – usually known as 'The Corner'. This was where they took their meals and played cards and billiards, and it also served as their postal address.

Axel soon won himself a place in the gang through the agency of Reinhold and Anna and their contacts, but also thanks to his own social skills, not least his singing and music-making. The Finnish sculptor Ville Vallgren remembered Axel's tuneful voice: 'When he sat down at the piano [. . .] and sang Swedish and Italian melodies in his attractive light baritone, women and men alike had tears in their eyes.' His constant companion was Puck, a Great Dane which he had obtained during his very first months in France.

On 17 June 1879 Anna and Reinhold travelled to Sweden for the summer, and two months later Axel was in Stockholm himself. On 14 August Reinhold wrote in his diary: 'Heard in a letter from mother-in-law that Axel had arrived and that he has completed his studies and is a fully-fledged doctor.'

It is an astounding piece of news – Axel was a 'fully-fledged doctor' after only five terms' study at Montpellier! He had certainly shown proof of his learning capacity on a previous occasion, when he had swotted for his school-leaving certificate in a few months – but a medical degree, after five terms? If the information is correct, it is yet another confirmation of the exceptional powers of study that Axel could mobilise at will. Considering that his studies were carried out in a foreign language, his achievement must be regarded as remarkable.

In October Axel was back at Montpellier. From there he reported that he seemed about to get more work at the Hôtel-Dieu than he could ever have dreamed of, but that he was quite content with that. Professor Dubrueil, 'who was to have the grey monster' (Puck, the dog), had left, and the responsibility had devolved onto a 12-year-old patient.

The comment about Professor Dubrueil and Puck is remarkable. If the famous professor looked after Axel's dog – and Axel allowed him to do so

– then there must have been a strong relationship of trust between them. Probably Dubrueil, like so many other people, had been captivated by Axel's charm and talent. As we shall see, there were several elderly gentlemen of good position in society who were charmed by Axel and who by their support and encouragement would come to play an important role in his career. One does not need to be a professional psychologist to see here a father–son relationship at work that replaced the original one.

Axel could not take Puck with him to work, but during his long wanderings in Italy the dog was always by his side. Fredrik Lund recounts an episode that must have taken place sometime before 1880 (when it is referred to for the first time). During a stay in Taormina Axel and Puck went out one day to look for the robber chieftain Leone and his gang:

> He did not find the robbers, but they found him and, despite Puck's protests, they took him off to their hiding-place up in the mountains. Luckily the gang had just had a brush with the militia and had many wounded men among them, besides which their grim leader, Leone, had been taken prisoner. Munthe's medical knowledge came in useful here – he plastered arms and legs, extracted bullets, sewed up gashes and became a close friend of the Gunelli brothers, Leone's adjutants, whom he declared to be complete gentlemen who at least understood the art of living, even if their education in good manners had not stretched so far as the art of allowing others to live.

Things may not have happened in quite this way, but that is not the important thing. The most interesting feature of this 'Munthe tale' is that it is so early. It shows that the desire for adventure that was so typical of Axel was already fully developed during his years of study in France – and that he was already famous for this.

I Am Not Here to Sing Your Praises!

On 10 April 1880 Aurora Munthe departed this life, having just celebrated her sixty-first birthday. Axel was not notified of his mother's death until two weeks later, but it is uncertain whether he would have gone to Stockholm even if he had been told in time; when word reached him he was wholly taken up with work on his doctoral thesis. After passing his preliminary degree in Montpellier, Axel completed his studies in Paris in the spring of 1880. He lived in a student lodging in the Hôtel de l'Avenir on Rue Madame, not far from the École de Médecine on Boulevard Saint-Germain. During the day he practised in the wards and at night he smoked copious amounts of cigarettes, reading Charcot's *Maladies*, Troussaux's *Clinique de l'Hôtel Dieu* and other text books.

Mornings in the wards of La Salpêtrière and Hôtel-Dieu and La Pitié, going from bed to bed to read chapters in the book of human suffering, written with blood and tears. Afternoons in the dissecting rooms and amphitheatres of L'École de Médecine or the laboratories of the Institut Pasteur, watching in the microscope with wondrous eyes the mystery of the unseen world, the infinitely small beings, arbiters of the life and death of man. Nights of vigil in the Hôtel de l'Avenir, precious nights of toil to master the hard facts, the classical signs of disorder and disease collected and sifted by observers from all lands, so necessary and so insufficient for the making of a doctor. Work! Work! Work!

The account comes from *The Story of San Michele*; no documentation from his period of study in Paris has been preserved.

On 2 August 1880 Axel defended his doctoral thesis. It was on a gynaecological topic: *Prophylaxie et traitement des hémorrhagies post-partum* – 'On bleeding from the womb after childbirth', in Axel's own translation. The chairman of the degree-awarding panel was Professor Depaul of the Paris maternity clinic; by his side sat Charles Richet, professor of physiology, author, inventor and later Nobel prize-winner for medicine, and Professor Jean Martin Charcot, nerve specialist at the Salpêtrière.

On the title page of the thesis it is clearly stated that the author was born in Sweden on 31 October 1857, a piece of information that was in no way accidental. It was an era marked by patriotic sentiments, and the disputation began with a nationalistically tinged attack on Axel, which his cousin Ludvig Munthe preserved for posterity:

The president launched into a bitter critique of the respondent and his thesis, a critique which characteristically enough was mostly concerned with the fact that 'when the author had sought the honour of being created a doctor in the famous faculty in Paris, he nevertheless seems to have despised the medical authorities in France, some of whom wrote in the field of gynaecology, and some of whom were even present here. Instead, he had cited Germans, like Spiegelberg and Scanzoni!' [. . .] [The young respondent] answered that if he had suspected that politics would constitute an important part of these scientific proceedings, then he would certainly not have omitted to include in his thesis on a branch of the art of obstetrics a declaration of political allegiance. Moreover, he would not shirk such a task even now, if such a declaration might contribute to deciding the correct method of handling the medical procedure in question. If the aforesaid authorities from Germany, whom he maintained were the most eminent living at the present time, were so unknown in this circle, that was something that he could only deplore, but this did not give him the right – nor did it imply any duty – to ignore them and, at the cost of the truth, praise only the French scholars whose importance, by the way, he would be the first to respectfully acknowledge. [. . .] However, the panel moved on at last from this type of comment to a more meticulous scrutiny of the work itself, which in the end, like its author's defence, received the most unstinting acknowledgement.

Axel's other cousin, Fredrik Lund, adds that 'the respondent [. . .] was so annoyed that, forgetting all academic decorum, he climbed straight up to the podium and began his reply with a declaration which was from an objective viewpoint totally justified but in form rather blunt: "*Messieurs, je ne suis pas ici pour chanter vos éloges!*" (Gentlemen, I am not here to sing your praises!)'.

One of Axel Munthe's defining characteristics was his tendency, in all kinds of situations, to speak his mind. It was a basic character trait that won him respect and friendship, but also gained him bitter enemies. In reality, Axel's obstinacy did not confine itself to citing German authorities: he also maintained that French methods of delivering babies were out-of-date and recommended instead a method named after the Leipzig professor of obstetrics, Credé – this had been put into practice in Germany, Austria, Britain and the Scandinavian countries, and had been proven to lead to fewer haemorrhages.

'I was the youngest Doctor in France when I defended my thesis,' he wrote several years later to his cousin Ludvig, 'which the old boys threw in my face as if it made my reckless behaviour during my disputation all the more shocking in their eyes.' The thesis was Axel's first published work. Although it was a publication with scientific pretensions, he found it difficult to keep his refractory ego in check. When he talks in the foreword about the danger that haemorrhages in childbirth pose for the mother, it is not so much the researcher's voice we hear as that of the daredevil doctor – and author:

Within the art of medicine there are hardly any instances which demand a greater combination of dexterity, cold-bloodedness and energy. It is not like in surgical interventions, where one can stand beside the patient calmly investigating his state of health, anticipate different eventualities, consider the complications which may occur and prepare oneself to combat them. In the case of a haemorrhage in childbirth one is suddenly faced with a life-threatening danger. Here, it is first and foremost a question of acting quickly if one wishes to succeed. One knows very well that the slightest hesitation, the slightest doubt, can lead to the woman's death. One also knows that one is usually the only person answerable. For our art is powerful in those cases we are discussing. The results achieved do not belong to those doubtful outcomes which our science so abounds in, and which an honourable person will wish to have nothing to do with.

Here, even the most sceptical of doctors still knows that his art is the art of curing, and that there really are cases where he has the right to say to himself: I have saved a life.

Axel's boldness and fighting spirit reflect the general development within medical science during the second half of the nineteenth century. In the 1870s and 1880s great medical breakthroughs were being made. In the same year that Axel defended his thesis, Louis Pasteur began his studies on rabies, and five years later a vaccine was tried out for the first time on a human being. The first successful operation on a gastric ulcer was performed in 1881; the first operation to remove a gallstone was carried out the following year; the first operation on an appendix in 1886; and the first electrocardiogram was in 1887. Cures for consumption and cholera were on the way. It was an epoch redolent of optimism and belief in progress.

Axel had already run through the greater part of his inheritance from his father, and his thesis had been printed with the help of money sent from Stockholm. But there was still some money left, and a week after Axel had defended his thesis he wrote to the notary in Stockholm to ask for the last of it. He needed to buy surgical instruments. The letter had the desired effect and Axel was allowed to draw out 1,002 kronor, which supposedly was the whole remaining amount due to him.

In the letter to the notary, who was an old friend of the family, Axel informed him that he had an offer to accompany one of the leading families in Paris to Italy, 'perhaps to Egypt', as their private physician. 'If things turn serious in the Orient,' he added, 'I'll apply to the Red Cross as a field-surgeon and will in that case travel down there from Italy, and then at all events I can't arrive completely empty-handed.'

What Axel did not mention was that he had become acquainted with a Swedish girl, Ultima Hornberg, born in 1861, the daughter of a chemist. She and Axel seem to have met in the summer of 1880, when Ultima was studying art in Paris. His secretiveness is not surprising. Why should he disclose his dealings with the opposite sex to an old codger in Stockholm, especially as he was asking for money? However, his silence about the relationship with Ultima is symptomatic, and part of a pattern that became clearer still with time. In his letters, Axel hardly ever names the women who surround him. In this particular case it might be thought rather remarkable, however, as three months later he and Ultima would become husband and wife.

In the run-up to the wedding Axel travelled to Naples with the French family and spent the autumn on Capri. In November he returned to Paris, where he celebrated his stag night with his artist friends. At the theatre and dance hall Elysée Mont Martre they misbehaved loudly in Swedish to such an extent that they were shown the door, suspected of being Germans. Axel had two gold watches on him, his own and another that he was going to give to his bride. The whole company ended up in jail, with Axel under suspicion of being a pickpocket. They were set free, however, presumably after the intervention of the Swedish legation.*

The wedding took place in Stockholm on 24 November 1880. The guests consisted mainly of the bridegroom's artist friends, including, among others, Carl Larsson. Axel's speech of thanks was by all accounts an object lesson in eloquence. Among other things he described how, as a child, he had believed that all married couples had the same date of birth, as his own parents always celebrated their birthday together (in actual fact his mother was born on 16 March and his father on the 17th). He had therefore often brooded over how he was going to meet a girl who, like himself, was born on the last day of October.

After the wedding Axel and Puck returned to Capri, this time with Ultima. But it was not a honeymoon. It was instead Axel's health problems that necessitated the stay in southern climes.

In March 1881 Axel travelled over to Ischia to lend his assistance in the aftermath of the earthquake that had devastated Capri's neighbouring island. In the spring a typhus epidemic broke out on Capri; Axel worked as a volunteer doctor but fell victim to the fever himself. 'Axel fell ill last week with typhoid fever,' Ultima wrote on 7 April in a letter to Axel's cousin Ludvig in Stockholm. 'He is certainly on the road to recovery now, but is still frail and will be so for a long time yet.'

It was during this first lengthy stay on Capri that Axel laid the groundwork of his popularity with the people of the island, who with the passing of the years would come to look on him as something of a saint. By 1881 the population was 4,848, of whom 2,827 lived in the island's lower town, Capri, and 2,021 in the upper town, Anacapri. There was no health-care to speak of, and only three doctors on the whole island. Axel's efforts were accordingly very welcome, particularly as he did not charge his patients.

When his artist friend Carl Skånberg visited Italy that same winter in an attempt to cure his asthma, he bumped into Axel: 'I met Munthe on my last day in Naples,' he reported to their mutual friend, the artist Johan Ericson. 'He pretended not to notice me, told me a bunch of anecdotes and was actually quite refreshing. He'll go far in future – devil take the fellow, he'll definitely wear an Italian ribbon one day.'

---

* In *The Story of San Michele* – the chapter entitled 'The Giant' – this story is transferred to Ville Vallgren's wedding in 1882, which is logical, given that Axel portrays himself in the book as unmarried.

Skånberg was right. Axel's contributions were noted in official circles, and in 1882 he was appointed a Knight of the Italian Order of the Crown.

His Excellency Georg Sibbern

In the summer of 1881 the Munthe family – Axel, Puck and Ultima – settled in Paris for good. Their first home was at 5 rue de Thann by the fashionable Parc Monceau, in the midst of the new middle-class Paris that was emerging from Baron Haussmann's city plan. The building was only two years old, and the apartment a large one. The choice of address indicates that Axel was aiming high. Certainly he was a French doctor, but he had only lived for short periods in the French capital and his circle of acquaintances consisted mainly of Swedes and other Scandinavians. Now that he planned to make his living as a doctor, he had to expand his clientele, and the choice of address was an important ingredient in this endeavour. His initial capital came in the form of a promissory note from Arnold for 2,000 kronor, around £7,500 in today's money. As already mentioned, Axel had already run through his inheritance.

Sometime around the New Year, Axel wrote a letter to his Norwegian relative, Bredo von Munthe af Morgenstierne, whom he had met several years earlier in Rome. Axel's main purpose with the letter was to ask a favour. Bredo's maternal uncle Georg Sibbern was none other than Sweden–Norway's ambassador to Paris and someone whom Axel was keen to meet. Georg Sibbern (1816–1901) was one of Norway's leading statesmen and diplomats. His postings included St Petersburg, Copenhagen, London, Washington and Constantinople before he became premier of Norway in 1858; his last post was as minister in Paris from 1878. He was married to an Englishwoman, Maria Soane, paternal granddaughter of one of England's leading architects, Sir John Soane.

Axel was received by Sibbern and one month later he came in his professional capacity to check His Excellency's heart; after this his visits became more and more frequent. The Sibberns seem to have fallen for Axel's charm, and the elderly diplomatic couple – aged 65 and 66 respectively – and the young doctor and his wife – he 24, she 21 – soon began to meet on a social basis. From March onwards Axel visited the Sibberns several times a week.

The relationship between Sibbern and Axel had clear parallels to that between father and son, and Axel himself explained that the ministerial couple treated him as if he had been 'their own son'. 'They are', Axel wrote, 'so kind' to himself and Ultima; Sibbern is 'a man of honour from head to toe and his wife is one of the kindest people I have ever seen – my wife is often invited out to drive with her and she is so extraordinarily kind towards my child-wife'.

From the very beginning of their acquaintance Sibbern and Axel had long discussions about the latter's 'occupation as a physician'. Axel saw the doctor's job as a calling and found it difficult to accept payment for his services. When Mrs Sibbern wanted to give him a fee of 1,000 francs (approximately £2000 in today's money) he refused to accept it, but Sibbern tried to persuade him that he needed something to live on, like everybody else. Until this point Axel seems to have subsisted mainly on inherited money and bills of exchange. After much hesitation Axel decided to accept the money.

Sibbern had for several years been in the habit of spending a few weeks in the summer at the spa of Bad Schwalbach, near Wiesbaden, and as early as this first summer of their friendship, Axel accompanied him there as his personal physician. Life in the spa was strictly regulated. Every morning one took the same stroll, drank the prescribed number of glasses of Weinbrunnen and Stahlbrunnen, took one's bath, ate one's meals and drank one's coffee at set hours of the day. Axel and Sibbern were together during all the waking hours.

The Artists' Doctor

Even though Axel assiduously cultivated Sibbern and other diplomats, this reflected only one side of his character and identity. Now that he was permanently resident in Paris, he also started seeing a lot more of the Swedish artists, who were 'as proud as could be of their fellow-countryman who had taken his doctor's degree in the French medical faculty'. All of them were in Paris to further their careers, and here was one who had enjoyed unprecedented success! Axel was a frequent visitor in these circles, both in Paris and in the painters' colony of Barbizon in the Fontainebleau forest, where he and Ultima used to go at the weekends. Ville Vallgren left the following portrait of him from this period: 'Doctor Munthe was a tall, slender, stately man with moustaches and a short goatee. He wore blue-tinted spectacles as he suffered from weak eyes. The most distinctive thing about him was his sympathetic manner. Wherever he went, one felt a sympathetic warmth radiate from his noble personality. So it was no wonder that he made so many friends.'

Another, painterly, portrait was signed by Ernst Josephson, whom Munthe treated for syphilis. According to Axel, it was painted in 1881 or 1882 while he was staying in Barbizon. Its value resides not least in the fact that Axel, throughout his life, harboured a strong distaste for being portrayed, either on canvas or on photographic paper. Apart from Josephson's painting there are only a few photographs of him that can be dated to this period. In Josephson's picture we see a pale-faced young man with sensitive features. One lens of his spectacles is frosted. His right eye had been damaged by a severe bout of scarlet fever in childhood, and his sight was adversely affected.

The artists' high regard for Axel depended in turn not only on his social skills but also on the fact that, like his Swedish colleague in the medical profession in Paris, Dr Gustaf Norström, he refused to accept payment for his services. 'If any of us artists were ill we always went to Munthe,' remembered Ville Vallgren. 'Not only would he never take any money from us; he would stuff 20 francs into our pockets. If it happened later that we artist-slaves came up with the idea of paying him, he would say: "Are you mad? You owe me nothing!"' A similar story is told by Carl Larsson.

LETTERS FROM NAPLES

Better to be Don Quixote than Hamlet! Better to be the self-sacrificing fool who battles against the sails of the windmills than the inert doubter who lives off his own melancholy.

Queen Elizabeth of Romania to Princess Stéphanie

THE YEAR 1884 began with Axel being appointed a Chevalier of the Légion d'Honneur: a symbolic prelude to a year that would bring a significant change in his life, the year in which he would gain yet another identity – that of an author. But before this, another important event took place. In the summer of 1884 Georg Sibbern retired, left his post as Swedish–Norwegian minister in Paris and settled in Stockholm. He was accompanied to Stockholm by Ultima and Axel, who was caring for the increasingly frail Mrs Sibbern.

On 3 August 1884 Axel went to Lunda. He travelled alone, Ultima remaining in Stockholm with the Sibberns. The manor house of Lunda had been in the Norstedt family's possession since the beginning of the nineteenth century and now belonged to Axel's brother-in-law Reinhold. The Norstedt family's musical talents made Lunda a centre of social life in the area. The guests included Sigrid von Aken and her husband, Baron Axel von Mecklenburg from the nearby estate of Högsjö.

Sigrid von Mecklenburg had been born in 1852 and was twelve years younger than her husband, a chamberlain who was 'quite fat' and 'an exceptionally jovial character', but only ten years older than her children's tutor, the young writer Tor Hedberg, who was afflicted by unhappy – and unrequited – feelings of love for her.

The baroness's coolness towards the inhibited and charmless Tor Hedberg was not because she saved her feelings for the baron – the marriage was not a happy one. The person who had captured her heart was Axel Munthe, who seems already to have fallen in love with her on the first occasions when he stayed at Lunda and Högsjö, when he was 20 and she was 25. They saw each other again during his repeated summer stays – but it is only now, in August 1884, that their romance stands out.

In a letter to his parents, Hedberg described Sigrid as 'a bit haughty at first but that disappeared on closer inspection, and she now appears to be very amiable. As regards her outward appearance, I can tell you that she is very sweet and pretty.' What struck Hedberg as 'haughtiness' might very well have been an expression of other facets of Sigrid von Mecklenburg, who was said to be 'rather taciturn and reserved', 'religious and serious, with a rather gloomy temperament'. After a few weeks, however, Hedberg's impression of the baroness was wholly positive, he called her 'a very amiable and loveable woman' and claimed to be very fond of her.

Apparently, Axel had married Ultima in the hope that he could thereby forget his feelings for Sigrid, but this had not worked. After little more than a week with his sister and brother-in-law at Lunda Axel went on to Högsjö where he stayed for two weeks. The number of letters and telegrams that were exchanged between Axel and Sibbern during his absence from Stockholm demonstrates that Axel's feelings for Sigrid were as strong as ever. The untenable nature of his relationship with Ultima was remorselessly exposed, and he underwent a severe emotional crisis. The care that the Sibberns lavished on Ultima during Axel's absence also bears witness to the problems in her marriage.

On 26 August Axel returned to Stockholm, but after only three weeks he was back at Högsjö. Before this second visit Sibbern noted in his diary that Axel was in 'a troubled mood' and that he and his wife were 'worried [. . .] about Dr Munthe'.

Axel left Högsjö on 29 September, but carried Sigrid von Mecklenburg with him in his heart; their paths would cross again. His next stop was Paris.

CHOLERA ASIATICA

During his stay in Sweden Axel could read almost daily reports in the biggest Stockholm newspaper, *Stockholms Dagblad*, about the cholera epidemic that had broken out in southern Europe and had cost thousands of lives.

The epidemic variant of cholera, an infectious disease with its roots in India, is called *cholera asiatica*. Despite several epidemics during the eighteenth century, it was not until 1817 that the disease spread beyond its area of origin. A few years later it reached Astrakhan, on the Caspian Sea. The next epidemic, in 1831, affected most countries in Europe. During the next few decades Europe was hit time and time again. In the 1870s it seemed that cholera had been pushed back into its original homeland, but in June 1884 it emerged that cholera had again reached Europe.

The infection is spread via drinking-water, food and clothes soiled by excrement. Therefore it is easily passed on by people on the move. The disease has a speedy course that consists of a high fever, violent fits of vomiting and diarrhoea, which dehydrate the sufferer; death often ensues after only a few hours. Cholera was a deeply undemocratic illness; it throve best in unhealthy slums and undernourished stomachs. In better-nourished people, the virus was destroyed by the stomach juices.

The cause of the contagion itself, *vibrio cholerae*, the 'cholera bacillus', was discovered in 1883 by the German physician Robert Koch (who the previous year had established that the cause of tuberculosis lay in the tubercle bacillus, a discovery that won him the 1905 Nobel Prize for medicine). It was in the course of a study trip to Egypt that he came across the cholera bacterium, yet he could not prove scientifically that *vibrio cholerae* was the cause of the illness and not just something that arose in its wake. This uncertainty led to strongly divergent views on methods of treatment, not to mention that in any case many French doctors refused to accept a German scientist's discovery. Mutual animosity and rivalry were still strong after the war of 1870–71. This time, in the summer of 1884, the epidemic was believed to have been carried to Toulon by a French warship, from where it soon spread to Marseilles. The first cases in the north Italian town of La Spezia were reported at the end of July.

When Axel opened his *Stockholms Dagblad* on 1 September he would have read, under the heading 'Cholera', that the epidemic had claimed its first victims in Naples: three people had fallen ill and two had died. Two days later, the daily toll of sick and dead in Naples was 122 and sixty-nine respectively, which accounted for more than half of all the cases in the whole of Italy. Naples was the epicentre of the cholera. Panic spread quickly among the illiterate and superstitious population, along with rumours – for instance, that doctors were being paid for each dead cholera patient and that they would receive a pension when the total reached 1,000. There were violent incidents and frequent outrages of various kinds.

On 8 September, barely a week after the first verified cases, the daily totals of sick and dead were 653 and 310 respectively; the following day it was 750 and 446, the day after that 966 and 474 – eighty per cent of all the cases in Italy! King Umberto defied his advisers and visited the newly established cholera hospitals and the most afflicted areas. The cholera now reached its peak and the masses were gripped by 'a frantic fear and despair'. According to the 18 September edition of the newspaper, they had an 'inborn antipathy towards medical care and the ordinances of the modern state', which evoked 'a wild ferment, a general madness which turned against doctors and police, against all authority'.

By the end of September, 150,000 people, a third of the population, had fled the city – that section of the population which had the means to do so and which, ironically, was at least risk of catching cholera. On 21 September, the Italian Health Commission reported 10,000 sick and 5,000 dead; *The Times* estimated that the total was double this. The bulk of the evidence suggests that the Health Commission's figures were wrong. For psychological reasons they did not want to admit the true amount of victims, but even if they had wished to do so, it would have been difficult. There were no reliable statistics and many people died and were buried without first visiting a hospital.

It was at some point during his reading of these reports in *Stockholms Dagblad* that Axel took the decision to set out for Naples. In Stockholm, Ultima waited anxiously for news from her husband. When, on 29 September, she at last heard from him, he wrote from Högsjö to inform her that he was travelling direct to Paris the same day. The following day Sibbern also received a letter. It clearly contained an appeal for money, for the very next day he instructed the consul at the legation in Paris to give Axel a loan of 1,000 francs.

VEDI NAPOLI E POI MORI

As late as a quarter of a century earlier, Naples had been the capital of the Kingdom of the Two Sicilies, which covered the southern half of Italy. Since the Congress of Vienna in 1815 the peninsula had consisted of a number of small states, of which the largest, after the Two Sicilies, was Sardinia – also called Savoy or Piedmont – in its north-western corner. On the opposite side of the mid-part of Italy stretched the Papal States, a secular possession tied to the Holy See.

In countries that were split up into smaller principalities – like Germany and Italy – the idea of a nation-state grew in strength during the nineteenth century. In Italy the dream of a national re-awakening, a *risorgimento*, had been called into being by the French Revolution and Napoleon I. The goal was the building of a modern state with a liberal stamp that could confer political unity and strength on the country, as well as re-creating something of the lustre of Classical antiquity and the Renaissance period.

Other important features of this *risorgimento* were the desire to break the power of the Church and to even out the economic and social differences between the north and south of Italy. Those who lived in the north regarded southern Italy, with some justification, as a backward outpost inhabited by illiterates, crushed by poverty and afflicted with gangs of bandits, the *Camorra*.

Italy was finally united, after years of strife, but also with the support of plebiscites that were carried out in the different states. In the Two Sicilies there was an almost unanimous will to unite with Sardinia, which had already been reformed by Camillo di Cavour; similarly in the Papal States – apart from the City of Rome itself. In 1861 a parliament met that represented the whole country (apart from the Veneto and Rome) and the Kingdom of Italy was proclaimed with Vittorio Emanuele II as head of state. The Veneto joined in 1866 and Rome four years later.

Many political goals were realised in the new Italy, not least the anti-clerical ones. But the other ambition, to reform the socially and economically backward southern end of the country, remained unrealised. Many far-sighted social projects were proposed in an attempt to reconstruct and clean up Italy's most populous city, but the economic means were lacking, and when the cholera broke out, Naples was just as ill-prepared as on previous occasions.

In actual fact, Naples in 1884 furnished the perfect conditions for an epidemic of *cholera asiatica*. Poverty was abysmal, living conditions were wretched, a drainage system was lacking, drinking-water was polluted and health-care neglected. These social evils did not, however, affect the whole of Naples but chiefly the lower, poorer and overpopulated parts of the city. In the upper part, situated up on the hill, where the richer people lived, the situation was significantly better.

In 1884 Naples had 496,000 inhabitants. Of these, 300,000 lived in the lower city, which meant a population density of 130,000 per square kilometre – compared with London's 13,000 and Rome's 28,000. In the very poorest quarters seven people were squeezed into a room of five square metres, and the ceiling was so low that one could hardly stand upright. According to the *British Medical Journal* the slums in Naples' lower city were the worst in Europe and could only be compared to those of Cairo. Others thought that Dickens's East End or the Manchester that had outraged Friedrich Engels paled in comparison to the reality of Naples. The cliché 'See Naples and then die' had received an extra connotation that was hardly suitable for tourist brochures.

By 5 October Axel was still in the French capital, but he seems to have set out for Naples via Rome the same day. In an undated letter written immediately after his arrival, he described his first impressions for Sigrid von Mecklenburg:

Morning in the cholera hospital instead of walks in the forest, the forenoon spent opening corpses in the search for cholera bacteria instead of cigarettes after coffee and a walk with the Baron to meet the postman. In the afternoon I sleep and the nights I spend making my rounds of the poor quarter, where a wretchedness that is nameless meets my eyes. [. . .] Don't be frightened by my awful letters, but what shall I write about – having a head full of thoughts about cholera is not the worst thing. I wonder if you can read any of this letter, Baroness – I hardly believe I could do so myself – perhaps I am also a little tired as I have had no rest at night since I left my armchair at Högsjö [. . .].

Although Axel was slaving away as a doctor round the clock, he found time to convey his impressions to Sweden. He wrote letters to the von Mecklenburgs, as well as to other addressees, among them Ultima and Sibbern. In addition he wrote letters of a less private nature: between October and December, no fewer than thirteen of Axel's 'Letters from Naples' were published in *Stockholms Dagblad*.

This was the first time that Axel had appeared in print since his doctoral thesis. What was it that persuaded him to take up his pen? In later life he explained that he had sent a letter about the cholera epidemic to a friend who 'happened to be the editor of the paper and he asked for more material he could publish'. But the letters also had a concrete source of inspiration, which was their addressee. He wrote to Axel von Mecklenburg: 'Your wife said that when I got here, she wished to know how things were for me in Naples. I could not write to her as often as I wished, but in this way she can see how things appear. Tell her that if the letters contain anything she likes, then it is written for her; if there is anything she finds droll, then it is intended to make her smile [. . .].'

The explanation is gallant but not entirely serious. For even if the baroness was constantly in Axel's thoughts, the impulse to write about the cholera outbreak should be sought nearer home, in Axel himself. There is some evidence that he had long desired to try his powers as an author and that the epidemic was the trigger. For his own part he waved aside his journalistic debut with a reference to his shortage of money: 'If I had not been as poor as I was [. . .] then I would have carried on as before, i.e. I would have kept my thoughts to myself and not exhibited them in print for payment.' But this apparent indifference was a defence mechanism that was rolled out each time Axel shrugged off his doctor's persona. In actual fact he had nothing against the attention he drew on himself; quite the contrary.

As for the actual decision to travel down to Naples, it can be explained by at least two reasons: one personal, and one existential. In a letter to the writer Anne Charlotte Leffler, whom Axel had met when she visited Paris in June of that same year, he wrote that the trip was a part of a private repayment plan. Ever since he had recovered his health in Italy as a tubercular young man, he had loved the country 'with a passion', and now he wanted to pay back his debt.

Axel also hinted to Leffler that there was a deeper motive, namely, that he hoped to be 'finished off' by the cholera. As he travelled to Naples direct from Högsjö it is tempting to see this death-wish in the light of the drama that had been played out there: death as the solution to the existential crisis he had put himself in. But the attraction to danger and death, to places and situations where life – including his own – was at risk, was so pronounced in Axel that we can see here something of a life pattern. This was the air he breathed, the mental atmosphere he needed to keep his melancholy in check; a melancholy that he made public for the first time in 'Letters from Naples'. Danger and human distress functioned as catalysts that stimulated his creative powers. The cholera outbreak in Naples was the first but by no means the last example of this.

PARTENZA PER NAPOLI!

The heading 'Letter from . . .' was the usual one for the foreign correspondents of the time. Axel's 'letters', however, had little in common with the newspaper's other foreign reports. His was a distinctive narrative voice that made no attempt to appear 'objective'. Several of the letters contain factual information (which corresponds well with stories printed in contemporary newspapers), but most of them were novelistic social reportage and subjective musings about philosophical and literary questions.

The tone is already set in the first letter, which was published in *Stockholms Dagblad* on 22 October. Axel describes his train trip from Rome to Naples. He is alone in the compartment, alone in the carriage, in fact, the only passenger on the entire train. 'A horrible stench of carbolic acid filled the compartment'; Naples has been placed under quarantine and no one is travelling there voluntarily. The train rushes on at a dizzy pace, past Velletri, Segni, Anagni, Ferentino – 'all friends of former happy days'. It begins to get dark and Axel dozes off for a while. An ice-cold draught wafts over him and extinguishes the light in the ceiling. He wakes with a shiver and has a feeling that he is not alone; he feels the cold sweat on his forehead. At the same instant he sees 'a funeral procession which is rapidly speeding across the dark plain, with Death and myself the only followers, and I felt under my closed eyelids how my sombre companion steadily watched me from his corner opposite . . . Slight carbolic acid poisoning + want of sleep + nervousness, eh, doctor?'

Gradually, as the train approaches more southerly climes, Axel revives; mild breezes float in from Sorrento and 'far away, like a beautiful mirage, floated Capri's blue island'. The smell of carbolic no longer disturbs him;

instead, 'old friendly thoughts of loving gratitude towards the beautiful country awoke from their winter sleep of long working days far away from sun and summer':

> Never before had I felt how strong was the link which bound me to this country; it is not in the moments of joy that one feels how much one cares for a friend, it is when one is told that he is unhappy, and in sorrow, that the secret voices of one's heart speak out and give utterance to the most silent thoughts of one's soul.
>
> Now Naples is in mourning, and therefore we long to hasten thither as to a brother in distress; we, who once were so happy here, who have learned how to like these childish, warm-hearted, poverty-stricken people; we, who have heard the mandoline sound at Santa Lucia to the strains of 'O Dolce Napoli!'; we, who from the heights of Camaldoli's convent have beheld the loveliest vision that ever greeted eye of man, when the sun goes down behind Ischia's mountains, and over Sorrento's hills hovers that rosy shimmer which no brush can paint, when Capri wraps its veil of blue mist around the fair island, and over the velvet green slopes of Vesuvius falls that tint of deep violet that can never be forgotten!

'*Je dois le peu de bonheur que j'ai eu à l'Italie*' (I owe the little happiness I have had to Italy), Axel claimed, '*et j'y suis allé cette fois pour dire merci*' (and I have gone there this time to say thank you). His love of Italy even overcame his fear of death: 'Should your own life be at stake, what of that? Is it then so sweet to live, and is it then so hard to die when one dies in the land of one's dreams, conscious that one has tried to help others to live, or' – and here his thoughts home in on a central tenet in his physician's code – 'if their doom is sealed, at least, has tried to help them to die?'

The train journey is depicted with an efficiency and concentration that indicate a significant degree of literary skill. In this first 'Letter from Naples' two major themes in Axel's life are introduced. One of them is Death (always spelt with a capital letter). Throughout his life Axel was 'curious about Death' and wanted to know everything about this force, which he describes in *The Story of San Michele* as 'the giver of Life, the slayer of Life, the beginning and the end'. The other theme is his burning, lifelong love for Italy, for the south, for the culture of the Mediterranean. These two themes are placed in the sharpest possible contrast to each other here: Death, stinking of carbolic acid, threatens 'the land of his dreams' where once he had lived in such happiness.

The first five letters were unsigned, but already in the second one Axel breaks cover. In the midst of a factual account of the authorities' unwillingness to reveal the true death toll, the author's *doppelgänger* pops up:

That the list of the dead is as inaccurate as that of the sick I was able to verify for myself yesterday evening when, *in the company of a French physician, a Dr Munthe,* I went up to the cholera cemetery; I remained there about an hour, and during that time alone eighty-three bodies were brought there (the official report announced only fifty-seven deaths for that day.

The corpses are laid in a row before they are buried; *the doctor leant over each and every one – they were all still warm, so there was no danger of mistakenly assuming that they were not all part of the day's toll.**

The author's *doppelgänger* follows in his footsteps, cropping up in one article as 'an obscure doctor' who works in the cholera hospital, in another as a man with grey spectacles who looks eccentric and 'homely'. On one occasion the man confronts the writer of the articles and complains that he has received 'scores of editions of the *Dagblad* full of letters containing more or less favourable reviews of these articles, which are generally ascribed to himself'. As if it was not enough that the articles are badly written, their tone is teasing, and they concern things that are sacred to him and that he has to make his living from, for instance cholera microbes. He therefore begs the author of the articles to stop writing about purely medical questions. Furthermore, he demands that the letters be signed so that he avoids being taken for their author.

All of a sudden the writer recognises the doctor, whom he had met in the churchyard but whose name he had forgotten:

Today he looked so angry and his spectacles bounced up and down; I thought he had caught rabies, and I rolled a cigarette – as an antiseptic. I didn't trouble to answer him. Otherwise I could certainly have made clear to him that I was not for a moment pretending to be a doctor and that I had realised long ago that I unfortunately would never make a doctor, and that, when all was said and done, I held that profession in as much esteem as he did – if not more.

The author of the articles promises, however, to discard his anonymity and henceforward sign his articles:

I have a dog-tax plate in Paris, in general I am innocent and harmless, but I bite back sometimes when people are nasty to me, and my name is

Ali.

The game of hide-and-seek is of a highly advanced nature. The author of the articles is not a doctor but he appears as such. Opposed to him is

---

* The words in italic are missing in the English translation from 1887 (second edition 1899).

a real doctor who is the author's alter ego. Axel Munthe is split into two personas: an author and a doctor, who rebuke each other for not mastering their respective professions. Since he is obviously unsure of himself in both roles, he is guarded: he is a doctor who dabbles in the writing profession and an author who is a doctor who is no use. In this way he avoids being held to account. To complicate everything even further, he appears under a pseudonym behind which there hides a dog. This game of identities was an elegant literary construction; there is reason to believe that it was also an expression of a serious personality split.

The *doppelgänger* motif was a popular literary concept at this time: we meet it in Dostoevsky, Strindberg and Maupassant. The concept originated with E.T.A. Hoffmann and Edgar Allan Poe, but became topical in the 1880s thanks to the research on the unconscious that was being carried out in France in particular, and which Axel was well aware of. The split personality that the doctors found in certain patients was used by authors as a literary concept. In certain cases the roles of patient and author merged, as for instance with Maupassant, who portrayed the split personality in literary terms in, for example, the short story 'Le Horla' (1887).

Axel's playful view of his two occupational roles reflected his alienation from established society as represented by the medical and writing professions. He asks, what do doctors know about illnesses and human suffering? Far less than they are prepared to admit, and less than patients believe, is his answer. The same holds true for authors, who sit at their writing desks and depict a reality of which they are ignorant.

This view of the Establishment sprang from Axel's own feeling of alienation, which in turn led him to identify with the weaker elements in society. During his stay in Naples he was able to observe the unique role played by religion, and he was strongly moved by the mystically tinged religiosity that pervaded the city. As he wrote later to an acquaintance, he was *comme fasciné par l'exaltation réligieuse* (almost spellbound by the religious exaltation) that surrounded him.

However much Axel was influenced by the atmosphere in Naples, he was too rational and sceptical to be swept along by it himself. Even if he was careful to preserve a certain amount of his own childhood faith, he saw religion mainly as a form of therapy. This was especially the case in the throes of death, a stage in human life that he had cause to study several times a day during his time in Naples. If one cannot help a fellow human being to live, one should at least try to help him to die, he believed. This holds true for the doctor just as much as for the guardian of souls. That was why he had such a favourable opinion of the care offered by monks and nuns – they gave comfort when nothing else was left:

I should like to get a deputation of newly fledged atheists out here, and to take them with me on my rounds in the poor quarters where sorrow and misery live. I would show them the peace which Faith brings to the closing eyes of even these poor creatures whom one really might excuse for feeling no special depth of gratitude towards their Creator; I would show them how the crucifix over the bed can better soothe the agony of death than the morphine syringe of the doctor; Ah! 'There are more things between heaven and earth, Horatio, than are dreamt of in your philosophy' – or in your chemistry either, for the matter of that, and maybe a sight like this might stir up the shallow source of their wisdom, and precipitate some of the pure gold of the childhood's faith to the bottom of their soul.

In the new anti-clerical Italy, Axel writes, monks have been 'hunted to death', but he defends them, although this is not popular. If he were king of a great kingdom he would divide it in three parts and share it out among 'monks, Laplanders and Red Indians'. He dreams of redress for these 'innocent victims of modern civilisation', and has a vision of a more just society. He wonders 'whether, after all, there could be any truth in the old legend that we shall all meet again on another planet in a sort of transmigration of souls, where all the *roles* will be reversed' – where those who were unhappy on earth will be happy, where the poor will feast while the rich stand looking on, where those who were punished here on earth will hold the whiphand, where 'The jailors are to sit in the cells while their former prisoners go round inspecting them!' In this promised land his other protégés, the animals, will go round being nasty to the humans:

small birds and butterflies will fly around on free wings, looking at cruel boys and butterfly catchers where they sit stuffed and enclosed in big glass cases, with long pins stuck through them. All the steep uphill roads will swarm with dead-tired old cab horses comfortably seated on the coach-boxes, pitilessly returning each bloody stroke of the lash to their former tyrants, the cabmen.

This passage is an eloquent expression of the misanthropy which many people would come to see as Axel Munthe's trademark, and which was well nourished during his stay in Naples. In several conversations with a philosophically inclined donkey he develops and clarifies his pessimistic view of mankind.

Axel describes how he wanders around the slums of the city with the orphan-boy Peppino, his donkey Rosina and the dog Puck, the Sancho Panza of the company. Axel himself is a Don Quixote who sits on 'the scraggy little donkey', with his legs – still weak after a bout of cholera –

dragging on the ground. (Axel's falling ill with cholera around 1 November is documented in letters to the von Mecklenburgs and Ultima).

Rosina – a short form of Don Quixote's Rosinante – had earlier been ridden from morning till night while a hail of whiplashes rained over her back. Gradually she realised that 'The world is not so pleasant a place as she had imagined, and that human beings are not so kind as they profess to be.' She became a bitter hypochondriac and adhered to that school 'where the broken-down old donkeys lectured upon their hopeless philosophy'. In the end she could no longer bear to carry tourists and ended up going around with Peppino's father, selling vegetables.

When Peppino's family succumbed to the cholera, Axel took responsibility for Rosina. She was now old and worn out. From time to time during her nocturnal rounds she stands still and ponders 'the missing link' in her philosophical system. While the donkey stands and ponders, Axel takes the opportunity to meditate on his own philosophy of life, 'which is not quite clear either'.

Munthe had long suspected that Rosina was an 'inveterate pessimist' and when she suddenly quotes the poet Leopardi, 'the poet of despair', he asks her if she has heard of Arthur Schopenhauer. She has, but Leopardi suits donkeys better as his pessimism does not lead 'into revolt against the principle of life, but to resignation, to silence, to contempt'. Axel agrees with Rosina and he whispers his motto into her ear: '*Seul le silence est grand, tout le reste est faiblesse!*' (Only silence is great, all the rest is weakness!).

Despite his respect for Rosina's search for the missing link, Axel urges her to stop seeking after the truth, as she would only be unhappy if she found it – 'for truth in itself is sad'. The more conscious we become, the more powerfully we experience the negative side of life. 'Suffering', Axel concludes, 'is an intellectual function, and is in direct relation with the development of the brain'. 'But we two,' asks the donkey, 'who have never felt happy, does that not mean that our brains are very highly developed, that we are misunderstood geniuses both of us?' 'No,' Axel answers, 'God knows we are no shining lights either of us; maybe we are not quite as big donkeys as some others – *voilà tout!*'

We should not let this whimsical grumbling obscure the tragic view of life that Axel is expressing here. As we have seen, he had a tendency to hide his identity behind stylistic refinements. Sometimes, however, the author of these melancholy thoughts peeps through the veil of pathos, humour and raillery in the text.

He describes himself as a 'fatalist', 'depressed with all the misery one is obliged to meet in this world, and which one can do nothing to relieve'. And yet this is why Axel has travelled to Naples – to do the best he can as a doctor to lighten people's sorrows. '[. . .] we have done plenty of mischief in our lives, and perhaps this is our only chance of making up for a little!' he writes. 'We' in this context may be taken as referring to the human race, which bears a collective guilt. There can be no doubt that Axel himself suffered from what could be called a feeling of 'original guilt'. What we see in this formulation is the embryo of the 'philosophy of duty' that would direct much of his life, and which there will be reason to touch on several times at a later stage. His work in Naples was a first repayment of this existential debt.

Axel's misanthropy was closely connected to his strong identification with animals; their isolation and subjection are Axel's own. But Axel does not see animals only as symbols; he views the world from their perspective – he looks at the human world with their eyes and speaks with their voice. His alienation is too great to be expressed by a human voice. This is why the donkey and the dog are at least as great philosophers as their master.

The first 'letters' were, as we have seen, unsigned. This was by no means an oversight. Behind the mask of anonymity lay an insecurity about which of his identities was the author. When Axel was finally forced to display a name, he chose that of his dog. But as someone in Stockholm was already signing articles as 'Puck', the editorial staff changed his signature to 'Ali'.

Axel perceived himself to be as alien in the human world as the dog. His identification with Puck, his 'only real friend', was total, and it would not be long before he bestowed his surname on Puck – or, to put it another way, borrowed the dog's first name. In any event, the 'beast' – to use Axel's own definition – who would soon bound into Swedish literature bore the name of Puck Munthe.

GRAU, GRAU IST ALLE THEORIE

Once Rosina and Axel had put the philosophical building-blocks in place, they went on to discuss literature, about which Axel had very decided opinions. In several 'letters' he directed ruthless criticism at the so-called modern school, whose representatives claimed to 'depict reality'. But modern authors were theoreticians who knew nothing about life outside their studies, and Axel quoted Goethe: 'Grau, grau ist alle Theorie,/Und grün das Lebens goldner Baum!' (Grey, grey is all theory/And green the golden tree of life!). Sitting in comfortable armchairs they describe poverty and distress and try to find efficacious ways of killing off children.

For Axel, it was self-evident that only someone who has experience of 'real life' can depict it: 'Go out among the poor, look their misery straight in the face, and lay your hands upon their rags and tatters. And you will bear witness to the fact that there is no romance so stirring, so thrilling – and so heartrending as Life's great epic!' He turns on the 'modern authors' who believe that their 'photographs, obtained by means of all the apparatus of modern realism, are truer to life than the naïve pictures of the old "idealists"'. His chief enemy, in other words, is 'realism' understood as a striving to convey nature without idealism.

> You talk of a return to *Nature* in literature as in art, but you entirely forget that *Nature herself is not realistic but idealistic*! Where will you find a symphony of which the romance can be compared to the murmur of the sea, where will you find a tragedy so impressive as the vast solitude of a pine forest, where will you find a poem so pure as the silent language of the violets, where will you find a sonnet so tender as the nightingale's song about Sorrento? And where will you find a greater idealist than the sun, where will you find a more incorrigible, sentimental, old enthusiast than the moon who, at this very moment, floats the glittering interpretation of her dream across the slumbering bay!

There is a contradiction between Axel's social radicalism and his aesthetic ideals and cultural conservatism. This tension, far from being unique to Axel, was widespread during this transitional ideological phase. What is interesting about Axel is that, at the age of 27, he hailed a stylistic ideal that many already saw as played out. At the same time it must be said that his literary style is not simply overburdened rhetoric but also – at its best – a model of economy and effectiveness. As in this description of the 'modern author's' creative pains, a masterpiece of concentrated sarcasm: 'Buried deep in thought our author lights his Havana cigar – and while he puffs the thin blue smoke across his manuscript, he allows the poor little castaway to discover a packet of tobacco at the bottom of the boat.'

Axel names no names, but even if his outburst was no doubt directed first and foremost against Émile Zola, it is highly probable that he also had the most prominent Swedish advocate of realism and naturalism in his thoughts, namely August Strindberg.

AVENUE DE VILLIERS

When Francis of Assisi, founder of the order of mendicant friars, attended a ball as a young dandy and was surrounded by notables' daughters who asked him: 'Now, Master Francis, aren't you going to take your pick of all these beauties?', he answered: 'I have chosen one much fairer!' – 'Oh, which one?' – 'La povertà' – shortly after which he left everything behind and set off on his travels as a beggar.

Arthur Schopenhauer, On the Suffering of the World

A XEL LEFT NAPLES on 13 November 1884, 'headlong', as cholera had broken out in Paris. Here too, it was the poorer parts of the city that were most afflicted, but the epidemic was both milder and shorter-lasting than in Naples. '*Ça ne vaut rien du tout le cholera ici*' (the cholera here is nothing to write home about), Axel wrote to Anne Charlotte Leffler, adding ironically that the prospects of his creditors having their demands met (his life was insured for 25,000 kronor, almost £100,000 in today's money) 'are getting less and less'. But he was broke after the Naples adventure and his brother Arnold came to his aid again with a new loan.

After his stay in Naples Axel gives his address as 90 Avenue de Villiers, where he and Ultima seem to have moved during the autumn. According to a Swedish artist it was 'a splendid boulevard where fashionable artists settled'. And writers too: at no. 98, for example, lived Alexandre Dumas the younger. This is the street that Axel gives as his work address in *The Story of San Michele*: 'Avenue de Villiers. Dr Munthe from 2 till 3.'

The move to Avenue de Villiers seems to have taken place on Ultima's initiative. The relationship between husband and wife was quite obviously under severe strain, affected by Axel's consciousness of the deception underlying their marriage. Ultima is noticeably absent from Axel's letters, where she is only named in the passing. One person whom Axel knew he could confide in was the writer Anne Charlotte Leffler (whose married name was Edgren). In a letter to her we get our first glimpse of the wife who was so anonymous:

> If you come to Paris, Mrs Edgren, and if one day you would like to look up a hypochondriac, there is one living at 90 Avenue de Villiers. My wife likes this district – and I like everything just as much. What is everything else compared to 'that peaceful contentment by the hearth' of which you authors talk so much! I shall of course be quite indescribably happy there. 'A nice home, everyone friendly towards you, a large medical practice – you have everything you could possibly want.' The cage is situated two floors up if you would like to come and view the prisoner it contains.

Axel's choice of words reflects his low opinion of the domestic bliss that a 'nice home' is supposed to confer; it also betrays a feeling of confinement and an alienation of a more existential nature. The word 'hypochondriac' is used here in the sense of 'a depressive', and the one who speaks is the same person who declared in one of his letters from Naples that he 'had never been happy'. Presumably the discord in Axel's soul was exacerbated by the contrast between the reality he had experienced in Naples and the utterly banal ideal of family life to which Ultima seems to have subscribed. After the terrors of the cholera he seems to have slumped into a daily routine that he thoroughly despised, and which his nerves could not cope with. Besides, he loved another woman.

Anne Charlotte Leffler had expressed her admiration for Axel's 'Letters from Naples', but he dismisses this in his usual way – he is no author, the letters had a purely practical purpose!

> Thank you for your kind opinion of the Naples letters, whose only purpose has been fully realised – they had no other goal than to enable me to go down there with my pockets full of money for those who were hungry. The letters do not lend themselves to publication, they are far too personal not to be private. Thrown together after sleepless nights (I was on my rounds every night for a fortnight so [illegible]) they are of course uneven and unpolished and will not suit literary connoisseurs. However, I continually receive letters about them from complete strangers – I knew, of course, that microbes are popular beasts, but I never realised that they are so to such a high degree. If people can see from them [the letters] that they are true, then I am content. I have bought several boats ('loaned out' to poor fishermen who have gone to the dogs), I feed my donkey and a whole bunch of boys as well – so they have certainly been of some use. I noticed to my surprise that I enjoyed this writing business and I almost think that I ought to go on with it, as it helps me not to succumb altogether to my melancholy, gloomy life here.

That Axel did not see himself – or pretended not to see himself – as a writer, was one thing. Others did see him in that light, and not only Anne Charlotte Leffler. When the editor-in-chief of *Stockholms Dagblad*, Erik Montan, asked

Axel for some articles, he responded by penning some 'Forgotten letters from Naples'.

'Golfo di Napoli' was printed in January 1885 and is first and foremost a celebration of the beauty of the Bay of Naples. Many Capri men, not least fishermen, are in Sorrento and are prevented by the quarantine from returning home. But one day they try to get there. With the enthusiasm of the dedicated sailor Axel depicts the crossing from Sorrento to Capri in a fishing boat. The wind freshens, the boat dances over white, foaming waves, the salt spray whips his face, 'finer than the richest wine'; the scales fall from his eyes, he sees that the world is 'beautiful as on the first day of creation' – and his heavy-heartedness subsides.

As so often when Axel reasons with himself, he does so via a *doppelgänger*, with whom he polemicises about thoughts he had aired in the earlier 'Letters from Naples':

> He who is at the helm I supposed to be a pessimist – well, if that is what pessimists look like, the disease cannot be so bad after all. It is he who believes that sorrow is positive and joy is negative in this world – have you any idea what that means? No, neither do I. It is he who declares that resignation to one's fate is the highest perfection to which man can aspire – no doubt it is resignation which sparkles in his eyes and plays about his lips. It is he who has written on the sly a long essay on the expression of melancholy which exists in all animals' faces. Look at the dolphins playing around the boat! have you ever seen anything so melancholy as their gambols amongst the waves! What would Schopenhauer say if he caught sight of you, pessimistic steersman, and you, sporting dolphins!

Apart from his music, it was the sea that was Axel's favourite refuge from his 'hypochondria' – especially on Capri, the island he had first visited in 1876 and which he was now bound for again, after four years' absence:

> Have you seen the loveliest pearl in Naples' crown, have you seen Isola di Capri, floating on the waters of the bay? The waves bathe shores richer than thine, fair island, softer breathe the winds that blow through the groves of Sorrento, and more bountifully Nature strews its verdant luxuriance over Ischia's hills than over thy summer-clad rocks. But never shines the sun as it does over Capri, never glistens the bay so brilliantly blue as round thy fair shores! [. . .] Ah yes, perhaps the poets are right, thou art unto like a sarcophagus! But leave the dead in peace, let silence shed its calm over thy departed joy! Here, beneath the roses and evergreens, a youthful dream lies slumbering.*

---

* The second part of the quotation was deleted in the second English translation of the sketch from 1899.

Eulogy was not Axel's best literary genre. Here, as in the more emotional social reportages, he was both verbose and high flown. Axel was most effective when he had scope for his humour, his irony and his social criticism.

However, the bathos would be even harder to take if it did not reflect a genuine feeling. This is not literature but a heartfelt and uninhibited homage to a dream that had not yet been fulfilled. For Axel, the Bay of Naples and Capri represented not only beauty but also myth and history, which stood witness to a time before the world was affected by modern civilisation: the time of 'the deathless ideal':

> Yes, the immortal Gods were here, and, living through the ages, they passed before me radiant in Pentelic marble. The broken temple columns rose anew against the heaven of the eternal ideal, and it was not the dawn of a new day – no, it was the afterglow of the sun of Hellas and Rome, which shed its lustre over the Golfo di Napoli.

The cholera reportages and the 'Forgotten Letters from Naples' made Axel a hot property in Stockholm's literary circles. His services were all of a sudden sought after by journals and publishing houses. But he was no easy catch. To one editor he wrote that his 'literary career' was probably over, adding: 'I suffer from a heavy and depressive mood, and have my reasons for it.' And when Anne Charlotte Leffler asked for a piece from Axel's 'so popular pen', he refused: 'I am no writer and will never be one so long as Our Lord allows me to retain my wits and my – self-criticism.'

THE NUNS' EXIT

What Axel says about being no writer sounds a little hollow when one thinks of the eleven 'Forgotten Letters' that were published in *Stockholms Dagblad* between January and March and five further articles that were printed in May and June. It is possible that some of them had been written earlier and that he could not in fact write any more at this time. But the problem lay not so much in the fact that he was an 'occasional writer', as he wrote to Anne Charlotte Leffler, but rather that he did not wish, or could not, write to order: the impetus had to come from within.

Another person who got wind of Axel's literary talent was the leading Swedish publisher Albert Bonnier, who wanted to publish 'Letters from Naples' in book form. Axel made the excuse that he had not yet made up his mind about a book edition. While still in Naples he had received several offers from publishers and in Paris he had received three more. 'It is unbelievable how popular cholera seems to be back home,' he stated. The matter strikes him as amusing, and the fact that 'hastily scribbled letters like these can be so well received' bears witness to 'the low level at which our literature stands'. He claimed to be known for his hopelessness in practical affairs, but these letters were a different story:

> I have earmarked the income from them once and for all for a bunch of former patients down in Naples. In these circumstances I am of course trying to get as much as possible out of them and as there has been an offer from another quarter to pay pretty well for them, I hope to collect a fair amount to send my patients down there. If it was just for myself, I would gladly let you have them, Mr Bonnier (if I decide to have them printed, which I have not yet done), but as the remuneration for the letters is not mine, I must give them to the highest bidder.

Self-confidence interwoven with feigned modesty – Axel was a skilful negotiator! Whatever Bonnier's answer was, it was not his firm that got to publish the Naples reportages in book form. Instead, Axel turned to Norstedts, who declared themselves willing to pay for a title vignette for such a book 'in any manner you indicate, it can be produced in Paris and with all possible dispatch'. They also promised that 'from a typographical standpoint too it will leave nothing to be desired', and that they would publish any 'letters or sketches' that Axel may write in future 'with pleasure'. The choice of publisher was not strange, considering that Axel's brother-in-law not only bore the same surname but was also closely related to the company's owners.

When the book came out at the beginning of March it contained, as well as the original 'Letters from Naples', two of the 'forgotten' ones – 'Golfo di Napoli' and 'Sœur Philomène'. This latter develops a theme that had already been aired in the Naples reportages: namely, the importance of religion as comfort for the dying. Dr Munthe did not share the faith of the nuns and priests, but gladly worked side by side with them in the Hôtel-Dieu hospital in Paris.

Like the Italian government, the leaders of the Third Republic pursued a strongly anti-clerical policy, with the goal of cleansing schools and hospitals of religious influence. *Laïcisation* (secularisation) was the order of the day. Between 1879 and 1888 seventeen hospitals in the capital were secularised, sometimes with great difficulty because of opposition by the doctors. The driving force behind the campaign was the president of the council, Jules Ferry, who ironically enough had signed Axel's doctor's diploma during his time as minister of education.

While reforms on the education front were both justified and well meant, *la laïcisation des hôpitaux* – which among other things meant that the Sisters of Mercy were to be replaced by lay staff – led to an abrupt reorganisation of the medical system, the advantages of which were less obvious.

When, after a period of absence, Axel returned to the Hôtel-Dieu, it was only to find that the Sisters of Charity and the hospital chaplain had been shown the door. The 'improvements of modern times' made him feel 'old-fashioned and strange'. Since 'the extinction of life is not synonymous with ceasing to *live*, but with ceasing to *die*', as he writes in one of the 'Letters from Naples', the nun and the doctor have a similar function to fulfil during the death struggle. The crucifix or the morphine syringe – it comes to the same thing. Now only the morphine syringe was left, which Axel regretted.

An Uncommon Human Being

Towards the end of March, Axel travelled to Italy, with Puck for company. In Florence he bumped into the Cederlund family from Stockholm. The Cederlunds belonged to the highest stratum of Stockholm society, lived in grand style and had now embarked on a six-week trip round Italy together with their son Edward junior. Four months earlier, Mrs Mathilda Cederlund had advised her son to read Axel's letters from Naples in *Stockholms Dagblad*, a recommendation she repeated when 'Sœur Philomène' was published in the newspaper in January. Now that she had the opportunity to meet the author in person, her enthusiasm knew no bounds.

Axel tagged along with the family and became their guide but asked them not to tell anyone that he was in Italy. They did not, but when the journey was over Mathilda Cederlund explained to her daughter in Stockholm that Axel had undertaken 'this month-long trip to try and get a little rest; highly strung and delicate as he is, his exertions here last autumn (in the cholera epidemic) have caught up with him'.

From Florence the company moved on to Rome. After a week there, they took the train to Naples; they drove through the slums and Axel showed them 'the poor people's churchyard', with 365 pits ending in an 'immense abyss'. Every day between six and eight in the evening one pit was opened up, into which the day's harvest of corpses was tossed without benefit of a coffin. After a few days in Naples they travelled on to Pompeii and Sorrento. On 16 April the company took a sailing boat over to Capri. They set up camp in the luxury Hotel Quisisana, visited the various grottos on the island, and rode up to Anacapri to the ruins of Tiberius' villa. The Cederlund family travelled around by horse or donkey while Axel always went on foot. On 22 April they returned to Naples.

The letter that Mathilda Cederlund wrote to her daughter the day after they left Capri conveys a vivid picture of both Axel and his standing on the island:

> To talk about the man himself is about as useless as talking about Capri – it would be equally dull! – suffice it to say that he is an uncommon human being, both in his heart and in his *caractère* – aesthetically cultivated beyond the norm, but nevertheless a natural man in the finest sense of the term. It was a proud feeling to be his fellow-Swede when stepping ashore on Capri – everyone embraced him, old men, old women, youths, children – all of them were happy to see him again, people of rank as much as the poor people – yes, it was touching – and he took this just as simply and humbly himself – for the very reason that he loves them in return – only when one has seen him coming ashore there can one truly understand his 'Golfo di Napoli' in the Naples Letters.

For Axel, the stay on Capri meant no rest since, according to Mrs Cederlund, he was 'overrun with patients from early in the morning till late in the evening'. Although he seemed to belong to the ranks of those 'who are destined from an early age for a better life', she feared that his life would not be a long one if he continued at this tempo.

Mrs Cederlund's misgivings were justified. Despite his weak lungs and bad nerves, Axel was always defying danger and fate, giving proof of his 'foolhardiness' (a noun he liked using about himself). One day Mr Cederlund and his son climbed Vesuvius in company with Axel. The cable car stopped just short of the crater, and the last stretch had to be completed on foot. But the volcano had been active for the last three days, belching out fire and stones, and the Cederlunds decided to stop where the cable car ended. 'But the doctor went right up to the edge', we read in the son's diary – a piece of information which by now ought not to surprise us.

When, two weeks later, the Cederlunds left Paris, Mrs Cederlund wrote to her daughter that it was with 'great regret' that they parted from their 'new young friends Dr Munthe and his wife', adding: 'He is impossible to describe – she is a little, simple, friendly soul, easy to understand and easy to like – both of them are very young, he 27, she 24 – therefore far too young for us – but nevertheless they have both awakened my interest and my affection.'

An Original and Independent Author

Axel returned to Paris just in time to scrutinise the first reviews of the book, published as *Från Napoli: Resebref* (From Naples: Travelogues). Before its publication, his attitude had been one of studied nonchalance. He was no author, after all; what difference did it make what reviews he got? Moreover he was, as he said himself, his own best critic: 'Aftonbladet has six people with doctorates, so I ought to stand a good chance of a hiding from that newspaper – the academics back home look on me as a renegade, and I imagine they will get heartburn from reading my book.'

Like the hypersensitive person he was, Axel tried to hide his unease behind a carapace of feigned indifference; but his fear was unfounded. The book's reception matched the sensation that the letters had caused on their publication in Stockholms Dagblad. The reviewers were unanimous both in their praise and in their opinions.

A quality that all reviewers emphasised was Axel's style. One reviewer claimed that the content of the letters was 'as captivating and interesting as their style is brilliant and fluent', and according to another, his style was 'pure', 'brilliant, lively and full of genuine humour'. It was also noted that Axel was 'to a great degree an original and independent author'.

Almost all reviewers concurred enthusiastically with Axel's attack on 'the sensation-seeking and impious detailed depictions with which the quasi-scientific novels of a Zola make capital out of human misery'. Munthe's own method of writing belonged neither to the 'new' school nor the 'old', but rather to the tradition of 'sentimental humour, the way it appeared in [the works of] the Englishman Sterne and the German Jean Paul'. What Munthe offered, they felt, was a 'genuine empathy', and the book was 'a kind of "Sentimental Journey"', where each page betrays an almost lyrically sensitive sounding-board'.

My Thoughts Fly

As well as the two 'Forgotten Letters' that Axel included in the book, another five articles were published during February in Stockholms Dagblad: 'Political Agitations in Capri', 'My Thoughts Fly', 'Only for Animal Lovers', 'From the Diary of a Hunter' and 'Enemies of the Light'. Of these, only the first two had a direct connection with Capri and Italy, while the others dealt with quite different topics.

'Political Agitations in Capri' describes a visit by the Prussian Crown princess that caused a great deal of trouble for the island's German residents, and gives Axel ample opportunities to air his anti-German sentiments. The German population of Capri has prepared a magnificent welcoming ceremony, but the Crown princess manages to give them the slip and instead meets up with Axel and Puck, who help her to avoid her pushy fellow-countrymen.

During the second half of the nineteenth century Capri had been discovered by north Europeans, especially the English and the Germans. By the 1880s a large number of foreigners were resident there, and the stream of tourists increased year on year. Especially noticeable was the invasion of Germans, who knocked back their German beer in the Zum Kater Hiddigeigei restaurant on the Via Hohenzollern (now the Via Vittorio Emanuele) to the accompaniment of German patriotic songs.

The German influence was hard to take for Munthe, with his romantic view of Italy. In fact, he went so far as to claim that Capri was 'infested with parasites'. He regarded himself as a 'Capriot', and saw the problem entirely from the perspective of the local population. Many years later, when he sent the English translation of 'Political Agitations in Capri' to the German-born Lady Walpurga Paget, he explained that she ought not to take it personally – if she lived on Capri she would soon be just as critical of the Germans as he was then, 'for they are distorting the harmony of the place a good deal, and those who have come here are as a rule not sympathetic'.

Axel's rabid anti-German sentiments were not entirely due to the German element on Capri. He grew up in a period when strongly anti-German feelings were prevalent in most European countries. The background to this can be sought in the two wars that directly affected attitudes to Germany in the rest of Europe. The first was the war of 1864 between Denmark and Prussia, which led to Denmark being forced to hand over Schleswig, Holstein and other north German provinces to Prussia. This conflict breathed new life into the Scandinavianist movement, and many Swedes wanted Sweden to come in on the side of Denmark.

Axel's negative attitude towards Germany grew stronger during his years in France, where the German occupation of 1871 was still fresh in people's minds and hatred of the Germans was deep-seated. The fact that the Swedes in Paris were often taken for Germans did not improve matters. Axel and his generation had feelings against all that was German just as engrained as those of the generation that grew up during and after the Second World War.

'My Thoughts Fly' is another paean to his 'beloved Italy'. Axel remembers with gratitude his and Puck's 'carefree vagabond days' down there, their canal trips in Venice, bathing at the Lido and encounters with art in Florence. They have drunk 'a toast to meeting again' from the Trevi Fountain in Rome and wandered through the Villa Borghese and the Villa Doria Pamphili; they have roamed around the Roman countryside and slept by campfires at night; they number both herds and watchdogs among their friends. They have sailed with coral-fishers to Sicily, where they strayed 'far from the marked paths that travel books trace out for inquisitive packs of strangers', they have lived among herds up in the mountains, 'where no echo of modern life has penetrated'.

However true or otherwise his reminiscences may be, they give us a good picture of the author's imaginative world. The same is true of his praise for St Francis, founder of the order of friars that bears his name, and, according to Axel, 'one of the greatest figures of the Middle Ages':

> Our age calls him a fool, and we dub his uplifting doctrine of self-sacrificing love for humanity 'religious fanaticism'. But his contemporaries gave him the name il Serafico, and Dante compared him to the sun which shines on everything and gives it warmth. And those master artists Cimabue and Giotto conveyed, in their magnificent high art, the rapture which the poor saint called forth. And as for us two, we hailed, with reverential wonder, the high-minded champion of the oppressed and the humble: the noble monk who was the friend of the poor and of animals.

The saint from Assisi, who was to loom so large in Axel's philosophy of life, appears here for the first time in his written works. For Axel, il Poverello with his simple lifestyle and his self-sacrificing goodness was an ideal Christian figure, beyond all articles of dogma and church walls. Francis's interpretation of the Christian mission corresponded well with Axel's own view of fellow-feeling for the rest of humanity and his unorthodox interpretation of the Christian message. In time it would emerge that they shared yet another point of contact, something that Axel was so far blissfully unaware of.

When Axel's thoughts flew, they mostly headed in a southerly direction. More recently, however, he had often seen how 'the dark-blue sky grows lighter, the mild air, with the poppy fragrance of gentle dreams, becomes bitingly cold but refreshing, like a bath in the cool spring of the forest'. The dark-green orange trees stretch out into sky-high firs and the brown bark shines, that bark 'which my poverty-stricken country has mixed with its bread'. And underneath, he hears the heartbeat of his native land:

> Greetings, proud cypresses of the North, which watch over the graves where linnaea and heather sleep, greetings, mighty giants of the forest with the robustness of the mountains in your veins, greetings, centuries-old bodyguards of my wintry homeland, grey old grenadiers with rime in your beards and snow in your locks! And from pine to pine I hear the wind murmuring a greeting to me again, a greeting to him who has been absent for so long, but who has never forgotten his native land.

The article concludes with a paean of praise to the Swedish Christmas, to goblins and creatures of the forest. The author is 27 years old but writes as if he were an old man; once again, style is one thing, the impulse behind it something else. Axel lived in a world that existed nowhere else but in his own imagination, the imagination of a child. 'There are people', he wrote, 'who do not believe in goblins, but this is something they should never speak of, for it shows that they are very ignorant and their senses are atrophied.'

The juxtaposition of Italy and Sweden can also be found in the article 'Enemies of the Light', although it mainly turns into a powerful critique of civilisation, romantic in tone but utterly uncompromising in its content. Axel describes a walking tour in the Swedish province of Dalarna, with its 'proud strain of upright men and healthy women'. The noise of everyday life does not penetrate this far, elves dance here and the water sprite sings, the pines murmur 'dark old tales of giants and trolls', and deep inside the cliffs nocturnal fires blaze, where the elves beat out their red gold. But the summer wears on, and Axel must return home again. Nature becomes more desolate and he sees 'a fire-breathing dragon flying over the plain' – the railway, 'one of the most destructive inventions there has been to date'. It is Beëlzebub who has come in the name of Culture, with his iron rails, his high-heeled boots and his steam sawmills. And when Axel enquires about an inn, he is told that there isn't one, only a hotel:

A serving wench came out onto the steps and asked what she could do for me. I asked if she could give me a room, addressing her as 'maid' – she turned up her nose and said there were no maids in the hotel, only misses. I looked at her slack cheeks and dull gaze, and told her she was right. In the dining room I was served with blue milk and blue Bordeaux wine by a sallow waiter with a white cravat, black frock-coat and black fingers. At night I slept in a room with a number over the door, like in the cells of a prison.

Axel's love of Italy and Dalarna and his belief in goblins and trolls were essentially expressions of the same thing; a longing for what was primordial and undisturbed, for a world to which the Evil One had not yet found his way. The ancient myths and the Swedish sagas symbolised ideal conditions that were the antitheses of the modern world. Capri and Dalarna had up till now been relatively spared from exploitation, but now they were threatened by streams of tourists and industrialisation. As we shall see, he would soon find new targets on which to project his romantic longing.

ONLY FOR ANIMAL LOVERS

The remaining articles, 'Only for Animal Lovers' and 'From the Diary of a Hunter', give added depth to a theme that was set out in the 'Letters from Naples': love of animals and campaigning for a more humane attitude towards them. 'Only for Animal Lovers' is a declaration of affection for Puck, Axel's constant travelling-companion, who never complains but always stands by his side, prepared to give his life for him if necessary. Puck's friendship passes the test in all kinds of circumstances. It is otherwise with human beings, who are jealous and selfish in relation to each other and indifferent to the suffering of animals.

Axel and Puck have travelled a good deal on Europe's railways and can confirm that here too, humans, 'who now push themselves forward everywhere and only think of themselves', have obtained significant advantages for themselves. While Axel, for example, is conveyed in a comfortable compartment, Puck has to travel 'with an utter lack of the simplest degree of comfort, with the sharp wind blowing right through his coach, tender in every limb from the incessant shaking, which is not mitigated by any springs, as black in the face as a sweep from the engine smoke'.

Axel's sympathy is not confined to Puck, but embraces the whole animal kingdom. Several of his views were very advanced for the time in which they were formulated. This is particularly true of his attitude to the transportation and slaughtering of animals, which betrays a degree of empathy uncommon even in our day. Who has ever asked the poor bullocks, he wonders, if it is

> too crowded there where they are standing on one another, poking each other in the eyes with their horns, and with the weaker ones already trampled to death before they have reached their journey's end, the depot, where, in the course of enduring untold suffering, they are to be shipped onto a steamboat in order to be taken to their death.

As for the slaughter, it ought to take place in controlled circumstances, and the 'executioners' – the slaughtermen – ought to be jailed as a punishment if they show the least sign of unnecessary cruelty.

Axel's love of animals was general, but there were two species of animal that were closer to his heart than any other: dogs and birds. He had owned dogs since childhood, and as soon as his economic and other circumstances permitted, he acquired several. As regards his attitude to birds, his biography was rather more complicated. As we have seen, he shot and stuffed birds as a child, and his hunting seems to have continued into his adult years.

However, at the age of 26, Axel seems to have swung completely the other way, and the articles 'Only for Animal Lovers' and 'From the Diary of a Hunter' take the form of an intense plea for kindness towards animals. It is hard not to interpret the intensity of Axel's commitment as a psychological reaction to the sins of his own youth.

Axel now regards the urge to hunt as a form of atavism which must be opposed: 'The great foundations of Creation are unchanged, hunting is nothing more than the application of that same right of the stronger to knock the weaker to the ground that permeates the whole of the natural world.' He does not wish to ban hunting altogether, but on one point he is 'immovable' – and here we can hear the voice of his own guilt-ridden conscience:

> *Children should not under any pretext hunt* because of the significant impact that a passion for hunting makes on children's instinctive cruelty and the tinge of coarseness it gives to the whole development of their character – as a child, one must learn gentleness towards one's subordinates; the world makes us hard enough. Nor should children take part in hunts as spectators, for people become so ugly when they follow a fleeing animal, and the child should be shielded as much as possible from the sight of everything that is ugly.

'Zoological Studies', the last part of 'From the Diary of a Hunter', is a paean to the miracle of Creation, from ladybirds and dragonflies, ants and other small insects, to birds, cows and donkeys. 'To observe a little donkey's physiognomy is something that I regard as a veritable delight for a psychologist,' Axel writes, with a form of words that suggests that the sight of a human mug is not. Axel's idolising of the animal world is, to be sure, in direct opposition to his dark view of the human world. In 'Zoological Studies' this misanthropy is set out for the first time in print:

> They say that love of mankind is the highest virtue there is. I admire love of mankind, and I certainly believe that it is vouchsafed to noble spirits. My soul is too shrunken, my thoughts fly too close to the earth to ever achieve it. And I must admit that the longer I live, the more I distance myself from this high ideal. I would be lying if I said that I love human kind.
>
> But I do love animals, those oppressed, despised animals, and I am indifferent to the fact that people laugh at me when I say that I am happier among them than among most of the people I encounter.
>
> When one has talked to a person for a quarter of an hour, one has generally had enough, is that not so? At least I usually wish by then to go away, and I am always surprised that the person I am talking to has not tried to escape long before.

In the course of nine months, from October 1884 to June 1885, Axel published no fewer than twenty-nine articles in *Stockholms Dagblad*. With these, he established himself as a headstrong new voice in Swedish literature – new, but at the same time markedly 'un-modern'. With his strident idealism and his uncompromising condemnation of modern society, he was on a straight collision course with the ideals hailed by the contemporary aesthetic. Stylistically as well as ideologically he belonged to a bygone world, and he would never take the step into the one that was dawning.

THE MISSES FROM
MEDSTUGAN

In reality he was a child, hungry and ever more hungry for notice and admiration.

Edith Balfour

THE SECOND HALF of the nineteenth century in Sweden was characterised by strong romantic patriotic tendencies and an increased interest in northern landscapes, with their undisturbed nature and pristine cultures. The Swedish north enticed not only Swedes but foreigners too, and especially Britons. Under the aegis of an empire that was at its zenith at the end of the nineteenth century, Britons explored the world not only in their capacity as mapmakers and railway engineers, but also as tourists. They travelled mostly to the Alps, the south of France and Italy, but there was also a certain interest in the undisturbed Swedish wilderness. British people were tempted most of all by good prospects for hunting, which they could read about in books like Captain Alexander Hutchinson's *Try Lappland* (1870).

A British family who decided to spend the summer of 1885 in northern Sweden were the Balfours from London. They arrived on the boat from Hull to Bergen and then continued along the fjords up to Trondheim, travelling in grand style: Mrs Balfour, her five sons and two daughters, Edith (nicknamed Miss DD) and May, several friends of the family and a maid. Among the fourteen members of their company was Maude Valerie White (1855–1937), a friend of the 20-year-old Edith. Miss White, ten years Edith's senior, was a singer and composer of songs. In 1879 she had been the first woman to be awarded the sought-after Mendelssohn scholarship, and in time she would achieve great success in her career.

During the voyage along the Norwegian coastline the company would gather on deck in the evenings and sing folksongs. After a while they noticed a young man who always sat nearby, listening. 'His face was extremely expressive, and he really seemed to love the English, Scotch, Irish, French, German, Italian, and Russian folk-songs which we sang softly to ourselves in our little secluded corner.' The man was a Swedish doctor who explained that he was on his way to Lapland.

The young Swede made a deep impression on the company, not least on Miss Edith and Miss Maude, who were enchanted by the doctor's stories about the cholera in Naples and other exciting adventures. In Trondheim their ways parted. The Balfour family took the train over the border to the village of Medstugan in northern Sweden. Axel took his rucksack and walking stick and set out 'in search of the Lapps'. He wished to learn their language and mode of thought, and to understand why they were oppressed, and he wanted to defend their interests.

Unlike many other enthusiasts for Lapland, Axel was not only interested in the Lapps from an ethnographical perspective; he was also deeply engaged in the question of their legal status. As we have seen, in the 'Letters from Naples' they are presented as 'some of the most blatant and blameless victims of civilisation', alongside Native Americans and monks. The common factor uniting these 'victims' was that they represented a lifestyle that was threatened by modern civilisation. It was such areas that Axel was drawn to, and that he sought out, in Sweden and abroad: on Capri, in Dalarna, in Lapland.

When Axel called on the Balfour family in Medstugan on his way back from Lapland they 'listened spellbound to his account of the little Lapps he had visited, their tents, their reindeer, and the kindly, simple hospitality', Maude Valerie White remembered: 'Again and again we made him repeat his experiences during the cholera epidemic in Naples, and again I told him to be sure and send me a copy of his book.' Axel also confided in the company that he wanted very much to travel to England, but that he did not dare to make any plans, as he had tuberculosis. He spoke like a 'world-weary and experienced man', wrote Miss Edith, adding insightfully: 'In reality he was a child, hungry and ever more hungry for notice and admiration.'

It is not difficult to see what made Axel so attractive to these female representatives of England's leisured class. He spoke about the suffering in the world; he said that one must have an ideal to live for; he spoke up for the Lapps and animals. What a contrast to the useless, meaningless life that they lived, and for which he reproached them! At last, someone who had realised what was important in life, someone who could help them to fill their lives with meaning!

Their ways parted in Stockholm. Axel did not forget Miss Maude's request; he sent his *Från Napoli* with the dedication '*Vous n'en comprendrez pas un seul mot*' (You will not understand a single word of it).

Seldom has such a short acquaintanceship resulted in so much printer's ink. Not only did Maude Valerie White devote about thirty pages to Axel in her memoirs; she even dedicated two of her songs to him: 'Addio Lucia' and 'Wird er wohl noch meiner Gedenken'. And forty years later Miss DD – under her married name of Edith Lyttelton – wrote a *roman-à-clef* about the Balfour family's Swedish trip entitled *The Sinclair Family*, in which Axel appears as the male hero under the name of Eric Tollander.

Edith's portrait of Axel agrees well with the picture of him that emerges from letters and diaries. This is how she depicts him:

> His personality was certainly picturesque, picturesque enough to influence all the males of the party – except Peter Fellowes – against him, and all the females in his favour. He had strange clouded blue eyes, with very dark pupils which were often dilated, giving him a look of inward fire. His lips were thick, though the actual mouth was small, his skin fair, and his long straw coloured, straight hair was always falling across his forehead, and he pushing it back with a weary gesture. His hands seemed to combine power and delicacy with a curious and ugly clumsiness, as if they would let a teacup drop, but could shift a microbe under a microscope; as if they could knock a man down, but pat a child's head with extreme tenderness.

Tollander/Munthe flirts with the young women and wins Mrs Balfour's heart and sympathy, not least by presenting himself as a deeply unhappy person. When Miss DD on a later occasion asked Axel to tell her more about himself, he answered with a counter-question: 'Isn't it enough for you to know that the person you met in Norway is one of the unhappiest you've ever met?' This high-flown declaration referred to his marriage, to his being 'tied to a woman who was uncongenial to him'.

Axel's complaint about his unhappy marriage made the Balfour sisters believe that he would have married them if only he had been free to do so. But 'did he really care for any of them?' Edith asked herself, and answered: 'I think he is just vain, and likes to make people fond of him. I don't believe he cares a bit.'

Despite their injured self-esteem, the sisters could not be really angry with the young Swede who had conquered their hearts. Miss White, who loved Italy, had in addition got it into her head that she was going to translate his book into English, without knowing a word of the language it was written in. Axel's interest in the young ladies may have been genuine or feigned, but his acquaintance with them led to a definite shift in his geographical focus – from Paris westwards, in the direction of London. Given the role that England would come to play in Axel's biography, it is no exaggeration to say that the meeting with Edith Balfour and Maude Valerie White was of decisive significance in his life.

Back to Högsjö

After a walking tour in Norway in company with the Swedish poet Carl Snoilsky and his wife, where they visited Henrik Ibsen, Axel returned to Sweden and Högsjö and the von Mecklenburg family. They had not seen each other for a year, but Axel's feelings for Sigrid had not cooled. This emerges from a long poem that he inscribed in her copy of *Från Napoli* and which is revealing in a manner unique for Axel. Since their relationship was socially impossible, he is forbidden to express his love for Sigrid. He is forced to sit like a stranger at her table, he wrote, and address her in the language of convention. His innermost thoughts can only be conveyed in the form of a poem that no one else may see . . .

Their feelings for each other could not be kept secret, and led to Baron von Mecklenburg asking Axel to stop writing to his wife. Axel obeyed, even though it was difficult for him. The reverse was also true; Axel not only filled an emotional vacuum for the beautiful but melancholy Sigrid, but with his talk of ideals and an active life of sympathy for others, he helped to lift her out of 'the artificial calm, the moral anaesthesia' in which she found herself.

At the beginning of October, after a period at Högsjö, Axel travelled to London on his way to Paris. He announced that he was 'utterly depressed by financial worries', something that is borne out by a letter that Mathilda Cederlund wrote the same day to her son: 'He seemed tired and melancholy – oh, if only papa could manage to sort out his affairs and he could find peace – the dear man.' Axel's 'financial worries' included, among other things, the debt to Arnold, which at this point amounted to 4,700 kronor (£17,000 in today's money). Mr Cederlund now lightened Axel's burden by paying Arnold a quarter of the debt in cash.

From the Paris Horizon

'Tremendous events in France! And it will be interesting to see what happens!' Axel wrote to Erik Montan shortly before he left Sweden. Journalistic activities had been at a standstill during the summer, but Axel had hardly set foot on French soil before he took up his pen again. Now, however, he sent his articles not to Erik Montan and *Stockholms Dagblad* but to its rival, *Aftonbladet* and its editor-in-chief Gustaf Retzius, a scientist and professor at the Karolinska Institute and one of the most celebrated scholars of his day.

The 'tremendous events' that Axel hinted at in the letter to Montan were the elections to the Chamber of Deputies. Ever since the Third Republic had been proclaimed in 1870 there had been serious conflict between supporters of the Republic and those who wanted to reintroduce the monarchy. At the elections, which took place in two rounds in October 1885, the right – which included monarchists and Bonapartists – made significant advances, but neither they nor the other two political blocs – the left and the republicans – were large enough to form a government on their own.

The right's success in the elections was seen by many as a victory for the monarchy, which, according to Axel, it was not. 'The republican principle survives undisturbed as the only possible durable form of government for France,' he asserts with some satisfaction in the article 'The Situation in France', which appeared in *Aftonbladet*. The reasonably unpartisan but stylistically loaded account of the different parties' positions closes with three asterisks, followed by some subjective passages where, finally, the third person gives way to the first:

> But it is not the republic of our own day that will give France back its greatness – it is another republic, one that is moderate and subject to the law; one that is sensible enough to suppress all parliamentary disorder, strong enough to know how to quell all revolutionary self-indulgence, truly tolerant in that it does not allow opposition to clericalism – let alone when dictated by political necessity – to spill over into religious persecution, or to let the proclamation of freedom of conscience to degenerate into enforced atheism. [. . .] France, so rich despite so many setbacks, so proud despite all the humiliation it has suffered, will, in the hour of peril, bear free-born sons raised to manhood by the gravity of the situation, who will know how to defend their free nation against both Cæsarism and external foes.
>
> And more than ever, I believe in a great, republican France.

Axel had already shown his political radicalism in the Naples letters, and he had given expression to his republican dreams in other connections. That he had problems with 'objectivity' was already clear in the reportage from Naples, and this was a complication when he wrote on political topics. Retzius therefore hinted that Axel reconsider his 'choice of themes'.

PARIS TOYS

Axel was extremely particular about the treatment of his texts. There were to be no abbreviations or changes in the manuscript without his permission, which was often accompanied by detailed instructions about the typesetting. The same was true of quotations, which were always introduced in the original language and which he seldom allowed to be translated, even in a footnote. All of this shows that his nonchalant attitude to his own authorship was simply a pose.

Axel stopped writing about politics, and instead published the sketch 'Toys. From the Paris Horizon', this time in his old stamping ground of *Stockholms Dagblad*. He extols a vanished golden age and criticises modern society, which, 'since the locomotives began to pant through the forests', has suppressed 'the hobgoblins' in reality as much as in fantasy. The sketch develops into an ingenious and humorous account of the battle that had been fought between France and Germany in the world of toys in the years after the real war of 1870–71, *l'année terrible*. Axel's sympathies are of course on the side of the French toys. These do not belong in the realm of the Great Powers, with one exception – the Paris doll, which 'bears the stamp of nobility on her brow, and she means to rule her doll world as before by right of her undisputed rank and her artistic refinement':

> It surely needs very little human knowledge to distinguish her at once, the graceful Parisienne with her *fin sourire* and her expressive eyes, from one of the dull beauties of Nuremburg or Hamburg, who, by the stereotyped grin on her carmine lips, and the staring, vacant eyes, immediately reveals her Teutonic origin. Should any hesitation be possible a glance at her feet will suffice – the Parisienne's foot is always shod with a certain coquetry, whilst the daughter of Germany is characteristically careless of her *chaussure – tous comme chez nous.*

Axel introduces representatives of different classes of society, from doll high society to the doll bourgeoisie to the pauper doll *à 13 sous*, which belongs to the *poupard* family, is normally made of papier-mâché or wood and has a head made out of a kind of dough. None of Bon Marché's charming coquettes has succeeded in capturing him 'in the net of her blond tresses'; it is the coarse features of the 13-sous doll that his eye dwells on with 'tender sympathy'. This weakness often leads him to those *quartiers* where he knows he will find her, to the dark hovels where the children of poverty live. 'The sparkling eyes of the little ones', 'the pale cheek of the sick brother' and 'the mother's ragged shawl' are depicted with a pathos that feels overdone today, but which struck a chord with the public of that time. This was what Gustaf Retzius wanted, not reports on the political situation.

'Toys' was Axel's first sketch from Paris and it impressed others besides Retzius. On 17 April it was published in the literary supplement of *Le Figaro* under the heading 'Paris Joujoux' – *en tête* – as the leading article. This was Axel's debut in a foreign language, but it was not without complications. When he sent a copy to Montan he informed him that the poor translation had been made without his knowledge. He had gone to the editorial office but arrived too late, and had 'the mixed pleasure of overseeing its printing in 90,000 copies'.

It is of course unthinkable that *Le Figaro* would have had the sketch translated and published without Axel's knowledge. It was no doubt Axel himself who was behind the whole thing, but this he could not admit. As usual, he did not want to take responsibility for his work. In his letter to Montan, he added, however: 'If you want to mention it [i.e. the publication in *Le Figaro*], please feel free.' As usual, he made sure that he attracted all the attention he claimed not to want!

However one regards Axel's complicated relationship to his own authorship, and however one judges his writings, the fact is that by this time he had earned himself a reputation both with the reading public and in leading literary circles.

THE SOUL OF THE MOUNTAINS

The days are so long, so long and the nights are even longer – but on the other hand the foot is a few centimetres shorter.

Axel Munthe to Edith Balfour, October 1886

ULTIMA SPENT THE month of June 1886 at the French seaside while Axel stayed in Paris, busy with 'a couple of troublesome patients'. 'My wife writes in very favourable terms about Villerville, where we have rented a house until September,' Axel informed Georg Sibbern, 'I shall perhaps pop over there one Sunday at the end of the month.' He was no doubt busy with his medical practice, but in view of his shaky relationship with Ultima the reservation 'perhaps' in his letter was not merely dictated by lack of time.

On 10 July Axel arrived in Bad Schwalbach, 'tired and downhearted'. There he met up with Georg Sibbern, who had just completed his move from Stockholm to Norway after his wife's death the year before. They passed the time as usual with drinking the water and going for walks. A few days after his arrival Axel received a letter that was hardly calculated to render him less 'downhearted'. It informed him that the majority of copies of his Naples book were still in storage and in booksellers' shops at the end of 1885, which, according to the publisher, was due to the fact that the book's contents 'were already familiar to the many readers of *Stockholms Dagblad*'. This did not, however, deter Norstedts from future commitments: 'If you were to write a similar book with material drawn from the lives of the poor in Paris and if you were to publish this exclusively in book form, you would find that your pen has already earned you a significant circle of readers who would gratefully seize the opportunity to acquaint themselves with yet another work of your hand.'

In August Axel and Puck moved on to Switzerland to walk in the Alps. While climbing the Matterhorn they were caught in the middle of a severe snowstorm. They survived, even though Axel found himself 'looking Death in the eye'; he lost his rucksack and their guide wanted to leave Puck to die: 'We sat under an overhang for a whole night and the following day we could see nothing for the mist until 2 o'clock. No-one died apart from an Englishman, Burkhart, whose body arrived here yesterday evening. [. . .] Puck cannot walk at all yet [. . .].'

Axel explained to Sibbern that he had a bad conscience about his 'rash foolhardiness' and he was grateful that it had all ended so well. But at the same time he realised the publicity value of the adventure and told both Montan and Retzius about it. Both of them sent Axel money and asked him for articles about the snowstorm. Axel chose *Aftonbladet* but had pangs of conscience about Montan, who had sent him 'lots of money'. The article 'Snowstorm' was published in *Aftonbladet* on 8 September.

The guides had been criticised over the accident with Burkhart, who had been left unconscious in the snow so that the rest of the company could be saved. But Axel defended them and laid the blame on the Englishman, who was made to pay with his life for his 'indefensible conduct in attempting to climb the Matterhorn without experience of mountain-climbing and without being properly prepared in terms of food and necessary provisions'.

The letter's literary merit, Axel maintained, was as good as zero, 'but it made no such claims; its whole point was to defend those mountain guides who were then having all the blame laid on their shoulders.' Later, when pressed about how true the story was, he admitted that he had written it down 'from the talk of the guides' and that it was 'stupid to write it upon so loose a foundation'.

A PERILOUS ASCENT

The article 'Snowstorm' reveals that this was not Axel's first encounter with the Alps, whose beauty had been discovered at the end of the eighteenth century and had been celebrated by many writers, among them William Wordsworth, Lord Byron, Percy Bysshe Shelley and John Ruskin. During the second half of the nineteenth century the Alpine countries became popular tourist destinations, not least thanks to the travel company Thomas Cook. But the mountain ranges attracted not only aesthetes, Alpinists and tourists. In the mid-nineteenth century it was discovered that the people of the Alps had immunity from Europe's great health scourge – tuberculosis – and that sufferers from consumption often regained their health in a miraculous way after a spell in that high altitude, with its dry air.

When 'Snowstorm' was published, Axel and Puck had already moved on and were at Champéry in the Valais, for 'a well-earned rest'. He had come here to meet up with the Balfour family, who were spending the summer in the little Alpine resort with Maude Valerie White. Axel was in no hurry to get back to Paris. Although the escapade on the Matterhorn very nearly ended in disaster, he was minded to make another 'trip over the mountains'. 'The thing was,' he wrote to Retzius 'that something tedious had happened to me and when that happens I always need fresh air.'

Whether it was the long drawn-out crisis in his marriage or something else that was making Axel depressed is unknown. This time, in any case, it was Mont Blanc that tempted him, although it was late in the season. After the first snowfall Mont Blanc should not be attempted because of the danger of avalanches. The bad weather and the lateness of the season also made it difficult to find guides. But it all worked out in the end – and if he had not found a guide, he would have set out on his own, he assured Retzius. If he reached the summit, 'i.e. as far from this vale of sorrows as Europe can offer', he would write about it, he promised Retzius, *otherwise the attempt must remain a secret between us* because it is so rash [. . .]'. In his next letter to Retzius, written in a hut belonging to the Alpine Club and postmarked 22 September, Axel asked for a loan of 250 francs for which he promised to write 'a couple of nice letters from Mont Blanc'.

Axel had expected to be back in Paris on 27 September. He arrived there a day later and in a different way to how he had planned. The ascent of Mont Blanc had almost cost him his life and instead of a peaceful carriage-ride from the Gare de Lyon home to Avenue de Villiers he was taken direct to the Hôtel-Dieu hospital for emergency treatment.

Only one day after his arrival in Paris, and despite being in considerable pain and having a high fever, he took the trouble to write to several people in Sweden about his adventure. One of them was Retzius, who immediately passed the information on to his readers:

> The day before yesterday we received a brief report from our correspondent Dr *Axel Munthe* in which he informed us that he climbed Mont Blanc, the giant of the Swiss Alps, at the beginning of last week, and in particularly unfavourable conditions. Unfortunately some of his toes had become frostbitten, and he was therefore obliged to seek medical help in [. . .] a hospital.

Munthe and his two guides had reached the summit of Mont Blanc but it was so cold – minus 18°C – that they could not even empty the traditional bottle of champagne. The fresh snow had already caused several avalanches, and they encountered one of them on the descent and ended up in a crevasse under a thick covering of snow. When, after some time, they fought their way out of the snow it emerged that they were on a little block of ice at the edge of an abyss. The two guides had lost their ice-axes but Munthe still had his, and it was this that saved them. By standing on the shoulders of the other two, one of the guides managed to swing himself up onto the edge of the crevasse and pull the others up after him.

In a letter to Retzius written directly after his return to Paris, Axel depicted the course of events as follows:

> Yesterday I was at the Hotel Dieu, went there straight from the station but am home now – the foot looks better today, in any event the old boys here (I have been seen by several of them Richet, Leblé and others and treated by the best surgeon in Paris, professor Tillaux, now chief surgeon at the Hotel Dieu and very fond of me although unfortunately he thinks I'm *fou*) say that if I'm *lucky* it will be 2 months before I can stand on the foot. The first phalanx of the big toe was amputated yesterday and they think we ought to be glad if I get away with only losing 3 toes [. . .]. I have a high fever and am incapable of writing printable words at the moment but you will get value for your 250 francs – never fear. The whole of Chamonix was in uproar at my journey which is judged unusual for 3 reasons: 1) It was looked on as crazy to go up just now when the first snow of autumn has been falling for 3 days and it hasn't had time to become compacted yet – as everyone knows Mont-Blanc's *only* (in my opinion *only* because I have climbed at least 4 mountains which I regard as more risky in respect of danger) danger is *avalanches of snow* and these are *constant* in the days following the 1st autumn snows. 2) The ascent, which in itself is fairly long, is doubly tiring when you have to plod through deep snow which moreover has obliterated all previous tracks forcing you to make many detours – from *Cabane des Grands Mulets* (3,050 metres) we were up to our knees in snow. 3) There is *no* instance among all Mont Blanc's miraculous rescues of individuals swept away by an avalanche of snow and hurled into a crevasse being saved, this is so *abnormal* that all the guides in Chamonix will for a long time hence tell the story of our marvellous rescue which can only be put down to a completely unique piece of luck.

What was it that made Axel defy fate in this way? The explanation he gave to Sibbern was that he climbed Mont Blanc, not out of 'thoughtless irresponsibility' (like the Matterhorn) 'but fully aware of the danger, and advised against it by most people, who thought it was impossible to reach the summit now, just after the autumn snow had fallen'. He said he was '*uncommonly* persistent' and maintained that he had undertaken the trip 'only after mature consideration of what I had to gain and what I had to lose'. So it was not Axel's usual 'impulsive foolhardiness' that persuaded him to undertake the ascent, but something else. 'You know, Your Excellency, that I have to be a little mad sometimes in order to calm down later,' he wrote, with an allusion to his manic streak. But is this the only explanation for the crazy climbing episode? As we have seen, Axel felt himself to be deeply unhappy, mostly on account of his love for Sigrid von Mecklenburg and the disharmonious marriage to Ultima, and there was a strongly asocial trait in his personality. Was the ascent of Mont Blanc *against all the odds* a suicide attempt, conscious or unconscious, like his stay in Naples two years earlier, when he hoped to be 'finished off' by the cholera? He did, after all, write to Sibbern that he had maturely considered what he had to gain and what he had to lose. What he had to gain was obvious – the distinction of having climbed Mont Blanc. But what was he risking? The only reasonable answer is – his life.

Le Roi des Montagnes

Axel was allowed home from the hospital after a day or so but could not stand on his foot. However, he was glad to have avoided the amputation that Professor Péan had wanted to carry out. Mr and Mrs Cederlund, who immediately called on him, reported that, although he had a fever and pain in his foot and was obliged to remain at home, he did not wish 'what was done undone, so delighted is he with his journey'.

Axel spent the time writing articles for *Aftonbladet*, the first of them being an account of his mountain-climbing mishap. Mont Blanc is personified here as *Le Roi des Montagnes* (the crowned king of the Alps): 'There was a time when he was sullen and cruel, but he has grown kinder-hearted in his old age, and now, like a venerable patriarch, he sits there, the white-haired Charlemagne, looking out in calm majesty over his three kingdoms' – France, Italy and Switzerland. When the summer day 'begins to darken into autumn, he goes to sleep in his white state bed', and does not want to be disturbed any more.

'The article dances away on the rope of a single metaphor,' Axel writes in a vignette, 'and dances over precipices'. It agrees well with the factual reports of the accident, despite a belles-lettristic packaging that can sometimes appear overdone. But, as so often with Munthe, the overwrought pathos is relieved by an economical and effective narrative style: as when the avalanche has erupted and Axel and both his guides are covered by the snowdrifts: 'Everything became silent and the chill of death fell over me,' he writes, continuing:

> But the instinct of self-preservation roused me, and half wake I sat up in the coffin and looked around. At the same moment one of my companions also crept out of his shroud, and by help of the ice-axe we forced the lid that had already been screwed down over our third companion. And

to our astonishment we discovered that we were not dead at all. We sat imprisoned in a subterranean dungeon waiting for trial, but we all agreed that we were in the cell of the condemned. Daylight fell through a narrow rift over our heads, and beside us yawned a great chasm – it was like the Mamertine prison in Rome. We had time to meditate upon a good many things. To complain was useless; to protest against our fate was useless too; all we could do was to hope that the judicial formalities might be conducted as quickly as possible – *der Tod ist nicht, aber das Sterben ist eine schändliche Erfindung*!

The German quotation – from Heinrich Heine – was absolutely not to be translated, Axel made clear in a follow-up letter to Retzius: 'Anyone who doesn't understand German is better off *not* knowing what it means.'

Sibbern had disapproved of the escapade on the mountain, but 'Le Roi des Montagnes' won his sympathy, which gladdened Axel. 'If only I was not so depressed and so concerned about my daily bread I would write a serious article,' he wrote to Sibbern, 'not about "The *King* of the Mountains" but "The *Soul* of the Mountains" – it exists and I have *felt* it – it is magnificent but melancholy, Beethoven tried to give voice to its tongue in his funeral march *Sulla morte d'un heroe* [sic] – on Napoleon's death – Your Excellency will remember that I have occasionally played it.'

Axel's ascent aroused both admiration and criticism. The secretary of the French Alpine Club wrote an article under the heading '*Une ascension perilleuse*' (A Perilous Ascent) and Axel became a member of the club. But several newspapers in both France and Sweden reproached Axel for having risked both his own life and those of his guides. The Stockholm satirical magazine *Figaro* wondered if the 'European fame' that Dr Munthe had won had really only cost him a big toe: 'There are also those who feel that this kind of undertaking demonstrates an even greater loss; for does this kind of foolhardiness not reveal something – mindless?'

BACILLUS NIGER

Axel's foot healed more quickly than the doctors had believed it would, but at the end of November he had himself carried to see a terminally ill patient and developed an inflammation in his leg. Not until the New Year could he begin to walk again with the help of two sticks, but his leg remained weak. His miserable state of mind had no stick to lean on. On the occasion of his twenty-ninth birthday on 31 October he announced that he had not felt so downhearted for a long time – *vie inutile, manquée*! – and he 'realises daily more and more how infinitely better it would have been to have remained in the crevasse on Mont Blanc'. The same theme is repeated in a letter to Sibbern written two days before Christmas Eve:

> I wish I could be up north with Your Excellency during the Christmas holiday. Here in Paris there is no Christmas holiday, because there is no spirit of childhood here. Never have I felt the desolation that surrounds me to be more hopeless than I do now. I have at last begun to limp around the room and tomorrow I shall go down to the street for a bit. But I have no desire to go out; on the contrary, I think that the life of the street is loathsome, all those people feel like vermin on my body [. . .]. I am so nervous that I cannot stand the company of other people for long and when it comes down to it, I almost think I got on better that time when I was lying in bed on my own than now when I am beginning to see people again.

At the same time, Axel writes, his brain is 'extremely active in a way that is not quite normal'. During his convalescence he indulges in intensive activity, as if to keep his melancholy in check. Miss White came over from London to discuss her translations; the Norwegian writer Bjørnstjerne Bjørnson, who had expressed his admiration for the article 'Le Roi des Montagnes', visited him almost daily. With the help of Retzius, Axel procured an Order of Vasa for a French colleague, Dr Thomas, 'who is very *poor*'. He wrote letters to friends and acquaintances, newspaper editors and publishers, and he wrote articles, among them 'Menagerie', which, with its fiery defence of animal rights and the pangs of conscience he suffered, corresponded closely to his earlier writings.

His life had certainly not turned out so well as he thought it would when he was a schoolboy, Axel wrote, but he had at least taught himself 'to feel tender' towards animals. One did not learn such things at school, where you exchanged birds' eggs for old postage stamps, shot small birds, raided squirrels' nests and were 'cruel to animals like all animals'. Now he wanted to make reparation for his sins, but an evil act never dies and he 'knows of bloodstains on tiny boys' fingers which have rusted to stains of shame in the childhood recollections of the man'.

The existence of zoos can be justified since there one can, like Darwin, 'study the customs and mode of life of different species of animal'. In the same way vivisection is justified when it is carried out by 'men who are serious researchers'. But travelling menageries have nothing to do with science and ought to be prohibited, being 'hotbeds of unspeakable and futile animal torture'.

As we saw, Axel felt that his brain was not 'quite normal'. He confided in Gustaf Retzius that he wrote down the 'worst idiocies' in a special little book. One of these 'idiocies' was an article that he deemed to be 'too crazy' for *Aftonbladet* and which he did not dare publish: Retzius would, he wrote, get to read it only in Axel's *œuvres posthumes*.

The article 'Hypochondria' deals with Axel's proven method of combating his lowness of spirits – by 'climbing up over the snow-line where "bacillus niger" is not found' – and it was written as a defence against 'all the abuse' he received after his ascent of Mont Blanc. Retzius did not need to wait until Axel's death before reading the article, but Axel sat on it for no less than nine years before releasing it (see the chapter 'Tiberio', below).

Why did he regard it as 'crazy'? Partly, one suspects, because he allowed himself to poke fun at medical science. But an even stronger motivation for not publishing it was its autobiographical character. It is in fact about Axel himself and the black sprite that almost always emerged victorious from the mental turmoil that had raged inside him since his youth. There is therefore good reason to pay some attention to it.

Hypochondria, we are told, is an infectious illness generated by a microbe to which its discoverer Dr Munthe has given the name *Bacillus niger*. The poison is spread, like rabies, along the nervous system; it results in 'constant and well-known disorders in the brain' and it ends in 'paralysis of the affected individual's intellectual and moral functions, and, at last, mental death'. The illness is difficult to identify but can, as with certain forms of tuberculosis, be diagnosed 'at the back of the eyes'. In a normal eye the visual impressions from the external world are broken up by 'illusions and never-dying hope' before being conducted through the visual nerves to the brain. But the *Bacillus niger* infection leads to morbid changes in the organs of sight that make the patient *see life as it is*. The bacillus is exceptionally hard to kill and can only be assuaged by four tried and tested remedies: alcohol, tobacco, ink and music:

> As for alcohol, its effect is indubitable, but unfortunately of very short duration. The microbe very soon – indeed, already the next morning, according to all experimentalists – regains its full vigour, and its temporary inactivity seems rather to have increased its virulence instead of decreasing it. Like most of the other anti-microbic agents, alcohol is in itself a deadly poison, and its application in the treatment of the disease is therefore very limited. It is to be used with the greatest precaution, for there are numerous instances of the individual having followed his microbe to the grave.
>
> May I here mention *en passant* a harmless old quack remedy – the common practice of smoking out the microbe. The home of the tobacco-plant is the same land where the poppy of oblivion blossoms, the silent shores between which flows the stream of Lethe. The fragrance of its leaf has deadened the microbe in more than one diseased brain, the clouds from an old pipe have hidden the reality from more than one sorrowful eye. (Do you remember Rodolphe in Henri Murger's *Vie de Bohème*?).

Ink as a bactericide is less known, but worth consideration. I know of a case [. . .] where a momentary amelioration was produced by an ink-cure. Contrary to alcohol, this specific can be used without any danger whatever to the individual himself – the danger being limited to his surroundings. The microbe is dipped in the ink-stand, and fixed on paper to dry. It maintains, however, its virulence long enough, and can, transplanted in a fertile soil, regain its vigour and grow. The preparation must, therefore, be strictly locked up in the writing-desk, which now and then must be disinfected, the surest disinfectant being here, as always, fire.

As for music, this treatment was known even in the childhood of science; it was already highly esteemed by the ancients – hypochondria is, as is well known, one of the oldest of all diseases; it resounds already in the choruses of Sophocles and Euripides. The new world of bacteriology was then undreamt of, but the discoveries of thousands of years have done no more than verify the experience of the ancients. Music still remains the greatest consoler of sorrow-stricken man.

After this account of anaesthetics, there follows a description of the patient. It is self-revealing in a manner unusual for Axel:

Man about thirty. The patient maintains an obstinate silence as to the origin of his sufferings; it is, however, evident that the evil dates from several years back. External examination nothing remarkable – on the contrary. Big dog at his heels. Energy but little developed. Active impulses wanting. Ambition rudimentary. Intelligence mediocre – maybe slightly above. Sense of humour well defined, as usual in these cases. Sensibility abnormally developed. Heart perhaps rather large. Tendency for idealism. Patient has hallucinations – fancies, for instance, he is surrounded by people who suffer and hunger; imagines seeing all sorts of animals oppressed and tortured to death. The doctor had in vain prescribed several things in order to calm and distract his diseased mind, rest-cure in Anacapri for a whole year; earthquake in Ischia, cholera in Naples, etc. etc., but without any enduring result. Returned to Paris, the patient had, though with visible aversion, gone through a cure of ink-treatment, and in the beginning had felt a little better for it, but had soon fallen back to his normal condition of hopeless dejection.

The doctor – Axel's alter ego – has a hypothesis that there is 'a region of immunity from hypochondria' and sends the patient to the Alps to study the influence of the Alpine climate on the affliction. Even on the summit of Mont Blanc there are significant numbers of microbes in the patient's brain, but after he has been left for a whole night in the raging storm on the Matterhorn the doctor thought he could identify 'an almost complete absence of bacillus niger in the benumbed thought of his patient'. When the patient slowly opened his eyes, however, he was 'more depressed than ever, and remained decidedly worse for several days', and the doctor was forced to abandon his theory.

'We are able to soothe sufferings of the hypochondriac, because we are able to deaden his microbe – kill it, we cannot,' Axel ends his reflection. 'After more or less time the bacillus recovers his virulence, and the diseased individual retakes his momentary interrupted course towards the sombre land where no traveller returns . . .'

The disease is life itself, which only death can cure.

SKETCHES FROM THE SLUMS OF PARIS

In 1887 Axel informed his publishers of his plans to write several sketches that he intended to collect into a book. The plans included, one imagines, the 'sketches from the slums of Paris' that were published in *Stockholms Dagblad* in the winter of 1887 under the general title 'Italy in Paris'.

One inhabitant of the Paris slums was the Italian organ-grinder who became the central character in the first sketch, 'For Those who Love Music'. Don Gaetano was so poor that Axel hired him to come and play twice a week underneath the balcony of the Hôtel de l'Avenir, where he had his study – 'it may, perhaps, appear superfluous for one who was studying medicine, but the old man's terms were so small, and you know I have always been so fond of music.' This sentimental story had a tragic ending – Don Gaetano's monkey died of consumption and its owner disappeared from Axel's view.

The second sketch, 'Raffaella', tells the story of a young girl from a town between Rome and Naples who had moved to the Italian slums of Paris with her mother and grandmother. After *la febbre* carries off her mother, Raffaella is forced to earn her living as a model. Nude studies of her meet with success in the Salon: 'Fame entered the young artist's studio, and a ruined child went out from it.' It is the beginning of the downward path for Raffaella. She goes from studio to studio and finally becomes pregnant. To be sure, the artist who takes the blame pays his dues, but her life as a model is over and she does not marry, 'for the people do not forgive one who has had a child by a *signore*'. Nor does she find any other work. Forced to choose between prostitution and poverty, she chooses the latter and ends up as a street sweeper.

So much for the actual story. The sketch ends rather abruptly with a suggestion that 'someone who writes well' should turn it into a short story – but it is not Axel who comes up with the idea but 'that doctor who liked Italians'. The *doppelgänger* motif again!

Write a story about the female models and dedicate it to the artists! Write it without distortion and without sentimentality. Write it without exaggeration, because none is needed, and without severity, because we all require indulgence.

Tell them – the artists – how fond of them we all are, those carefree, good-hearted comrades, tell them how proud of them we are, those fortunate interpreters of our longing for beauty. But ask them why they despise their models so much, ask them if they know what happens to the originals of their female figures.

They know perfectly well.

If they answer that they are young, that their temptation is greater than anyone else's, then ponder whether you yourself have the right to say any more to them.

But if they answer that it is the models who are to blame, tell them to their faces that they are lying. Tell them that the majority of female models in Paris become prostitutes – the statistics are there, and they brook no opposition. [. . .]

You who know how to write well, you know what else you must say to them. But is he altogether wrong, the doctor, in thinking that the artist stands in the same relation to his female model as the doctor to his female patient? [. . .]

Yes, you who can write, you certainly know what else you must say to them – take with you those doctor's reflections of yours if you think they amount to anything. They have at least the characteristic of being grounded in experience, experience of the Parisian artists' world as well as that of Rome.*

This outburst against artists collectively is surprising, considering that most of Axel's friends in Paris were painters and sculptors. Their ethical responsibility is now being compared to that of doctors, to the latter's advantage. Why this excursion into the field of manifesto writing? Axel must after all have realised that the sketch could be taken the wrong way. By maintaining that his reflections were grounded in his own experience he also deprived himself of the possibility of claiming that the whole thing was fiction.

The attack was of the same type that we have seen examples of earlier, in outbursts against authors and doctors. Axel himself belonged to no collective; he was always the loner standing on the sidelines.

The third sketch, 'Monsieur Alfredo', is set, like the first one, during Axel's student years. The hero is an unsuccessful dramatist who has little time for successful colleagues like Racine or Corneille, and who openly despises practitioners of the lighter genres like Lecoq or Offenbach. But on

---

* None of these paragraphs were included in the English translation of the sketch.

one occasion Axel comes across him during a performance of Offenbach's *Les Brigands* at the Varieté theatre, where he joins in the vociferous bravo-ing of the claque, the hired applauders. Axel sees the underlying tragedy of the whole affair and decides to take theatre lessons from Monsieur Alfredo, who at the same time is working on his *magnum opus* for the Théâtre Français (the Comédie Française). But before he can finish his drama he falls ill with consumption and dies. At the moment of death he believes he can hear the echo of 'his life's fondest dream', the Théâtre Français 'ringing with applause', and 'slowly the curtain sank upon the old author's last tragedy'.

With its muted sentimentality and accomplished tragi-comic construction, 'Monsieur Alfredo' is more successful than the first two sketches. The same is true of the fourth and last sketch, 'From the Impasse Roussel', the story of the poverty-stricken Salvatore family and their backward son Petrucchio. Here, it is Axel's passion for social justice and his empathy with the family that carry the story. The father of the house drinks but has Axel's full sympathy:

> Those who watch the lives of the poor closely cannot be very severe upon a working man who, after he has toiled twelve hours a day the whole week, sometimes gets a little wine into his head. It is a melancholy fact, but we must judge it leniently; for we must not forget that here at least society has hardly offered the poorer classes any other distraction.

After Salvatore falls from a bricklayer's scaffold and breaks his arm, he can no longer pay the rent and the family are evicted. The landlord is known for his ruthlessness, and Axel sees it as necessary for his own 'study of human nature' to make his acquaintance. During the conversation he erupts in full-blown rage: 'I pointed to the crucifix which hung against the wall, and I said that if any divine justice was to be found on this earth, vengeance could not fail to reach him, and that no prayers could buy his deliverance from the punishment that awaited him, for his life was stained with the greatest of all sins – namely, cruelty towards the poor.' On the following day the landlord hanged himself and Axel saw himself as 'the unwitting herald of a judgement'.

In a letter to Anne Charlotte Leffler, Axel claimed that he never 'invents' anything – 'It is extraordinary, I only write *historically*, and that is a great error.' To what extent this claim is valid is hard to say, but there is plenty of evidence that there were nuggets of truth in most of what Axel wrote – sometimes more, sometimes less. The story of the Salvatore family, Axel assured both Montan and Sibbern, included 'a rather dramatic moment which has the great advantage of being true – I still bear the dreadful impression of it'. And when later he offered *Blackwood's Magazine* the English translation it was with the same assurance that it made 'rather depressing reading [. . .], but truth, as a rule, is not particularly merry'.

ARABIA

I do not wish to be his *wife*, but I should like to be his *mother*, in order to look after him!

Mathilda Cederlund to her son Edward, 1887

AXEL'S LONG CONVALESCENCE took its toll not only in the form of frostbite in his legs and face but also as depression and nervousness. So when in January he received an invitation from Mr Cederlund to accompany his son Edward to Algeria, he accepted immediately. The boy had been afflicted by a persistent catarrh in his chest and throat and his parents were extremely concerned, as his sister had died of consumption. The offer was a generous one: all his expenses paid, and payment for a locum in Paris.

Although Axel could not leave Paris immediately, the Cederlunds relied blindly on him, especially Mrs Cederlund: 'Convey my *particular* greetings to the dear Doctor,' she wrote to her son, 'thank him for accompanying you, tell him that I am relying on him, next to God, for a good outcome from this trip; I know that if he will not look after himself, he will nevertheless look after you as long as he is able.' Of the Cederlunds' six children only two were still alive. Axel became like another son for her and brought out all her maternal instincts: '[. . .] how often have I said "I do not wish to be his *wife*, but I should like to be his *mother*", in order to look after him!' she wrote to her son Edward. 'But ask him sometime if he would not like, with regard to his own Mother's memory, to take a little more care of himself – how she would grieve if she was alive to see her beloved, talented child going to rack and ruin – because of his pride and obstinacy [. . .]!'

One of the reasons why Axel could not leave Paris was that one of his patients, the Swedish consul Ullman, was mentally ill and his condition had worsened. But Consul Ullman's illness was only one of the obstacles to Axel's trip. At about the same time as Axel received the offer from Cederlund, the 21-year-old Prince Eugen of Sweden and Norway arrived in Paris to study painting and Axel was asked by King Oscar II's physician-in-ordinary to be his doctor. In a letter to Sibbern, Axel commented that the proposal was 'flattering to my royalist ego, which, as Your Excellency knows, is highly developed'. Despite the ironic tone, it is probable that Axel did indeed feel flattered.

Despite the prince's reputation as a liberal in both political and aesthetic questions, he was met with scepticism and mistrust by several of the Swedish artists. Nevertheless, this opposition gradually disappeared and the prince became friendly with many of them. The general scepticism was shared by Axel, whose initial attitude was one of wariness. After the welcome lunch for the prince hosted by the Swedish–Norwegian minister, Sibbern's successor Count Carl Lewenhaupt – later foreign minister – Axel reported back to Sibbern:

Yesterday I was graciously invited to the minister's dinner for the prince – this was definitely intended as a great honour, for the rest of the company had been invited to a soirée at 9 o'clock. I sat there on my own representing the 'underclass', but at any event I sat up straight. The prince looks pleasant and kindly but perhaps a little stupid. He came up to me immediately and asked about my foot – so my Alpine reputation seems to have even reached the royal castle.

Why this accentuation of class? Axel, after all, did not come from the underclass but from a solid middle-class background, and he was himself the legation doctor, an author and, in 1884, appointed a Chevalier of the Légion d'Honneur. One answer is that Axel was in fact 'underclass' in relation to the aristocratic circles he often associated with. The gulf between the aristocracy and the middle class was at this time enormous. By designating himself as 'underclass' he was in a way also expressing solidarity with his friends in the artists' and writers' colony.

In Axel's case the class issue was exacerbated by his own social unease, the problems with his own identity. On several occasions during the Paris years he gave out that he himself was of noble birth. The diploma from the Légion d'Honneur was made out to 'Axel de Munthe, Swede, Doctor at the Swedish legation', and he often signed his name as 'de' or 'von' Munthe, for example on his visiting cards. To Edith Balfour, Axel explained that he belonged to an old aristocratic family and really ought to have a 'von' before his name. On being asked why he did not, he answered, in his phonetically and syntactically still not quite perfect English, reproduced as follows by the authoress: 'I do not believe in triffling tittles, if I earn a tittle I will not spurn it away, but I must make it.'

It is not quite clear what it was that made Axel play around with his name in this light-hearted way. According to a source of 1657, Munthe was a noble family in Flanders, but it was never introduced into the Swedish House of the Nobility. Axel must have been aware of this, but he still took the risk – in the age of aristocracy, a noble prefix might well come in useful.

I'm Looking Forward to Getting a Little Air

The prince remained in good health and Ullman was committed to a madhouse – at last Axel could get away, a month late. He had great expectations of the Africa trip: 'I have admired Arabs for a long time and if my admiration stands the test I shall try to come here [to Paris] in the autumn for a few months and write a book about them,' he told Retzius, who was apprised that Axel also planned a riding tour in the Sahara and had with him letters of recommendation to 'the chief of one of the Arab tribes there'.

Axel prepared himself as best he could during the short time available to him. He wrote down in a notebook the titles of books about Algeria: *Mountain Life in Algeria, Chasse de l'Algérie, Le Sahara, Tableaux algériens*, among others. He also put together a little Arabic–Swedish/French phrasebook containing everything from 'Bring the coffee here!' to 'There is no other God but God and Muhammed is His prophet'. He made notes about customs and practices. And he took with him on the trip the most trusted travel guide of the time, *Murray's Handbook for Travellers in Algeria and Tunis*.

On 23 February Axel took the train to Marseilles. Ultima stayed on in Paris where Puck 'is staying with her to guard her'. Waiting for him in Marseilles was Edward Cederlund junior, with whom he boarded the steamer *Ville de Rome*, which was to take them to Algiers.

During their five days in Algiers Axel and Edward returned each evening to the Arab neighbourhoods, where among other things they had an opportunity to 'take a closer look at the Arabs' domestic life', something which was difficult otherwise ('Their wives were of course not allowed to show themselves'). In an Arab café with 'splendid coffee' they also imbibed experiences of another sort: they smoked 'the intoxicating but delicious kif, a kind of tobacco or opium'. Kif was the same as hashish, and the fact that Edward noted the event in his diary demonstrates that its use was not particularly guilt-laden. (At a later stage of the trip when Axel again smoked hashish, he wrote to Retzius: 'Yesterday I studied physiology or pathology or whatever you want to call it – lay on a mat and smoked "kif" (= hashish) with a nightingale singing in the cage alongside – a most interesting form of intoxication.')

The goal of the trip was Biskra, an oasis 144 miles further on in a south-westerly direction. As the railway had not yet been extended as far as Biskra, passengers had to disembark at El-Kantara, the gateway to the desert. Since the *diligence* was full, Axel and Edward had to cover the last thirty miles in a little peasant cart.

Biskra was the group name for five villages spread over a five-kilometre-long oasis. The climate is very pleasant during the winter half of the year but in summer the temperature is often around the 40°C mark. 'On the 6th we awoke to the finest summer weather which meant that we strolled to our hearts' content through Biskra's streets and pretty parks. We passed the time by writing during the hottest hours of the day, for it was certainly hot, and otherwise we enjoyed a *dolce far niente*,' Edward reported to his mother after the first day at Biskra: 'During the course of the afternoon we went to a couple of Moorish cafés where we managed to see Negro-Arab dancing in its full splendour.'

For Edward the health resort of Biskra may have been the final destination of his journey, but for Axel it was only a temporary halt. His destination was the desert. Before setting off he wrote almost identical letters to Montan and Retzius, both of whom were enjoined not to give the contents 'any publicity whatsoever': 'My name is not to be further made fun of in any way.' He asked Montan to send the fee for 'From the Impasse Roussel' to Ultima in Paris – although the journey itself was costing him nothing, the desert trip was outside the programme and would be 'expensive but interesting'. 'Today I have hired a superb Arab horse,' he wrote to Retzius:

> a camel for the tent and provisions, and I have an Arab for a guide and a negro too – a manservant, *s'il vous plaît*. But in fact he is really coming with us because he is so droll to look at, a fine Darwinian type and as innocent and happy as a puppy.
>
> The goal of our journey is Tuggurt, 4 days' march *en plein* Sahara, 205 kilometres from here – I hope to return via El Oued. Here again in 12 days' time and so direct to Paris where I will be on the 25th. I have had a Swede with me on the way here and am glad that I will be doing the desert trip on my own – exceptionally enough 2 Italians were murdered the day before yesterday on their way home from there – and that has made him rather wary. I am telling you this so that you will not think it is me if you see some news item about what happened to them. [. . .] I have a revolver and the Arab has a carbine (with flintlock) and I am far too interested in the desert to have time for silly nightmares. [. . .] Anyway the Arabs are much nicer than we think and there is a good deal to be said about the propagation of the blessings of culture by military terrorism.

Le négro, by the name of Boularez, was – according to Edward – 'Munthe's special friend and brother' and a master of negro dancing. He fascinated Axel, who devoted several pages to him in his notebook:

Glistening skin almost black. They had taught him to smoke and with his black claws he snapped up cigarette butts as I threw them away and took a few puffs, accompanying this with much spitting and grimacing. He also had other skills, striking a match, carrying a parcel well enough, – & if you gave him a sou he laughed contentedly [and] immediately stuffed it in his mouth. [. . .] He had been taken captive at quite a young age [. . .] far out in the desert. He was now completely tame & piety shone out of his trusting, doggy eyes. He slept in the negroes' village beyond [Biskra] among the palms [. . .] & during the day he crouched in the sun outside some of the Arab cafés. After I found him he followed me faithfully like a dog for days at a time, ran after my horse when I rode out into the desert & crouched under my window while I ate my lunch.

At 7.30 on the morning of 10 March Axel set off on his journey southwards, straight into the Sahara. The ride was full of risk and, according to *Murray's Handbook*, it should only be done by persons with good health and the capacity to endure 'considerable fatigue and privation'. Nor should it be undertaken without consulting Biskra's *commandant-supérieur*. But this was a piece of advice that Axel airily disregarded – on the contrary, he defied the military commander, who, after the murder of the Italians, opposed the trip and refused him an escort. Edward did not go with him. 'We both sincerely approved your staying in Biskra,' wrote Mrs. Cederlund to her son, 'but we can well understand that Dr Munthe wishes to go deeper into the desert! – for him, danger simply does not exist – and he longs to see just what no-one else has seen or experienced.'

Axel made a few stray notes about the excursion in his notebook but gave no consistent account of it, but the route he followed is described in *Murray's Handbook*. It consisted of four daily stages of about sixty kilometres each. He spent the first night in Ain Chegga, a caravanserai that offered a roof over his head but no food. However, the surrounding area is rich in gerbils, which, *faut de mieux*, offer a far from unappetising meal.

On the second day the traveller rides via floodplains up to the oasis of El Meghaïr. During this stage he will encounter the first desert sands. In El Meghaïr he is highly likely to be taken to the house of the sheikh, where he will be offered whatever hospitality the house can afford. 'On leaving, a present will be expected, though never demanded.' The third stage, with its many oases, is the most pleasant part of the ride, but the caravanserai in Tamerna, where the traveller will spend the night, is worse than any other stage of the journey.

On the evening of the fourth day one reaches Tuggurt, after covering the last twenty kilometres in metre-deep loose sand that threatens to bury your horse. With its twenty minarets piercing the sky over the thousands of palm-tops, the oasis presented a picturesque sight to the traveller. The population was extremely homogeneous, the 7,000-strong French garrison consisted wholly of natives of the region, and visiting foreigners were immediately surrounded by crowds of people in colourful costumes. It is easy to imagine that Axel got his fill of ethnographic authenticity and exoticism here.

Axel arrived in Tuggurt on 13 March but only stayed for a day or so. On the morning of 18 March, Edward rode out into the desert, accompanied by a guide, to meet him. 'It was a pleasant meeting, for my travelling companion was hale and hearty after the long and strenuous journey he had made.'

A few days later Axel and Edward went back to Algiers, from where Axel took the boat to Marseilles while Edward remained in Algeria for another month. 'I think', wrote Mrs Cederlund to her son, 'that he could well have taken a bit more time off – now that he was abroad and it wasn't costing him anything – and also, he knew that each day he spent with you was dear to us – but he no doubt has his own thoughts, that one, which no-one else can read!'

Axel was in a hurry to get home – his thoughts, 'which no-one else can read', were centred on debts that had to be settled. In a letter to Mr Cederlund he admitted that it was the poor state of his finances that made him leave Edward in Algiers. 'I have such heartfelt sympathy with him,' Mrs Cederlund wrote to her son,

> and I emphasised to papa how much I wished to help him, according to my poor ability, the upshot of which was that papa took my little sum and added the rest to it, so that he sent him the amount he had mentioned as being most difficult to find, viz. 1,000 francs. We have not heard from him since then, and I so earnestly hope that he has not taken offence now, as sometimes happens, but that he realises it is the most sincere friendship and concern for him that has characterised our dealings with him.

No, Axel 'did not take offence', but gladly accepted the sum of money, on condition that he was permitted to convert it into a loan.

'I do not regret my trip as it was extremely interesting and gave me an insight into a new world – the old, patriarchal, biblical life,' he reported to Sibbern after having returned to Paris on 28 March: 'I have the greatest admiration for the Arabs, they are both more God-fearing and more genuine than we civilised folk and the Koran is, next to the Bible, the most remarkable book that has ever been written – its morality is in any case the same as that which the Bible gives us.'

LETTERS FROM A MOURNING CITY

Axel did not stay in Paris for many weeks before he was longing to escape again. The name of his saviour was, like so many times before, Georg Sibbern, who yet again – for the seventh year in a row – invited him to spend a few weeks in Bad Schwalbach, where, according to his own account, Axel had always felt 'calm and free of care' and 'uncommonly healthy': 'I feel as if I were still in the Sahara and the oasis which I long for is called Schwalbach. As regards the rest of my summer, I do not know, I do not dare to think any further ahead. Home in Sweden there is nothing for me to do.'

Axel had no desire for his homeland; instead, his thoughts were on England: 'I eagerly desire to learn the English language and *if* I can afford it financially I want to try to find a cheap place in the country-side on the Isle of Wight or elsewhere [. . .].' Axel's wish to learn English had doubtlessly been inspired by work on the English edition of the Naples book. *Letters from a Mourning City* – as the English edition was entitled – came out in April 1887. The book's contents correspond to those of the Swedish edition but include in addition the sketch 'When Puck was Lost', which tells how Axel saves a young woman from cholera. As thanks for this he unwittingly acquires the protection of the *Camorra*, who help him to retrieve the stolen dog. With the publication of the letter about Puck, the first phase of Axel's authorship was at an end.

The English translation had been finished during the late autumn, when Miss White travelled to Paris to join with Axel in putting the finishing touches to it. As she knew no Swedish the English text was hammered out by author and translator working in tandem. Under the Swedish words Axel wrote their meaning in French, or he dictated aloud to her.

A female friend of Miss White's encouraged her to show her translation to John Murray, one of the oldest and most respected publishing houses in Britain, with Lord Byron, Walter Scott and Charles Darwin among their authors. Apart from their literary output Murray specialised in travel literature and guidebooks, which made the Naples book perfect for them. The firm expressed their willingness to bear all the expenses of printing and advertising and to share the eventual profit with Miss White. Axel himself said that he did not want to see the letters in print, but this attitude, as we have seen before, was simply a reflection of his neurotic approach to his literary work.

Relations between author and translator were in fact extremely strained. Miss White was just as fanatical about translating the book (according to Axel she 'suffered from *Monomania*') as he was difficult to work with. In a letter to John Murray she complained that she had 'grown thin over his bullying and my own efforts at satisfying him' and in the summer of 1887 she informed Axel that she was handing in her 'resignation' and 'ended a chapter' in her life. Axel, in his turn, could pretend to be indifferent to the book's fate, but when it came down to it he made detailed demands, just as with his Swedish publications, both on her and on the publishers. Among other things, the texts were not to be exposed to any editorial intervention whatsoever.

Maude White's attitude to Axel was a combination of boundless admiration and awe-struck respect. When she described him to John Murray she did so in the following terms: 'He is *so* original and with all his "cleverness" is the most simple-hearted fellow I ever met. He is only 29 and still looks like an Uppsala student. He talks *very* funny English such as for instance "my hat who I lost on Mont Blanc" etc.' In another letter she writes that he is 'so *frightfully* natural that no one can stand him', adding in brackets, 'I mean he's sometimes such a tiger!'

Miss White was not only driven by ambition to see her translation in print, as Axel believed. Like so many other women who crossed his path, she had made his ideals her own and become a medium for his voice. Her letters to Murray borrow elements from Axel's style, and she asks the firm to forgive her for being so 'mercenary' – but, she assures them, all the money she receives will go to an Italian family in Paris whom Axel is caring for and which 'is literally dying of starvation'.

Letters from a Mourning City was well received and the first edition of 1,030 copies sold out. The reviews were generally in accord with those of the Swedish edition. The critic of the *Athenæum* wrote that readers ought to be grateful to Miss White for her translation of these letters of 'the quaint-minded idealist from the extreme North', 'a sort of Scandinavian Sterne in Italy'. *Blackwood's Magazine* noted that 'Dr. Munthe is much more of a philosopher than a doctor', he 'himself and his opinions are the essence of the book, the cholera is simply the accident that has called him before the public.' And the *Saturday Review* thought that there is 'scarce a line of it but should be read and pondered'.

The most flattering judgements for Axel came from private quarters. One was signed Matthew Arnold, who in a letter to the translator 'spoke very highly both of the *Letters* and the author'. The other comment came from the former (and future) prime minister Gladstone, who was gripped by Axel's depiction of the dreadful conditions in the prisons of Naples. According to his own account Axel even met the 'Grand Old Man' of British politics.

Axel's English-language career could hardly have had a better start.

A Semblance
of Married Life

Ye gods, what a crazy institution marriage is when it is meant to unite two people who do not love each other!

Anne Charlotte Leffler

AXEL WAIVED HIS rights to any payment for *Letters from a Mourning City*. But he was keen for the Swedish artist Hugo Birger to illustrate the frontispiece, and asked Murray to remunerate Birger for this to the tune of 100 francs. Birger was in dire need of money. He had been seriously ill since the autumn of 1886, his tuberculosis had entered its final phase and he wished to return to Sweden before he died. Axel had been his doctor for many years and it was he who took care of the practical arrangements for the artist's last journey. In situations like this Axel never hesitated but gave proof of his genuine and active sympathy for others, despite the price he himself had to pay; in this case the price was to be exceptionally high.

The journey took almost a whole week because of Birger's state of health, which necessitated a stay of several days in Hamburg. Hugo Birger died in a hotel in the south of Sweden on 17 June 1887. After his death Axel went to Gothenburg in a determined attempt to obtain funds to provide for Birger's wife Matilda: 'It is a question of persuading some Gothenburg millionaires to convert their ostentatious patronage of the talented artist into discreet compassion for his widow,' he wrote to Sibbern. The 'millionaires' were the art collectors James Fredrik Dickson and Pontus Fürstenberg, Birger's principal patron. We do not know to what extent Axel managed to cultivate the industrial magnates during his short stay in Gothenburg, but despite the fact that he was in poor shape both physically and mentally as well as financially, he did not give up the idea of helping Matilda; indeed, he put great effort into this self-imposed mission during the next few years.

At the beginning of July, Axel went to Bad Schwalbach, where Sibbern was waiting for him. After their stay there, Axel planned to travel with Sibbern to England and then on to Ireland 'to have a look at the Home Rule question which has interested me for a long time', he wrote to Retzius. The question of Home Rule for Ireland went back a long way but it had become topical again since Axel's admirer, Gladstone, had put it on the Liberal Party's manifesto the previous year.

The trip never came off. On 22 July Axel suffered a haemorrhage of the lungs. He coughed up three potfuls of blood and was forced to lie still on a sofa. After a few days he was able to move out into the garden, where he spent whole days in a deckchair. He was weak but not so bad that he could not work with Miss DD – who was staying with her mother in the nearby health resort of Königstein – on her English translation of the 'Sketches'. 'Dear Dr Munthe more agitated today', Sibbern noted in his diary on 27 July. 'I noticed how careful one must be.' Sibbern did not want to leave Axel, but Axel persuaded him to go.

Part of the reason why Axel was able to stay on in Bad Schwalbach was Mrs Balfour, who soon came to his rescue. 'The English are an incredible people – this is almost too much, and I would rather have been alone, however kind she is.' A few days later Axel was installed in Königstein, where the air was better than at Schwalbach, and he slept better too.

The 'Sketches' that Axel and Miss DD were working on during his convalescence were 'Roi des Montagnes' and 'Italy in Paris', the English version of which was now given its final polish. In actual fact Miss White and Miss DD both seem to have contributed to the translation work. Axel's relations with Miss White and the Balfour family had become more and more intense during the two years they had known one another. Miss White and Miss DD were important for Axel's introduction to the British market, both as a writer and as a doctor. Apart from their usefulness to him, his relationship with the Balfours also meant that Axel came into contact with a family remarkable for its solidarity and warm feelings: 'I am almost flabbergasted by all this friendliness, which I do not deserve – she signs her letters "Mammy" – which is what the children call her, and she treats me exactly as if I were one of them too.' In her relationship to Axel Mrs Balfour was guided by the same maternal instincts as Mathilda Cederlund and Mrs Sibbern. They were Axel's surrogate mothers and they gave him something that he had missed out on during his early years, namely, friendliness – they were 'so kind' to him.

Särö

After a few weeks in Königstein Axel travelled to Sweden. He had to go to Gothenburg again to settle Hugo Birger's posthumous affairs. He was forced to travel slowly, he wrote to Sibbern, for he was 'extremely agitated and depressed': 'My whole nervous system is abnormal and I feel I can no longer rely on my body.'

Axel's destination was the island of Särö, south of Gothenburg, a popular holiday resort frequented not only by west-coast society but also by the royal family. Several of the 'Gothenburg millionaires' lived on Särö; apart from James Dickson there was James Keiller, an industrial magnate from a Scottish background. Keiller's younger brother Alexander was also renting a house on the island, and one of the first people Axel bumped into after his arrival was his daughter Alexandra. 'He was not handsome, he walked badly, but his teeth were dainty and he appears to be very interesting,' were Miss Keiller's comments on the 'famous person' she had heard so much about and now 'at last managed to see'. On 31 August, she noted in her diary:

> We were sitting sewing on the veranda, when, to my great surprise, I saw Puck Munthe and his master down in the forest. I was bold enough to approach him and I really do not think he was offended, although he is very shy of people. [. . .] He has been confined to bed by illness again in Paris and is depressed and strange, but he has such pretty teeth – I could be platonically in love with him! – but he has a pretty wife whom he doesn't like! I have just been singing up in the inn and he stood down there and listened. In the evening we had music up there. [. . .] Munthe was there. I have always respected him and did not particularly want to sing for [him]. I noticed him quietly clapping his hands behind the others and looking at me and I can hardly express how happy that made me! He praised me afterwards: 'It would be worth making something of that voice, – shall you not come to Paris?'

Alexandra thought that she was 'the only one he cares about on the island after Puck, the only creature he really cares about in the whole world'. Although she was courted by several young men, she could not stop thinking about Axel, who 'talks mostly about animals and plants and a whole heap of things that I with my poor understanding have trouble grasping'. They lay in the grass studying 'the ants and other small creatures on their travels, working away without a break', and Puck, 'who right from the beginning has been jealous of me, wanted to lie between us and growls whenever I come too near to the Doc'. 'A shiver literally runs through me when I see that ugly, shabby physiognomy with the matted hair,' she confided to her diary.

The erotic charge became stronger each time they saw each other. After an evening stroll Alexandra noted in her diary:

> In the evening we sat on my bench in the moonlight. He was like a different person then, he talked about his wasted life, referring to his unhappy marriage, something I would have loved to discuss, but which out of delicacy I never dared to. This is what happens when children go and get married. He was so gentle and so sad, oh if I had only been able to do something for him. He does not wish to meet me by moonlight any more, he *does not dare to*! So this is where we have ended up!

Alexandra Keiller's notes about Axel end here; she did not wish to confide anything further to her diary. In the autobiographical 'sketch' (the description of the genre was no coincidence!) 'An Autumn Saga' – also written in her diary – she was more frank. Here, she described her infatuation with Axel and her disappointment when she 'felt a pair of warm lips passionately pressed to hers' and realised that he was 'like other young gentlemen'.

The Divorce

On 7 September Anne Charlotte Leffler came to the island to visit her brother Arthur. Axel and Anne Charlotte had met in Paris in the summer of 1884 and had been corresponding since then. Anne Charlotte Leffler lived in a marriage of convenience with a district judge and had for several years been carrying on an intensive – but not erotic – relationship with Adam Hauch, a Danish headmaster. Thus there was no shortage of talking points when Axel and Anne Charlotte met again for the first time in three years. After only two days on the island she sent Hauch the following description of Axel:

> He is only 29 years old but already broken by natural melancholy and an unhappy marriage, from which he wishes to free himself, although he has been unable to get his wife to agree to this. It is one of those meaningless marriages which can sometimes be more burdensome than those which are truly unhappy. He is based in Paris where he works as a doctor, he is a gifted writer and a very unusual and very sympathetic personality. [. . .] He belongs to that breed of men who, with their manly independence, unite a woman's gentleness and delicacy; a very rare variant of the species *man*, of whom I have previously known only a few examples. Such men are always congenial comrades. [. . .] He is a little reminiscent of the heroes of English sentimental novels insofar as he seems to be unconfined

by any restraints and pops up now here, now there all over the world. [. . .] To me, the man is an interesting psychological study which relieves my melancholy. [. . .] I am [. . .] quite gripped by Dr Munthe's story now. [. . .] Ye gods, but what a crazy institution marriage is when it is meant to unite two people who do not love each other!

On 15 September Axel took the steamboat direct to London, where he stayed as a guest of the Balfour family at 65 Pont Street – 'The Balfours are so kind to me.' After about a week in London he travelled to the Isle of Wight to stay with the Calthorpe family, relations of Sibbern's wife who were also Axel's patients. Before leaving, he wrote a letter to Anne Charlotte Leffler. She seems to have been the first person to become aware of Axel's decision to ask for a divorce, which testifies to the depth of the trust she had inspired in him:

I told you I had written to my wife and her parents to tell them that I thought it was far better to openly acknowledge the spiritual and physical isolation in which we lived than to continue, from fear of the criticism of others, to try to keep it secret under a semblance of married life – a life which my whole nature helplessly rebelled against – which incidentally suggests that nature is chaster than the law. My aim was and is to spare my wife as much as possible and I understand enough psychology to know that wounded womanhood assuages the pain of a loss which in this case is not really a loss at all. My wife believes that I have been a lot worse than I have been and I have laboured to portray myself in these terms. Otherwise she would not have been able to agree to our lawful divorce. For myself, I am not greatly worried about it as I feel unfree in any case, but I think it will be much better for her.

Axel returned to Paris on 9 October. Two days later it was Sibbern's turn to be told what had happened. In the letter to him Axel wrote that he felt that he was 'doing the right thing here in the very name of that morality that people will now regard me as offending against', adding:

If I were to lose Your Excellency's friendship I would be profoundly sorry, but my decision has now been made once and for all, not in a moment of rashness but during the agony of sleepless nights. I committed a great sin when I married, but what I intend to do now cannot be a sin. In any case I have left the final decision to Ultima, and if she prefers, then as far as I am concerned we can continue to conceal our mutual isolation under the deceptive *lie* of marriage. But I do not wish us to try to live together any more; it is immoral and unjust.

Sibbern assured Axel of his continuing goodwill, which made the latter heave a sigh of relief: 'I thank you with all my heart for your friendly letter.

I am so depressed in body and soul now that I truly do not need more grief from losing the affection of those I am fond of.'

To the poet Carl Snoilsky Axel explained that what had 'destroyed' him was that he had married with his 'thoughts and feelings dominated by another than the one I was marrying' and that one day he would tell him 'the story'. To Gustaf Retzius he complained that there was no other woman involved – 'I almost wished there were, as I would perhaps feel less unhappy then, but such is not the case.' He says he has no difficulties in justifying the break with Ultima and will be able to do it 'on *physiological* grounds the *psychological* consequence of which is as inexorable as fate itself'.

The letters give a good idea of Axel's thoughts and motives but Ultima's image remains indistinct. Her anonymity can best be explained by her 'innate physical and mental apathy' – Axel's only known characterisation of his wife and a description that seems close to the truth. The passive streak in her personality is also brought out by the ballad singer Sven Scholander, who saw in it one of the reasons for the breakdown of the marriage: 'He was an unpredictable neurasthenic who admittedly was not easy to live with, but who in casual company could be quite charming in a beguiling and spiritual way. [. . .] Ultima Munthe came across as rather indifferent to music, and, in her whole being, perhaps rather indolent, something which unfortunately was clearly irritating to her lively, highly-strung and versatile spouse.'

That life with Axel was a torment to Ultima was obvious to everyone around them. Mathilda Cederlund praises her son in a letter for having invited Mrs Munthe to 'a little entertainment' during his stay in Paris. 'She needs that, poor thing,' she adds, 'however tempered she may be by her sad life!' Rumours about the Munthes' marriage reached as far as the Swedish capital. The art collector and cultural historian Fredrik Martin remembered how as a young boy – this must have been around 1883 – he heard his upset mother repeating what her friend Mrs Hornberg, Ultima's mother, had told her about her daughter, married to 'a dreadful Swedish doctor' in Paris.

Everything was dreadful, both the man himself and his behaviour. They wanted a divorce. At that time this was something unheard of among decent people in Stockholm. [. . .] Four years later I saw the dreadful doctor at a seaside resort on the west coast. I could not understand that such a sweet girl could fall in love with such an ugly man, badly dressed, trousers baggy at the knees and with delicate but unwashed hands, very intelligent eyes.

One example of Axel's 'dreadful behaviour' is given by a friend of the couple, who tells us that Axel used to leave Puck to guard Ultima and her maid when he went out on house calls, so that they could not leave the house. If this is true, it points to an almost pathological need to control. We will find plenty of instances of Axel's need to be obeyed during later phases of his life, when even heads crowned with something other than servants' caps were subjected to his inflexible craving for obedience.

In his letters Axel provided several explanations for the divorce, but there were only two people who were allowed to know the true reason. One of them was Snoilsky, to whom Axel confessed in the letter quoted earlier. The other person was the Norwegian writer Bjørnstjerne Bjørnson, with whom Axel was even more open and to whom he confided that the marriage had broken down 'because he was helplessly in love with a married woman with several children (outside Stockholm) and therefore could never love another'.

It was thus the episode with Sigrid von Mecklenburg that had 'destroyed' Axel. It was because of his love for her that the marriage with Ultima was not consummated and it was this that turned him into a brooding melancholic, a hypochondriac. The change in Axel's temperament can be dated with almost mathematical exactness to the moment when he fell in love with the baroness: 'The inclination to live alone was not in my nature – ah! I was so happy when I was 20! – but it has slowly taken possession of my character, my mood and my habits during the 6 years when I lived through the hardest form of loneliness there is – when we were two.'

'His whole nature' revolted 'helplessly' against a married life that 'did not exist and never could exist', he wrote to Anne Charlotte Leffler. Why could there never be a married life? Was it only chastity that forbade him to carry out his obligations in the marriage with Ultima? Or were there other reasons too? What were the '*physiological* grounds whose *psychological* consequence is as inexorable as fate itself'? To Bjørnson Axel confided that 'He had had syphilis and therefore did not indulge in intercourse with his wife.'

If this information is correct, it gives us yet another explanation for Axel's melancholy and hypochondria, as well as for his obvious death wish. A shameful and usually incurable illness could be reason enough for wanting to be 'finished off' by the cholera in Naples or for setting out on life-threatening mountaineering escapades. The question that presents itself is whether Axel told Ultima about his syphilis. It is hardly likely that he did: if she had known he was ill he would not have needed to hit on other stratagems, such as portraying himself as 'much worse' than he actually was – that is as an unfaithful husband – with the aim of arousing her 'wounded womanhood'.

Perhaps both explanations were true. Axel could not have sexual relations with his wife because of his feelings for Sigrid and on some occasion he had been infected with syphilis. Bjørnson, however, suspected that he had not been told the full truth. If he had stayed longer in Paris, he wrote to his daughter, he would have 'gradually been given another four editions of reasons' why Axel could not live with his wife. The letter develops into a sharp characterisation of what Bjørnson saw as Axel's essential nature:

> A kinder, nobler disposition does not exist, nor another talent so fine and great and so capable of versatile thinking that it could accomplish wonderful things. And a loveableness, a sweetness in character and eyes and smile which makes him eternal for anyone who has been exposed to his image.
>
> But so insecure from introspection, so preoccupied with vain coquetry, so preoccupied with his whims aimed at self-admiration and that of others, that he can no longer be at peace with himself. And so sanctimonious on account of his ambition to appear in a favourable light that he tells everyone a different version of the same story!

Perhaps the talk of syphilis was only men's talk, a convenient and plausible explanation at a time when this ailment affected so many. Perhaps there were deeper reasons for the divorce, too sensitive to discuss even with Bjørnson. The reference to 'physiological grounds' points in the direction of a sexual problem of some kind. There is a great deal of evidence that Axel suffered from impotence – an impotence conditioned by the nervous problems that followed in the wake of an unhappy love. This is why 'nature is chaster than the law': his love for Sigrid von Mecklenburg made it physically impossible for him to have sexual intercourse with his wife.

This suspicion is strengthened by the fact that Munthe seems to have suffered from problems with impotence at later periods of his life. Among his papers are extracts from German medical literature about cures for impotence such as erection exercises and various kinds of aids to achieving an erection (one of which, ironically enough, bore the name 'Ultima'). His notes can of course have been of a purely professional nature, but the unconsummated marriage with Ultima suggests that Munthe's lifelong interest in sexual pathology was at least in part grounded in his own emotional problems.

Small Sketches

Axel wished to leave behind everything that reminded him of his ill-fated marriage – including the actual scene of the disaster, Paris. In a letter of December 1886 to Carl Snoilsky he had formulated his view of the French capital: 'Things are the same as usual here, as happy as ever for those with something to celebrate and as miserable as ever for those who have taken a knock – I have always thought that Paris is only suitable for success, and I think I'm right in that.' Now, a year later, he wrote to Sibbern: 'I had my 30th birthday the day before yesterday and I feel that my young days have gone and my illusions with them, and that life is not a game but a serious business.' When his period of success was over Axel drew the logical medical and spiritual conclusions from his analysis of Paris and left the city.

As regards the goal of his travelling, he hesitated, largely out of financial considerations. All he knew with certainty was that it would take him in a southerly direction. In conversations with Anne Charlotte Leffler he confided that he had thought of moving to Rome for the winter. For a while he thought about Tangier in Morocco, before realising that he was 'too frail for that trip now'. In the end his choice fell upon Capri, where he could live cheaply and where he hoped to be able to make enough by writing to pay for his expenses.

Axel had always seen to it that he was well paid for his writings, and with the forthcoming stay abroad in his thoughts he was more preoccupied than ever by the question of fees. *Letters from a Mourning City* had done so well that Murray offered to pay him for it, Axel told Sibbern. But he needed to make more money and during his stay at Särö he set to work on the book of 'sketches' that Norstedts had offered to publish.

In the letter in which Axel informed Norstedts of his decision to publish his newspaper articles in book form he mentioned that he was also negotiating with another firm about publication. To Norstedts this came as a total surprise. Axel's action was a pure negotiating tactic, with the aim of obtaining the best possible conditions. Norstedts accepted the challenge and made him an offer he could not refuse, 50 kronor per printed sheet: 'These conditions apply to the original works of Ibsen and Bjørnstjerne Bjørnson and should be seen as the most advantageous that any Swedish author has hitherto enjoyed [. . .].'

With the book out of the way there remained only one task to perform before Axel could leave Paris: making provision for Matilda Birger, which he did by arranging for her to be 'the guest of an English family of friends of mine' who were 'heading south'. One of these 'friends' was none other than Axel's translator Miss White, who was to spend the winter months in Italy.

Axel left Paris in the days before Christmas Eve 1887. In his last letter to Sibbern before departing he wrote:

I [. . .] hope that in future I shall come to see life with other eyes than I do at present, for as I see it at present, it would be better not to live it. Hypochondria is caused by anomalies in the nervous system and if the body is sounder then one's thoughts are bound to become lighter. As regards Ultima, I am not aware of anything new apart from the fact that she has written to Mrs Birger and asked her to buy her gloves and a silk dress. It will not take long, I hope, before she realises fully how much better it is for us to live apart. I have been quite open about this business with those people I have to do with here [. . .] and a few others and their view seems to be that this ought to have happened long ago.

To his friends Axel said he would be away during the winter months, but to Sibbern he confided that he did not intend to return to Paris until he 'had become calm in his mind and better in his chest'.

Hysteria and Hypnosis

The eighteenth century saw many great scientific discoveries, but not until the 1800s did the breakthrough in science and technology achieve a wider influence. Scientific explanatory models now began to be applied in other areas too, not least within literature. Aesthetic doctrines such as Realism and Naturalism built on scientific theories that were re-interpreted – and often misinterpreted – by writers, historians and philosophers. Balzac, Zola, Flaubert, Maupassant, the brothers Goncourt, Ibsen – all of them joined in the scientific discussion, ever ready to re-cast the latest findings in literary form.

During the 1880s the dominance of Naturalism in prose began to weaken. In its wake there followed a current that is usually known as 'Late Naturalism', characterised by a pessimistic outlook on life, influenced by German philosophers such as Arthur Schopenhauer and Eduard von Hartmann. Deterministic belief in progress and optimism were about to be replaced by a dejection and a pessimism marked by the same deterministic fatalism.

In Naturalism the depiction of human beings had been reduced to physiology. Now the psychological interpretation gained the upper hand. Hence the unique influence that Jean Martin Charcot's research into hysteria and neurosis came to exert. The period was said to be marked by a pathological uneasiness and the fashionable illness was hysteria. In the same way that physiological research had given rich stimuli to the efforts of the Naturalists, psychiatric research now came to influence the way in which authors treated the object of analysis that they shared with physicians – the human being.

Jean Martin Charcot (1825–93) was one of the leading neurologists of his time. A trained pathologist, in 1882 he was appointed to a newly instituted chair of neurology in the Paris medical faculty. La Salpêtrière, where he worked for the greater part of his industrious life, was an old saltpetre works that had been transformed into a hospital. It had 5,000 patients, most of whom were chronically ill women – 'a living museum of pathology', in Charcot's own words.

Charcot was not only a brilliant researcher but also a successful practitioner and an inspirational teacher. Many of the most outstanding neurologists of the next generation began their studies with him. Among the foreign students attending his lectures was Sigmund Freud. But Charcot addressed himself not only to students and colleagues but also to a wider public. Authors, journalists and other interested parties flocked to his lectures in large numbers and he became an outstanding scientific celebrity.

It was during these sessions that Charcot set out his ideas about hysteria and hypnotism. For him, the causes of hysteria were physiological. If the patient was a woman, the attack could be unleashed by pain in the area around the ovaries. In men, the 'hysterogenic zone' was in the testicles. Many of the movements and poses were of an erotic nature (for example *arc de cercle*), and some patients experienced sexual release during their attacks. In order to demonstrate what happened during an attack of hysteria, Charcot put his patients into a hypnotic sleep and then induced hysteria by means of suggestion.

Charcot's hysteria sessions were tremendously popular and could rather be likened to theatrical performances. The clinic had its 'stars', who were better than others at having – or simulating – attacks. When Charcot's ideas began to be criticised, this was one of the things that people fastened on: that the hypnotic trances were the result of the training of hysterical women, the most 'psychoplastic' of human beings, as someone had called them. The most vehement and accurate criticism was fired off by two other nerve specialists, Hippolyte Bernheim and Ambroise-Auguste Liébeault, leaders of the so-called Nancy school. Unlike Charcot, they believed that hysteria was not a physiological but a psychogenic condition, that its causes were mental, and a reaction to feelings that for various reasons had not been integrated into the psyche.

As for hypnosis, it could be applied not only on those who suffered from hysteria, as Charcot maintained. Hypnotic sleep, Bernheim and Liébeault claimed, was in principle identical to normal sleep and could therefore be induced in almost anyone. Under hypnosis, the patient could then be made well by the power of suggestion. Hypnotic suggestion was a method of treatment that Liébeault in particular practised with great success.

For a whole decade a downright war raged between the Nancy school and the school of Charcot. It was won by the former, whose key concept of the role of suggestion had the future on its side. But even if Charcot's ideas about the physiological bases of hysteria turned out to be false, one cannot overlook his historic contribution as a researcher into the phenomena of hysteria and hypnosis. The same holds true of his enormous influence on those authors who read him and attended his lectures, and for whom he was a veritable oracle. 'After parting with him I no longer have any desire to engage with my own stupid concerns,' wrote Edmond de Goncourt. 'My brain is saturated like after an evening at the theatre. Whether the seed will bear fruit, I do not know. But what I know for sure is that no human being has ever affected me in a similar way.'

Axel also read Charcot's books and attended his lectures, but he was critical of Charcot's theories and instead supported Bernheim. In *The Story of San Michele* he states that he visited Bernheim on several occasions. A week-long visit to Nancy is confirmed in a letter to Sibbern from the summer of 1890, but otherwise our information about Axel's interest in hypnosis and hysteria is garnered from his own book, written forty years later. Although the chapter about Charcot is one of the central chapters of *The Story of San Michele*, there is no documentation to flesh out his account. Charcot is not mentioned in a single letter of Axel's out of the hundreds that have been preserved from his Paris years.

When, in *The Story of San Michele*, Axel wants to provide a motive for his decision to leave Paris and take himself off to Capri, he refers to his disagreements with Charcot, which ended with his being banned from La Salpêtrière. After visiting Bernheim he claims to have had an article published in *Gazette des Hôpitaux*, which made Charcot ignore his presence for several days. When, some time later, Charcot was about to be elected to the French Academy of Sciences, *Le Figaro* published an article on 18 April 1883 with the heading 'Cabotinage' (Play-acting), written by the journalist Félix Platel under the pseudonym 'Ignotus'. The article condemned Charcot's lectures as theatre performances and contained so much biographical detail that the author was assumed to have had sources close to Charcot himself. According to Munthe, Charcot put it about that he was the source, and 'from that day his usual cordial attitude to me had changed'. However, no such article in *Gazette des Hôpitaux* has been found, just as there is no confirmation that Charcot reproached Munthe for supplying 'Ignotus' with material.

What finally persuaded Charcot to break with Munthe was the episode with a young female patient, Geneviève. According to Axel's version of the story, he had wanted to help the young girl to flee from La Salpêtrière, but the attempt failed and he was thrown out of the hospital by Charcot himself, accused of having wanted to exploit the girl. It was 'one of the bitterest [blows] I ever received in my life', Axel wrote in *The Story of San*

Michele. There is no documentary account of any such attempt at flight. Presumably the story is the result of Axel's usual mixing of fact and fiction according to a recipe of his own making. Geneviève was – just as Axel described her in the book – one of the 'stars' at La Salpêtrière – but the real Geneviève was, firstly, considerably older than the girl of the same name in the book, and secondly, she had a quite different family background from the one described there.

Why did Munthe choose to tell a story which in all likelihood was made up and which moreover showed him in a dubious light? His motive had to do with narrative technique: he needed a plausible explanation of why he suddenly left his promising medical practice in Paris and moved to Capri. Since Axel is a bachelor in *The Story of San Michele*, he could not mention the true reason, his divorce. His wife is as absent from his book as Charcot is from his correspondence. Yet by blaming himself for the fact that he had to leave Paris, he came close to the psychological truth.*

Even if the episode with Geneviève is a product of Munthe's imagination, it does not have to be totally untrue; it would tally quite well with Axel's literary method. In this case, the kernel could be an actual conflict with Charcot, which he chose to dramatise in this way. In the manuscript of *The Story of San Michele* there is a piece about Charcot that Munthe deleted before the book was typeset: 'Jealous to ferocity of anybody high or low who dared to touch his special hobbies, his grande hystérie, his catalepsy, his somnambulism, his spinal cords, he silenced all opposition with his indisputable authority and broke ruthlessly the brilliant promise of more than one young doctor.'

Was Axel one of the promising young doctors whose career Charcot so ruthlessly destroyed? And if so, why? Did Axel on some occasion give vent to a dissenting opinion, did he express the same scepticism about Charcot's methods in reality as he did in the book? Diplomatic finesse was not Axel's most obvious talent. There is reason to believe that there really was a conflict between Charcot and Munthe, but that it found rather less dramatic expression than the one described in the book.

The fact that the account of Geneviève and the articles mainly seem to have had a narrative function does not alter the fact that Axel's views about Charcot's professional qualifications are largely in agreement with the judgement of posterity. The remarkable thing is that in *The Story of San Michele*, alongside the professional criticism, he allows himself to characterise the French doctor, and not only him, in terms that are sometimes

---

* Munthe's marriage problems are hinted at in the book, but in coded form: 'It was not overwork but something else that had reduced me into such lamentable conditions; but don't let us talk about that here.'

downright libellous. Axel's outburst of professional jealousy – examples of which we saw earlier – was on this occasion so violent that it drew protests from Charcot's family. But that story belongs to a later chapter.

EXILE ON CAPRI

I have learned the great rule of wisdom that we ought not to try to satisfy our needs, but rather to reduce our needs. The old philosophers did this, and so did Christ.

Axel Munthe to Georg Sibbern, summer 1889

THE ROAD TO Capri was more winding than Axel had imagined. On his way south he stayed several weeks in Cannes, where an old friend from Uppsala, John Freundt, was terminally ill with lung cancer. 'He needs me both as a doctor and as a friend and I have done too much evil in my time to be able to afford to pass up a chance to do some good.'

During his stay in Cannes Axel received the proofs of the preface to *Små skizzer* (Small sketches), which the publishers found 'far too modest not to in some degree damage sales'. It is not hard to understand why. 'The appropriateness of publishing these small articles in book form has long seemed to their author rather doubtful,' runs the opening sentence. The person who wrote the articles is no author, the preface continues, his time 'belongs to the real world and gives him no peace to try his hand in earnest at literary composition', his inclination 'has once and for all confined his best thoughts and endeavours within that specialised type of writing whose circle of readers consists exclusively of pharmacists'.

The self-effacing foreword was yet another indication of Axel's angst-filled attitude to his own writing. When the book came out the usual obeisances were made. 'It is not out of discourtesy to you that I am not sending you a book (Small sketches) by that beast Puck Munthe to be published in a few days by P.A. Norstedt,' he wrote to the well-known literary critic Karl Warburg: 'After much hesitation I have now agreed to the publication in book-form of these trifling newspaper articles [. . .]. I am under no illusions, and if your demanding role as a critic obliges you to even glance at this book – then I beg you to read the foreword.' He does not want to send the book to Warburg, but more or less urges him to review it!

Tarantella on Capri

Freundt died at the end of January and Axel travelled to Menton, where Miss White and Matilda were staying. As he was coughing, he remained there for about a week before travelling on to Capri, which had by now become a popular travel destination for people with weak chests. In that same year of 1888, for example, one could read in *Harper's New Monthly Magazine* that visitors to Capri 'find in the deep-blue sky, the clean air and the mountain tops a refuge from bronchial troubles, fever and other physical ailments.'

When Axel arrived on the island in February 1888 he hoped that his stay there would do him good:

> I am well again now but have really been quite poorly this time. I am on Capri and these climes which once recalled me from the dead will perhaps even now succeed in restoring my will to live. I have never dared to hope for *joy*; one has to be thankful if one avoids pain occasionally. I live economically and hope to be able to get by without making obeisance to debit and credit till I feel healthy enough for Paris. [. . .] I haven't written much yet but am pondering. There are some Englishmen here whom I am often with and who are extremely kind to me. Otherwise, I have plenty of old friends from very modest social backgrounds but of a friendly disposition. I miss so-called social life less and less the longer I live.

Miss White and Matilda passed the winter in Florence but also spent some time with Axel on Capri. Axel hired a fishing boat and they sailed over to the mainland, where they visited Sorrento, Amalfi, Ravello, Praiano and Paestum. In Sorrento the horse pulling their coach bolted, the coachman jumped off, but Axel stayed where he was and managed to halt both horse and coach two metres from the edge of a precipice. 'We were all of us very nearly killed,' Miss White remembered. In Anacapri they danced the tarantella the whole night long, encouraged by Axel.

Axel danced the tarantella and sailed in the Bay of Naples ('He adored the sea and everything connected with it,' according to Miss White) but in the letters a different person emerges: he is 'sick and gloomy and at this rate will soon be heading in the same direction as Hugo', 'his spirits are shattered for good' and he 'has become as shy as a wild bird lately, doesn't see people very often and has less and less need to speak'. Both pictures are true – Axel was basically a 'hypochondriac', and his mood shifted between periods of depression and a need for solitude and a hyperactivity and elation of an almost manic nature.

However, Axel's wish to isolate himself should not be exaggerated. He had both *Stockholms Dagblad* and *Aftonbladet* sent to him wherever he happened to be, even to Capri – all his life long he was a keen and well-informed newspaper reader; and the outside world was always impinging on him. On 20 March 1888 his divorce became legal. From what he heard Ultima was apparently 'in good spirits', which reinforced his conviction that she 'will very soon feel a lot better than she did before'.

WHAT A BASTARD!

Small Sketches came out in January 1888, and as soon as he heard that Karl Warburg had written a review Axel got in touch with him:

> I have not heard a single word of what people have said about it nor am I in the least bit interested – with the exception of your verdict, as you are a phenomenon in our press, viz. since you understand what you are writing about. You would therefore be doing me a great favour if you could send me your verdict as a press cutting or as printed matter – especially if it is harsh; praise does not affect me, but censure interests me.

Warburg of course saw through Axel's manipulative turns of phrase, but he also saw the genuine insecurity behind the pose and was very appreciative in his notice. Axel was said to be 'an individual authorial voice of a remarkable kind', 'a refined, sensitive, rather wayward individuality' – despite his obvious 'hatred for mankind'. Warburg concluded that Puck Munthe was '*quelqu'un*', 'someone', in Swedish literature, but this conclusion was not shared by everyone. At the same time as Warburg was singing his praises, Axel became the object of a review of a quite different kind. But this criticism was made privately and he would never know of it. It was August Strindberg who, two days after Warburg's review, poured his gall over Munthe in a private letter:

> I have just been reading Puck Munthe's infamies and I found myself roused to indignation by a heartless individual's skulking behind love of animals to hide his malevolence and his hatred of the human race. It was the most loathsome, most hypocritical book I have ever read! Not to shoot grouse, but to slaughter oxen! There you have naïvety, stupidity, showing-off, and villainy! Coquettish as a whore, despising decorations when his chest is full of them, identifying himself with such lowly forms of life as dogs, yet spitting at naturalism and naturalists! What a bastard! Bloody hell!

I Don't Give a Damn About People

When, in mid-April, Swedish newspapers gave wings to the rumour that Countess Snoilsky had left her husband and run off with Axel, Strindberg picked up the scent again. But this time Axel got off lightly, as an even more hateful strand was woven into the case. The main guilty party was seen as 'the woman', for whom the misogynous Strindberg suggested that corporal punishment be re-introduced.

After an account of how Count Snoilsky in 1879 divorced his first wife, remarried and left the country, a Swedish newspaper publicised the 'deplorable rumour' that he himself had now been abandoned:

> Another heart broken! One, no, perhaps two! For the man who is now playing the usurper's role also had a wife whom he divorced a few months ago after an eight-year marriage. [. . .] This 'third' man is also a widely known if not yet so renowned man of the pen as the other. At the same time a man of the pen, and an experienced wielder of both Aesculapius' staff and – an alpenstock.

'I am not worried about what is attributed to me, as it is a long time since I stopped acknowledging the public's right to judge my morals – but I am sorry as it will hurt Snoilsky if he gets word of it,' Axel wrote to Gustaf Retzius: 'And why was I chosen to be the villain of the piece? Perhaps because my own divorce leads others to presuppose that there was another woman involved there – which is not the case.'

The source of the rumour seems to have been Claes von Mecklenburg, elder brother of Axel von Mecklenburg and hence the brother-in-law of Sigrid. He knew Axel, and of course he was aware of the emotional drama that had played itself out at Högsjö manor. Resentful of Axel's encroachment into the von Mecklenburgs' matrimonial bliss, he would no doubt be glad to see him compromised.

Axel's alleged abduction of Countess Snoilsky was not the only rumour of that kind. In the wake of this affair there was some gossip that Matilda Birger and Axel had run off. Behind the gossip lay Axel's energetic attempts to help Matilda materially, but there seems to have been no more substance in it than in the Ebba Snoilsky case. He applied constant pressure to the 'Gothenburg millionaires' and with the help of Miss White he managed to gather together enough money in England to provide Matilda with an annuity for life.

Perhaps, as Axel suggested in his letter to Retzius, it was his own divorce that inspired and precipitated the dissemination of the rumours. The fact that Axel was allotted the role of Don Juan in two dramas simultaneously

– one of them having Sweden's most celebrated poet in the other leading male role – shows at any rate that despite his long sojourn abroad he really was *quelqu'un* in his homeland.

This is also borne out by a bizarre episode that took place at the same time, with King Oscar II and Axel as leading men. The king was on a state visit to Italy and called in at Capri with his boat on 29 April. According to a Swedish newspaper, 'the inhabitants of the island had assembled in large numbers on the streets and paths and gave a warm welcome to the visitors'.

That Axel was not among those who gave the royal party a 'warm welcome' should not come as a surprise given his anti-royalist sentiments. The remarkable thing is that he deliberately avoided the king: 'His Majesty was on the island yesterday, he asked for me, but I did not present myself,' he wrote to Sibbern: 'Kings absolutely do not belong in the landscape here. He looked well – I saw him from a distance.' A remarkable scene: the King of Sweden and Norway asks after his subject, who hides in the crowd or behind a bush and refuses to make himself known!

A LITTLE HOUSE IN ANACAPRI

The house that Axel rented was in Anacapri, the upper and quieter of the island's two villages. Most of the foreigners lived down in Capri itself, where the large hotels were. 'I feel more at home here and live completely on my own and extremely cheaply, eating like the locals, good wine but very seldom meat which is dear here. I sleep well, go to bed at 9 o'clock and get up at 5.' But he is 'in a bad mood', and has not written anything. Instead, he becomes more and more gloomy: 'It is as if I had distanced myself more and more from all the interests of an active life and also from people, and the need to talk to others is becoming less and less important to me.'

Despite his lethargy and his 'bad mood' Axel was not at a loose end. He had a considerable practice among the people of Capri, and some foreign patients as well. One of them was a Mr Milberg-Godeffroy, another a secretary at the German legation who had typhus and whom Count Solms, the German ambassador in Rome, had asked Axel to look after.

Whether Axel would be able to leave Capri or not depended on 'the state of his finances', he wrote to Georg Sibbern – 'There is typhus here on the island and I am everybody's doctor, night and day.' Axel, however, suffered from the heat and wanted to leave.

Sibbern took the hint: when Axel reached Champfer in Switzerland, a cheque was waiting for him. Thanks to that cheque he was able to live in 'rather better style' than he had expected. But it was 'horribly cold' in

Champfer and he continued on to Grindelwald, which is 800 metres lower down, at the foot of the Jungfrau.

Despite the accident on Mont Blanc the mountains still held an irresistible fascination for Axel and he wanted to try his luck again on the Jungfrau. The snow was so deep that it was doubtful if he and his guides could reach the top, but they were nevertheless going to try. 'No-one has been there this year so far,' he wrote on 11 July to Retzius, who was told that Axel's motives were purely therapeutic:

> I had an unpleasant illness on Capri – a sort of cadaveric infection, according to an English colleague's diagnosis, and my own, and I had to take myself off to colder climes. Then my hypochondria returned and sat on the edge of my bed and stopped me from sleeping as usual and once again I was obliged to resort to my old cure of climbing up over the snow-line where, according to my observations, 'bacillus niger' does not flourish [. . .].

However, Axel had to abandon his plans to climb the Jungfrau – the snow was too deep, he wrote to Sibbern, whom he met up with in Bad Schwalbach on 22 July.

On the positive side, the ink began to flow again for the first time in ages: 'Luckily I have got involved in some English writing and they pay so well that I can survive on it until I regain my health again.' Miss DD was also in Bad Schwalbach and Axel continued working with her on the translation of his 'sketches' into English.

On 15 August Axel and Sibbern travelled to England, where they remained for a month. Axel stayed in a hotel in London, and also for a while at Mrs Balfour's house in Pont Street. But 'the din and the noise of humanity' made him 'so alarmed' that he scarcely dared go out, and he left the city without regret, once again to visit the Calthorpes on the Isle of Wight where Sibbern was also staying.

In that very year, 1888, George Eastman introduced his new Kodak camera with rolls of film, a technique that made the art of photography accessible to a wider public. Axel bought a camera, although it cost half of all the funds he possessed. He took his first pictures on the Isle of Wight, after which he became a diligent photographer. Axel's interest in photography is paradoxical, given his unwillingness to be snapped himself; but on the other hand there was no shortage of paradoxes in Axel's mental larder.

During his stay in England Axel received a passionate declaration of love, the first known of all the countless ones he would receive during his life: a 'Sturm und Drang letter', as he put it, from a Miss Poth, 'Frida' by name, with 'dynamism and roses, Amor and Bismarck in a bizarre union – she is either mad or in love or both'. Although he did not answer her letters, the bombardment continued. In the end he decided to rebuke her. If 'Frida' had not realised before that she was German, she did now. Her poetry, he wrote to her in French, was characterised by the same 'lack of distinction' that was so typical of the German people: 'The Germans have no concept of *grace*. Their imagination lacks style and urbanity. As a race they are poetic and intelligent but common and unrefined. They are honest but have no idea how to behave.'

The wording was elegant but not Munthe's own, having been borrowed word for word from the Swiss philosopher Henri-Frédéric Amiel, whose *Fragments d'un journal intime* Axel read with his pen at the ready.

'I really believe that she is in love with me,' Axel wrote to Sibbern, 'but as she is superficial, flirtatious and vain, that should soon pass. Strangely enough I am the only person she listens to, according to what her mother writes, and despite the fact that I do not write to her, her mother says that this peculiar influence is increasing rather than diminishing.' Frida's attacks were so powerful that, forty years later, Axel found them worth commemorating in *The Story of San Michele*.

PUCK IS DEAD

From England Axel travelled to Paris to deal with some matters of business. He was very unwilling to undertake the journey and spent only two days there. 'I found Paris painful,' he confided in Sibbern, 'I wasn't even in the area round Avenue de Villiers and everything looked at me so strangely and indifferently.'

After a short stay in Paris Axel moved on to Grindelwald, where after a few weeks' rest he felt the pull of the mountains again and set off with Puck on 'a longish mountain trip of a more serious kind'. A few days later they encountered heavy snow and were forced to spend twelve hours on a glacier on Monte Rosa 'in very difficult circumstances'. Puck became lame and Axel and his guide had to carry him down to Zermatt. Five days later Axel sent a short message to Sibbern from the Hôtel de la Poste in Simplon: 'I am so sad that I cannot write at any length – Puck is dead. I left Zermatt yesterday and have come here over a mountain pass. Spent the night with the monks at the Simplon hospice.'

Axel was devastated. It was not only his best friend that had gone, but a part of his identity. 'I am depressed in spirits and have plenty of reasons for that, and the "struggle for life" finds me with ever weaker weapons as much for attack as for self-defence,' he wrote, 'but one has to live after all, although to be sure Richelieu's words often come to mind – "Je n'en vois pas la nécessité" [I don't see the need for it].'

By this time 'Puck Munthe' was such a well-known 'beast' that his death was mentioned in the Swedish press. Even former prime minister Louis de Geer commented on the unfortunate circumstance in a letter to his friend and colleague Georg Sibbern:

Well now, what do you say about Dr Munthe, who has climbed up into the mountains again and lost his dog. Poor Mrs Munthe is supposed to have contracted consumption and to be devastated by grief. It will put a particular strain on her that he has had the misfortune to lose his faithful dog, for she is still supposed to love him unselfishly.

By the end of November Axel was back on Capri. He was glad to be back. 'It is *silence* that I now value above all else – and it is so peaceful and still here and I see no tedious, vain people.' He was now entering his second year in Capri and was beginning more and more to live the life of the local people. The house he was renting belonged to the French artist Édouard Sain, who had come to Capri in 1865, married a young local girl and fallen in love with the island. The Villa E. Sain – as the house is still called – was situated in the Le Boffe part of town and offered a ravishing view from the pergola out over the Mediterranean.

Axel worked his land for several hours a day. He sowed barley, made his own wine and made every effort to live on 'the simple food of the people'. It was difficult at first. Even if his digestion was better than before, thanks to the coarse bran loaves he had baked for him, he still had problems with his stomach.

It is a sad thing that one's body is aristocratic when one's finances are plebeian – but such is the case, unfortunately. By conviction and taste I am inclined to live on the simplest of food, since I regard luxury as immoral, but it doesn't work – the food of the people here costs no more than half a franc per day and my food costs up to four times that amount.

In a long and open-hearted letter to Carl Snoilsky in the spring of 1889, Axel summed up his life and his thoughts:

In my solitude here I am watching the slow fulfilment of my fate. It is not the judgement of other people that is dampening my spirits: I became accustomed to that many years ago and have never recoiled from that spectacle. I was well aware that my life abroad would subsequently be branded as a kind of moral exile, that I myself would become an outlaw whose name must be accompanied by a denunciation. – But it is my own fate I grieve for, I grieve for my lost enjoyment of life. What I did was done too late. Yet the desolation around me never comes near the desolation inside me. Your thousands of friends have never let you feel the former, and you have never even suspected the existence of the latter, for you have your fine soul and the love of your family. And I have no-one and I cannot even look for someone, because contact with others is becoming ever harder for me. The inclination to live alone was not in my nature – ah! I was so happy when I was 20! – but it has slowly taken over my character, mood and habits during those 6 years when I lived through the hardest form of loneliness there is – when we were two. I got used to living by myself then, grieving and rejoicing for myself, and now when I want to live with others, I cannot. [. . .]

I live here in almost the same conditions as the poor people who surround me and the artificial barriers which separated them from me are falling one after another. I eat the same food as them, go around in much the same clothes and my formerly so unquiet mind now sticks calmly and meekly to the beaten track where the contadino's [peasant's] thoughts, slow and sluggish as a draught-ox, are fixed on the day's labours for the material needs of the moment. I work several hours a day in field and vineyard, look after the sick people up here, write their letters for them and read the welcome replies (almost every family here has a father or brother in America) and weeks go by without my exchanging a word with anyone who can read or write. The active life out yonder seems to me like a dream but I am well aware that it is I who am dreaming and the others who are awake. Reading is becoming harder and harder for me, the newspapers lie unopened for weeks and letters ditto sometimes. The days fly past in a kind of painless calm whose proper name I suppose is lethargy. The only sensation I have which can be defined is my growing love of nature, and I have come to realise that a close relationship with her is a vital necessity for me – I do not believe I could live in a large city again.

Axel had his work cut out as a doctor on the island, not least because of an epidemic of smallpox, 'introduced in a ship from Sicily and spread by the ignorance of the doctors and the people'. In the spring of 1889 he reported that 'all the sick people on the island' were in his care, 'with very few exceptions'.

In the evenings he practised reading with his 14-year-old maid Giovannina, whom he was instructing in the alphabet. No one on the island was literate apart from the priests, but they were 'egotistical, dishonest individuals, unable to comprehend God's words about love of one's fellow man and most of all of the poor', and they were 'shockingly ignorant'. Despite his sceptical view of the priesthood, Axel played the organ in the village church on feast days, which says something about the respect he enjoyed. On Easter Day 1889 the priests arrived in full vestments and asked if they could bless his house:

They knew I was Protestant, but did not think I would take offence. Naturally, I replied that I would be grateful. And so they sprinkled holy water over all the rooms, over my bed and over the garden, and read a little prayer. It is an old custom here on Easter Day but of course they do not go to foreigners. This was an expression of their friendly feelings towards me.

If the priests harboured 'friendly feelings' towards Axel, the local population's attitude towards him could best be described as 'adoration'. 'He seemed to know all of them, and he was obviously their best friend and protector,' noted a Swedish visitor, whose description of Axel's status on the island is a pure echo of Mrs Cederlund's paean of 1885:

After San Costanzo in Capri and San Antonio in Anacapri, 'il Dottore' was definitely the patron saint of the Capriots. He treated the old people with kindness and respect, joked with them and relieved their pains for them. And the young girls (the men are almost permanently out coral-fishing or in America) looked up to him as their help and comfort, yes – to some degree – as their father-confessor.

BLACKWOOD'S MAGAZINE

Axel seems to have found a kind of *modus vivendi* that made his life bearable. But he wanted to write and was tormented by his writer's block. To the extent that he was willing to confide something to paper, it was not literature: 'I did not want to write novels or short stories, but a little philosophy. And that kind of thing is out of date nowadays; nobody has the time to think.'

However, the fact that Axel was not writing anything new did not mean that he was abstaining altogether from literary exercises. During his stay in Bad Schwalbach, as we have seen, he had 'got involved in some English writing'. What he was hinting at was the task of rendering already published 'sketches' into English. His success with *Letters from a Mourning City* had inspired him and he was now pinning his hopes on establishing himself in the English-language market. At the same time as he was complaining about his creative drought he was sending two sketches, 'Paris Toys' and 'Mont Blanc', to William Blackwood, editor of *Blackwood's Magazine* in Edinburgh.

'The article about "Toys" is to be published in *Blackwood's Magazine*,' Axel informed Sibbern, 'he wrote to me in terms that were very flattering to my vanity. I hope I will get paid for it. An English publicist who is here just now says that *Blackwood's M.* is now seen as no. 1, but I don't know.' Mr Blackwood took 'Paris Toys' but not 'Mont Blanc'. However, he asked if he could see some more articles, and Axel sent him 'Political Agitations in Capri', with the following reservation: 'I do not deny that its author is not entirely guiltless of making a little fun of the Germans, but the article is written in a good temper and no malice was intended. And I believe that most of the English visitors would subscribe to my indignation about the 'Germanisation' of Capri.'

Axel's intuition was proved right: Blackwood found the article too strong for his stomach and Axel offered to edit it. He also forwarded 'Menagerie', which was printed along with 'Paris Toys' and 'Political Agitations in Capri' in the November 1889 issue of the magazine; the last piece was indeed printed with some of the most anti-German comments deleted. The sketches were introduced under the general heading 'Diary of an Idle Doctor', a title that was Axel's own, but which nevertheless led to an outbreak of self-pity:

> God knows that the epithet is wrong in any case! I have killed myself with overwork, and here I sit in my solitary Anacapri like an hermit, with destroyed health and a future of incurable hypochondria before me, a future which may be long and weary, for I am only 32 years old. But this your readers do not care about and neither do you, and I will not tell anybody that this epithet is a lie.

Just as he had done in his dealings with Swedish publishers, Axel skilfully played off Blackwood against other potential interested parties: in this case, Mr Harper, who according to Axel had 'expressed his wish to have something' from his hand. But Mr Blackwood was still interested and the sketch 'Impasse Roussel' was printed in the issue of September 1890 – the same issue, incidentally, that carried a story by another literary doctor, Conan Doyle's 'A Physiologist's Wife'.

The contact with Blackwood was maintained during the following years and in 1893 a further three sketches were published in the magazine: 'La Madonna del Buon Cammino', 'Rafaella' and 'Zoology'. In all, Axel managed to get seven articles published in *Blackwood's Magazine*, but there were also a few that were turned down: not only 'Mont Blanc' but also the sketches 'The Protestant Cemetery in Rome' and 'The Dogs in Capri'.

'The Dogs in Capri' – a reflection on the island's dogs and at the same time an attack on *il cacciatore*, Capri's quail hunter, who was Axel's deadly enemy above all others – was the last fruit of the creative harvest that had begun with Axel's stay in Naples in 1884. With the exception of medical prescriptions, he would write nothing new for two whole decades.

A Man who Does Whatever Occurs to Him

In the spring of 1889 the Danish-born Swedish author Helena Nyblom and her daughter Ellen came to Capri. The day after their arrival, they had lunch with Axel. 'Everything was quiet and still. – I can't help liking Munthe,' Ellen remembered. 'He gives the impression of being good, and melancholic, and that he certainly is too. Then mama played his piano. I lay in the hammock and rested, and Munthe came with cushions, books, lemons and a large parasol for me, then he placed a dove on the edge of the hammock and was kind and nice.'

In his letters Axel emerges – and presents himself – as a hypochondriac in both senses of the word: deeply melancholic and at the same time extremely focused on his bodily functions. What impression did he make on those who came into contact with him at this time? Anne Charlotte Leffler found him both interesting and 'strange', and Mrs Nyblom and her daughter thought highly of him – he was 'a man with an unprecedented knowledge of humanity, imagination and a rare talent for story-telling [. . .] who amuses himself by saying whatever he feels like. All in all, that is exactly what he was: "A man who does whatever occurs to him"'.

At the same time, Axel had an 'impulse towards melancholia, which one sympathised with and believed in'. His outward appearance had 'nothing especially fascinating' about it, his eyes, already fragile by then, 'really had nothing engaging in their expression'. His gaze was 'tired and strained', his face neither youthful nor attractive, but he was 'captivating and loveable, and people "wondered" about him':

> All this time I had a distinct feeling that his stories were often somewhat 'overdone', and occasionally I sensed this when he was talking, as if I was walking through a quagmire. [. . .] At any event there were a few areas where we all met in complete harmony. Doctor Munthe had a sense of humour, a happy, childlike sense of humour which contrasted with his otherwise precocious nature. He thoroughly enjoyed anything comic, and his own jokes lacked venom. And he loved music too. He often played for us at twilight, in an attractive and melodious way, and on occasions when my mother sat down at the piano in his study, he listened to her with delight.

The Goal of an Individual's Life

The 'Capri exile' gave Axel time for deeper reflection on philosophical and religious questions. His simple lifestyle was not only the result of economic necessity; it also had an ideological dimension. In November 1888, immediately after his arrival in Capri, Axel informed Sibbern that he had read Leo Tolstoy's *Ma réligion* (Paris, 1885), 'a sober and thought-provoking book by a man who is a Christian but not orthodox'. Tolstoy was sharply critical of the Church – not least of his own denomination, Russian Orthodox – which sanctioned war and the death penalty in the name of Christianity, and the book could not be published in its author's homeland. However, it soon circulated in several foreign-language translations and appeared in English in 1886 under the title *What I Believe*. It came to be a major subject of discussion in cultural circles during these years – Miss White, for instance, read it during her Italian trip, and it may very well have been her copy that Axel had borrowed.

For Tolstoy, the fundamental contradiction was that between 'the teachings of Jesus' and 'the teachings of the world'. He suffered in his worldly existence with its torments and temptations, its 'unbearable, unnatural conditions', far from the natural and simple life lived by the people. Whilst 'the teachings of the world' exhort people to leave the countryside and take themselves off to 'an unhealthy, corrupt town', a disciple of Jesus, according to Tolstoy, should be poor: 'Being poor means not living in the towns, but in the countryside, not sitting shut in a room but working out in the forest or the fields and taking delight in seeing the sun, the sky, the earth and the beasts of the field.'

Tolstoy's personal interpretation of Jesus' teaching and his critical view of the clergy and the Church appealed to Axel. If in his sketches he had identified himself – ironically –with Don Quixote, the figure of Christ now crops up more and more in his letters. Only by living an ascetic life one comes close to Christ, Axel believes. The fact that he had no 'daily worries' is because he had taught himself 'the great rule of wisdom' – that one ought not to try to satisfy one's needs, but rather to reduce them: 'The old philosophers did this, and so did Christ.'

Even if Tolstoy's ideas were nothing new for someone who revered St Francis, it is clear that Axel, in his ideas as much as his wording, was inspired by the Russian author. Both his observations about town life and his view of guilt and duty have direct parallels in Tolstoy's book. 'Every attempt to give meaning to life which is not founded on the sacrifice of one's selfishness, which does not have as its goal to benefit mankind', wrote Tolstoy, 'is merely an empty illusion which will fall apart on its first contact with reason.' Axel wrote:

[. . .] I find myself well in both body and soul through living outside 'society' and I am doing more good here than I ever did in Paris from a general human and Christian point of view. And in any case the goal of an individual's life is surely to seek to bring some benefit or happiness to others in some small degree [. . .] You seem to think, Your Excellency, that my future life must necessarily be lived out in a large city but who knows, perhaps *happiness dwells in the countryside*, and I am sure that God does. It is simply a question of doing one's duty, i.e. to seek to serve, to the extent one's disposition and individuality show the way to the fulfilment of this duty. The word 'duty' is no more an absolute concept than the word '*happiness*'.

What we see here is the contours of a *philosophy of duty* that caused Axel consciously to turn his back on the life that, in his own words, he had been 'accustomed to by my upbringing'. Jesus' teaching, according to Tolstoy, was not an 'indeterminate, vague ideal'; rather, it consisted of *action*. This view was shared by Axel, with his strong feeling of 'original guilt'. The medical care he provided free of charge was a way of assuaging this guilt. When Axel helped an old woman whose husband had just died by working their field, he did it, revealingly, 'not for her sake but for my own'. Another instalment was his decision to present 'a worn-out old man' with a piece of land that he could live on 'till the day of his death'. 'After lengthy hesitation and consideration' Axel had worked out for himself that it was his 'duty', even if the field cost him half of the capital he had saved up – but the man's 'neediness was distressing in the highest degree' and Axel saw it as his 'duty to make this sacrifice'. On this occasion his duty was instantly rewarded: that very day a cheque arrived from Sibbern for five times the amount he had paid out.

Axel's fascination with religion had its origins in the religious environment in which he had grown up. But although he was deeply influenced by the Christian message, he shared Tolstoy's scepticism about the clergy and the official Church. He had seen too much feigned piety to accept Capri's *parroci* or Swedish clergymen as the ideal interpreters of Jesus' teachings. As we shall see later, Axel also shared Tolstoy's attitude towards individual immortality and the Church's defence of war and killing.

Axel's interest in Christianity was complemented by his admiration for Arthur Schopenhauer, a philosopher who was so famous during the second half of the nineteenth century that according to Axel even the donkey Rosina had heard of him. What made Axel see a soul mate in Schopenhauer was no doubt the philosopher's 'pessimistic' world-view. 'Pessimism' can lead to contempt for humanity. But pessimism is also and principally clear-sightedness, penetration, lack of illusion – by contrast with 'optimism', which flatters people in a hypocritical way and is therefore 'a bitter mockery of mankind's nameless suffering', in the words of the philosopher. Anyone who is affected by *Bacillus niger* 'sees life as it is', Axel wrote in 'Hypochondria'.

Human life is a 'disappointment' – Schopenhauer uses the English word – yes, even a deception. It oscillates between two poles: ennui for the upper class, who are always bored, and suffering for the working classes, who are always working. 'Just as suffering is the constant scourge of the ordinary people, so is ennui for people of rank.' In reality, we ought to address each other not as 'monsieur' or 'sir' but as 'fellow-sufferer'; that would be more in keeping with the real order of things.

If we are able to see through the veil of phenomena that hides the true reality, however, we can attain resignation ('equanimity') and achieve the insight that we are a part of everything living. Then we will be filled with a moral strength and solidarity with everything that is alive which Schopenhauer expresses with the Vedic formula *That twam asi* (This is you): 'My real, most inward being is present in every living creature as immediately as it makes itself known in my self-consciousness.' If egoism is to Schopenhauer the ultimate evil, the insight that 'This is you' is the basis of all morality. We ought not to hurt anyone, but must help everyone as much as we can. By dealing with others out of motives of compassion and philanthropy we are acting in a genuinely moral way.

Compassion for all living things includes animals too. Schopenhauer is just as furiously eloquent as Axel when he speaks on their behalf. Like Axel he was a dog lover not only in theory: he had several dogs, a room full of dog pictures, and he was one of the founders of the Frankfurt animal protection society. 'Man puts his most faithful friend, the dog, in chains,' Schopenhauer wrote, continuing with a form of words that could just as easily have been Axel's: 'I can never see a chained-up dog without being gripped by heartfelt sympathy for it and a strong feeling of indignation at its master.'

It was not only with regard to animals that Axel and Schopenhauer had almost identical opinions. Both of them also regarded music as the highest form of art, both of them accused the clergy of taking advantage of people's metaphysical needs, and they both had similarly patronising views on women. Moreover Schopenhauer, as he describes himself in letters and as is depicted in memoirs, has a striking number of personality traits in common with Axel. He was a 'hypochondriac' and 'shy of people', 'had a sombre sense of humour', 'loved being alone', was 'utterly honest', 'calls everything by its proper name to friend as well as enemy', was 'full of humour' and donated money to the needy. To the degree that Axel was familiar with Schopenhauer's biography, he could identify not only with his philosophical system but also with the man.

But the Future?

The constant philosophising deepened Axel's melancholy. 'I am a little afraid of these long tête-à-têtes with myself,' he admitted. And at the same time as he was claiming that most of all he wanted to live close to nature and believed he was no longer fitted to live in a large city, he was conscious that this way of life was a threat to his intellect – and to the other side of his personality, which was drawn exactly to that.

> [. . .] if I begin to think, then I am lost, and then I ask myself if one has 'the right' to regress back into this unconscious life which ought really to be called a refined form of spiritual suicide. Does one? Then I see clearly that my situation is frightful, for there is something sick in my thought-processes themselves, *I can only think gloomy thoughts*. And if this is the case, tell me if one has the right to seek a cure for this, even if the consequence of the cure is that one *ceases to think* – I am well on the way there.

It was not only the risks of 'spiritual suicide' that made Axel think of a life beyond Capri. The heat of the summer months was intense and he suffered from the *'fiercely* strong light': 'I see my patients in the early morning and as early as 9 o'clock I retire to my darkened room which I do not leave until 7 in the evening.'

The future was uncertain. The house he was renting was to be sold and he could not afford to rent another one. It had been his dream since 1876 to own a house on Capri but he felt he would never realise it. Nevertheless, it would be a good investment as the site would increase in value many times over. Capri was becoming 'more and more modern and attracting more attention', a large English company had bought an old ruin for a song and was going to build a hotel with 300 rooms and English standards of comfort. 'When this is finished, Capri will be an ideal place for a doctor like me, but then everything will also cost several times as much as they will lay claim to all the island's products.' At the age of 31, he confided to Sibbern, he was missing, more than ever before, *'a home'*.

As regards the immediate future, Axel pondered leaving Capri for the summer. As usual it was the mountains that drew him, more specifically the Val d'Aosta in the Italian Alps. He had no money and Sibbern sent him a banker's draft that, however, Axel returned. He did not want to use the money for 'pleasure trips' and he had subdued his bodily needs to a level appropriate to a man of his poverty. He had other, more long-term plans that he intended to use 'every farthing' to try to implement – therefore he would remain on Capri, although on one occasion he had gone down with sunstroke.

As we have seen, Sibbern was of the opinion that Axel ought to live in a large city: a viewpoint that Axel countered with the argument that 'Happiness dwells in the countryside.' But the other side of his personality was seduced by the thought, and in August 1889 he drew up a long letter to Sibbern:

> But the future? Yes, that is the big question, because although I am not hard-up now, it is still impossible for me to prepare the way for a change in my existence. From the moment I leave my home here, everything will fall apart and I will face the insoluble problem of how to earn my living without being able to subject myself to circumstances which will make this possible. [. . .] I think I would make a serious effort as a doctor in Rome if I had the means to establish myself there. But here I can never put a sou aside to prepare for such a contingency as my source of income consists of potatoes, fruit, rye, eggs etc. which I eat up day by day. [. . .] I am popular with them and they wish me well in their way. I would even go back to Paris if I could – I might find it easier to maintain myself there than in Rome the first time since several people know me in Paris but I am unknown in Rome. On the other hand, my sympathies as a human being lean more towards Rome, which has a stamp of *grandeur* that no-one can uproot. – So it is not out of reluctance to work but out of pure necessity that I am continuing my life on Capri. My intention however is to try to manage a stay of a month or a couple of months in Rome in the winter in order to form an opinion of the prospects there might be for me if I settled there as a doctor – my knowledge of Rome is of a purely aesthetic nature and dates back 10 years, and it is a fact that no large city in Europe has changed so much as Rome in recent years. My prospects would be better if I could speak fluent English as the English colony there is pretty large and Your Excellency knows of my warm feelings towards that nation. I read as much English as I can but that is not enough – nevertheless I have improved my knowledge since we last met in the expectation that 'something might turn up', as Mr. Micawber hoped.

Finally Axel was offered an opportunity to stay in Anacapri. The guardian angel was a Salvatore Farace, with whom on 6 August 1889 Axel signed a ten-year lease on the Villa Damacuta (right next-door to the Villa Sain). The rent was so 'ridiculously low' – 100 lire a year – that he could afford to have the house standing ready to flee to whenever he felt himself 'too ill at ease out in the world': 'And if I leave Capri that will be a lot easier for me if I have this little pied à terre here, since I will know that I have not been uprooted from the rocky island that is so dear to me.'

The house in Anacapri also to some extent decided Axel's choice of town when he chose to establish himself as a doctor. Although he nursed 'a kind of *grudge*' towards Paris, where he had lived 'a more unhappy life than anyone knows for 7 years', he still felt that his place would have been there if he had had 'a resilient nature and a little more joie de vivre' in his heart. Rome, he wrote, 'is a kind of middle way in the struggle for life – a prudent general thinks about his line of retreat, and Capri is close in case I get beaten'. In Paris he would starve to death if he failed.

The decision was made. At the end of October 1889 Axel Munthe left Capri to establish himself as a doctor in Rome. His life had seen many changes of fortune, but none so dramatic as this.

Victoria

1889–1930

Piazza di Spagna

> I am not forgetting that I have Your Excellency to thank for everything.
> *Axel Munthe to Georg Sibbern, September 1890*

WHEN IN THE summer of 1889 Munthe returned Georg Sibbern's banker's draft, it was on the grounds that he did not think he could afford any 'pleasure trips'. The move to Rome, however, was no holiday but rather a venture on which Axel's whole future turned. To establish himself as a doctor in the Italian capital was a big undertaking. He would have to rent somewhere to live as well as a doctor's surgery, preferably with a good address, and the rags he wore on his beloved island would have to be replaced by presentable clothes. Visiting cards would have to be printed and a series of other marketing strategies adopted.

All this, of course, cost money, lots of money – money that Axel did not have. If it had not been for Sibbern he would hardly have dared to take the plunge. At the end of October Sibbern sent Munthe a draft for 4,000 francs; 4,000 francs corresponded to around £160, which is worth about fifty times as much at today's values.* But the money seems not to have gone very far. Two months later Sibbern received a letter from Munthe that resulted in yet another cheque, this time for 2,000 francs.

In mid-November Axel went to Capri to fetch his maid Giovannina and the dog Tiberio. 'I was forced to take Giov[annina] with me for she had changed so much since the day I told her I was leaving,' he wrote to Helena Nyblom: 'She said nothing but hardly touched her food and became so pale and thin that I thought she would be seriously ill and go the same way as her brother who has consumption.'

His parting from Capri was emotionally trying both for Axel and for the islanders, whose payments in kind continued even after *il dottore* had moved to Rome. He received cheeses, hams, figs, oil and flour, among other

---

* From 1865 Italy, France, Belgium, and Switzerland belonged to the Latin monetary union, and the lira and the franc had the same value. 25 francs/lire corresponded to £1 or $5.

things, and on one occasion he managed to persuade the postal service to return a Christmas gift in the shape of 'a little live piglet'.

KEATS'S HOUSE

After only a few months in Rome Axel took up residence at 26 Piazza di Spagna, right in the centre of Rome. The house by the Spanish Steps had formerly been a boarding house. It was here that the English poet John Keats had lived for three winter months with his friend the artist Joseph Severn, before dying of consumption on 23 February 1821. On 3 January 1890 Axel wrote to Mr Blackwood:

> Since I wrote you last time I have returned to active life, have been in Paris to fetch my things and am now settled as a doctor in Rome in the very same appartement [sic] where Keats and Severn lived and where poor Keats died. However I still keep my little house in Capri where I intend to spend my summers.*

Even if Axel intended from now on to concentrate his literary efforts on writing prescriptions, he would, according to what he told Blackwood, have plenty of time to formulate his more profane thoughts in the 'Diary', some extracts from which had already been published in the magazine. During the winter of 1889 and the spring of 1890 he prevailed upon Blackwood to publish several 'sketches', and 'Impasse Roussel' made it into the September issue. At the same time he pretended in his usual way that he was not in the least interested in seeing his work in print.

Axel's 'active life' could have had a better start. It was a cold winter and he caught influenza. When in addition he was struck down with a new and severe haemorrhage of the lungs, hypochondria took a firm grip on him again. His lungs were admittedly healthy, he wrote to Edith Balfour, but one fine day he would catch a chill, get consumption and keep Keats company in the Protestant cemetery:

> Perhaps you will think I am in very bad temper but I cannot say that I am – I am worse than so, I am more indifferent than I knew myself. Some years ago I would have cried like a child over my sad destiny but I cannot honestly say that I am very much impressed by this – it came about 5

---

* The small room where Keats died is on the second floor. According to a list of tenants drawn up by the Keats–Shelley Museum, Munthe rented the first floor and a part of the third, and in a letter to Helena Nyblom written the same month he gives his address as '1mo piano', i.e. first floor. It seems unlikely, however, that he should have lied about something that was so easy to verify.

o'cl. in the morning and I laid [sic] quite alone until 7 when the servant
came and then I thought over the whole thing with a calm which almost
frightens myself now – do you know what that signifies that I was so calm
this time? – I do.

Moreover, the illness had been a hindrance in his career. 'I am [. . .]
deeply depressed about the series of misfortunes which have followed my
decision to start working and which at any event are delaying my prospects
of finding my feet here,' he confided to Sibbern. On the other hand, his
expectations were extremely modest: 'I will not of course find much of a
practice now, but if I can just find food for myself, Giovannina and the dog
then I will be satisfied – and if things go really badly then we can retire to
Anacapri.' Giovannina, who had never been outside Capri before, had a
more original solution to the problem of earning a living – she thought they
should buy a cow, which could graze in the Villa Borghese and live in the
dark little room that served as a lumber-room.

At the end of June Axel returned to Capri. He now received yet another
cheque from Sibbern: not for 1,000 francs as he had expected, but for 1,500.
On 15 July he left Capri in order to take himself off to Paris for 'scientific
matters'. In a letter to Sibbern he explained why he had returned to that city
which, only a year earlier, he had claimed to have such a grudge against:

I have already begun working and have just come home from a 6-hour
shift in the hospital with mentally-ill patients. I managed to tranquillise
one of them after they had tried in every possible way to calm her, but in
vain. She was living in a cage like an animal and had sat there bound hand
and foot for over a month. We are on the threshold of a new world here
and the history of mental illness has entered a new stage. She fell asleep
after 10 minutes without my touching her, apart from on the forehead. I
hope to be able to remain in Paris for at least 3 weeks. Unfortunately the
summer is far advanced and all the professors will soon be taking their
leave. However, I hope to benefit greatly from this trip if I can keep my
health.

It is not clear which hospital is meant here, but the very fact that Axel
wanted – and was able – to work with mentally disturbed patients in Paris
bears witness to the fact that the business with Geneviève and his dismissal
from La Salpêtrière either were not known to anyone other than Charcot
and Axel, which is not very likely, or was – which is more likely – strongly
slanted. Which Paris professor would otherwise let him practise in his
hospital after such a faux pas?

Axel's interest in mental illnesses was still strong. After his stay in
Paris he planned to travel to Nancy to Professor Bernheim, 'an important

authority on those subjects that now occupy me'. The subjects in question were suggestion and the possibility of curing illness without prescribing medicines. In a letter to Sibbern in August of that same year Axel described how he had made a 'young, charming and exceptionally pretty' patient with suicidal tendencies better 'without directly hypnotising her', 'merely by *suggestion*'.

Whether or not Axel made it to Nancy is unknown, but his ambition to do so is worth noting. At about the same time, Sigmund Freud was on a study visit to Bernheim.

Lord Dufferin

On the way to Capri Axel passed through Sorrento, where a diplomatic delegation led by the British ambassador to Rome, Lord Dufferin, was taking a break after an international conference on Africa that had been held in Naples during the summer.

Axel booked into the Hotel Victoria, the most elegant and expensive hotel in the town, where he had lived once before in the spring of 1885, at Mr Cederlund's expense. Sibbern had sent money again, and after returning to Capri Axel felt that he ought to explain the reason for his stay in Sorrento and why he planned to return from time to time 'despite the expensive lifestyle there':

> Lord Dufferin and his wife – who are living there – are exceptionally friendly towards me and clearly this is very useful to me. Some other families, among the most distinguished in Rome, are also living in the same hotel and it is no doubt to my advantage if I show my face there from time to time – especially as I am in such good company as that of the British attachés, all of whom are personal friends of mine: well brought-up, fine young men. [. . .] I intend to set off for Rome around the 15th of October, which will be in good time – if I can stay healthy then my prospects are not bad, it seems to me. I am not forgetting that I have Your Excellency to thank for everything.

Nothing could be more true. Without the constant handouts from Sibbern Axel's life would have turned out quite differently. Sibbern's aid would continue, but now, during this week in Sorrento, Axel struck up an acquaintanceship that would be just as vital for him as the meeting with Sibbern in Paris six years earlier: with Lord and Lady Dufferin.

Frederick Temple Hamilton-Temple-Blackwood, fifth Lord Dufferin and first Marquess of Dufferin and Ava (1826–1902) was one of the great British statesmen and diplomats of the late nineteenth century. Among other things he was the governor-general of Canada, ambassador to St Petersburg from 1879 to 1881 and to Constantinople from 1881 to 1884, and viceroy of India from 1884 to 1888.

Lord Dufferin belonged to the Liberal Party, was known for his political skill and tact and was often called on to resolve conflicts and monitor the fulfilment of international agreements. During their time in India his wife, Lady Hariot Dufferin, made major contributions in the medical field by helping to introduce modern cures for women's and children's ailments. Lord Dufferin was also a passionate sailor who in 1856 had sailed as far as Iceland, an adventure which he described in his book *Letters from High Latitudes*. (It was at this time that Burma was annexed and Dufferin was promoted to Marquess of Dufferin and Ava, after Burma's ancient capital.)

In other words, all the preconditions were there for a match between the personal chemistry of the Dufferins and the charming young Swede: their liberal outlook on society, their engagement with social questions – and sailing. In all probability, the Dufferins also knew Axel's writings. *Blackwood's* and *Murray's Magazine* were reputable journals and if the ambassadorial couple did not know *Letters from a Mourning City* before, they undoubtedly soon became aware of the book's existence. In any case, they promptly took the young doctor under their wing. Axel's conscious efforts to acquaint himself with the English language and culture had begun to bear fruit.

During Axel's absence, an important event was taking place in the Swedish colony in Rome. In September, Sweden–Norway's ambassador to Italy, Baron Carl Bildt, married none other than Alexandra Keiller – 'an old flame', as Axel put it in a letter to Sibbern. If Axel and Alexandra still had any feelings for each other they were pretty well forced to conceal them as they were now meeting, if not daily, then weekly, in the ministerial couple's elegant apartment or elsewhere in Roman society, where the minister's wife, 'la bella bionda baronessa di Bildt', as she was called, soon came to occupy the position of one of the city's leading beauties.

On 31 October 1890 Axel reported to Sibbern:

Today I start work in Rome and today I celebrate my 33rd birthday – yet if anything I feel younger than I did a few years ago. Thanks to Your Excellency I can look forward to this coming winter without too much anxiety. *Socially* speaking I have every reason to be content with my position here in Rome and I feel I am entitled to hope that on the economic front too things will be satisfactory here once I have got over the early stages. My health seems to be quite good, by which I mean that I can always fear for what happened last year, but that seems not to be dangerous, only tedious for as long as it lasts.

Around the New Year Axel received another cheque from Sibbern, and on 16 July 1891 he drew up a new report:

> My sincerest thanks for the latest cheque, which arrived in good time. I hope and believe – insofar as my health holds out – that this money will bring good fortune and will turn out to have been put to good use. I have good prospects here, I see a fair number of patients these days and I seem to have a certain 'luck' with them – mieux vaut un médecin heureux qu'un médecin savant, as they say in Paris. [. . .] After long hesitation I have decided to hire a carriage – it will cost a lot of money, but on the one hand the risk of maintaining my health is increased thereby, and on the other hand it will give a certain *eloquentia corporis* in which unfortunately I am completely lacking. I was the only one among all the foreign doctors here who lacked one. I have already realised that I acted wisely and I am quite sure that I already have the carriage to thank for more than one patient – la comédie humaine! The day before yesterday I was at a magnificent ball at the Dufferins' which was attended by the [Italian] king and queen as well as the Duke of Cambridge, who looked very shaky. Lady Dufferin is the most distinguished lady I have ever seen. They are kind to me and often invite me there. I am also often at the Austrian ambassador's – but very seldom at the Swedish–Norwegian ambassador's. I don't like him. – I continue not to smoke and feel calmer in my nerves than before. There is no question of writing as I don't have the time – but the desire is still there and I truly believe that I am inclined that way by nature.

'The latest cheque' was the second that year and it did not come as a surprise to Axel. Sibbern had in fact promised to put a sum of money at Axel's disposal at regular intervals, so that he could 'obtain a satisfactory and independent position'.

Thanks to the Dufferins Axel was introduced into Roman society and in the course of a few months he had become established as the new shooting star in the social and Aesculapian firmament. Only a month and a half after the last letter, he could write as follows:

> The other day I was invited to Princess Roccagiovane's (née Julie Bonaparte) where I met Plon-Plon, who talked to me for ages; among other things, about his travels in Norway. When I mentioned Your Excellency's name he said immediately – 'je me rappelle très bien de lui, c'était un long gaillard'. My health is bearing up, thank God, I am still a non-smoker and am drinking *no* alcohol apart from red wine, but about a bottle of it with each meal. Italy's current minister of education has shown me great kindness, goodwill even. In a speech couched in very flattering terms he quoted my views on the sanitary conditions in Naples and he has asked me to write on the subject – which I do not think I ought to do. I have also had an audience with the queen, 'forced and compelled so to do'. Lord

Dufferin held a banquet for the King & queen to which only those who had already been presented were invited, but they insisted that I should go there in any case and be presented afterwards, which duly happened. There were about a hundred people being presented at the same time and I was greatly surprised when the queen had me summoned out of my corner, talked with me for ages and seemed to know a great deal about me. She still looks very well but the Little Prince is small and unimpressive. I don't see much of Swedes and don't miss them much either. I mostly socialise with Englishmen and also get on best with them. [. . .] I don't see Bildt very often, and I believe he is not well-liked among his colleagues here. [. . .] I am not forgetting that I have Your Excellency to thank for enabling me to come here and I hope and trust that you have put your money to good use. I myself live very frugally, too frugally, I think.

Roman social life was rich and intense. The city had long since ceased to be a centre for artists – it had been succeeded in that respect by Paris – but it retained its former power to attract society.

Lady Victoria

The role that the Sibberns had played for Axel in Paris was played in Rome by their British counterparts. Lord Dufferin was a cultivated person and his lady was not only a diplomat's wife but also the author of several books, including the two-volume *Our Vice-Regal Life in India*. Moreover, in her past life she had been an actress, a talent she had the opportunity to practise every Saturday during the carnival season, when ambassador von Bruck put on theatrical performances, directed by himself, at the Austrian embassy. The British embassy was housed in a palace that had formerly belonged to Prince Torlonia, the richest man in Rome, and the Dufferins' parties were among the high points of the social scene.

'I am very successful here in Rome,' Axel reported to Sibbern at the end of March. At the beginning of April he travelled to London for a week to see a former patient. 'It was a tiring journey but I thought it was the right thing to go – moreover I succeeded as a doctor, for my patient is now almost well again.' He had not received any fee, but they were 'rich people', so he would no doubt be paid sooner or later.

Now, in April 1891, Munthe was able to inform Sibbern that he was the doctor 'to a large number, if not the majority, of foreigners based here in Rome, and this is a solid basis'. That he did not yet have such a large hotel practice, he wrote, is due to his 'impractical temperament'. On the other hand he had many American patients and had met many 'particularly agreeable Americans, both men and women'. 'Frida' continued to bombard him with letters and 'poetic effusions' – which however remained unread as a rule – but he gave 'little thought to women' and was glad to have his 'head clear in that respect'.

In mid-May Axel travelled to Capri to enjoy his *otium cum dignitate*. The Crown Princess of Sweden and Norway, Victoria, was staying at the Hotel Quisisana. She had spent the winter in Egypt and on the return journey stayed for a few weeks on Capri. The fact that Axel was both invited to breakfast and granted an audience with her shows how keen she was to make contact with him. The audience was in fact a medical consultation. 'She made conversation with me for a long time,' Munthe wrote: 'I do not believe she is dangerously ill now – but she will certainly want to come south again next winter too.' There are no more details of what, as far as we know, was the first meeting between Axel and the Crown princess. But the contact testifies to the fact that Axel's name was already widely known.

Victoria left Capri and Axel travelled to England, where he was asked to care for a patient during the summer – an H.G. Watkins in Dorset – who suffered from 'a bone-marrow illness, *tabes* (Heine's disease)', for which Axel had earlier successfully treated an English lady in Rome. Axel had accepted the offer because he would get his trip paid and 'maybe a bit more on top'. Most of all, though, he was attracted by Mr Watkins's suggestion that they should spend a whole month on his yacht while Axel treated him.

At the beginning of June Axel travelled to London to buy clothes and underwear – 'as everything is shoddy in Italy' – and on 12 June he boarded Mr Watkins's yacht *Astræa* at Southampton. She was a schooner-rigged pleasure craft of 130 tons with a crew of twelve. For once he slept very well and felt his old 'love of the sea and sailing more keenly than ever'.

They set their course along the west coast of England up towards Scotland, where the scenery reminded Axel of northern Sweden. They visited Loch Lomond then carried on to the Isle of Skye. Here they stayed at Armadale Castle as guests of Lord MacDonald – 'the Lord of the Isles', according to Axel – and Dunvegan Castle, which was owned by the Macleod of Macleod, whose granddaughter was on board with them.

To judge from the size of the fee, Axel must have succeeded in curing Mr Watkins's bone-marrow ailment. Even more important, however, was the gift with which Mr Watkins unexpectedly honoured him, 'a little cutter roomy enough to live on': 'Since 10 years I have yearned to have one on Capri.' He sailed the cutter down to Cardiff himself, where he put it on a Norwegian vessel bound for Naples. The transport of the cutter turned out to be more expensive than planned, but thanks to an 'unexpectedly large fee' from a patient, Axel managed to 'balance the budget'. Now he could indulge in sailing competitions with Lord Dufferin, that 'master of watermanship', who was steering his *Lady Hermione* in the Bay of Naples that summer too. The ambassador's yacht was named after one of his daughters; Axel christened his cutter *Lady Victoria*, after the other one.

JAMES RENNELL RODD

Axel was now firmly established as Rome's leading foreign doctor. He had also made a name for himself as a cultivated and charming individual and an original conversationalist. Now, in the autumn of 1891, he made the acquaintance of a man who would remain his friend and confidant for the rest of his life: James Rennell Rodd, who in 1891 took up the post of second secretary in Her Majesty's embassy in Rome.

James Rennell Rodd (1858–1941) was not only a gifted young diplomat but also an author who had brought out a collection of poetry called *Songs in the South* in 1881 and had been published in Axel's house publication *Murray's Magazine*. He had been educated at Balliol College, Oxford, where he was a contemporary of several of England's coming men in politics and diplomacy, like Lord Curzon and Cecil Spring-Rice. Oxford was also a literary and cultural centre, where Walter Pater and John Ruskin lectured on fine art – and it was here that Rodd got to know Oscar Wilde, with whom he came to be on such familiar terms that his family's suspicions were aroused.

The young James's first journey abroad took him to Italy, when he was only 6 years old. Like so many Englishmen of his generation he would be loyal to Italy throughout his life. A few years before he arrived in Rome to take up his post at the British embassy, he became involved, among other things, in a diplomatic game with the aim of saving Keats's grave from disappearing. The authorities in Rome wanted to demolish the Protestant cemetery in order to drive a road through the area. However, their plans were averted, thanks to protests by British authors and the intervention of Queen Victoria.

Now Rennell Rodd met the renowned doctor who inhabited the house where Keats had died. They became friends. 'The mysterious Swede inspired warm friendships and bitter enmities,' he wrote: 'I unhesitatingly joined the category of his friends [. . .].'

In November 1891 Rennell Rodd received a visit from the Tennant family, Sir Charles and Lady Tennant and their daughter Margot. The Tennants were typical representatives of 'the brilliant and powerful body', as Churchill put it, which had ruled Britain for generations – around 200 families united by both personal and economic ties. One of Margot's sisters was married to Lord Ribblesdale, a well-known Liberal politician. Her other sister, Laura, had been married to Alfred Lyttelton, one of England's leading cricketers and tennis players. Alfred Lyttelton in his turn was not only an outstanding sportsman but also a nephew of Britain's prime minister William Gladstone, and he would later follow a political career himself within the Unionist party and the government. When he re-married in 1892, the bride's name was Edith Balfour, Axel's friend and translator.

Rodd had been one of Laura Lyttelton's closest friends and now he received her family, who were spending a couple of days in Rome on their way to Egypt. On 19 and 20 November Margot Tennant noted in her diary:

> Mama, papa and I dined with the Slades. I sat next to Dr Axel Munthe, whose *Letters from a Mourning City* Maude White had translated. I found him really original and interesting, full of fancy, with a kind of lurid humour. We got on very well indeed, and I think he liked me. [. . .] Dr Munthe called, and drove me to the Pantheon, which I thought hideous inside. We went to two or three other churches, and then he took me to see the room Keats died in – where he lives. [. . .] He is an artist and a poet; he said I had flown across his path like a brilliant little bird that comes quite close and then flies away. He said that I surprised him, and brought him back to life; that I was dreadfully spoilt, which was a pity; he wished he had met me before I was spoilt. I assured him I was unchanged; I was born what he meant; I had not improved! He said my brain worked at lightning speed, and that I must not think his indifferent English precluded him from judging of this, as he saw scepticism in my eyes. He took me to the station, and kissed my hands.*

This was Axel's first meeting with Margot Tennant, whom he would meet in many different contexts in the future. In 1894 she married the British home secretary – and later prime minister – Herbert Asquith.

In the winter of 1892 Lord Dufferin was appointed ambassador to Paris. He asked Rodd to come with him, an offer that Rodd could not refuse although he had looked forward to a few more years in Rome. Within the course of a few months Axel had lost both his principal patron and a new but cherished friend. He was apprehensive about Dufferin's departure, fearing that he might lose his position as doctor to the British legation. But his misgivings were unfounded – the new ambassador, Lord Vivian, was if possible even more favourably disposed towards him.

---

* The diary was published in 1892 as a private print. In Munthe's copy, with the hand-written dedication 'Axel Munthe from his friend Margot Tennant', there is a comment in Munthe's hand commenting upon the last sentence of the quotation: 'Do you remember what you did yourself?' In Margot Asquith's *Places & Persons* (1925; pp. 21–22) the paragraph is reprinted in a slightly different version.

Despite his professional successes, Axel found it just as difficult as before to bring some order into his personal finances. The fact that he was permanently in need of money was not just because he was poorly paid but because he could not keep his spending in check. He seems to have been completely incapable of looking after his own financial interests. 'How many times have the banks not been able to get a signature of Munthe, for a paper which was very important for himself', wrote a person with inside knowledge of his carelessness in financial matters. Money ran through his fingers.

I'M AFRAID OF HIM

When in 1892 Ultima married the Swedish manufacturer Gustaf Richter, Axel was glad for her sake and hoped that 'she is making a more suitable choice than last time'. But his own pressing financial straits made it hard for him to accept that the silver that belonged to him and which Ultima's family took when they divorced should end up on another man's table: 'I myself own only *one* teaspoon – that was all I was allotted out of the pretty substantial amount of silver I had.' Richter, who according to Axel was well-off, gave Ultima not only financial security but also the child that Axel had denied her. In 1893 a boy was born to them. She died two years later, apparently in childbirth.

Axel also thought about marriage, but money problems made him hesitate. His position in society required him to find a wife, but he was afraid of the costs. He had also had his fingers burnt after the marriage to Ultima, which he often referred to in his correspondence as an example of captivity and his unsuitability as a husband.

Many women fell for Axel's charm; we shall return to that topic in a later chapter. But one who definitely did *not* was the young Swedish writer Sophie Elkan, who met Axel in December 1891 when she visited Rome with a friend. She was terrified of Axel, although her only experience of him was way back in 1879, when he was only 22 years old. But even then she had heard 'so much (bad) about him' that she had no wish to be introduced to him. On Christmas Eve, she wrote home to her mother:

He is a bad character – I can believe anything of him, and certainly that he hypnotises people. There is not an honest drop of blood in his whole body and he is extremely dangerous. He began by asking where we intended going and when I said 'Naples and Sicily', he said, then you ought to ask advice about hotels and everything else from a man who knows the whole of Italy better than anyone else, a fellow-countryman. Do you wish to go and talk to him? Yes, gladly, if you introduce me. Here is his card – and with that he took out his own. Come up to me between 2 and 3 and I will be your guide. At first I said yes – because he really is the most able person you could think of to get information from – you know, mamma, that he is the one who wrote the letters about cholera from Naples. But after thinking about it more carefully, I didn't go to see him. It would certainly have been interesting to see and hear what he intended saying to me – it all depends on what he was really up to – as a writer I could certainly use him, but I'm afraid of him, literally afraid, so his addresses can wait. That fellow has played far too big and far too unpleasant a role in too many women's lives for me to wish to admit him into mine.

The letter is quite hysterical, and how much of it should be attributed to Sophie Elkan's overstrung psyche and fear of men, and how much to Axel's reputation as a lady-killer is hard to say. What is clear is that the charm and radiance that made so many women fall at his feet provoked the opposite reaction in this case.

LORD VIVIAN

Despite his misgivings, Axel retained his position as doctor to the British legation, and the new British ambassador, Sir Hussay Crespigny Vivian, the third Baron Vivian, became his patient. Vivian had trouble swallowing and Axel suspected from an early stage that he had cancer of the throat. He travelled with Lord and Lady Vivian to Heidelberg to consult a famous specialist, Professor Kussmaul. After their return to Rome in October a rumour spread that the German doctor had distanced himself from Axel's method of treatment: the introduction of a tube that led to an irritation of the throat, which now in its turn had to be cured.

When the rumour reached Axel he wrote to Lord Vivian saying that he still maintained his method of treatment was the correct one, enclosing a letter from Professor Kussmaul which bore out that there had been a 'unfortunate misunderstanding', and explaining that he was absolutely in agreement with Axel about his method of treating the patient: 'I can expressly confirm that you have recognised the nature of the illness in good time and that you have treated it appropriately; also – and this is of the greatest importance – that you have regulated the course of treatment in such a way that the patient has received sufficient nourishment.' But Axel's reputation had already been damaged and he offered to resign as Lord Vivian's doctor, an offer that, however, the ambassador turned down.

The case of Lord Vivian is interesting for several reasons. In the first place, it represents the first known assault on Axel's position in Rome and his authority as a doctor. There would be more – Axel's short and incomplete medical training made him vulnerable to attacks of this kind. But it also says a lot about Axel's methods of treatment and his view of the doctor's function in cases of incurable illness.

Axel's silence did not of course mean that he found a little criticism justified after so much undeserved praise, as he coyly maintained. What it was really about was his oath of confidentiality as a doctor, and not only towards the general public but also in his relationship to his patient. In his letter to the ambassador he explained that the scientific details of his illness 'cannot be explained to you and cannot be understood by you or by anybody else who is not a doctor'. What Axel could not or would not explain was that Lord Vivian was incurably ill. From a letter to Frederick Curzon – an employee at the British embassy who, according to Axel, was the person who spread the rumour – it emerges that Axel's main ambition was to represent the case to the patient in the best possible light, in order to 'spare himself as much anxiety as possible'. As an example of the importance of the psyche for a patient's well-being, he cites the benefit that Lord Vivian had received from the Heidelberg trip, which is 'a purely mental one':

> In a chronic disease of, let us hope, slow evolution, his doctors *cannot* deceive him by saying that he shall be all right in so and so many months. This would produce a contrary effect, make him mistrust everybody and open his eyes to the real state of his health. He must know that his disease is long and difficult to get rid of entirely. I have never said more to him, and I never shall.

Lord Vivian died one year later. Axel had not been able to help him to live, but – true to his philosophy of doctoring – helped him to die: by refusing to explain 'the details' of his illness, by giving him a certain amount of hope (without waking false expectations), probably also by easing his pain with the help of a morphine syringe.

Soccorso e Lavoro

Three years had passed since Axel had left Capri and his hermit-like existence there. He had been very successful, far more than he had expected. His earlier reluctance to live in a big city seems to have evaporated. Had Axel, who honoured Francis of Assisi, *il poverello*, and who admired Tolstoy for his penetrating thought, completely denied the other side of his character, which was expressed at such length in his letters to Sibbern?

There is no doubt that Axel let himself be sucked into Roman society with alacrity. But at the same time his conscience dictated a parallel plan of action. Just as in Paris, he had a practice among the poor of the city alongside his official practice. 'I have been round to see all my humble friends yesterday and to-day,' he wrote to an English woman friend –

and more than ever I am struck by the terrible misery here and by my impossibility to help as I wanted to do and ought *to do* according to my unfortunate theories of life and its duty. When I see sights like this I feel ashamed to keep a penny to myself, although those few who now and then share my meals say no. What I would like to do would be to start a dispensary here. I could then have the feeling of being useful to somebody which might restore the harmony of my mind – always thinking of myself again. Up till now I have been able to give away a good deal of medicine and money – all I have earned in fact [. . .].

One of Rome's leading cultural figures at this time was the German archaeologist Wolfgang Helbig, author of a number of works about Greek and Roman antiquity. His wife, the Russian princess Nadina Shakhovskaya, had read *Letters from a Mourning City* and since coming under Axel's care for a throat ailment she had also fallen under his spell. In company with a leading Italian doctor and expert on hygiene, Professor Angelo Celli, Axel and Mrs Helbig decided to do something for the poor of the city and 'set the whole of Roman society in motion' in order to found the organisation Soccorso e Lavoro – Help and Work.

Bazaars and charity balls at the Grand Hotel were organised to finance the project. The money raised was enough to finance soup kitchens, unemployment benefits, children's homes and a children's clinic, and an *ambulatorio* in the poor quarters of Trastevere. Between 1896 and 1902 the clinic dealt with eleven thousand patients, but the total number was significantly larger as statistics from the years 1892 to 1895 are not available.

Axel's efforts on behalf of the poor also extended to an involvement with Le Piccole Sorelli dei Poveri (The Little Sisters of the Poor), to whom he regularly gave money and material help. The Sisters had – and still have – their hospital and home for the elderly beside the church of St Peter in Chains in the centre of Rome. Axel's contacts with the Sisters of the Poor are not cited anywhere other than *The Story of San Michele*, but there is no reason to disbelieve what he says. This activity was completely in line with his ideas about charity, which he was happy to see exercised with religious overtones, though preferably not under the auspices of the Church.

GENTLEMAN AND MAN OF THE WORLD

'My position in Rome is good,' Axel declared in a letter at Christmas 1892. He was treating the British ambassador and was doctor in 'the best British and American households in Rome' – despite the fact that there were no fewer than seven British doctors in the city. However, there was still no trace of any 'increased prosperity', he admitted, hinting that this was due to 'something amiss with my brain'. His unwillingness to accept payment for his services had led to his being forced to dispense with his carriage, although given the state of his health he ought not to 'dash about in cabs'. He was once more suffering from inflammation of the large intestine, he had lost a lot of weight and was having trouble digesting his food. We recognise here his problems from the summer of 1888. His chest and nervous system were, however, 'fairly good' and his 'head is all right'.

At this stage of his career something happened that was to turn Axel's life upside-down. Crown Princess Victoria planned to spend three months of the winter in Italy and needed a doctor to attend her on the trip. The Swedish court turned to ambassador Bildt to ask 'if he would be so kind as to say whether Doctor Munthe could be regarded as a suitable person for appointment as physician to Her Royal Highness' – and, if the answer was favourable, to ask Munthe if he would be willing to accept the commission.

Carl Bildt immediately contacted Axel and replied by return of post that 'Doctor Munthe is both a gentleman and a man of the world,' and that he has 'every reason to believe that HRH the Crown Princess will be most satisfied with him' since 'he is regarded as an exceptionally skilful doctor and has without question the best clientele of all foreign doctors in Rome.' Bildt had talked to Munthe, who asked him to reply that he 'would be delighted to take on the duties in question and he left it to HRH herself to decide on the terms'. However, one stipulation he made was that he would also be allowed to care for his other patients as he earned almost ninety per cent of his annual income during the winter months.

The Crown princess was keen for Munthe to accept the offer and prepared to accept his terms. When Axel told Sibbern the news he explained to him the deliberations that made him say yes to the offer, despite the financial loss that the position entailed, viz. the long-term advantages:

> This is certainly an honour of a sort but it is during these three months that I have to earn everything *I live on for the whole year* – for that is when the season is in full flower. The acceptance of this offer means for me *a financial loss* which is quite significant and my absence will in itself be a minus point for my standing here. A *plus* point is of course the undoubted

publicity inherent in this, as a result of people's snobbery. She wrote in very kind terms and I'm sure I would enjoy good conditions, without pressure and ceremonial. I replied via Bildt that I accepted, but only on condition that I be allowed to return here from time to time so as not to have *disappeared* completely – 'les absents ont tort' [the absent are wrong]. She has agreed to this and now even wishes to stay here for a while, in which case we will not travel to Sicily until February. In *any case* I suffer a financial loss – for they are not going to pay me what I am currently earning in Rome – *during the remaining 8 months of the year I don't earn a penny.* Now I am wondering to what extent I ought to budget for this incipient loss of income. Does Your Excellency think I ought to *refuse* absolutely, or, because of the indirect advantages (which I do not acknowledge) accept, and put up with this loss of income which will probably bring my budget to – again?

Axel turned to His Excellency for advice, but it was only a gesture as he had already accepted the offer from the court. From the winter of 1893 onwards he was the Crown princess's doctor in Italy. Things would never be the same again.

THE CROWN PRINCESS

We are both of us orphans of the heart, you in your royal prison and I in my humble surroundings.

Axel Munthe to Crown Princess Victoria in 1893

CROWN PRINCESS VICTORIA of Sweden–Norway, who in December 1892 asked Axel to be her doctor during her stay in Italy, was born in 1862 as Princess of Baden. In 1881, at the age of only 19, she was united with the heir to the throne of Sweden–Norway, Crown Prince Gustaf, in a marriage that from a dynastic point of view was extremely advantageous to Sweden. Victoria's father, Grand Duke Friedrich I of Baden, actually had a Swedish mother, Sophia Wilhelmina, the daughter of Gustaf IV Adolf, which meant that Victoria was a lineal descendant of a Swedish king. The thinking was that, through her marriage, she would inject a little Vasa blood into the veins of the young Bernadotte dynasty, thereby conferring on it a greater historical legitimacy. On her mother's side Victoria belonged to one of Europe's leading princely families. Her mother, Grand Duchess Luise, was the daughter of Kaiser Wilhelm I of Germany and the sister of Kaiser Friedrich III.

Despite the fact that the marriage was entered upon with obvious political designs, Gustaf and Victoria seem initially to have entertained warm feelings for each other. During the 1880s the Crown princess presented her husband with three sons. The first was Gustaf Adolf, who was born in 1882 and who became Sweden's king sixty-eight years later, taking the name of Gustaf VI Adolf. His mother was utterly exhausted after his birth and took a long time to recover. When Prince Wilhelm was born two years later it became clear that the frailty that previously had been seen as a temporary state of ill-health was in reality constitutional. On several occasions she visited health spas in Central Europe and England (Eastbourne). This was the start of a constant toing and froing that would result in Victoria spending most of each year beyond Sweden's borders for almost fifty years.

EGYPT

The state of chronic ill-health to which the Crown princess had succumbed was to some extent a consequence of bronchial infections that she had been prone to since childhood, when to toughen her up she had been made to sleep in unheated rooms in the ice-cold family castle in Karlsruhe. After the birth of her last son Eric in 1889, her state of health deteriorated even further, mentally as well as physically. Eric was born epileptic and was also slightly retarded. The prince's poor health was a hard blow for his mother, who, to crown it all, was struck down with pleurisy.

Her Swedish and German doctors did not take long to conclude that the Scandinavian winter was directly detrimental to the Crown princess's health, and she was sent to Egypt. The dry Egyptian climate was indeed beneficial to the Crown princess, who became visibly better. Her sojourn in Egypt also afforded ample scenic opportunities that Victoria immortalised with her photographic apparatus and in drawings and watercolours. She had a considerable artistic talent, which she cultivated first and foremost in the realm of photography.

The journey home began on 20 April 1891 in Cairo. The Crown prince travelled to Sweden while Victoria stayed for a couple of weeks on Capri. It was on her last day on the island that her first meeting with Munthe – described in the previous chapter – took place.

There were great hopes that the Crown princess's winter in Egypt would have made her so healthy that she would be able to endure the Swedish climate. But the summer was unusually damp and the palace she and the Crown prince inhabited, Tullgarn, was far from an ideal residence. At the end of August Victoria became ill with such a high fever that her doctor could offer no better advice than yet another winter in Egypt.

As well as her bronchial problems, extra complications had set in which no change of climate could cure – Baron von Blixen-Finecke, adjutant to the Crown prince, who 'made a particular impression' on her during her stay in Egypt. Gustaf von Blixen-Finecke was of royal blood: his mother was born a Princess of Hessen-Cassel and his aunt was Queen Louise of Denmark, who because of her children's intermarriages with other European princely houses was often referred to as 'Europe's mother-in-law and grandmother'. Blixen-Finecke was also an unusually stylish fellow whose 'appearance, figure, bearing and manner were quite simply enchanting', according to a contemporary.

During their stay in Egypt it was the baron who carried Victoria's camera equipment and helped her with developing; it appears that it was not only negatives that were exposed in the special tent that was used as a darkroom. On the eve of the next Egyptian trip, the baron's name was deleted from the list of Victoria's companions – 'so that people will not have a gratuitous excuse for gossip', as Gustaf wrote to his father.

When Victoria returned to Europe from her second trip to Egypt at the end of April 1892 she began by spending fourteen days in the Bay of Naples, taking in Amalfi and Capri, among other places, and followed this with a few days in Rome. During those days in Rome Victoria talked about her 'great longing to return to Rome next year and stay there for some time'. She longed *towards* Italy and *away from* Sweden – and from her husband, her relationship with whom had deteriorated drastically in recent years.

The royal couple spent the autumn in southern Sweden, where they planned to stay until the end of November. But on 22 November it was announced in the official press that the Crown princess had left Sweden the day before and travelled to Karlsruhe. The fact that the Crown princess had gone to see her parents was not remarkable in itself. What was startling was that the journey was reported in the newspaper as an accomplished fact and not announced in advance, as was the custom. That something exceptional had happened is borne out by the letter that the Crown prince drafted to his mother on the same day that he was reunited with Victoria in Karlsruhe on 20 December 1892:

> As soon as we reached the castle and I was alone with Vicky I talked to her and told her *everything*, the whole truth straight out, *very* seriously and calmly, not in a dismissing way but with as much loving admonition and words of caution as was possible for me under these trying conditions. I finished by telling her that my feelings for her were not the same as before after everything that had happened during the autumn, but that at the same time I still hoped in my heart that if she really wanted to change her whole demeanour and behaviour, everything could be fine again at some time in the future. She sat the whole time, silent and cold, let fall scarce a tear but asked my forgiveness and acknowledged everything without evasion, as well as saying that she realised how unjustly she had acted.

Precisely what had 'happened during the autumn' is unknown, but there is scarcely any doubt that it was Gustaf von Blixen-Finecke who continued to make the Crown princess's heart flutter. They often met when the royal couple stayed in southern Sweden, among other times, during the Danish king and queen's visit in October 1892. Gustaf and Victoria lived apart for much of the year and the 30-year-old Crown princess was both sexually frustrated and emotionally and intellectually starved. She was ill at ease in the Swedish court and, besides, the Crown prince had begun 'to seek other company', as Victoria's biographer puts it. Whether Gustaf's bisexuality had already revealed itself or whether it was more traditional erotic escapades that threatened their relationship is unknown, but their ten-year marriage was on the point of breaking up.

Whatever the exact background to the conflict of autumn 1892 may have been, the Crown princess of Sweden–Norway was in an excitable state of mind and an unstable state of health when, in December 1892, she turned to Dr Axel Munthe and asked him to be her doctor and her companion during her stay in Italy the following winter.

You Are the Lady of my Heart

When the Crown princess arrived in Rome on 4 March she was immediately examined at her own request by Munthe – so that he would be able to make a comparison 'between her state of health on arrival in Italy and later on her departure therefrom'. The next day the Crown princess gave a lunch for the Bildts, the Swedish papal Marquis Claes Lagergren and Munthe. According to Lagergren, Axel came, 'extravagant as always', half an hour late, 'when we others had already eaten both the soup and the fish'. His lateness can certainly be described as 'extravagant', but it may well have resulted from a call to a sick-bed – in which case it ought rather to have impressed the Crown princess. Considering that it was a member of the royal family who had issued the invitation, however, Axel's behaviour testifies to an astounding frivolity on his part.

The following morning Victoria continued on to Amalfi. Axel remained in Rome. In Amalfi, Victoria contracted a 'slight cold' but Munthe was summoned and she recovered. Her stay lasted for about five weeks, with a break of a few days for a trip to Capri. From reports in the press it was clear that the Crown princess had found a new doctor: 'The days pass tranquilly in Amalfi, and little changes. Longish walks and occasional excursions by carriage or boat are the only interruption to the daily calm.' Munthe's cure – long walks – was radically different from the former methods of treatment, which prescribed that Victoria should remain indoors and in bed.

After her stay in the south of Italy Victoria returned to Rome and continued with her daily long walks: 'Doctor Munthe, who is employed as HRH's doctor during her stay in Italy, takes pains to ensure that her régime is strictly adhered to.' During her month-long stay in Rome Axel had his first opportunity to socialise a bit more with the Crown princess. They met daily, he won her trust, she confided her marital problems to him and told him of the man who occupied her thoughts. The intimacy between the Crown princess and her doctor gradually turned into warmer feelings, but her emotions regarding Blixen-Finecke gave Victoria pause.

On 8 May the Crown princess and Axel travelled to Venice, where they had planned to stay for a week. However a 'slight cold' ensured that Victoria remained there twice as long as planned. This time it was not a question of some run-of-the-mill fever, but of a rise in temperature of a quite different kind. A letter that Munthe wrote after Victoria's departure shows clearly that something had 'happened' between them: 'I have gone through more than you will ever know these days I have been here, but I have never failed towards you in my loyal devotion and chivalrous friendship. Remember that my only aim is to help you.' He wrote of his longing for his 'sweet friend' and thanked her for everything she had given him. 'I shall not write like this any more,' he finished – 'Don't be afraid'. The letter lacks both a salutation and a signature.

The letter exudes remorse and anxiety. Had he gone too far? Victoria's reply has not been preserved, but was obviously of such a nature that in his next letter Axel burst out with an open declaration of love:

I have been away to Naples and last night on coming home I was greeted by your letter and the photos. I kissed the dear, sad face under its veil of mourning, for I love this photograph, it is the only one worthy of you. But I am so thankful you allow me to keep them all, each of them contain [sic] something of you. – Bless you for your dear letter, so like yourself as you were in Venice! Yes, you are right, those were happy days we spent together in beautiful Venice with Life's hard reality far away and merciful forgetfulness in our mind. Ah! we had both of us so much to forget, not who you were, because to me you are the lady of my heart and nothing else; but forget that your thoughts went to another man. I said here in Rome that I could never forget this, but I did forget it, so help me God, for a few short moments. And you did forget it too, while the gondola moved slowly over the shimmering waters and the old world was gone and we sat there silently gazing out towards the beautiful green-clad island of dreamland far away in the distance. Bless thee, fair Venice, who gave us the forgetfulness of ourselves. Italy can do this, and so can your beloved Eastern land [= Egypt], but my country cannot and neither can yours [= Germany]. And it is for that reason that we feel homeless there, for we were born with wings, it is for that reason that you laid your hand in mine for we are both of us orphans of the heart, you in your royal prison and I in my humble surroundings. And it is for that reason that we shall meet again, I know we shall, for you will need my frank devotion and chivalrous friendship even when you do not care anymore for the manly tenderness of my heart which is now all yours, for the beautiful emotion of love which now fills my soul with joy and sorrow. I cannot believe that we did wrong in forgetting who we were, that God could disapprove of us poor human beings, who dared to feel happy and thankful for a few hours' silence and peace in the midst of the noise and clamour of our daily life – wasn't it like Sunday for the tired thoughts, this beautiful, long day of Venice[,] after a hard week of toil and labour.

After Victoria's departure, Axel wrote, he spent the whole evening lying on the beach. He fell asleep and Victoria came to him in a dream: 'You came at last, dearest, in a beautiful dream which was granted to me by God and you said that you cared for me a little.'

The letter is a remarkable mixture of sincere feelings and turgid rhetoric of the kind that Munthe so easily lapsed into. But at the same time it is the most self-revealing declaration of love that we know of from Munthe, along with the poem to Sigrid von Mecklenburg. In Victoria's reply – which has not been preserved – she urged Axel to be 'sage' which does not, however, mean that her feelings were cooler. But she was afraid to give way to them, fearing the consequences. That the Crown princess of Sweden–Norway had had an affair with Blixen-Finecke, who was of royal blood, was bad enough. That she had taken a fancy to a low-born chemist's son was even worse. The very fact that she was deceiving her royal spouse was something unheard of.

In actual fact Victoria was experiencing what had happened between them just as intensely as Axel. Six years later, when she visited Venice on her own, the gondolier's song woke memories of their first lovers' meeting: 'Guglielmo has been singing several times to evoke all the dear remembrances of those bright, happy days here the first spring, *our* spring! never to be forgotten! It is like a beautiful ray of sunshine through my dark miserable life! bless you for it d[arlin]g.'

Victoria and Munthe had only known each other for a few months when the Crown princess chose to confide her most intimate secrets to him. Shortly thereafter their hands, and probably not only their hands, were united for the first time. What was it that attracted them to each other? For the Crown princess, Munthe's psychotherapeutic skill, his ability to listen and explain, his empathy, was an important factor. He filled her life, which she felt to be so empty, with content and meaning. As for Axel, one can assume that Victoria's rank and position exercised a considerable enchantment on him. For someone who has been striving all his life for recognition, it is hard to imagine a better testimonial of success than the favour of a Crown princess.

Yet this does not suffice to explain the union of souls that took place in Venice in May 1893 and whose true significance would be revealed in the last words uttered by Victoria on her death-bed thirty-seven years later. Axel and Victoria were united by a shared attitude to life, the main ingredients of which were melancholy and resignation. In both cases it was illness that set its stamp on their view of life. Around the beginning of the twentieth century young people with lung problems did not expect to live long, and their lives were lived in the shadow of illness, in hospitals and sanatoria. It was an environment to which melancholy and resignation were appropriate responses. This created a feeling of being an outsider, which was strengthened by the alienation Victoria felt in her Swedish family and Axel in society in general. But in both of them melancholy was balanced by a strong vein of humour, which in Munthe's case was revealed in his writings, not least in *The Story of San Michele*. Victoria has been depicted as a haughty, class-conscious, stiff German, which indeed she also was – in official contexts. In private she was a completely different person, at least when she was in good health: 'an exceptionally genial personality' who could be 'terribly funny', noted Alexandra Bildt.

Apart from this basic similarity in temperament and attitude to life, there was a great deal more that brought Victoria and Axel together. They were both intelligent, creative people with a highly tuned sensitivity. By contrast with Gustaf, who lacked cultural interests and ambitions, Axel was a well read and stimulating person with whom Victoria could converse about art, literature and archaeology. They were also both enthusiastic photographers, in Victoria's case to a professional standard.

Another link that united them was their great love for animals – so common among people who feel like outsiders in their human environment. At the very beginning of their acquaintance Axel gave Victoria his dog Tom, and she in turn gave him the dogs Tappio and Jallah. Over the years there would be several gifts of this kind.

An equally strong bond was music. There are innumerable witnesses to Axel's musicality. He had an attractive light baritone voice and was an accomplished amateur pianist. But he did not make music in order to entertain. Music was for him a way of escaping from the world and from his melancholy. 'Sometimes', his cousin Fredrik Lund testified,

> he could bury his intelligence in the nocturnal abysses of hypochondria and let his conversation drip with wounded humanity's, *præsertim* his own heart's, blood. If you then annoyed him sufficiently, you could occasionally induce him to do something which was just about impossible to achieve by the route of persuasion – namely, to sit himself down at the piano. Although he was completely self-taught, he improvised freely and tastefully and had an exceptional musical memory; and with the notes, his bad mood dissolved into harmony. Schopenhauer had to give way.

The composer who was most effective at helping Axel to keep the black dog at bay was Franz Schubert, who in *The Story of San Michele* was hailed as 'the greatest singer of all times'.

Victoria for her part had grown up at the court of Baden, a European centre of culture. Even as a young girl Victoria had demonstrated a significant musical talent and she was introduced at an early age to Wagner's world (which was also Munthe's). The conductor of the Karlsruhe Opera was the famous Felix Mottl, and several of the period's leading musicians played as guest artists there; on one occasion the young Victoria was allowed to turn the pages for Franz Liszt. She received a solid grounding in the piano and over the years developed into a very good pianist. When the Crown princess and Axel made music together it was she who played the piano while Axel sang.

Treat Me with Greatest Indifference

'We shall meet again, I know we shall,' Axel had written, in a form of words that exuded confidence. However, that they would see each other again was by no means a foregone conclusion. Axel's task had been to accompany the princess during her stay in Italy; nothing more had been agreed upon. But he turned out to be right. Victoria had no intention of waiting until her next trip to Italy before meeting her new doctor and friend again – Axel was already in Sweden by the summer. Not only that, but on 1 July Oscar II appointed him a Knight of the Order of the Pole Star, a distinction that was normally bestowed as a reward for long and faithful service. Axel had only been in royal service for two and a half months. What praise Victoria must have lavished on Axel in her reports to her father-in-law the king!

In Italy Axel and Victoria had been able to see each other in relative freedom, but in Sweden they were permanently surrounded by courtiers. The Crown princess was busy with official duties and under the constant scrutiny of her attendants. In order not to arouse suspicions, Axel and Victoria entered into a role-play that involved showing as little interest as possible in each other. Their strategy was outlined by Munthe in a letter to the Crown princess: 'Remember that you must treat me with greatest indifference, rather as a bore.' Another precaution was that they always spoke English to each other so that the servants would not understand what they were saying. In the same way, their private, secret correspondence was conducted in English while Munthe's official letters, 'very correct and very dull', were composed in Swedish. It is important to keep this double-entry book-keeping in mind when judging Munthe's often offhand or downright disparaging comments about Victoria over the years. They were a way of removing any suspicions about the true nature of the relationship.

Munthe was now sucked into a life whose rhythm was determined by the routines of the Crown princess. His agreement with Victoria specified that he would not have to take part in court ceremonial. But the days on Sofiero, the royal family's castle in southern Sweden, were filled with visits and courtesy calls and Axel could not entirely avoid the ceremonial side of court life. In addition, this first autumn on Sofiero offered 'a fair amount of interest', as he reported to Sibbern. One day the Crown prince and princess received a visit from from 'Europe's mother-in-law and grandmother' with her husband, the Danish King Christian IX, the Crown Prince and Princess of Denmark, the princes of the Danish royal house and Princess Alexandra, who was married to Edward, Prince of Wales, the future Edward VII. They were accompanied by another son-in-law of the Danish royal couple, the Russian Tsar Alexander III. The company also included several Russian grand dukes and grand duchesses, including the imperial couple's son Nikolai, who the following year would succeed his father on the Russian throne. Thus on 12 October 1893, the current and future rulers of four European countries – Sweden, Denmark, Great Britain and Russia – converged on Sofiero.

At the end of October Axel was invited to Kristiania (now Oslo) to meet King Oscar II of Sweden–Norway and Queen Sophia, who were his actual employers and who were eager to make his acquaintance. On his journey down to Rome Axel stayed briefly in Baden with Victoria's parents, Grand Duke Friedrich I of Baden and Grand Duchess Louise, who also wanted to meet him. The impression he gained was a positive one, his stay was 'interesting' and they were 'extremely friendly' towards him, he wrote to Sibbern. Munthe had promised Crown Prince Gustaf to report on his stay in Baden as soon as he got to Rome. In the report he gave an amusing account of his hour-long conversation with the grand duchess about her daughter's state of health. They met on several occasions but he seldom got a word in edgeways:

> I tried all the languages known to me in hopes of finding one where at least the technical difficulties of the language itself would give me the chance to get a word in from time to time – in vain, the Grand Duchess's French was even faster than her English, and her German rendered me completely speechless. She knew everything, had studied everything, could foresee everything.

The report survives in only fragmentary form, but we get an indication of the nature of the conversations from a letter that Munthe wrote at the same time to Carl Snoilsky: 'Unfortunately I do not believe that [the Crown princess] will recover, she is also mentally ill and medication for that is not sold in the chemist's.' Presumably it was this insight that Munthe passed on to Victoria's parents. The form of words was part of the camouflage game that he and Victoria were engaged in, but it also mirrored the true situation: Victoria not only had a weak chest, but also weak nerves. 'Yet I believe I could have been of some use to her,' he concluded in his letter to Snoilsky, 'a fraction of what she herself believes is enough for me not to regret my summer.'

If the Crown princess valued the new medical thinking that Axel's appearance on the scene implied, then the royal couple's official doctor, Anselm Werner, had all the more reason for displeasure. Here came the Crown princess dragging behind her a young doctor, surrounded by rumours, who had hardly had time to set foot in his homeland before he was hailed with royal favours! To many Swedish doctors, Axel, with his short formal medical education, was simply an upstart. In his report to the Crown prince, Axel summed up his impressions of his first summer with the Crown princess:

> My experience from Stockholm is [. . .] of such a nature that I feel it likely my time will be short. The great friendliness I have met with from the Crown Princess's family cannot take away the bitter aftertaste that unmotivated jealousy and ill-will have left in my mind. I am not saying this to the Crown Princess as it would counteract my own objective if I was to let her know how I have been slandered and calumniated by several colleagues at home. I am not a Swedish doctor but I am a Swede, and I have tried in my way to help the Crown Princess to become Swedish too – we both know that she is not there yet. I have *in every way* behaved absolutely correctly towards the Crown Princess's doctor in Stockholm, but he has not behaved correctly towards me. During the days I spent in Stockholm I was exposed to more slander than during the whole 13 years that I have been a doctor – I have no answer to that. But were it not for my personal fondness for and scientific interest in the Crown Princess, which has multiplied since I got to know her in the summer, I should now see myself obliged to refuse any further co-operation – however temporary it might be – with my colleague in Stockholm.

Munthe was eager to stress that his interest in the Crown princess was mostly of a scientific nature. But, as we have seen, this was a way of diverting attention from the real situation. At the same time as Axel was composing his lines to Gustaf, Victoria was writing a letter to her doctor that testifies to the fact that quite different questions were occupying them. She has, she confesses, no intimate relations with her husband ('*Nothing* between the Crown Pr. & myself except quiet talks') but feels she has entered into a union of souls with Munthe: 'Do you know, I begin to think it is quite natural & quite as it ought to be, that I cannot sleep, because *you* cannot either! And as a certain communication exists between our souls, I suppose it is a natural consequence.'

MUNTHE MORE IN CLOVER THAN EVER

Even before his meeting with Victoria, Munthe had a unique position within Roman society, but after she came under his care – and he under her protection – his career took a qualitative leap. As early as during Victoria's first stay in Rome after the declaration of love in Venice, Bildt reported that Munthe was 'more in clover than ever'.

Even if Victoria and Axel could not show their feelings openly, it was obvious to most people that the Crown princess took a particular delight in her doctor. And the gossip circulated, in Rome as in Stockholm. 'She must have taken quite a fancy to her doctor, that's what they believe here too,' Sophie Elkan reported from Rome. Few, if any, could have guessed how intimate Victoria and her doctor were, but the fact that Axel so openly enjoyed the Crown princess's favour was enough to elevate him in the eyes of his contemporaries – and in his own. When the Swedish poet Verner von Heidenstam met Munthe in Rome, the latter is supposed to have given 'eager hints' that the Crown princess was his 'mistress'. The liaison was of such significance that it was hard to keep to oneself…

Claes Lagergren, who was in a position to follow Munthe's blooming career at close quarters, was impressed by his status and power:

[We had] breakfast with Dr. Munthe in his apartment in the Piazza di Spagna, which to be sure was small but not without a certain elegance. Munthe was by now such a celebrity in Rome that one was bound to feel oneself particularly honoured by an invitation to his table. Everybody ran after him, and with his irresistible charm he dominated the whole of Anglo-Saxon society. It is supposed to have been Munthe who arranged the marriage of Francesco Massimo and Prince Brancaccio's daughter. As the bride's grandmother Mrs Field was completely under Munthe's influence, it was only after submitting themselves to his conditions that the Massimo family managed to conclude this alliance which has rescued them financially.

One visitor to Rome who was not so easily persuaded was Bjørnstjerne Bjørnson, Munthe's friend from his Paris years. Bjørnson had condemned Axel's treatment of Ultima, and his depiction of their first meeting for seven years is coloured by this attitude. To Bjørnson, Munthe was a boastful upstart whom he wished to have no more to do with. On 11 December 1894 he wrote to his daughter:

On the outside, completely unchanged. But now it's no longer possible to talk to him without his immediately interjecting that he has just been called to Stockholm to the queen, who didn't want to let him go. He had to make up that he had to go to London for a consultation, and strangely enough, just as he was about to set off, he got a telegram from Lord Dufferin. The same Lord Dufferin sailed with him in the Bay of Naples in the summer, but Munthe had to put him ashore on Capri as he was summoned to Princess Ruspoli in Rome. The first time I talked to Munthe after that, the young son of an American millionaire had just arrived in Rome. His sole reason for coming was to consult Dr Munthe, he was a drinker and would obey no-one but Dr Munthe. Now he was obeying his mother since Dr Munthe had ordered him to do so; he is expecting a fee of 10,000 dollars.

He lives by the Spanish Steps 'in the apartment where the English poet Keats died; Shelley lived above him'. When you enter Munthe's apartment Keats' and Shelley's poems are lying open, just by chance. Both are bound in de luxe binding of the utmost elegance. In the hall you find an excessively large dish for visiting cards. Gladstone's card lies uppermost. You are supposed to believe he was at Munthe's yesterday. Dr Munthe drives round the city, sometimes with two magnificent horses, sometimes with two ponies. Beside him sits either the Crown Princess of Sweden or his two dogs, one small, one big, of England's noblest blood, the little one on the back-seat and the big one on the front-seat. A groom sits alongside the coachman, both of them in uniform. Munthe himself, on the other hand, is as simply dressed as Napoleon. Never do you see him wear a decoration, and seldom gloves. Without further ado, as if in the passing, he tells you how important he has been to the queen, the Crown Princess, the princess Ruspoli, the American millionaire's son, or he talks about the consultation which preceded the British ambassador's death last year, when Dr Munthe proved to be right and everybody else wrong. This comes out just as uncalled for as when we sometimes say that we *have* already had lunch or we *have* already had coffee. For a visit, he can get 50–100 lire (£2–4) or more. There is money lying all over the room, some of it crumpled up. He often charges no fee at all. What is he doing other than his duty?

He has three maidservants, all of whom belong to a family in Anacapri whose members he has saved. The remainder of the family now live in his villa in Anacapri. There is only one name that is known in Anacapri, and it is his. (A Norwegian was there recently and met no-one who knew where Munthe's villa was.)

I have been at Munthe's once – *one* time. Thereby my visiting-card also ended up in his dish. Since then he has had no use for me nor I for him.

UNDER DOCTOR MUNTHE'S CARE

Because of her poor health, Victoria's existence in Rome was almost completely uneventful. The risk of infection meant that she was cut off from any social life as well as from the world of the theatre and music – 'It would actually be easier to describe what the Crown Princess does not do rather than what she does,' Bildt reported in a newspaper article.

During the 1890s Victoria suffered a couple of genuinely serious health crises. The first occurred in August 1894 when Dr Werner and Munthe recommended that she submit to examination by Professor Erb in Heidelberg, 'the most outstanding specialist in the area of neuropathology in Germany'. 'The result of this will be = 0 but it's necessary for her mother's sake,' Axel wrote to Sibbern: 'I have been invited to participate in the consultation but have excused myself as I have other things to do and I know it's only a farce.'

Axel himself went to see Queen Sophia in Norway, 'at her earnest request'. After visiting the queen and paying a quick call on Sibbern, Axel set sail for London with English friends whose yacht was lying in harbour in Norway. He put up at the Savoy, but London, he reported, was 'a horrid town', he was unable to sleep at night and he travelled out to the country to call on some patients and friends, including Lady Carnarvon at Pixton Park (in Dulverton, Somerset). By 1 October he was back on Capri, where he spent most of his time out on the sea: 'Since I came back I have spent my days in the boat although the weather has been horrid and we would have gone to the bottom more than once had not the boat been good and the helmsman watchful – myself if you please.' As usual bravura and self-pity contend for the mastery in Axel's situation reports: 'I sleep so badly and have constantly that ominous disturbance with the heart's condition which shall kill me one day.'

Axel did not remain long on Capri – he had given in to the Crown princess's wish that he be present during the consultation with Professor Erb. He was the only person the Crown princess relied on, he wrote; she had 'officially declared that she would set her face against anything they suggested if I was not of the same mind' and this 'naturally vexes her 2 German and Swedish doctors'.

The consultation took place as planned, in Axel's presence. The medical report was unequivocal in its recommendation for treatment: 'As far as one can now predict, her condition will continue to necessitate a stay in the south during some of the winter months during the next few years.' The form of words used was an indirect admission that from now on she was in Munthe's care: something which was reinforced by the following conclusion: 'H.R.H. will depart for Rome around the 15th of November and will remain there under Dr. Munthe's care.' That 'Dr. Munthe's care' was a metaphor for a relationship of a quite different kind was something that only those directly involved were aware of.

The power struggle over the Crown princess's health was over. Axel had won and Victoria was finally placed under his supervision. Dr Werner's position from now on was purely nominal.

I Am With You in my Thoughts the Whole Day

'My journey to Baden was very troublesome and a complete failure for me personally as notwithstanding all my efforts to have her sent elsewhere and another doctor with her the other 3 doctors agreed to send her to me again and again I shall have the entire responsibility and the whole bother for the whole winter,' Munthe complained. It was under cover of this smokescreen that Victoria arrived in Rome on 20 November 1894.

Otherwise, Axel had nothing to complain about, he was 'still regarded as a good doctor' who despite his independence was still well trusted. For once he had not had to borrow money – this was as near as he would ever come to 'financial independence' and he was glad to have got so far. He is 'as highly-strung as ever' but now, thank God, 'I am the master of my mind / I am the captain of my soul'. The quotation comes from the poem 'Invictus' by William Ernest Henley, but it is not quite correct. Henley wrote 'master of my *fate*', not 'mind'. Whether or not the misquotation was a conscious one, it is revealing for someone who confessed that he did not always have full control over his 'mind'.

In November, when Victoria was about to set out for Rome again, Axel complained to Warburg: 'the Crown Prince never speaks and seldom thinks, but he is a man of honour and I like him and feel sorry for him – the best proof of that is that, yet again, and despite all the inconvenience it involves, I have agreed to take the responsibility for his wife on my own shoulders. She is coming tomorrow and will remain with me throughout the winter.' The smokescreens were becoming even denser.

Axel and Victoria lived separate lives for large parts of the year and exchanged not only letters but also presents. Victoria sent him silver objects and – crispbread. Axel's presents were of another kind. The silk stockings he bought for Victoria in London give an indication of the intimacy of their relationship. It was a gesture with a quite different erotic charge at that time compared to today. He asked Victoria to let him know her size, but best of all, of course, would be if she could send him a stocking as an example ... but he was unsure where to send the parcel, and to whom

– it could not be sent direct, but only via a third party; they were afraid of awakening suspicion: 'It is not safe any more.' The romantic game they had entered upon was a gamble for exceptionally high stakes. When could they see each other?

I am longing to come to Sweden = to you, but when? [. . .] End of July? Or early in August. I wonder if you will continue to be as kind to me as you are now once after having returned to Sweden with its associations and souvenirs – only be *true*, that is all I ask of you. [. . .] I am with you in my thoughts the whole day. Remember me in the hours of need and try not to forget me altogether when you are happy.

The last sentence was fishing for compliments; Axel had no reason to doubt Victoria's feelings.

Victoria spent the following winters in Rome too. In the autumn of 1896 Axel wrote to Sibbern from Capri:

I have been here the whole summer and my only outing was to Venice last spring with the Crown Princess, who spent last winter in Rome under my care. I am almost sure she will go there again, although the families are not in favour. They have asked me if I will travel with her, to which I have replied no. She obeys me completely and I try to keep her feeble body and soul intact – old, bad blood. She gets no support in Sweden from her own people.

Axel did not mince his words, but that his services were appreciated emerges from the fact that in 1898 the Grand Duke of Baden awarded him the Zähringer Order of the Lion, Second Class.

I Am Becoming a Worse Courtier Every Day

Axel's intimate contacts with royalty had not made him modify his anti-royalist attitude; if anything, the result was the opposite. His sceptical view of the monarchy was underpinned both by the insights he gained into the stultifyingly conventional Swedish court and by Victoria's antipathy towards her Swedish relatives. 'My ideas are [. . .] not in sympathy with the royalist comedy and I am becoming a worse courtier every day,' he confided to Sibbern.

The Crown prince is described in Axel's letters as 'decent' but 'languid', 'not particularly gifted' and 'not interested in anything', 'a kind, honourable but *insignificant* person, ignorant and limited'. He had the same ironic, condescending attitude to Oscar II as many other intellectuals at this time: 'His father – the king – n'est pas un homme sérieux and it seems incomprehensible to me that the myth of royalty can be upheld by such pathetic representatives.' With reference to the Crown princess too, Axel often adopted a nonchalant tone of voice, saying that she interested him mainly as a psychological case study.

The rabid radicalism that Axel permitted himself in relation to his royal employer drew nourishment from the very special relationship he had to his highborn patient – and the confidence the royal family placed in him in general. As for his view of the Crown prince, it was derived both from his own impressions and from information received from Victoria, who did all she could to reduce her dealings with her husband to a minimum.

The fact was that the royal couple had little in common, apart from their children; they had widely divergent notions of how they should be reared. Victoria's relationship to the princes was heavily guilt-laden as she saw them so seldom. On one occasion she appealed to Gustaf in an instance involving one of their sons. Gustaf's answer, in the shape of a telegram, was 'no', and he added that the doctors were also against it. Victoria immediately wrote a despairing letter to her 'darling' Munthe. 'I really feel sorry that "our" country could produce such idiots!', she burst out, with a sarcastic dig at the country in which both she and Axel saw themselves as aliens, and went on:

> I shall not so easily forgive the Prince his unkind ways. As to sitting alone with him in Tullgarn after this, really I *cannot*. Then I prefer decidedly to bore myself in Franzensbad. But I don't see my way quite clearly yet, & more than ever I miss *you* d[arlin]g, & your good advice. But I know you will write to me and advise me in the matter.

Towards the end of the 1890s the relationship between Gustaf and Victoria degenerated to the point where, one day, Victoria declared that she wanted to 'celebrate the end of 1881' – that is, her marriage to Gustaf, which had begun in 1881. The choice of verb says everything about the atmosphere between the spouses. Relations were now so poor that no one could fail to notice, not even the Crown prince's own mother: 'To what extent circumstances at home will improve as a result of her protracted stay there, Doctor, you no doubt know better than I,' Queen Sophia wrote to Munthe in October 1898, reluctantly drawing the conclusion herself: 'I merely suspect and fear that such will not be the case.'

THE DREAM OF SAN MICHELE

A creation of the most fantastic beauty, poetry, and inutility I have ever seen clustered together.

Henry James

AXEL'S YEARLY RHYTHM was as regular as that of his royal patient: the winter half of the year was spent in Rome; in May he took his little cutter *Lady Victoria*, which had been moored in the harbour at Anzio, over to Capri: 'Miss Hall with Giovannina and Rosina and all the dogs went by rail to Naples as usual,' he wrote in *The Story of San Michele* – 'I, together with Billy the baboon, the mongoose and the little owl, had a glorious sail in the yacht.' During the summer he sailed and raced in the Mediterranean. He usually spent some time in Sweden and England and he would normally return to Rome at the beginning of November, when the winter season began.

Munthe's 'villa in Anacapri' that Bjørnstjerne Bjørnson referred to in the letter to his daughter in 1894 was the Villa Damecuta, which Axel had managed to rent before leaving Capri in the autumn of 1889. In October of the same year he was invited to buy the house, which was situated in the centre of Anacapri and lacked a view. Soon a better alternative came along, perhaps the one he was looking for: the old carpenter Vincenzo Alberino – 'Mastro Vincenzo' in *The Story of San Michele* – decided to sell his little house on Capodimonte, 'the crown of the hill', 325 metres above the harbour, with a ravishing view over the Bay of Naples. The contract was signed on 1 June 1895. On the same day Axel bought an adjoining chapel from a Count Papengouth and a few pieces of land in the immediate neighbourhood from the Ferraro family.

Although Axel was a newly fledged houseowner, he travelled around that summer in his usual manner, like a bird of passage. He raced in the Bay of Naples, he sailed to Monte Cristo and Elba and according to eyewitnesses he was very up-beat: 'He is on the water constantly, either racing or cruising, and seems to be in high spirits,' he 'is looking very well, browned by the sun [. . .], laughing and joking the whole time'.

In July Axel travelled to Cowes on the Isle of Wight, where he stayed with the Duchess of Manchester, whose daughter was his patient. Cowes was the headquarters of the Royal British Sailing Club, large-scale regattas were held in August between the island and the mainland and it was presumably the sailing rather than the duchess and her daughter that lured Axel to these waters. In any event, sailing was the theme of that summer. In mid-August he travelled up to the west coast of Sweden to join the Crown prince and princess on the *Lady Sophia*. In September he returned to England and Scotland as Lord Dudley's guest and also took the opportunity to visit some British patients.

After his stay in Britain Axel returned to Capri, where he seems to have spent the autumn working in his newly acquired vineyard. In a letter to Karl Warburg he claimed to have 'dug up a couple of rooms with the most beautiful mosaic floors and frescoes like the finest in Pompeii – and marble floors on which imperial feet have trod – Tiberius had a palace there and these rooms were part of it.' He had found 'superb Greek coins and fine marble fragments'. Everything was now covered up again but he would continue digging next summer.

The facts were not plucked out of the air. The vineyard he had acquired concealed the remains of an imperial villa, perhaps belonging to Tiberius, who ruled the Roman Empire from Capri during the period 26–37 AD. According to the Roman historian Tacitus, Tiberius is supposed to have had no fewer than twelve villas on Capri. From Capodimonte one can look out towards the ruins of the Jupiter Villa (Villa Jovis), a colossal structure on the north-east tip of the island.

The ruins under Mastro Vincenzo's vineyard had been unearthed in 1830, then gradually destroyed by the various owners of the land. Through his efforts in digging up marble fragments and other remains, Axel contributed to halting the continuing destruction. In a letter to Sibbern in the autumn of 1896 he described the plot he had acquired:

This last year, I have been wholly taken up with the realisation of an old dream – the acquisition of a refuge on Capri where I can live out my last years and die in peace. I have succeeded in buying an old church situated on the loveliest point of the island all to myself and am now busy converting it into a dwelling-house. A vineyard lies round it and conceals one of Tiberius's palaces, a significant part of which I have excavated, finding many antiquities and hundreds of Roman and Greek coins. The church was formerly a temple of Isis, then it became part of Tiberius's palace (I have excavated a room with a mosaic floor and frescoes from his time), then it became a chapel again, later dedicated to St Michael, which was destroyed by the Saracen Barbarossa in 1560, then in 1804 it became a fortress, when Britain occupied Capri, it was stormed by the

French in 1806 (it dominates what was then the only road to Capri), then it was made into a powder magazine and now it is my home. I have gone into debt in England in order to get it ready but there's no danger there as the place will be worth quite a bit. If all goes well I will move in next year.

The letter shows that the building that was occupying Axel's thoughts at this time was the chapel dedicated to St Michael – San Michele. It was here that he would make his dream come true, it was here that would become 'home'; Mastro Vincenzo's house was not mentioned at all.

When Axel took over the chapel it was a ruin; the floor, according to *The Story of San Michele*, was 'covered to a man's height with the débris of the fallen vault, the walls were covered with ivy and wild honey-suckle and hundreds of lizards played merrily among big bushes of myrtle and rosemary [. . .]'.

A year later, in the autumn of 1897, Axel sent yet another report to Sibbern: 'I have now built my little house here, high up on the cliff-face (1,000 feet high) and completely isolated and surrounded by the sea on all sides, and here I have been sitting all alone in a kind of dream-state since the end of May.' The 'little house' in question is most likely the chapel, which in his letter written in the autumn of 1896 Axel said he hoped to be able to move into 'next year'.

When Axel decided to rebuild Mastro Vincenzo's house, and when it was finished, is unclear. *The Story of San Michele* hardly helps to clear up the mystery:

> What had once been Mastro Vincenzo's house and his carpenter workshop was gradually transformed and enlarged onto what was to become my future home. How it was done I have never been able to understand, nor has anybody who knows the history of the San Michele of to-day. I knew absolutely nothing about architecture, nor did any of my fellow-workers, nobody who could read or write ever had anything to do with the work, no architect was ever consulted, no proper drawing or plan was ever made, no exact measurements were ever taken. It was all done 'all'occhio', as Mastro Nicola called it.

Elsewhere in the book we are told that 'After five long summers' incessant toil from sunrise to sunset San Michele was more or less finished.' Five summers counted from 1895 is 1899, which is probably about right – the first recorded mentions of the completed villa relate precisely to 1899.

From the little chapel and vineyard to the magnificent villa that was erected in the grounds of Mastro Vincenzo's house, surrounded by its orchard, was a big step, mentally as much as financially. Even if labour on

Capri was cheap and Axel was a notorious dreamer, it is hard to believe that someone with such a well-developed business sense could throw himself into a project of this nature without financial guarantees of some kind. Axel was *always* short of money and, besides, his bank in Rome went bankrupt in 1894 and he lost all his savings: 7,500 francs.

A few years later, however, a radical change occurred in his living conditions. In 1898 he told Margaretta MacVeagh, daughter of the American ambassador to Rome, that he was now financially independent: 'Since I saw you a change has taken place in my life. I am now independent and can live where I like, undisturbed by the idea that I must earn my living.'

Since Axel said he was financially independent, a substantial sum of money must have been involved, much bigger than any doctor's fee, however generous. Was it someone who was anxious to assure themselves of Axel's affections? A grateful patient, a lovesick admirer? But it is hard to believe Axel would accept the degree of dependency that such a monetary gift would imply. Could it have been a gift from the elderly and childless Sibbern? Was it Victoria who ensured that Axel could make his dream come true, so that they could meet far from the gaze of the world? If so, it could have been done through her cousin, Prince Max of Baden, who was also his patient (see the following chapters) and who, according to a reliable source, provided Axel with large sums of money.

Whatever the answer may be, the fact is that, after this date, Axel significantly extended his domains. In 1899 he acquired land below Mastro Vincenzo's house and, that same year, the ruins of the Barbarossa castle on the hill above. Two years later he bought La Foresteria (the foreigner's lodging), which lies fifty metres from the villa and which had formerly served as the summer residence of the bishops of Capri. In 1904 he concluded his land purchases on Capodimonte by buying the Barbarossa hill itself.

THE SOUL NEEDS MORE SPACE THAN THE BODY

The architectonic ensemble that developed over time consists of the main building, the Villa San Michele, the chapel and the remains of a rest-room – a *cubiculum* – with wall-paintings and mosaic floors diagonally under the chapel which may have been used by Augustus or Tiberius. The two main parts of the structure, the villa and the chapel, are connected, partly by the beautifully curved pergola, and partly by a cypress alley that, before Axel acquired the area, was a public right of way. His own description of the finished work is as follows:

The house was small, the rooms were few but there were loggias, terraces and pergolas all around it to watch the sun, the sea and the clouds – the soul needs more space than the body. Not much furniture in the rooms but what there was could not be bought with money alone. Nothing superfluous, nothing unbeautiful, no bric-à-brac, no trinkets. A few primitive pictures, an etching of Dürer and a Greek bas-relief on the whitewashed walls. A couple of old rugs on the mosaic floor, a few books on the tables, flowers everywhere in lustrous jars from Faenza and Urbino. The cypresses from Villa d'Este leading the way up to the chapel had already grown into an avenue of stately trees, the noblest trees in the world. The chapel itself which had given its name to my home had at last become mine. It was to become my library. Fine old cloister stalls surrounded the white walls, in its midst stood a large refectory table laden with books and terracotta fragments. On a fluted column of giallo antico stood a huge Horus of basalt, the largest I have ever seen, brought from the land of the Pharaohs by some Roman collector, maybe by Tiberius himself. Over the writing-table the marble head of Medusa looked down upon me, fourth century B.C., found by me at the bottom of the sea. On the huge Cinquecento Florentine mantelpiece stood the Winged Victory. On a column of africano by the window the mutilated head of Nero looked out over the gulf where he had caused his mother to be beaten to death by his oarsmen. Over the entrance door shone the beautiful Cinquecento stained-glass window presented to Eleonora Duse by the town of Florence and given by her to me in remembrance of her last stay in San Michele.

'The soul needs more space than the body.' It is a noble sentiment, and as regards the Villa San Michele it is also true. To be sure, the villa was big enough in its external dimensions, but there was not very much usable space. The ground floor was dominated by the kitchen and dining-room. The upper floor consisted initially only of a bedroom and study – and a terrace with pergola. After a few years the terrace was walled in and converted into the new and largish bedroom which can be seen today, and a bit later again the villa acquired an extension in the mid-part of the building.

The architecture does not follow any accepted style, but shows traces of eclecticism and wilfulness. Yet the villa adhered both outside and inside to the 'symbolist pessimism' that hailed retrospection as 'protection against the future'. 'I want to have white loggias and arcades with antique marble fragments, worthless fragments of sculpture from past times strewn throughout my orchard,' Munthe wrote: 'I am going to make the chapel into a quiet library with monastic seating along the walls and melodious bells ringing Ave Maria over each joyful day.' Hypnos, Medusa, the Sphinx, Artemis Laphria, 'with Death's swift arrow in her quiver' – the choice of sculptures was made by a sleepless hypochondriac searching for an answer to the riddle of life and death.

In *The Story of San Michele* Axel tells us that he himself was the architect of the building, and he told Sibbern that it was built *à la sueur de mon front* – 'from the sweat of my brow'. That Axel was involved in the planning and building of the house is beyond any doubt. As far as the technical side was concerned, however, he had help from his good friend, the prominent Italian artist Aristide Sartorio. Sartorio was a many-faceted artist – a painter, graphic artist, architect, sculptor – known among other things for a monumental frieze on the parliament building in Rome.

There has been a great deal of speculation about how Axel came across all the antique objects with which he filled the house and orchard. In *The Story of San Michele* he gives more or less imaginative explanations. For instance, he is supposed to have spotted the Medusa head in his study on the seabed one day as he stood looking down from his pergola. And as for the famous Sphinx, which looks east from the chapel balustrade, he had seen it first in a dream and then fetched it from Calabria. Perhaps we will never know where the Medusa head came from, but neither is it particularly important. The story of where his artefacts came from is part of the myth that Axel spun around San Michele, and a part of our experience of the villa.

Axel enjoyed telling cock-and-bull stories about his collections. However, he admitted to the archaeologist Amedeo Maiuri that most of the artefacts came from antique dealers in Rome and Naples – a detail that is borne out by receipts preserved in the archives of the Villa San Michele. Most of the tombstones and Latin inscriptions also originate from places and epochs that make it impossible that they can have been dug up in Mastro Vincenzo's vineyard. Some of the objects were picked up from local people, sometimes as payment for medical care. Axel also had copies of sculptures made, something he made no secret of.

Villa Tiberiana

Axel's villa was soon as well known and talked about as his surgery at the Spanish Steps in Rome. One of the very first visitors was Oscar Wilde, who in October 1897 spent a few days on Capri with his friend Lord Alfred Douglas. Wilde had just served his two-year prison sentence for 'homosexual immorality' and not many people were keen to be seen in company with the couple. But Axel had a liberal attitude to sexuality and invited them to his home. Wilde reported: 'We both lunched with Dr. Munthe, who has a lovely villa and is a great connoisseur of Greek things. He is a wonderful personality.' And in a letter to his mother, who had distanced herself from him, Douglas wrote:

When Munthe asked me to go and see him, I said I could not come without my friend. He immediately replied that he would be pleased to meet him and hoped I didn't think him so ignorant and so brutal as to be unkind to anyone who had suffered so much or been so shamefully treated. He added, 'his condemnation was always to me utterly absurd'. And yet I think you know enough of Munthe to know that he is a good man, and a humane man as well as a clever and enlightened one.

The house that Wilde admired must have been either the chapel or an earlier version of the villa. The first person who commented on the completed building was Henry James, who came to Anacapri on 13 June 1899 to experience the Feast of Saint Anthony. Munthe had met James in Rome during the spring and had invited him to his house. 'On their way to the Marina [the band] halted at daybreak under the windows of San Michele for their customary "Serenata d'Addio" in my house,' Axel remembered in *The Story of San Michele*: 'I can still see Henry James looking down from his bedroom window, shaking with laughter, in his pyjamas.'

Henry James spent only twenty-four hours on the island but the villa made a deep impression on him: 'A creation of the most fantastic beauty, poetry, and inutility I have ever seen clustered together', he wrote in a letter to friends. As for the owner, he noted in the same letter that he had an 'unnatural simplicity'. In the story 'The Saint's Afternoon and Others' James praises the villa and its creator:

> [. . .] here above all had the thought and the hand come from far away – even from *ultima Thule*, and yet were in possession triumphant and acclaimed. Well, all one could say was that the way they had felt their opportunity, the divine conditions of the place, spoke of the advantage of some such intellectual perspective as a remote original standpoint alone perhaps can give. If what had finally, with infinite patience, passion, labour, taste, got itself done there, was like some supreme reward of an old dream of Italy, something perfect after long delays, was it not verily in *ultima Thule* that the vow would have been piously enough made and the germ tenderly enough nursed? For a certain art of asking of Italy all she can give you, you must doubtless either be a rare raffiné or a rare genius, a sophisticated Norseman or just a Gabriele D'Annunzio.

According to James, Axel's villa was a glaring contrast to Capri's 'restorations and breweries' – a metaphor for the strong German input to the island. The Germans and Austrians walked around clad in Tyrolean hats and lederhosen and it was not for scenes like this that other tourists came to Capri.

Another visitor to the villa was the Swedish social reformer Ellen Key, who was mightily impressed by what she saw: 'Munthe's villa here', she wrote to friends in Sweden, 'is a miracle of taste; with the choicest things he has collected – medieval and antique – and a location – well, it cannot be described!' Ellen Key was also delighted to discover that the islanders spoke very highly of Munthe, and she quoted an oarsman: 'We all doff our hats to him, he looks after all the sick people and never takes anything from the poor.'

Neither Wilde nor James used the name 'San Michele' to describe the villa. In actual fact it had not yet been given that name, which really belonged to the chapel. When the Crown princess visited the villa on 17 March 1899, it was mentioned in the *Corriere di Napoli* as the 'Villa Tiberiana'. This is an interesting piece of information, which confirms how obsessed Munthe was with the fact that the house had been erected on the ruins of an old imperial villa – and with the emperor himself.

What an Astonishing Man He Is

On 20 April 1902 Alexandra Bildt visited Munthe's villa with her daughter Blanceflor and immediately wrote down her impressions of the house and its owner in her diary. The detailed description of the villa's material and human interiors makes it unique:

> What an astonishing man he is – incorrigibly rude, almost coarse in the manner in which he treats people. Anyone who wants to win his heart really ought to be a monkey! These creatures were tied to the trunk of an olive-tree with a chain which went round their bellies, and they are not allowed to be untied as they sneak into the rooms and eat up the flowers. The big one grinned and pulled Blanceflor's hair and clothes and screamed frantically when Blanceflor ate 'nespole' as she wanted them herself.
>
> At table we were waited on by the lovely Maria, Munthe's ward, who was not allowed to come to Rome and who never leaves the house in order not to be corrupted. The charming expression in her childlike eyes is like that of a madonna from the 6th century by Apolloni, and it conveyed, like her whole being, that she was a virgin and not yet touched by hand of man. Extraordinary! He pays her no wages; instead, she belongs to 'la famiglia' and gets everything she needs from him. He has had many Capri girls at his place – all of them pretty – during these years, and one does not hear an ill word about it. Poor Doctor – he is not happy, despite his harem in this divine seraglio. In three rooms there were skeletons of children that he likes to look at and think of death.
>
> The lovely Maria looks after his finances, i.e. he simply never has any money, but when he gets paid by some admiring patient he hands the sum over to her without knowing how big it is. She is as honest as she is innocent – or so he believes! Yet building the villa with all its treasures has

cost a great deal. He has furnished the old church with its mosaic floor as Faust's study: mystical, with the lovely antique volumes on the massive worm-eaten table. Nowhere is there a rug or a curtain, only window-slits with Florentine pillars. Several antique fragments are built into the walls along the loggias and paths, and there are climbing roses between the arches and pillars. The view from the terrace is the most beautiful in the world, without exaggeration. The sea far below is an ultramarine blue, and the whole island can be seen as from a balloon. The road to Anacapri is in itself perhaps the loveliest I have ever seen, easily comparable to the Bay of Salerno.

High up on a hilltop lies 'Il Castello Barbarossa', an old ruined castle which he bought and where he sleeps at night. Every day now he has to climb 300 metres vertically from his boat, which he keeps in 'Marina grande'! This has strengthened his heart and lungs.

When Blance and I were strolling past the white house, which has only one [upper] floor, we heard him playing [the piano] with feeling and sensitivity and we did not ring the bell but went past the door and stopped under a sort of window out of which a long white dog's head soon stuck out and barked. The doctor hurried down and opened the door and it was really a moving experience to step into this sanctuary. It was as if I felt myself too unworthy to be allowed in, though there may well have been worse people than me in there. Four metal bells covered in verdigris, which were taken from the church, hang in the hall and the servant shall ring them to signal the category of visitor. The doctor sits upstairs and can hear from the noise what kind of visitor he has. Unbelievably crafty!

He was friendly and agreeable but showed us through the little house at a rate of knots and as soon as we stopped he urged us on with 'Come on now', 'Hurry up' etc. Maria served us and the favourite dog at the table in the strange little dining-room – everything was antique. All three courses we got were prepared in the same way, by frying. The wine is his own and is excellent. He sat at the end of the table and told us that the Crown Princess and Stéphanie were once in his house. He can now read the former like a book and understood that she was wondering what the seating arrangement would be, since the other person was a 'Kaiserliche Hochheit' – so he sat down in his usual place and said: 'Well, this is my place, so you can sit where you please!'

TIBERIUS

In the sketch 'Political Agitations in Capri' Axel had uncritically repeated Tacitus' and Suetonius' view of the Emperor Tiberius as a sensualist and tyrant who abandoned himself to sexual perversions and threw his enemies off the cliff by the Jupiter villa. But this was an image of the emperor which he would revise and which in *The Story of San Michele* was turned into its opposite: 'Augustus was a great man and a great emperor, but mark my words, Tiberius was the greatest of them all!'

Axel's re-evaluation may have been inspired by another foreigner on Capri, John Clay MacKowen, an eccentric American who had been a colonel in the Confederate army and had studied in Heidelberg, where he obtained a doctorate in medicine and also acquainted himself with Classical culture. In 1876 he settled in Anacapri where he acquired a medieval tower, which he rebuilt and to which he gave the name 'Casa Rossa'.

Because of his racist opinions and his irascible temperament, MacKowen soon earned the nickname 'Colonel Slavedriver' in Capri's Anglo-Saxon colony. Like Axel, MacKowen was an industrious amateur archaeologist and just like him he filled his home with fragments of sculpture from the ruins of the island's imperial villas. The conflict was inevitable: MacKowen quarrelled with Axel about a grave which he claimed contained the remains of a Roman slave, while Axel insisted that it held the dust of the Emperor Commodus' wife Crispina. MacKowen challenged Axel to a duel and suggested pistols, but Axel explained that a riding-whip would be a more suitable weapon; whether or not the duel ever took place is unknown. In 1900 MacKowen left Capri and returned to his birthplace of New Orleans, where in the wake of a racist incident he was shot by a fellow-countryman.

Not much more is known about Colonel John Clay MacKowen – except that in 1883 he brought out the book *Capri*, which on 24 November 1888 he presented to Axel 'with kind regards of the author'. The book contains a long chapter about Tiberius in which the author attacks the Roman historians' one-sided description of the emperor, which he sees as 'a gross injustice to a great statesman and general'. MacKowen fastens on the only existing portrait bust of Tiberius as emperor: 'His cup of happiness ought to have been full,' he states, thinking of all the outward successes the emperor had had during his lifetime – 'but on examining the face, what a tale of misery it tells!' This is a motif that Axel goes on to develop in *The Story of San Michele*, where Tiberius is described as follows: 'He was a gloomy old recluse, a weary ruler of an ungrateful world, a bitter idealist – today he might be called a hypochondriac – but his brilliant mind and sense of humour outlived his belief in humanity.' The image is a self-portrait. Axel had previously identified himself with Christ – and, more ironically, with Don Quixote; now there was a third figure. Like the emperor, he would over the years acquire the rights to several properties on Capri. Nor would it be long before 'Tiberio' became his nickname on the island, an alias he took a liking to and gladly used himself.

Like an emperor, Axel received one royal visitor after another in his villa. But the list of royals in *The Story of San Michele* is a mixture of facts and *conscious* fiction, as when the author claims that Crown Prince Rudolf of Austria had lunched at San Michele. He did not, as he had already committed suicide in 1889 at a hunting lodge outside Vienna – the so-called Mayerling affair. Such an openly erroneous detail can only have had one purpose: to warn the reader against being too trusting. 'I do not ask for better than not to be believed,' as Munthe wrote in the foreword to the twelfth edition of the book.

On the other hand, Rudolf's *widow* was there – Crown Princess Stéphanie, who accompanied Victoria during her visit in March 1899. As daughter-in-law of the Emperor Franz Joseph and Empress Elizabeth of Austria–Hungary ('Sissi'), the princess was incredibly ill-fated. Nine years after her husband's suicide, in September 1898, her mother-in-law fell victim to an Italian anarchist who stabbed her to death. Just before this, according to *The Story of San Michele*, the empress had put in an offer for the villa via the Austrian ambassador. In a letter of 1937 Munthe revealed that the offer was for 4 million lire. If Elizabeth visited San Michele, it was probably during a Mediterranean cruise in 1897; but at that time the villa was not yet completed.

One thing that is sure is that the former Empress Eugénie, Napoleon III's widow, visited Capri in the summer of 1899 and asked Axel to spend a few days with her on her yacht *The Thistle*. Also on the voyage, which was to Sicily, were, among others, her relative Joseph Napoleon (Giuseppe) Primoli, whose maternal grandfather Charles Bonaparte, Prince of Canino and a well-known ornithologist, was a nephew of Napoleon I. Count Primoli was a cultivated and eccentric gentleman who lived in a large palazzo in Rome with his even odder brother Louis (Luigi). Nowadays the palazzo houses Rome's Bonaparte Museum. Among Primoli's friends and acquaintances were Alexandre Dumas, Théophile Gautier, Paul Bourget, Gabriele d'Annunzio – and Axel. The Spanish-born former empress, who had fled to England after the fall of the empire in 1870, was a legend already in her own lifetime.

Eugénie spent the fifty years between her flight and her death in 1920 at the age of 94 constantly travelling between her own homes and palaces in Europe and those of others. She was known as an original and outspoken woman. When someone on board complained about the bad air that sometimes swept in over the Bay of Naples, Count Primoli explained that it depended on the wind. 'No,' elucidated the empress, 'it depends entirely on what you ate for lunch.' 'She is', Axel reported to Sibbern,

interesting to be with because of her history. She has survived everything that has happened to her and seems to be doing well – despite everything and despite her great friendliness towards me I judge her fairly harshly and I cannot deny that there is something of the successful 'adventuress' about her. She talked a great deal about 1870 and gave me a detailed account of her flight.

The former empress invited Axel to stay on board for the rest of the voyage, which would continue to Norway, but he declined. He had to go to London, where he had been invited to a ball at Buckingham Palace on 7 July, in 'full dress'.

ANNA AND ARNOLD

Axel had many guests on Capri, but they did not include his sister and brother, who never visited him in Italy. Nor did they meet all that often when Axel was in Sweden.

Relations with Arnold were complicated, and they were undermined by unresolved financial affairs. In November 1898 Arnold wrote to Axel complaining about his intractable gastric and intestinal catarrh. As Axel had still not repaid his debts to Arnold, the latter had been forced to sell Axel's life-insurance policy (which since 1881 he had paid the premiums on) in order to cover the expenses for his health.

> The reason I wrote to you with such urgency in the spring was because of my state of health, and if you had known how genuinely ill I was and how worried by my pains, you would surely not have been so hard as you were in your letter. For the last 3 months I have [been] forced [. . .] to borrow money. If you can help me now, it will not come amiss.

The last part of the letter shows what a financial and mental gulf divided the brothers: 'I have heard from [people] talking about how well-off you are. When we got on to talking about your house on Capri he said it's a palace and the finest on the whole of Capri. You might send me a photograph of it, for otherwise I don't suppose I'll ever see it.'

Axel was notoriously negligent about financial matters, but given his position, the fact that he did not repay his debts to his brother is most surprising. Can there have been some other underlying reason? Axel complained to their cousin Ludvig that Arnold was a 'difficult person to deal with' who despite his long years of hardship remained 'quarrelsome and difficult to be with' – 'what is it? Lack of intelligence?'

Arnold's health problems seem to have been at least partly mental. His career had got off to an illustrious start. He had spent the years 1884 to 1887 in the French navy, and on leaving the service had been awarded the Légion d'Honneur. But in 1902 he was forced to leave active duty at sea because of nervous problems. He ended his service career as a captain and thereafter devoted himself to his writing. Arnold Munthe became one of Sweden's leading maritime historians, with works such as *Swedish Sea-Heroes* and *Charles XII and Russian Sea-Power* (in which he contradicted conservative historians by questioning the king's talent as a statesman) to his credit, not to mention historical dramas.

Nor did Axel's sister Anna, who was by now an accomplished painter, visit him in Italy, although their relationship was considerably warmer. 'I love my only sister dearly,' Axel confided to Charlotte Payne-Townshend. But Anna did not have particularly close contact with Axel: 'I seldom hear anything from Axel,' she complained to cousin Ludvig. Axel believed himself to lack *ésprit de famille*, family feeling. To him, there was no difference between family members and other people:

> I simply see human beings and feel myself as close to – or as distant from – the one as the other. Their *personality* can inspire me to feel fondness, gratitude or love for them, but the coincidental, external link which binds them to me does not spring from the heart. The heart's affection is probably to one's mother or the woman one loves or has loved.

The qualifier 'probably' is a clear indication that Axel was not acquainted with this feeling – there had never been any 'heart's affection' between his mother and himself. And this lack of warmth and understanding between mother and son would in its turn characterise Axel's relationships with the other sex – which is the subject of the next chapter.

A Demonic Talent

Strangely enough I often meet women who wish to marry me and I observe with mounting amazement that their number is increasing rather than diminishing.

Axel Munthe to Georg Sibbern, 1897

THE CROWN PRINCESS was not the only one, in Sophie Elkan's words, 'enchanted by' Axel – the same could be said of many of his female patients. At this time contact between doctor and patient was much closer than today. Doctors visited their patients several times a day in a psychological and social game in which both partners had well-defined roles.

Munthe explained away the exceptional popularity he enjoyed with reference to external circumstances: 'Despite my impracticality and my increasingly misanthropic mood, resulting in a dictatorial and brusque manner, I still have a fair amount of luck.' Success as a consequence of 'luck' was something he was prone to emphasise, then as well as later. But as an explanation it is superficial and disingenuous: Axel knew very well that no luck in the world can help except in the short term. The other explanation he proffered, in a letter to Sibbern, has more substance to it:

> I do not actually enjoy my profession but I do have a certain aptitude for it and am regarded as a 'competent doctor'. However, I have discovered the secret and it is simply that I have a certain ability to *lead people* and they submit themselves, almost unconsciously, to my will. What this actually is, I do not know, but it is so striking that I cannot avoid pondering over it – can Your Excellency give me an explanation for this phenomenon? I do believe that it depends on a definite talent for *judging* people, but this is not enough. Sometimes it almost seems to me to be 'demonic' and there is no doubt that this ability has markedly increased in strength in recent years. I have a considerable weapon in my hand there, but I cannot deny that it worries even me sometimes.

The authoritative or authoritarian doctor's role was not unique to Axel. Around the turn of the last century a doctor's authority was taken for granted as much as the patient's subordination. This was particularly true of the doctor's relationship to his female patients, whose rights in society were strictly limited – women were not allowed to vote, they could not inherit, in the higher social classes they were not supposed to work either. The doctor's dominant position vis-à-vis female patients was therefore a mirror image of the man's superior role in social life in general. To be ill was a way for a woman to be seen and illness became an identity, almost a profession. This applied particularly to lung diseases, which, because of their prolonged nature, are especially prone to affect a person's identity. As we have seen, this also applied to Axel himself, who readily took on the role of a victim of tuberculosis.

In order to 'lead people' one must have their trust, and in order to build this up one must be able to listen to them. Axel had this ability in spades. He did indeed have 'a definite talent for *judging* people', he saw his patients and they felt they had been seen. When, accordingly, he prescribed fresh air, walks and the purchase of a dog instead of pills, it was a shock therapy. But it was appreciated and he acquired the reputation of a miracle doctor. Not for nothing was *il dottor Munthe* described in the contemporary Rome press as 'a literary and artistic spirit, one of these modern doctors who are more occupied with healing the soul than the body'.

Axel won Victoria's love and trust through his way of talking and being with her, quite simply by being just who he was. Behind the Crown princess's strict exterior lurked an artistic temperament and a living intellect. She also had her fair share of humour and could be both 'nice and fun'. Given the background of the spiritual barrenness of the Swedish court, her acquaintance with Munthe was a shattering and liberating experience.

The relationship between Axel and Victoria was based, among other things, on the fact that they told each other the truth – a commodity in short supply in the circles in which the princess had grown up and now dwelt. Honesty was an essential, perhaps the most essential, component of the treatment that Axel offered. In fact it was not in spite of his 'dictatorial and brusque manner' but because of it that Axel exerted the influence he did. In a letter to Sibbern he admitted that by nature he was 'used to giving orders', and he turned this character trait into a method of treatment. He had tremendous willpower – 'demonic' in his own words – which he transmitted to his patients in a bid to mobilise their own will to fight their illness. It was an aid to curing themselves, in which the patient's unconscious did most of the therapeutic work.

Sophie Elkan hinted that Axel had hypnotised Victoria, but he himself maintained that she had never undergone any hypnotic treatment either from him or from any other doctor. However, it is feasible that he made use of some form of suggestion. He had learned about suggestion from the disciples of the Nancy school, and in *The Story of San Michele* he writes about his diligent use of the methodology. During the First World War he gave dying soldiers hypnotic pain relief by laying his hand on their foreheads and repeating 'words of hope and comfort'. Where did the power come from? he asked himself: 'Did it come from the stream of consciousness within me below the level of my waking life, or was it after all the mysterious "odylic force", the magnetic fluid of the old mesmerists?' He claimed to have possessed this power, 'whatever name is given to it', since childhood.

This treatment, which in Axel's words was intended to 'inspire confidence', has been described as 'a combination of charismatic presence, an eye for psychology and an authoritarian image'. The patient's confidence in the doctor was in itself a prerequisite for a successful treatment. This meant that the patient must put blind trust in him. The Crown princess was herself a strong-willed, single-minded and stubborn person who was used to giving orders and being obeyed, and to begin with she found it difficult to submit herself to Axel's will: 'She is very "entêtée" but very kind to me,' he confided in an acquaintance. In this case the treatment was complicated by the fact that the relationship between Victoria and Axel was not only a doctor–patient relationship. For the most part the Crown princess deferred to her doctor/lover, but it was a struggle between two iron wills. Victoria's other doctors did not dare to oppose her will or her wishes, and for them Axel had only contempt; all patients should be treated alike.

His influence over Victoria was strengthened by his insights into the problems afflicting the royal couple's marriage. Sexual problems in general and sexual deviations in particular were the subject of regular discussion in medical circles around the turn of the previous century – the classic text was Richard von Krafft-Ebing's *Psychopathia sexualis* of 1886, a source Munthe often referred to.

As Munthe writes in *The Story of San Michele*, during his first years as a doctor he had tried to cure 'sexual inversion' with hypnosis, but he gradually came to realise that homosexuality is not a disease but 'a deviation of the sexual instinct natural to certain individuals where an energetic interference often does more harm than good'. It is unclear whether Gustaf and Victoria's abstention from sexual contact was due to simple indifference or whether the Crown prince's homosexuality, to which he gave in later, had already manifested itself at this time.

WOMEN NEVER OCCUPY MY THOUGHTS COMPLETELY

Apart from her mental problems, Crown Princess Victoria also suffered from genuine physical illnesses. For many of Axel's patients, though, their problems were not primarily of a physical nature but were rooted in their lack of useful employment and ennui – they were quite simply *malades imaginaires*. True to his doctor's oath of confidentiality, Axel was close-lipped about his clientèle, but in *The Story of San Michele* he gives a generalised picture of his hysterical female patients and their relationship with their doctor:

> It is easy to be patient with lunatics, I confess to a sneaking liking for them. With a little kindness one comes to terms with most of them as often as not. But it is not easy to be patient with hysterical women, and as to being kind to them, one had better think it over twice before being too kind to them, they ask for nothing better. As a rule you can do but little for these patients, at least outside the hospital. You can stun their nerve centres with sedatives but you cannot cure them. They remain what they are, a bewildering complex of mental and physical disorders, a plague to themselves and to their families, a curse to their doctors. Hypnotic treatment, so beneficial in many hitherto incurable mental troubles, is as a rule contra-indicated in the treatment of hysterical women of all ages young and old, hysteria has no age limit. It should in any case be limited to Charcot's suggestion à l'état de veille. It is besides unnecessary, for these helpless women are in any case already too willing to be influenced by their doctor, to depend on him too much, to imagine he is the only one who can understand them, to hero-worship him. Sooner or later their photographs begin to turn up, there is nothing to be done.

It would be easy to see this as unashamed boasting: the successful doctor who is idolised by his female patients and forced to defend himself against their attacks! But the account Munthe gives in his book is no exaggeration, but rather a faint reflection of the true situation. The amount of love-letters that have been preserved confirm that his attractiveness to women was quite unique. Through his medical practice and his social life he came into contact with innumerable women who were only 'too willing to be influenced by their doctor' and to 'hero-worship him'.

The women whom Axel met all belonged to the European leisured class. If they were not economically independent themselves, then their parents or husbands were. They were 'idle', but in many cases wished to be of use and longed for a purpose to their lives. Just as he had done with Baroness von Mecklenburg, Miss White and Miss DD ten years earlier, Axel talked to them about his ideals, which were fundamentally based on Christ's teaching.

One has a duty to give away or at least share money one has not worked for oneself. One ought to live a simple life, not buy expensive clothes nor indulge in gluttony. One should live the life of the spirit and refrain from worldly things. He talked about his charitable projects and persuaded the women to donate money to them. He argued very convincingly for his ideas and with pronounced distaste for the world they lived in. If they wanted to associate with him they had to change their lifestyle in order to become what he wanted them to be.

Often it took only a single meeting for the women to be head over heels in love with Axel, whom they felt to be a Christ figure. They bombarded him with impassioned letters that he seldom answered. Or if he did, the answer was measured and chilly. For the most part their impression that the feelings were mutual were unfounded, but sometimes Axel encouraged their interest, at least initially. Once in a while the relationship led to physical contact. Even if in some cases Axel was fond of the woman, the relationship could never develop into a full-blown affair, let alone marriage, for reasons he could not reveal. He could hardly explain that his lukewarm interest was because of his intimate connection with the Crown princess of Sweden – a *liaison dangereuse* that had to be kept secret at all costs.

Many of Axel's patients were indeed hysterics, but it was not only clinically ill persons who clamoured for Axel's attention but also perfectly healthy women. In the spring of 1894 the 37-year-old Charlotte Payne-Townshend arrived in Rome. She met Axel at a lunch with mutual friends, fell for him and before long became his patient. He prescribed valerian but pointed out that she was not actually ill and that she ought to try to get the better of her nerves. He suggested a change of air. Why not Venice, where he was about to travel himself with the Crown princess?

Charlotte was flattered that the famous doctor should wish her to be in Venice at the same time that he and the Crown princess would be staying there. She travelled to Venice, unaware that her main function was to serve as a cover under which Axel could go around with Victoria without awakening suspicion. They met on several occasions, Axel visited her at her hotel and they had long conversations. Back in Rome Charlotte realised that she was in love, for the first time in her life. Accustomed since childhood to restrain her feelings, she was now, as her biographer writes, 'painfully aware that Munthe knew she was in a growing state of emotional upheaval'.

Axel was stimulated by the admiration he inspired in women but at the same time he despised them for the meaningless lives they led, for not doing any good with their inherited wealth. Charlotte was rich but she also had a social conscience. Back in Rome Axel invited her to lunches and dinners. Charlotte told him of her search for a faith that would bring peace to her soul and fill her life with meaning. Axel for his part talked about his ideals, about the clinic for the poor in Trastevere, and the like. Charlotte was transfixed; this was the kind of thing she had been longing to hear.

When the invitations eventually dried up, Charlotte became desperate, and when she had not heard from Axel for a week she arranged a dinner at her hotel and invited Axel. He declined and countered by inviting her to lunch at his home:

> Thanks for your kind invitation to dinner. I am much too far gone for a table d'hôte dinner and know the people you are inviting – their inside and outside – since 10 years. But it might be good for you to lunch here any day you like when I can manage to be at home – simple food. Tomorrow I shall be out of town and today no time for luncheon: but after tomorrow I shall be in if you like. No preparation whatever will be made for you except that I will try to appear myself.

Charlotte rushed off to the lunch, Axel displayed his best side and they started to see each other again. He took her with him to the Little Sisters of the Poor and induced her to make a large donation to them. He did not thank her once, her biographer tells us; he took for granted that she, who was rich, should open her purse and share its contents. Summer was approaching, Axel travelled to Capri and Charlotte went to England. Before their departure he asked her for a photograph to remember her by. Charlotte did not have one but asked Aristide Sartorio to paint her portrait and send it to Munthe when it was finished.

While Charlotte sat in London waiting for a letter, Axel was sailing around the Mediterranean in his cutter. Charlotte wrote to him to ask if he had received the portrait but got no reply. Her state of mind was such that a female friend encouraged her to travel to America as soon as possible just to have something else to think about. But it was as if Charlotte was paralysed. She wrote to Axel again and reminded him of his promise that they would see each other again in England. In the end she received an answer, from Capri. He thanked her for a book she had sent and went on:

> As to your other present, Sartorio's picture, I have given orders to have it sent to your house in London. I cannot and will not accept it. If you do not want it I shall make Sartorio take it back if you like. [. . .] I am off again for a cruise after tomorrow down to Calabria and probably Sicily. My further plans are very dim – you ask when I am coming to England, I wish I knew myself. I ought not to go there at all but to remain here till I go to Sweden, because the state of my finances is very seriously alarming me now when I have time to think. However, maybe I can manage it, if I turn up it will be in August. Of course I shall let you know in time – we might go and have a sail somewhere.

The brusque rejection of the portrait shows that Axel thought it was high time to dampen down Charlotte's feelings. He came to England, a few more letters were exchanged, but they did not meet. Charlotte, on the other hand, was bewitched by Axel and hoped he would ask for her hand in marriage. When she realised that this would not happen she understood that she must try to break the spell. It took time, as Axel had appealed not only to her feelings but also to her conscience. Her talks with Axel and the ideals he championed had influenced her profoundly. When she visited Rome the following year she made a point of calling on the Little Sisters of the Poor and once again making over a large sum of money to them. Axel did not meet her again until much later, in the 1930s, by which time she had long been Mrs George Bernard Shaw.

A couple of years later the same story unfolded again, this time with the daughter of the American ambassador, Margaretta MacVeagh. In the course of a tête-à-tête with Axel under an olive tree in Beaulieu on the French Riviera, Miss MacVeagh came to see life through new eyes, and during the coming years she strove her utmost to try to live up to Axel's ideals. He reproached her for living on money she had not earned herself – she assured him that she was not interested in money, that she had only 10,000 francs a year (£20,000 in today's money) at her disposal, but that was enough for her to be able to help others; her own needs were becoming smaller and smaller. When on one occasion Axel rebuked her for buying expensive clothes in Paris, she answered in bewilderment that there was a very simple explanation for this open flouting of his ascetic ideals: '*I had to have some things to wear!!!*'

Axel is the only person she thinks about, 'waking and sleeping', he alone is '*Real*'. In the life that she wanted them to live together she would serve him in his 'over-worked, over-worried life'. Her parents were initially opposed to the match but have now begun to see it in a different light, and she can see no obstacle to their union:

I had such a glorious dream last night. You came to me, and taking both my outstretched hands in yours said: 'You have learned to love me as I wish.' [. . .] Today, for the first time, I don't hate and regret every hour of those terrible years – years in which you know I was suffering almost as cruelly as you. I know you loved me and you promised you would wait – and I felt you must know I loved you, and understand and forgive my silence. [. . .] You are the central fact of my life, you are in my every ideal, in every fine thought I ever have. I am forced to admit you are with me always. [. . .] I don't want to marry, *in the abstract*, any more than you do. But I want to be with you, as you have told me you want me to be – and to be together as much as we would wish we should have to be married – that's all. As to where you live, whether in a crowded city, on a desert island or in lovely Anacapri – what does it matter. We should always be in earnest and very busy and yet find time to make our inner life as deep and beautiful as possible.

There was to be no marriage, either conventional or unconventional, between Axel and Margaretta MacVeagh; the dream of marriage was one-sided. But Axel had made an indelible impression on her. She married later in the USA but kept in contact with him. After her death in 1938 Axel received a long letter from her husband: 'She was very fond of you, Axel. There is no way to measure these things, but I think she cared more for you than for anyone except her mother.'

LADY OTTOLINE

At the same time as Margaretta MacVeagh was composing her love letters to Axel, he was the object of an emotional storm emanating from the British Isles and bearing the name of Ottoline Bentinck.

Ottoline Bentinck (1873–1938) was a half-sister of the seventh Duke of Portland and belonged to the higher aristocracy of England. She lost her father at the age of 5 and the search for male role models came to occupy a large part of her childhood. One such early model was Charles Kingsley, who preached a kind of Christian socialism and believed that the landowning class had a duty not to misuse their inherited privileges. If one had been favoured by fate one ought to help those who had been dealt a poorer hand.

Ottoline's mother survived her husband by fifteen years and she and her daughter came to live in close proximity to each other. Ottoline's biographer writes that she inherited two things from her mother, 'her religious fervour and her appalling health'. Deeply pious, Ottoline gradually came to see religion as an exercise in asceticism. She even spent some time in a nunnery, where she neglected her meals and clothing to such an extent that the abbess advised her to exchange Thomas à Kempis's *Imitatio Christi* for H.G. Wells, her own favourite writer.

It was this overwrought 25-year-old who in the summer of 1898 met Axel for the first time in the Duke of Portland's London home in Grosvenor Square. Ottoline was immediately captivated by him:

He was a rather mysterious figure, very ugly, but with great charm, and he had an athletic, supple figure, very remarkable hands, was devoted to children and animals, and was said to have done extraordinary quixotic deeds – for instance, when the cholera was raging in Naples. [. . .] At last I had met someone to whom I could talk freely, who was not cut on the ordinary cardboard pattern, who was subtle and free and daring and sympathetic. He came to see me sometimes in my room, and I remember the last party of the season when he circled round me, and as we parted by the door he made me promise to come and stay with him at Capri.

Ottoline had planned to spend the late summer in Savoie with her companion and distant relative Hilda Douglas-Pennant, but when they arrived at their hotel in Brides-les-Bains, a letter from Axel was waiting for her. He invited her to Capri, where he offered her La Foresteria to stay in. Ottoline found it hard to make Hilda share her enthusiasm for the Capri trip, and therefore told her that the doctor was an elderly gentleman. When they were met by Munthe on Capri, Hilda was appalled to discover that, far from being 80 years old, he was about half of that and moreover – in Ottoline's words – 'a fascinating satyr in appearance with an alert figure'.

The days passed, time ceased to exist, Ottoline was transported by this 'enchanted land'. It was harvest-time and the girls with their huge baskets of grapes on their backs were reminiscent of Greek nymphs. Ottoline and Hilda took all their meals with Axel, who entertained them on the piano. Axel and Ottoline made a habit of sitting chatting in the chapel, which was now a library. The intimacy between them was so obvious that Hilda began to be uneasy. The happier Ottoline appeared to be, the more convinced Hilda became that she had been bewitched by Munthe, whom she saw as a 'necromancer'. Hilda persuaded her to leave Capri. It was when she told Axel of her decision to leave, Ottoline wrote, that she realised she loved him. 'I had been filled with a spiritual and transcendental desire to pour love into this man, had poured out everything in my heart to him, but now for the first time in my life I realized the usual feelings of love.'

By the time she reached Florence Ottoline was beginning to feel the pain of separation. She suspected their love was not mutual, or that Axel did not want to admit his feelings for her. During her stay in Lucerne she received a letter couched in very formal tones ('Dear Lady Ottoline'), but in the same envelope was a note in which Axel made clear that he had been waiting for her all his life. 'I was sure he loved me,' she wrote later, 'but lurking underneath was the instinct that he would not undergo the ordeal of facing my family to get me.'

Despite the uncertainty, her passion had an uplifting effect on Ottoline. Before the friends moved on, Hilda Douglas-Pennant wrote Axel a letter heavy with guilt in which she asked his forgiveness for not thanking him for his kindness when they left the island:

The fact was that I had heard you spoken of (as I now see falsely) as a mesmerist who acquired great influence over people, & when I noticed that from the moment Ottoline saw much of you she became in some respects a changed being, the recollection of what I had heard about you & thought nothing of at the time, flashed across me & I confess I began to feel anxious about the influence. [. . .] I see now that I was quite mistaken & had no cause for anxiety & I feel very sorry at having for one moment mistrusted you or imparted motives to you on mere hear-say which are entirely contrary to your nature. Now that I realize the true state of things & all that it means to Ottoline I am particularly anxious that you should feel that she is entirely free from any outside influence or bias during this time when she is making up her mind. [. . .] If she has found a man truly worthy of the entire love of her great nature the thought of the immense happiness which I see it has brought her will be to me also a great joy, for after all the only thing I care about is that she should be deeply & lastingly happy.

Ottoline could not understand the irresolution of this man who said he loved her. To Axel's vacillation was added Ottoline's own doubts and feelings of guilt. Could she really marry a non-believer?

When they met again in England their relationship clearly entered a more intimate phase. Encouraged by this, Ottoline began to attack Axel with love letters, sometimes several a day, penned in a handwriting which betrays despair, frayed nerves and hysteria. As can be seen from the following example, the letters were extremely high-pitched:

I feel often in my remembrance & [illegible], your dear hands passing all over me – as they did at Guildford & Folkestone. Oh will they again – my heart seems breaking with Desire – – – for you my Axel.

Do you know it is over a fortnight [. . .] & I have had 1 letter from you! How many have you had? I am beginning to think you are *Selfish. Are you*? [. . .] I feel as if you had forgotten me when you do not write [. . .]. I [illegible] you will think this is *low* of me & that I ought to rest content & *trust* your love. [. . .] by my love to you I should keep you *in* me always. What one loves – one cannot lose. One loses it when one ceases to love. It passes out of one's life – but one possesses what one loves & so *I* should *go on possessing you* even if you cast me away. I have just had my nice [?] hot bath & am in bed – with your 'Blue' Shirt. *I do love it.* It is quite a part of you now. *It is a real comfort.* (13 October 1898)

Ottoline's cousin Violet Bentinck, who saw how she was suffering, wrote to Axel that Ottoline 'has given herself so entirely to you and nothing else in the world is now of any consequence to her'. Axel replied with a letter that is central to an understanding of his mental world – in it we hear a clear echo of Tolstoy's religious opinions, both with regard to his view of the Church and the question of the individual's immortality.

Lady Ottoline is right – we are living in two different worlds. I shall never be as she wishes me to be and I maintain my words that she is not healthy the way she has worked herself up to abnegation. – *I do not even admire it. I only dislike it.* I shall never accept many things she looks upon as coming from God and so long our official church has prayers of thanksgiving to be read on battlefields and can find priests thanking God for having helped them to shoot or massacrate [sic] so and so many thousands innocent people – the God of mercy and forgiving – so long I shall [look] upon them and their creed with suspicion. I shall never believe in the Devil, never in hell, never in the power of a priest to procure absolution for my sins. I believe perhaps in a life after death but not in the survival of the individual. I believe that Christ was a man like myself but he was the greatest expression of perfection and beauty and as such he is the right leader of men and will remain so. I do not believe that his suffering death had anything to do with 'Adam' – who I always think was badly treated – nor that it can save me from the fulfilment of my destiny. I am constantly brought in contact with a great deal of hypocrisy and fraud committed by the clergy and it would never occur to me to go to *confess* to one of them *because he is a priest.* – I might do it to a man I respected and admired but he might be just as well by profession a lawyer, a doctor or a carpenter. The Holy Communion is to me a beautiful function as reminding us of the death of the greatest of men – but that is all and the curse which our Lutheran church has thought fit to add to it is horrible and disgusting to me and would prevent me from partaking in it. God is love and mercy. I do not believe in an angry God.

I write all this as quick [sic] as the pen can run along the paper and I am wrong in doing so, for it is too important a subject to discuss in this way. But it is enough for you to see the gulf which separates me from your cousin and yourself and that her hope shall never be fulfilled, for I am not a savage, I have read and thought a good deal. She has judged me by the rigid laws of the church and I have failed to be admitted to her heaven – and what is more I fear I would not wish to. I shall never surrender my thoughts to any man. [. . .] I think you now can see what a bad man I am and you will thank God that your cousin has escaped to fall into my claws.

When a few years later Ottoline married the lawyer Philip Morrell she was so afraid that the memory of Axel might sour their relationship that she decided to tell her future husband about her affair with him: 'About that my dearest I would rather no one told you except myself. Hardly anyone knows and very few people care for the man or understand him and I should mind if you heard him abused. [. . .] indeed I love you very deeply but I am not sure that is enough.' They married in February 1902, but for Ottoline the marriage was unsatisfactory sexually. Five years later she had a love affair with the artist Augustus John and in 1911 she began a passionate relationship with Bertrand Russell. Although the affair with Russell lasted for five years and occasioned thousands of letters, on 24 August 1919 she confided to her diary that she had only known happiness once, with Axel Munthe on Capri. And when Rebecca West visited Munthe in 1922, Lady Ottoline was 'green with envy'.

In distinction to Charlotte and Margaretta, whose passion for Axel remained unanswered, it is clear that Ottoline awoke feelings in him that were not only motivated by his psychological interest. There was a great deal about Ottoline that struck a chord with Axel: her idealism, her distinctive beauty, the circles to which she belonged. One sign that the relationship was also serious for Axel is all the gifts they gave each other: clothes, rings and – not least – timepieces; Axel was a fanatical collector of watches. In October 1900 Ottoline wrote to Munthe that he was welcome to keep all the watches she had given him with the exception of the one that had belonged to her father and which she thought should remain in the family. On the other hand she asked if she could keep a watch that Munthe had given her: 'I always wear it & if parted from it would miss it very much. But of course if you ever want it you must ask me for it – until then I wear it always.'

When Ottoline died in 1937 Axel wrote to Philip Morrell and asked for his watch back. Morrell promised politely to hand back the watch if he could find it, but in reality he was upset by Axel's request. Their daughter hid it so that her father could not fulfil his promise: after all, it was a present. She had no way of knowing that, thirty-seven years earlier, Ottoline had promised to return the watch when Axel asked for it.

WHERE WILL ALL THIS LEAD?

Those around Axel naturally wondered why the popular doctor never married, despite being surrounded by rich women eager for marriage. When, on numerous occasions during the 1890s, Axel felt he had to clarify his position to Sibbern, he consciously portrayed himself as an unsuitable candidate for matrimony – an argument that sounded particularly plausible to someone who was aware of his ill-fated first marriage:

> If it was not a question of *living*, I would withdraw completely from the world without any sense of loss. Not even women have any power over me, I have never managed to 'fall in love' with anyone to the extent of being able to live with them – where will all this lead? (1896)

> I feel myself so old – coming up to 40 – and the future strikes me as gloomy and miserable. I suppose I ought to marry but my mood is so inward-looking and *my nature so accustomed to giving orders* that I fear I am

hardly suited to living with anyone. By the way, poverty becomes quite a different and serious matter from the moment one is alone no longer. Strangely enough I often meet women who want to marry me and I observe with mounting amazement that their number is increasing rather than diminishing – but the climax has surely been reached now and soon that delight will be over. I do not believe I can be what the poets call *in love*, unfortunately I am too critical for that. (1897)

My personal life is the same, I live alone, have no mistresses and unfortunately! never fall in love – women never completely occupy my thoughts and I have never succeeded in losing my head over anyone. However I realise the purpose of nature and would gladly marry and there is no lack of opportunity but it is hard for me to do it à froid and I am still waiting for the female Messiah – who never comes. (1899)

The reason why Axel's flirtations never led to marriage was of course that he was otherwise engaged. At the same time as he was complaining to Sibbern that he had 'never managed to fall in love with anyone' he was assuring Victoria, as we have seen, that he was longing for her and thinking of her 'from morning to night'. This double-entry book-keeping was a part of his and Victoria's strategy, however painful it must have been for the Crown princess. But since their relationship had to be kept secret at all costs, the presence of other women in his life helped to deflect gossip. All these flirtations, however, won Axel a reputation as a cynical ladies' man.

There is also another plausible explanation for the double game. Axel realised that the relationship with Victoria could not possibly be maintained in the long term, and he therefore left the door open to alternatives – one of which was perhaps Ottoline Morrell. Victoria was also aware of course that the relationship between herself and Axel was doomed, but the alternatives open to him were not available to her.

TIBERIO

The Crown Prince, the King and I all repose the utmost confidence in you.
Queen Sophia to Axel Munthe, 1901

IN ROME MUNTHE mixed with the highest society, but he also had many friends and acquaintances in the artistic and cultural spheres. These included, apart from the archaeologist Wolfgang Helbig, the Italian artist Aristide Sartorio and the American sculptor Waldo Story, son of the sculptor William Wetmore Story, whose home in the Piazza Barberini was one of Rome's leading salons during the later part of the nineteenth century. Axel's artist acquaintances also included the legendary actress Eleonora Duse, regarded by Munthe as 'the greatest actress in the world', who was also his patient.

One would think that the intensive social life of Rome in the 1890s and the building of his villa in Capri would have helped to lift Munthe's depression, but such was not the case: the effect was rather the opposite. 'The laws of propriety tormented him,' recalled a Swedish diplomat who served in Rome in the years after the turn of the century. He could be 'very agreeable and entertaining, when he was in a good mood', but he was unpredictable, spoilt and 'capricious'. When he was invited out he often declined, making the excuse that he had to see to some old man or woman who was at death's door. When Claes Lagergren had heard that excuse several times, he issued a jocular warning to Axel that he would be forced to stop inviting him to lunch 'so as not to increase the mortality rate in Rome'.

As usual it was mainly to Sibbern that Axel confided his hypochondria: 'I am a hopeless hypochondriac these days and nothing can save me. What is worse is that I am shy of people and more and more lonely – this is highly inappropriate for a man who depends so much as a doctor on his immediate surroundings' (September 1897). 'Besides, I am a complete hypochondriac and getting to be more and more so. And in addition I am beginning to feel old and am well aware that I have already received the best gifts that life has to give' (June 1899).

Axel's hypochondria was exacerbated by his persistent writer's block. He complained that the Crown princess took up all his time, but the reasons lay deeper than that: he had written nothing for ages and, as we saw, found it difficult to handle his authorial identity. Axel was not wholly inactive, however. As he had done many times before, he turned his gaze towards Britain in order to try to place some already written articles there. 'Mont Blanc, King of the Mountains' had been turned down by *Blackwood's Magazine* in 1889 and in the spring of 1894 he offered the magazine 'another paper on Mont Blanc'. But this was not to the publisher's taste either.

The article was 'Hypochondria', which he had deemed 'too crazy' to publish in *Aftonbladet* nine years earlier and which had been turned down by *Blackwood's Magazine* in 1889. When in March 1898 Axel offered Murray's in London a volume with 'sketches', however, it turned up in the choice of pieces. As Murray's had published Axel's last book it was natural to turn to them first, but at the same time he made it clear that there were others who were interested too: 'Some of the sketches were printed in Blackwood's Magazine several years ago and I possess on their account some letters from Mr Blackwood himself of so flattering a nature that I have little doubt that his firm would be most willing to print the book.' Axel had improved his English considerably since the last time but his style of negotiation had not changed, and he cleverly played off different interests against each other.

John Murray rose to the bait and on 2 March Axel sent the manuscript from Rome. 'Here and there the English may seem a little peculiar, but so am I, and it has to be taken as it is or not at all – involuntary faults of course not included.' Blackwood had chosen not to publish the sketch 'Blackcock Shooting' and Axel was afraid of John Murray's reaction: 'I know well that if your reader is a keen sportsman I am done for [. . .].' Although it contains a violent attack on one of England's most revered sports, fox hunting, the sketch was included in the book, which Axel wanted to call 'Diary of an Idle Doctor'. However, when it landed on the bookshop counters in September 1898 it was under the title *Vagaries*. Axel did not expect any income from the book, which he regretted as he had 'a fine idea' which he wanted to realise:

Above my house in Capri there is a big mountain-slope, famous since centuries for the quantity of passing birds which are caught there in the nets every year – I have *seen over 5000 caught there in one night*. I want to buy this mountain, surround it with a big wall, plant pine-trees there and turn it into a sanctuary – a sort of holy mount where thousands of tired birds, quails, larks, pigeons, thrushes etc. etc. may rest in peace before crossing the big sea or on their return in the spring when they are so tired that often they are caught by the hand. Isn't it a fine idea? But I cannot keep any money I make as [a] doctor and writing books does evidently not pay. I have a great number of friends in America and am *certain* the book would sell well if attended to – will you remember the birds if you decide about an American edition?

The Times (5 November 1898) thought that the value of the book 'is diminished by the air of self-consciousness' but in general the reviews were very positive. The *Daily Telegraph* (23 November 98) wrote that the author had 'a pleasant colloquial style, a keen sense of humour, and considerable imagination' and *The World* (26 October 1898) found that he 'makes a very pleasant companion for a stray half-hour'.

Encouraged by the publication of *Vagaries*, Axel suggested a new book project to his publisher, namely a new edition of *Letters from a Mourning City*. When he had still not received an answer from Murray by the beginning of November he wrote to him again. Certainly he had seen only 'uninteresting reviews' of *Vagaries* but was 'amazed at the quantity of letters I received from known and unknown people in praise of the book'.

Murray's answer was evasive. He agreed that *Vagaries* 'has been well received, and extremely well spoken of by those who have read it, but so far it has not moved off quite so quickly as I had wished and hoped'. He asked to be allowed to 'leave the decision as to Naples open till the end of the year' – if a decision had not been taken by then, Axel was welcome to contact other firms.

Although sales of *Vagaries* were not that bad – at the end of January 1899 only 209 copies remained unsold out of a print run of 1,000 – Murray could not make up his mind. But Axel was impatient and on 2 April he sent him the manuscript of *Letters from a Mourning City*, 're-written by myself in my own crooked english':

> My idea concerning the Letters from a M. City is to have the book printed in a *small* book but dainty and without an illustration. Countess Feo Gleichen who is actually here wants to make a drawing for the book but I suppose better not – or a nice design for the binding – if you want to have it she will do it at once. It seems to me important that the little book should be published in the spring – if so I take the responsibility that it will sell.

This is a remarkable letter. The publisher has not even read the manuscript, let alone accepted it, but Axel is drawing up clear demands regarding the book's design and publication! And the fact that he is shouldering responsibility for its sales shows that there was nothing wrong with his self-confidence. His name was quite simply a guarantee that the book would circulate in those circles he now moved in.

One person who belonged to those circles was Feodora ('Feo') Gleichen, a German countess closely related to Queen Victoria's husband, Prince Albert. As relatives of the British royal family the Gleichen sisters had rooms in St James's Palace. Lady Feo was an artist and painted a fine portrait of Axel at this period.

Feo Gleichen was commissioned to do the frontispiece to *Letters from a Mourning City*, which, John Murray informed Axel on the 8th of April, he was 'delighted' to publish. However, one precondition was that Axel should first tell Maude White about the new edition and obtain her permission. Axel agreed terms with his translator and the book came out in October in an edition of 1,200 copies. The promised foreword contained several phrases that – given that Axel more or less foisted the book on Murray – can only be seen as a unique show of hypocrisy:

> These letters were brought before the English public twelve years ago by a courageous English lady who, in collaboration with the author, had translated them from the Swedish. The little book has long been out of print and is forgotten, and I am not aware of any particular impatience on the part of the English readers to be reminded of its existence. Still, it has now been deemed opportune to issue another edition. Having re-written the book in my own English, guided by the Swedish original, without availing myself of the former published translation, it would not be fair to make the translator share the responsibility of this new version, which rests with its author alone.

Axel's English earned Murray's admiration, but also a few cautiously worded objections: 'There are a few (wonderfully few considering the circumstances) expressions and phrases to which I should like to call your attention for it seems to me that they may require alteration,' he pointed out. Axel, for his part, was well aware that it really was his own 'crooked' English:

> I know well that many of my expressions are rather uncommon, not to say un-English, but I am not afraid of them so long [as] I do not commit a *fault*. So for instance where I when speaking of the children living in the dusky slums, quite consciously invented the word 'light-shy' children – well, I like this expression. But I need not tell you that I gladly accept your veto where you consider that I have gone too far in this direction.

It hardly needs saying that the expression 'light-shy' was allowed to remain. What could Mr Murray do with an author who in the same letter, almost by the way, mentioned that Henry James had visited him in Rome and said 'all sorts of nice things' about his *Vagaries*?

1–2 Axel's parents, Fredrik and Aurora Munthe

3 Axel (left) and his brother Arnold   **4** Axel's sister Anna

5 This photograph of a very young Axel Munthe was taken in Naples during one of his first visits there – perhaps in 1876, when he also visited Capri for the first time.

6 Marina Grande, Capri's harbour, at the time of Axel's first visit to the island in 1876. Along the mountainside one can see the road between Capri and Anacapri which was opened in 1874.

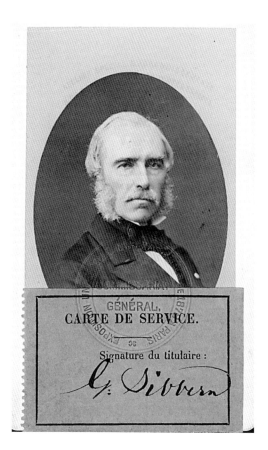

7 Georg Sibbern in 1878, when he took up his post as Swedish–Norwegian minister in Paris

8 Sigrid von Mecklenburg, Axel's great love

9 'Assistants', frontispiece by Hugo Birger to *Letters from a Mourning City* (1887)

10–11 (above) Edith Balfour ('Miss DD') and (right) Maude Valérie White, whom Axel met in the summer of 1885 and who meant a great deal to his English orientation

12 Axel on Capri, probably during his 'exile' on the island in 1888–89

13–14 Axel's servant girls, the young sisters Giovannina (left) and Rosina Alberino (right), photographed by Munthe. Rosina remained in Axel's service until his death. 'Giovannina and Rosina belonged to the San Michele household, better servants I have never had, light of hand and foot, singing the whole day at their work' (*The Story of San Michele*).

15 The Spanish Steps with its flower sellers. Munthe had his studio in the house to the right, where John Keats died.

16 Lord Dufferin, photographed by Munthe

17 Munthe was an inveterate sailor and enjoyed taking his guests cruising in the waters around Capri. 'My beautiful cutter *Lady Victoria* was as fine a boat as Scotland could build,' Munthe writes in *The Story of San Michele*, 'teak and steel, ready for every emergency, safe in all weather if properly handled, and if ever I knew anything worth knowing it was how to steer a boat.' The photo shows Princess Marie Louise of Baden sailing with Munthe in the Bay of Naples.

18 This panoramic view of Villa San Michele, the chapel and the Sorrento peninsula was taken by Crown Princess Victoria with a special camera lens in 1903.

19 Crown Princess Victoria in a gondola, possibly during her and Axel's first visit to Venice, when she had pains in her right arm and wore a sling. The photo was in all probability taken by Munthe.

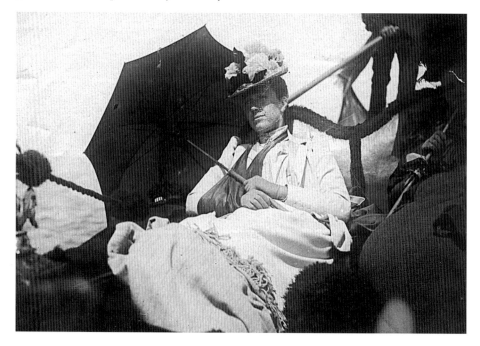

20 The study with the head of the Medusa, which, according to his own account, Munthe found at the bottom of the sea, but which possibly has a more prosaic provenance (photo Crown Princess Victoria 1901–2).

21. The sculpture gallery, photographed by Prince Max of Baden 1901

22 The sculpture gallery continues in a bow-shaped pergola which offers an enchanting view over the Bay of Naples (photo by Crown Princess Victoria in 1903).

23 Torre di Materita as it looked when Munthe bought it in 1902

24 Prince Max of Baden and Axel looked so alike that the local population had difficulties distinguishing the one from the other. On this photograph they are seen outside Torre di Materita.

25 Munthe with his and Victoria's dogs at the Barbarossa fortress

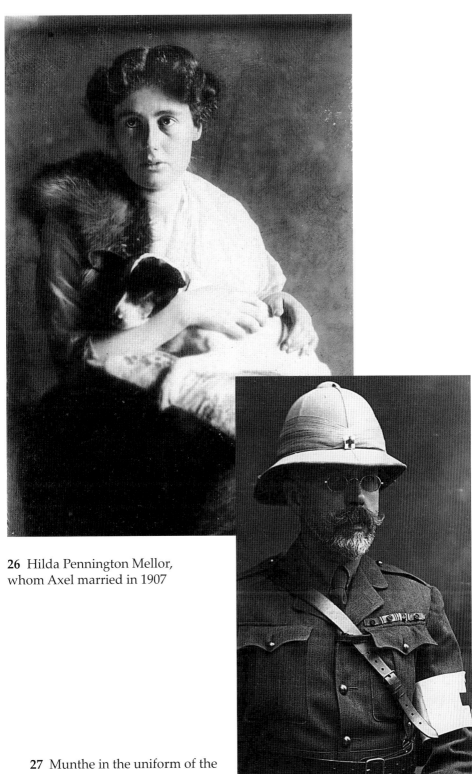

26 Hilda Pennington Mellor, whom Axel married in 1907

27 Munthe in the uniform of the British Red Cross

28 The photograph of 'the boys' that Hilda sent Axel in 1924

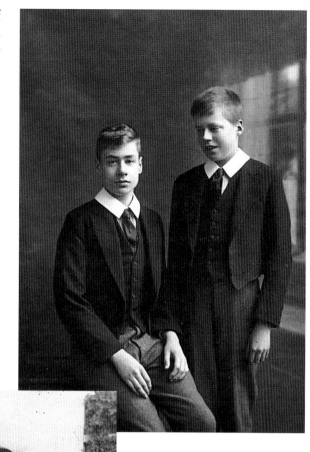

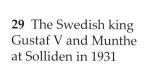

29 The Swedish king Gustaf V and Munthe at Solliden in 1931

30 In 1937 Hermann Goering visited Munthe with the intention of buying the Villa San Michele.

31 In March 1938 Greta Garbo visited Capri with the conductor Leopold Stokowski. In a letter to Jock Murray, Munthe reported that he found the actress 'surprisingly nice, simple, and natural'.

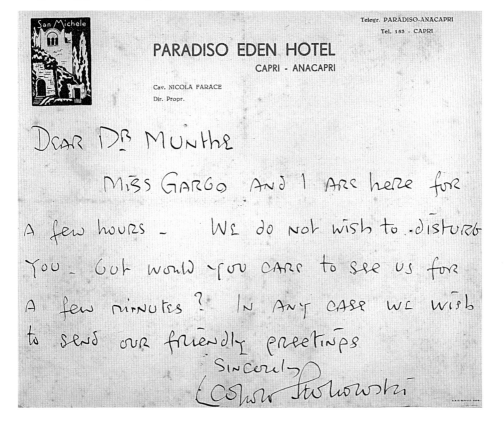

Telegr. PARADISO-ANACAPRI
Tel. 153 - CAPRI

PARADISO EDEN HOTEL

CAPRI - ANACAPRI

Cav. NICOLA FARACE
Dir. Propr.

Dear D.R Munthe

Miss Garbo and I are here for a few hours – We do not wish to disturb you – but would you care to see us for a few minutes? In any case we wish to send our friendly greetings

Sincerely
Leopold Stokowski

32 The 80-year-old Axel Munthe and his publisher Jock Murray at Albemarle Street in 1937

33 Axel Munthe photographed in his rooms in the Royal Castle in Stockholm with his son Malcolm and his five-month-old grandson Adam in October 1946

FROM THE SPANISH STEPS TO THE FENICIAN

In the year 1900 Munthe's and Victoria's annual rhythm was broken. For the first and last time Axel crossed the Atlantic, for a consultation in Newport. Another break in the routine occurred the following year, when Victoria's eldest son, 19-year-old Gustaf Adolf, accompanied his mother to Rome and Capri.

The prince was ill and 'is in absolute need of my care', wrote the PR-conscious Munthe in passing to a patient. But the prince's doctor was not well himself. The haemorrhages continued: one of them in the spring of 1897, another in the autumn of 1900. Axel began to think about leaving behind the hectic life of Rome and retreating to Capri. It was a hard decision to take since there were many patients who relied on him. But in the spring of 1901 he left Rome behind and moved to Capri for good.

There were several reasons for Munthe's decision to leave Rome. He was overworked and ill. Hard work was a way of paying off his moral guilt, but Axel's nervous system could not stand the stress involved in being both a serious practising doctor and a sought-after society darling. The life he was living accentuated the duality in his character and tore him apart. He was tired of all the filthy-rich patients, the lukewarm friendships and the empty society prattle. On Capri he would get rid of his Rome patients and be able to devote himself to his old clientele of the poor. The recluse in him took revenge now for the defeat of 1889, when the other side of his personality was tempted to settle in Rome.

The decision to leave Rome had been maturing since at least 1898, as emerges from a letter from Queen Sophia to Axel:

> I have been greatly dismayed to hear that you may have to give up your work in Rome. My belief is that if such a misfortune were to happen, the Crown Princess would try to find somewhere to live close to you. If this is impossible, I suspect she would remain in Rome, where after all she is so happy. How she will then be cared for is a mystery to me. If the Crown Princess knows anything of your coming departure from Rome, she will already have made her plans, which we will certainly not be able to influence.

The queen realised how dependent Victoria was on her doctor, and perhaps she also suspected that Victoria's need for being 'close' to Axel was not only geographical. Rome – and Stockholm – were buzzing with rumours about the nature of the relationship between Victoria and her doctor. Perhaps it was time to escape from the world's gaze? The decision to move to Capri would in that case have been taken by Axel and Victoria in concert. On Capri they could go about together far more freely than in Rome. Now that the Villa San Michele was ready and Axel had a home of his own, it was time for the furniture van.

LEX BACCELLI

However, there was also another circumstance that may have influenced their decision to leave Rome. Munthe's position within the city's medical profession was so unique that in 1900 the Italian government proposed a law whereby all foreign doctors wishing to practise in Italy must pass an oral and written examination in the Italian language. According to the *Berliner Tageblatt*, this would radically reduce the number of foreign doctors, several of whom lacked academic qualifications. The newspaper gave as an example 'a certain Scandinavian doctor', a 'charlatan' who 'without possessing an academic title practises in the most prestigious foreign colony and is supposed to be earning about 150,000 francs a year'. The doctor in question was course Axel, who, the paper alleged, had solicited the help of the queen of Italy to enable him to continue practising as a doctor. The queen, however, was supposed to have said that she could not influence the legislation. Dr Munthe, the correspondent wrote, would instead have to turn to Baccelli.*

Guido Baccelli was a legendary Rome doctor, the holder of an honorary doctorate in 1852 at the early age of 20 and thereafter the occupant of several chairs of medicine. After the union of Rome with the kingdom of Italy in 1870 he became professor of medicine at Rome University. Baccelli was also politically active and in 1881 he became minister of education, a post he held on three separate occasions, the last one being from 1898 until June 1900.

The German journalist's suggestion that Munthe should turn to Baccelli was pure malice. The suggestion of a language test for foreign doctors was not only motivated by concern about the Italian medical profession, who at this time had a particularly bad reputation. Alongside his duties as a minister, Baccelli was also a celebrated doctor whom Munthe, with his miracle cures, had deprived of several rich patients. In Rome it was rumoured that the *Lex Baccelli* in reality was directed against Munthe and really ought to be called the *Lex Munthe* – the law about language-testing was allegedly a convenient way of getting rid of a troublesome rival. The fact that it was Munthe and no one else who was hung out to dry in the article gives credibility to this rumour. Yet the criticism of Axel was without

---

* *Berliner Tageblatt*, 27 March 1900. The notice was unsigned but written by the newspaper's Rome correspondent, Dr Hans Barth.

foundation as he demonstrably had a diploma from the medical faculty in Paris. The information about Axel's income (about £300,000 in today's values) was of course pulled out of thin air and basically intended to arouse jealousy among the newspaper's readers and Munthe's colleagues, but it is interesting as an approximation.

The item in the *Berliner Tageblatt* bore witness to the fact that Axel had powerful enemies and rivals, especially within the Italian medical establishment. When Munthe recounted the story in the chapter 'Doctors' in *The Story of San Michele*, he transposed it – like so many other Roman events – to Paris:

> A large number of foreign doctors were practising in Paris in those days. There was a great jalousie de métier amongst them, of which I got my share and no wonder. Nor were we much liked by our French colleagues for our monopoly of the wealthy foreign colony, no doubt a far more lucrative clientèle than their own. Of late an agitation had even been started in the press to protest against the steadily increasing number of foreign doctors in Paris, often, it was hinted, not even provided with regular diplomas from well-recognized universities.

Physician-in-Ordinary
Axel Martin Fredrik Munthe

Queen Sophia guessed correctly when she assumed that Victoria would try to spend as much time as possible close to Munthe. In the winter and in the spring of 1902 Axel as usual took care of the Crown princess, this time in southern Italy. They spent two weeks together in Taormina and a whole month on Capri before she set off for Baden via Venice. This was the first time that Victoria had spent a lengthy period on Capri during the winter. She had been on her way to Sicily before but on that occasion her family put paid to her plans. Now, after ten years as her doctor, Axel's authority was undisputed.

In a letter to Grand Duchess Luise Axel reported that 'The expedition [. . .] was a great success and as H.R.H. alas! cares for so little of Sweden her liking of the Navy has to be encouraged in every possible way and it will besides contre-act her growing impopularity at home.' Since she arrived in Capri she had 'improved in every way'.

The Crown princess's feelings for Italy were not only nourished by her love of the country's culture and climate. Italy was also a mental and emotional refuge for her, not least because of Axel. She was not happy in Sweden nor with her Swedish family, her marriage to Gustaf lay in tatters and she did everything in her power to spend as much time as possible beyond the country's borders. As Axel pointed out in his letter to the Grand Duchess, Victoria was unpopular in Sweden because of her constant sojourns abroad, which were seen not only as inappropriate but were also very expensive.

By this time Axel enjoyed the unbounded confidence of the royal family. In the summer of 1901 Victoria was 'frail and poorly and highly strung', and the Crown prince placed all his hopes on Munthe: 'I will expect you here around the 18th to 20th of August, and that will be a great help to me.' But even Axel seems to have found the task overwhelming on this occasion, and he indicated that he wished to resign. Queen Sophia's distraught reaction says it all:

> I hope and most sincerely beg that you will never again consider giving up the care of the Crown Princess. I certainly do not underestimate the difficulties and unpleasantness that you have to cope with, but only consider that you have a great mission to undertake on her behalf, and I do not need to add that the Crown Prince, the King and I all repose the utmost confidence in you.

Hitherto Axel had lacked official standing at court, but on 21 January 1903 his role was formalised and he was appointed physician-in-ordinary. As well as the change of status, his appointment meant a change in Axel's routines. From now on he was to spend much more time around the Crown princess than he had previously done, and not only in Italy.

In 1903 not even the stay in Capri could cure Victoria's fragile nerves, and to escape from her melancholy she wished to travel to Baden to celebrate her father's birthday on 9 September; however, she was not allowed to take such decisions on her own. Every foreign trip was regarded with suspicion by her Swedish family who thought she was away too often. When she was forced to abandon the trip, she reacted with despair: 'The dear 9th is approaching & they will all be near my Father & I sit here in my loneliness,' she wrote to Axel. She was more depressed than ever and hurled dreadful reproaches at her husband:

> I am in a desperate state of 'lowness', it is a little better now when the Prince is away, but when he is there I simply cannot stand it. When I read in a paper of a divorce-case, I envy the partners! – How this will go on I know not; but it will take some fatal turn sooner or later; that I am convinced of. No preaching will help, & it is all I can do not to run away. I am so low that my strength & courage are all gone; I dread to see people & prefer to go to bed than to assist at a dinner. Now that he is gone I live up a little & try to be with the others again. But when he comes I am not

capable of it. I only want to be left in peace. [. . .] Even as I write this the tears are flowing; I cannot help it, I feel so dreadfully miserable, alone & forlorn. Why must one be chained like this?? it is so terribly hard. God bless you. I beg you to forgive my writing like this, but I must pour out my heart, or else I cannot live on. [. . .] Bless you ever. Do help me! I am crushed to the ground. Hug the dear dear dogs. Bless you d[arlin]g. Oh, how I long to hold your hand!

The letter reveals chilling facts about the deteriorating royal marriage. Despite Axel's fondness for Victoria and his insights regarding Gustaf's shortcomings, it was his ambition to help the Crown prince and his wife to find a modus vivendi that would enable them to carry out their public duties although their life together was over and their relationship had hit rock bottom. The Crown prince was passive by nature and thought that most of what Victoria tried to do was 'unnecessary'. Axel did his utmost to ensure that Gustaf would not be placed in situations where he had to say no to his strong-willed wife, who was unwilling to give way even when she knew that she was at fault. He therefore tried to divert her from ideas and projects that would force the Crown prince to put his foot down.

Axel's actions were dictated in large part by his concern for the Crown princess's reputation and her position in the family and the country. He could not go against her expressed will, but he could try to direct it by means of his own and that of others. He was a master at this kind of psychological jigsaw puzzle.

At the same time as Axel was trying to halt projects that the Crown prince would feel compelled to reject, he realised as a good psychologist that the Crown princess had to have something to occupy herself with during her sojourns in Sweden to avoid sinking into depression and dejection. This was why he was so keen to support what he called 'the Borgholm project', asking the Grand Duchess of Baden to convince Queen Sophia of its excellence.

Victoria had visited the island of Öland in the Baltic in the summer of 1901 and she went there several times the following year. It was now she chose it as the site of the 'Borgholm project', the building of a large villa. The foundation stone was laid in September 1903, in the midst of Victoria's severe depression. The villa was christened Solliden, 'Sunny slope'.

The Crown princess wished the villa to have a 'Capri-character' and that San Michele served as a model for Solliden is evident both from the architectonic details and the general concept: a combined villa and planned garden. Plaques in relief and other artworks were incorporated into the façade and the park was filled with antique sculptures, several of which were copies of those that stand in the sculpture loggia of the Villa San Michele. Tables and the floor of the terrace were constructed out of marble fragments that were sent there from Italy and the walls were covered in paintings with motifs from Capri and Venice.

A CROWN PRINCESS IN ROPE SANDALS

From 1901 up to the outbreak of the First World War, the Crown princess visited Capri almost yearly. During the years 1903–4 she lodged in the Hotel Molaro, which lay a few hundred metres from Munthe's villa and had an equally fantastic view over the Bay of Naples. Closer to her doctor she could not come. The hotel – which nowadays is called San Michele – had stood empty for several years and so Victoria and her suite had it all to themselves.

The person who arranged for the Crown princess to live in the Hotel Molaro was of course Axel, who, according to Victoria's lady-in-waiting, was 'all-powerful on the island'. He also arranged a cleaning lady, a cook and a kitchen maid. The cook was annexed quite ruthlessly from a pair of English ladies on the island who on several occasions had expressed a wish to be able to repay Axel for his services: 'Now you have a chance to show your gratitude, the Swedish Crown Princess needs a cook, I am engaging him at once.'

When the hotel opened to the public in 1905, Victoria no longer wished to live there and Axel rented a private villa belonging to a doctor colleague, Dr Vincenzo Cuomo. During the next few years Victoria lived with her suite at the Hotel Paradiso in the centre of Anacapri. In this case too the owner let the whole hotel to the Crown princess and her attendants – although this was not done voluntarily, but only after Axel locked him in the toilet until he relented.

Their time on Capri passed quietly and according to fixed routines. In the morning the Crown princess attended to her correspondence and afterwards walked with her dogs, the poodles Tom and Pussy and the Lapland dog Gioia. When Munthe was with her, he and the Crown princess walked by themselves a little way in front of the others. During her excursions Victoria wore her 'Capri uniform', which consisted of a white dress of Capri wool, a straw hat and shoes with soles of woven raffia.

GERMANS IN CAPRI

Royalty and other celebrities enjoyed visiting Capri but whether it was Victoria or Munthe who was the attraction is hard to say. In any event, a visit to the Villa San Michele was obligatory for most of them.

In the spring of 1903 Count Zeppelin, the airship designer, called on the Crown princess, and in March 1904 Kaiser Wilhelm II, Victoria's cousin, paid her a visit. Victoria met him at the harbour and they made their way straight up to the Villa San Michele, where, according to an eyewitness, Axel showed them round 'without much enthusiasm', although the Kaiser was in excellent humour and, to his host's relief, in civilian clothes. When a member of the Kaiser's entourage suggested that, as a souvenir of their visit, Axel ought to make the Kaiser a gift of 'the funny old eagle' – the Horus falcon in the chapel – Axel was filled with horror as the falcon was one of the most treasured objects in his collection; needless to say, no gift was ever presented. But Munthe had been provoked, and when Wilhelm, with the air of a connoisseur, picked out a torso as the most valuable item in his collection, Axel replied: 'Your Majesty, it is not my custom to value my art treasures in monetary terms, but with regard to this torso I have quite by chance chosen to make an exception. I happen to know for certain that it is the only object in the whole of this house which is completely worthless. It is not even of marble – it is of plaster.'

One German royal whom Axel on the contrary welcomed as a guest was Victoria's other cousin, Prince Max of Baden, born in 1867. Max was close to Victoria, he knew about her real and imaginary ailments, and he felt sorry for Axel but realised at an early stage that his heart, as he put it, 'is set upon the saving of this poor lady'.

Axel was also the prince's doctor. Their correspondence shows that Max was at least as dependent as Victoria on Axel as a friend and doctor. During the 1890s he endured bouts of severe depression, he suffered from a 'sensibility in sexual things', claimed to be plagued by 'perverse ideas' and in 1898 he underwent a cure administered by Professor Krafft-Ebing in Vienna which included, among other things, hypnosis. A couple of romantic poems addressed to Munthe give an indication of the nature of his 'perverse ideas'.

However strong the prince's feelings for Munthe were, there is no evidence that this homoerotic attraction was mutual. However, they had much else in common, both politically and culturally. Max was a convinced liberal and would come to play an important role in Germany's development in the closing stages of the First World War (see the chapter 'Red Cross & Iron Cross' below). Another common interest was music. Max played the piano, and they often visited the Bayreuth festival together. 'You have the talent to tempt me most horribly,' was his reply to Axel's invitation to come and call on him in Capri: 'Most people bore and tire me in the long run, you never, and to talk to you is one of my greatest joys.'

Max and Axel would remain friends throughout their lives, despite the trials that the First World War would expose them to. That their friendship endured depended in no small measure on the fact that Axel helped Max in a situation where others might have hesitated to put up their resources.

In 1900 Max married the young and pretty princess Marie Louise of Cumberland, granddaughter of 'Europe's grandmother', the queen of Denmark. From the prince's point of view the marriage appears to have been a purely practical arrangement intended to guarantee the succession. As he confessed to Axel, 'This marriage question is only one of duty', 'duty to my house and country'. If he had to choose between the 'happiness and peace' of his fellow-creatures, and 'family politics', the latter would have to come second.

In the summer of 1901 Max and Marie Louise spent their honeymoon on Capri as Axel's guests. The marriage was childless, presumably because of the sexual disorder from which the prince suffered. The main reason for the lengthy stay on Capri seems to have been to find a remedy for this condition. They sailed in the bay and visited the coastal towns on the Sorrento peninsula. Max and Marie Louise took photographs and filled two albums, one for themselves and one that they gave to Munthe before they left Capri. On the cover of Munthe's copy they had printed 'Germans in Capri' – a humorous allusion to Munthe's dislike of the Germans. 'The Germans in Capri leave him no peace, / They bore him and hurt him and torture and tease', Max wrote in his rhyming dedication. After his and Marie Louise's visit, however, Max hoped that Munthe, this 'hermit' on his 'rocky height', had reconsidered.

When the princess became pregnant, rumour had it that Munthe had been of assistance. During her visit to Munthe in April 1902, Alexandra Bildt noted in her diary:

> Prince Max and his young wife, who had been grieving over the fact that they could not have a child, lived in a house directly opposite [San Michele] – simply to be near him [= Munthe]. This had the desired effect, insofar as the princess is now to become a mother in July and the whole of Baden is hailing Munthe as the 'indirect' cause of this great joy. He is going there himself to help in the great event.

Their daughter, Maria Alexandra, was born on 1 August 1902, so she must have been conceived around 1 November 1901. According to a dating in the royal couple's photograph album they stayed on Capri between May and August, but the phrase 'What happened then I cannot tell' in Max's dedicatory poem testifies that something occurred later in the autumn. That Munthe's contribution to the pregnancy was anything but 'indirect' is borne out by Alexandra Bildt's ironic quotation marks around the word. And Munthe *did* visit the royal couple around the date of the conception.

By hinting later in life that the royal couple's second child, Berthold, born in 1906, might have been his, Munthe acknowledged that he had had an intimate relationship with Princess Marie Louise. If the rumours about Munthe's sexual intervention are true, this testifies to a significant openmindedness in all the parties concerned. In any case, his possible contribution to the happiness of the Baden royal family seems to have been made with the greatest degree of mutual understanding. Like her husband, Marie Louise maintained a close friendship with Munthe throughout her life and their castle in Salem, where Axel was a frequent guest, was decorated with bronze casts of busts and statues from San Michele.

COMMANDER OF THE VICTORIAN ORDER

During the first period of Axel's time as physician-in-ordinary, the Crown princess's case record was constantly filled with new ailments. To the recurrent depressions were added all kinds of physical pains. In the autumn of 1902 Victoria was afflicted with an inflammation in the left eye that resulted in her often wearing blue spectacles like her doctor. The affliction turned out to be a chronic one.

Strangely enough the same fate affected her physician too, and almost at the same time. In Axel's case it was the right eye that was the weak link. He suffered a retinal detachment and he needed to shield the eye totally from light. He seems to have retained a certain amount of vision, even if from now on he suffered from periodic, severe pains in his eye.

Although the Crown princess was at a low ebb on account of the continuing treatment to her eye, she travelled to Rome at the beginning of February 1905. At the same time, her eldest son Gustaf Adolf was engaged to Princess Margaret, daughter of the Duke and Duchess of Connaught and granddaughter of Queen Victoria. Margaret's father, Arthur, was a brother of King Edward VII and her mother was Princess Luise Margarethe of Prussia. Gustaf Adolf was heir to the Swedish throne and Queen Sophia had long been advocating a union with the British royal family. The choice fell on the eldest of the Connaught daughters, Margaret, who was 23 years old.

The wedding took place at Windsor Castle on 15 June the same year. The day before the wedding the British royal couple gave a splendid lunch. Axel, who on account of his poor sight never took part in evening engagements, was called for by King Edward: 'I should like to meet that doctor who is with you and whom I have heard so much about. Where is he?' The phrase with which the king greeted Axel is worthy of note: 'We have many friends in common.' On the day of the wedding, Axel was appointed a Commander of the Victorian Order.

TORRE DI MATERITA

At the same time as the Crown princess was devoting herself to 'the Borgholm project', Axel was fully occupied with his own building plans on Capri. As we have seen, the Villa San Michele underwent constant alterations during the first years of the century, but Axel had not lived in the villa for many years before he started to look for something new. One important reason was his worsening eyesight. He had raised San Michele as a temple to the sun, but his eyes, which had been weak since childhood, could not tolerate the strong light. 'I have been driven out of San Michele, the labour of a lifetime', he wrote in *The Story of San Michele*, and went on:

> I had built it stone by stone with my own hands in the sweat of my brow, I had built it on my knees to be a sanctuary to the Sun where I was to seek knowledge and light from the glorious god I had been worshipping my whole life. I had been warned over and over again by the fire in my eyes that I was not worthy to live there, that my place was in the shade, but I had paid no heed to the warnings. Like the horses returning to their burning stables to perish in the flames, I had come back, summer after summer, to the blinding light of San Michele. Beware of the light, beware of the light!

There were other reasons too. One of them was the steadily growing stream of tourists. The house and its owner had been transformed into tourist attractions but Axel had not retreated to Capri to become a sight for tourists but to find peace. The other reason was that it was the building process itself that came first with him. Once the villa was built, his restless ego sought out new visions to implement.

Half an hour's walk from San Michele in a south-westerly direction lies a medieval tower, Torre di Materita, which Axel obtained in May 1902 from the Englishman Arthur King for around 25,000 lire (£2,000, or about £100,000 in today's money). The house has a unique west-facing position. Here, Axel's eyes were not met by the strong forenoon light, as at San Michele, but by the duller light of the setting sun. Moreover, Torre di Materita was much more suitable as a home than the Villa San Michele.

Torre di Materita was only one of Axel's new acquisitions during these years. In 1903 he bought a second medieval tower, Torre della Guardia, which lay even further to the west, on a clifftop with a fantastic view over the sea. And at roughly the same time he acquired the ruins of yet another imperial villa, Damecuta, on the north side of the island, where he immediately began to excavate.

He also did all he could to get his hands on Mount Barbarossa above the Villa San Michele. The reason, as we have seen, was that he wanted to put a stop to the hunting of the migratory birds that rested on Capri before continuing their flight. Quails in particular were seen as a culinary delicacy and they were snared in nets before being sold to restaurants on the mainland. In order to lure them men set out cages with decoy birds in the shrubbery under the nets. Putting out their eyes with a red-hot nail ensured that they would sing day and night. Victoria and her attendants would conscientiously destroy all the snares they discovered during their walks.

In *The Story of San Michele* Axel describes his battle with the owner of Mount Barbarossa, a former slaughterman from the mainland, who kept forcing up the price so that Axel would not be able to buy the mountain. The whole thing led to continual arguments and lawsuits. On one occasion, when Axel asked the Crown princess to invite the highest official of the municipality, *il sindaco* [the mayor], to lunch in order to work on him, Victoria's lady-in-waiting, who spoke no Italian, was encouraged to 'at least make eyes at him'. The mayor was said to have become 'as yielding as wax' under the spell of the royal favour. What importance the lunch had is not known for sure, but in May 1904 Axel managed to acquire the mountain from Francesco Gargiulo and made it into a sanctuary for birds. This was not popular with the locals, for whom fowling was an ancient custom, a right, and an important part of their livelihood.

Thus, within a few years of his move to Capri, Axel had obtained for himself a mountain and three towers – Materita, Guardia and Damecuta. His ambitions were truly Tiberian.

Miss Ankarcrona: A Case Study

A person who observed Munthe at close quarters and bore witness to his complex personality was Wivica Ankarcrona, who had been born in Stockholm in 1863 and had left the parental home at an early age in protest at an arranged marriage. In 1900 she arrived on Capri where she converted to Catholicism.

Wivica Ankarcrona had no profession but was nevertheless fully occupied day and night. She was in fact a professional invalid who spent a large part of her life in bed. She showed symptoms of tuberculosis in her lungs and abdomen and had an irregular heartbeat, but her problems were basically imaginary. What she really suffered from was the major female ailment of the period: delicate nerves and hysteria. In other words, Wivica Ankarcrona was a typical 'Munthe patient'; she died in 1953, at the age of 90, which shows that you need a good constitution if you want to allow yourself a lifetime of being ill.

As Wivica lived down in Capri town and Munthe in Anacapri, they did not meet all that often. However, in a letter to her brother in the winter of 1906 she gives an interesting glimpse of her fellow-countryman:

> Yesterday I met Doctor Munthe, whom I have not met for a year, I think, & he walked with me uphill to Anacapri where he lives, & we compatriots had so much to chat about that I walked so far & so quickly that today I am quite worn-out & aching all over. Despite his coarse manners & love of truth in the guise of rudeness, he is nevertheless engaging and interesting & it is a great shame about his loss of sight in one eye & the other so sensitive that he seldom goes out in the sunshine except early and late & then the day can be miserable for a lonely gentleman.

Her physician on Capri was Doctor Cuomo, whom she abandoned after a few years in favour of Giorgio Cerio. What she wanted above all was a doctor who was prepared to underwrite her own diagnoses – that she was mortally ill. What she absolutely did not want to hear was that she was looking well or – God forbid – that she was completely healthy.

According to Wivica's sister, Dr Cerio had been all too accommodating 'with new injections and other tricks'. When Munthe took over – 'thank God' – everything changed in a trice:

> Dr. Munthe has been with her today. Saw to everything very thoroughly, said there is no danger to her lungs, *possibly* tuberculosis in the stomach, but not to any significant degree. Nothing organically wrong with her heart, but weakness in the nerves round about & what's wrong with her is that her nervous system is completely topsy-turvy, which is illness enough he said. I shall meet him again one day. However he said to me that he already told Vica 5 years ago that in order to become healthy she would have to leave Capri & the whole environment of priests etc. – 'but then she became angry with me & would not obey me and then I wanted nothing to do with her.' – 'To make her *obey* is the most difficult thing, I have now told her what she has to do to become healthy – in a few days I will return & then she must give me a definite answer.'* [. . .] Yes, poor, wretched little Vica – now she has to start again in a new phase and be made to obey a definite set of rules instead of reacting as she has been

---

* This story is told in a slightly different version by Baroness von Uexküll (1953), according to whom Munthe asked for an answer in five minutes. To the Crown Princess Victoria's lady-in-waiting Munthe explained that the Italian doctors preferred that the patients died since they received 2,000 lire for each embalming.

used to. When her heart begins to pound, instead of injections she has to say to herself: 'Dr. M. has said it isn't dangerous.'

The reason why Miss Ankarcrona had difficulties in keeping up with Munthe on the slopes up to Anacapri was that her muscles had atrophied from all her bed-rest. When she came under Munthe's care she could not walk without severe pain. She was then just over 40.

Munthe's cure altered Miss Ankacrona's whole identity as a professional invalid. When he told her she was perfectly healthy, she became extremely upset. In a long letter to her brother in Stockholm she poured out her feelings about Munthe's way of handling her and her illness. The letter sheds light on the way in which a recalcitrant patient reacted to Munthe as a doctor, with his 'dictatorial manner' and insistence on total submission:

As you know, Dr. Munthe has on several occasions concerned himself with my person & I may say from the beginning without being asked. About a month ago he returned to Capri & called on me & now he wishes to interfere far too much with my personal freedom & right to make up my own mind & I get the impression that he wants to exert a hypnotic influence over me. For time and again he forces me instantly & against my will to obey his orders which he takes my word that I will follow down to the last detail. Since I first met him I have felt an uncomfortable sense of unease, constraint & repulsion & my nerves have been so strained that on those occasions when I have met him I have been unable to sleep & have heart palpitations.

He strikes me more than ever now as highly-strung to the point of abnormality. What on one occasion he ordains as absolutely essential, like for example a companion at home, which I believe I have already found, is now altogether unnecessary. I feel I must be free of him & this is what I hope you will help me with & now I will tell you how. He has ordered me to travel to Sweden and stay in Dalarna & I am happy to do this. [. . .] Then this suggestion was thrown out, companion & all, & I had to give my word of honour to set off alone with his maid & on the way to stop off in Karlsruhe for nearly 2 months at a German pension & there to have the pleasure of meeting him & possibly travelling the rest of the way in his company. [. . .] He also never stops making a fuss about where I stay here in Italy, first it has to be Rome, then Anacapri, then Capri will suffice, sometimes in this apartment, sometimes elsewhere, until I am at my wits' end. [. . .] Do you find that normal? [. . .] On the last few occasions when I would not instantly bow to his wishes he was so furious and so rough that I shudder all over and have had several heart attacks which I did not have until he came and argued with me.

They argued and quarrelled but did not fall out with each other, the professional invalid and her heartless doctor. Rather, they were actors in a play of two roles, which they infused with life at regular intervals. When Munthe once called on Wivica unbidden she was lying in bed as usual and he came 'with his usual theories that I *want* to be ill & he mocked me for my fancies & everything could be cured with sour milk'. Nevertheless she thought it kind of him to take an interest in her health, although he never examined her but had his diagnosis ready in advance.

HILDA

She is clever and good, and a lady.
Axel Munthe to Baroness Ebba Åkerhielm

A ROUND THE TURN of the century, political and social reality cast long shadows over life on sun-drenched Capri. On the other side of the Atlantic the USA and Spain were at war over control of Cuba, in South Africa the British were fighting the Boers, and in the Far East the Russo-Japanese War was raging, eventually resulting in a humiliating defeat for Russia. The Russian revolution, which followed in 1905, bore witness to the fact that a new era was dawning – something which was underlined by the wave of assassinations and attempted assassinations that swept over Europe during these years and which affected individuals whom Victoria and Axel knew personally. In September 1898 Empress Elizabeth of Austria–Hungary fell victim to an anarchist's knife; two years later the King of Italy, Umberto I, was murdered, and in the same year there was an attempt to murder the Prince of Wales. The world in which Axel and his patient lived was being slowly but surely undermined by new social and political forces.

On 20 September 1906 a double anniversary was celebrated in Karlsruhe: the silver wedding of Victoria and Gustaf and the golden wedding of the Duke and Duchess of Baden. The celebrations were lavish, but the part that concerned Victoria herself left only emptiness in her heart. Twenty-five years together with a man she despised – what was there to celebrate? As soon as the festivities – which recommenced a week later in Stockholm – were over, she fled to Solliden, which was now ready.

If the silver wedding was a torment, the inauguration of Solliden was pure triumph and a joy. The villa was Munthe's and Victoria's joint project. They now had two islands where they could be together and be relatively undisturbed: Capri and Öland. When Munthe was at Solliden he stayed in the villa itself, in a guest apartment that was entered from the pergola. Gustaf for his part shunned the place, which had been built more or less against his will.

Axel did go to Öland for the official inauguration on 15 October but left for London a few days before. As soon as Victoria reached Solliden, she wrote him a passionate letter that reflects the temperature of their relationship at this time:

> I wish I could go on my knees to thank you for that dear dear letter before you left Sweden. Oh how it warmed my heart, how it made it shrill with joy to hear such loving words from you darling, you who fill my heart & soul & my whole life for ever. God bless thee for every one of those dear blessed words, they went straight home to my heart & it was as if light had spread about me, when I read them. And I felt so near to you. Yes, thank God I know that neither time nor space can sever us, & I feel more than ever that I am yours, *thine*, for ever. Thank God I may hear the echo in your heart that thou art mine too! – My thoughts have followed you so closely the whole time, praying for my darling at sea, & now I hope & trust that you are safe in London & not the worse for your long journey. – When you left me [at the railway station] in Gnesta [close to the Tullgarn Palace] I felt that my all in life was going from me, & I cried bitterly. But then there came peace over me & I felt that my darling had not left me though he was gone for my outer eye.

By the end of November Victoria was back in Germany, this time in order to undergo a minor nose operation in Berlin. After the operation she spent Christmas as usual with her parents. On 29 January she fell ill with influenza, and developed an inflammation of the lungs and an irregular heartbeat and suffered fainting fits; the planned Italian trip was postponed.

Munthe was 'very concerned, occasionally seemed to be genuinely worried, kept repeating "weak pulse", "poor heart function", etc.', remembered Victoria's lady-in-waiting. 'Previously, e.g. on Capri, I had often thought that he did not take the Crown Princess's ailments seriously enough, did not devote enough attention or real care to her, but now that it had become serious, I found that he became wholly absorbed in his calling. I saw that he was suffering, and I felt sorry for him.'

Victoria's condition was in fact very serious. Axel issued daily bulletins on her state of health, in Stockholm the palace ball was cancelled and on 22 February the Crown prince travelled to Karlsruhe to be at his wife's side. But five days later, when Munthe informed him that Victoria was feeling better, Gustaf immediately went home; he did not stay a day longer than appearances demanded.

On 19 March Victoria set off for Italy accompanied by Axel and her suite in a direct train coach paid for by her mother. 'God grant that this trip will be of benefit to my daughter,' wrote the Grand Duchess: 'I had set aside the 3,000 marks which the extra coach cost me to pay for a large number of poor children to spend some time in the countryside.' It was not only Oscar II who groaned under the financial burden that Victoria's poor health entailed.

This time Victoria's general state of health was so poor that the improvement that usually took place on Capri was not forthcoming. On 11 April Axel informed Professor Adolf Passow, one of the Crown princess's German doctors, that her nose continued to run and that the secretion sometimes had blood mixed in – Victoria suffered from a chronic nasal catarrh called *ozæna*, or 'stink nose'. The situation was judged to be so serious that, in a letter to the Swedish foreign minister, Carl Bildt already spoke of the Crown princess in the past tense: 'Be prepared for the fact that the news about her cannot be other than bad. It is a great shame, for after all she had plenty of grit and she could have been a real boon to Sweden. Fate has not so decreed.'

RILKE, KEY AND GORKY

Things were not as bad as that. But they were bad enough for Victoria to be unable to see the Austrian poet Rainer Maria Rilke, who since February had been living with his friend Alice Faehndrich in the Villa Discopoli, down in Capri town. In March Ellen Key came to the island. There she met a new resident of Capri, Maxim Gorky, who had come to the island in November 1906. She was quite taken with the Russian writer, and wrote that he was 'the typical Russian artisan, full of goodness, honesty, genuineness . . . His whole demeanour is very subdued, awkward, extremely simple; his voice low and mild, he shuns any kind of social life, everything "bohemian", he lives in the greatest quietness, drinks milk and eats very little; loves his simple Russian food, which his wife sometimes cooks.'

If Gorky impressed Ellen Key, his appeal was less for Rilke, although the Austrian poet looked on Russia as his 'spiritual home'. The fact that Gorky allowed himself to be celebrated as an agitator on Capri and in Naples, Rilke wrote, 'has hardly endeared him to me'. Accordingly, despite Ellen Key's best attempts to try to induce Rilke to get to know Gorky, it was several months before the meeting took place. It was unexpectedly relaxed, but Rilke's impression that Gorky the revolutionary stood in the way of Gorky the artist remained unshaken.

Ellen Key had also asked Rilke to convey a greeting to Munthe (who was in Baden), a task which the poet carried out with far greater enthusiasm. After first having been up at the Villa San Michele and admired the view without meeting the owner, on 17 April Rilke was finally able to deliver the greeting. His mixed impression of Gorky stands in stark contrast to the unmixed enthusiasm he felt for Axel:

The meeting with *Munthe*, on the other hand, whom I visited yesterday, gave me *very* much. And I also have his best regards to convey to you. He is a remarkable human being, who understands life and whose innermost being must be a rare, empathetic goodness. He has really surrounded himself with the most beautiful objects, out of which he has made, not a museum, but a real home. – I will probably see him again.

On 29 April Axel and his patient left Capri and returned to Karlsruhe. Although Victoria's state of health was still very poor, Victoria insisted on returning to Stockholm. It was duty that called: on 6 June King Oscar and Queen Sophia would celebrate their golden wedding.

June was an unusually eventful month for the royal family. A week after the royal couple's golden wedding Victoria's second eldest son Wilhelm became engaged to the Russian princess Maria, daughter of Grand Prince Pavel Alexandrovitch. Russia's former emperor Alexander III was her uncle, and the present emperor, Nikolai II, her cousin.

If the royal year had begun in a major key, it ended in darkest minor. In October the 81-year-old Grand Duke of Baden died, and two months later came the turn of Oscar II. Victoria was now the Queen of Sweden and Axel had another title to add to that of physician-in-ordinary: physician to Her Majesty the Queen.

I Was Married in London a Month Ago

It was not only in the royal family that the year 1907 signified big changes. At the same time as Prince Wilhelm was getting engaged in St Petersburg, Axel sent the following letter to Baroness Ebba Åkerhielm, mistress of the robes to Queen Sophia:

> You have been so good to me that I wish to inform you myself about an important change in my life that nobody else knows about yet. I had my reasons for not rushing to announce it. After having tried in vain two years ago to find someone to be with me and read to me – I am now forced to abstain completely from reading – I have after long indecision accepted the generous offer made to me by a good woman immediately after I lost my eye, to marry me and help me. She is English and has known all my faults and weaknesses for twelve years. She is 30 years old and far too good for me. Since I lost my eye she has learnt Swedish in order to help me. I have taken a house in England from Sept. and shall then begin my new life. It was of course rather hard to get my patient here to see things from my point of view, but it has happened and the matter is now settled and nothing to keep secret. I was married in London a month ago. [. . .] She is clever and good, and a lady.

The form of words he adopted was a mild euphemism for the difficulties he must have had trying to persuade Victoria of the rightness of his decision. Her feelings for Axel were as strong as ever, as emerges from the loving letter to him of October 1906 in which she writes that he will fill her 'heart & soul [. . .] for ever'. There is no documentation to shed light on the Crown princess's reaction to the news that her 'darling' was going to marry and no longer be hers, or only hers. Fourteen years of a relationship which on Victoria's side was characterised by pure and passionate love now had to end, or at least be recalibrated.

After suffering a detached retina, Axel had a real need for someone who could help him and who would always be by his side. But why did he take the plunge just at this time? There were several reasons. For one thing, it was only a question of time before Victoria would become Sweden's queen – King Oscar was ailing in the spring of 1907 and was not expected to live for much longer – and their relationship even more difficult to sustain. For another thing, he may have found her 'courting' irritating, just as he did with other women who were in love with him. At heart, he was a lone wolf. Another motive may have been a desire to have heirs – after all, he had accumulated a fair amount of property and antiquities over the years.

In any event, there seems to have been no question of passionate love on Axel's part. One's thoughts inevitably return to his first marriage, with Ultima – was this marriage also an attempt to flee from another, impossible relationship?

The clever and good lady was called Hilda and was the daughter of John and Catherine Pennington Mellor. The father, who died the following summer, belonged to a wealthy English business family that owned a merchant fleet plying the route from Liverpool to Brazil. The family also owned cotton plantations in Egypt. His wife Catherine, née Wilson, was American and a divorcée. Their first child, their daughter Hilda, was born on 2 October 1876 – though she would later, for some reason, claim to have been born in 1882.

The family belonged to the contemporary equivalent of the 'jet-set', and Hilda – like her brother John who was three years younger – spent her childhood and teenage years on the move. In the course of a grand tour that lasted several years and was undertaken in their own railway coach, they visited Paris, Athens and Rome, the French Alps and the Wagner festivals in Germany. Mr and Mrs Pennington Mellor were great Italophiles, their honeymoon was spent in Rome and it was probably in that same city that Hilda and Axel saw each other for the first time. Axel was the Pennington Mellor family's doctor, as he was the doctor to so many other English families in Rome. The first prescription in Munthe's hand that has survived is from 1898, and the first one written out for Hilda is dated August 1903.

The Pennington Mellors owned a palatial Tudor-style country house near Biarritz, on France's Atlantic coast, known for its mild climate and health-giving saltwater baths. Ever since Napoleon III had built a chateau there for the Empress Eugénie fifty years earlier, the resort had been a playground for the aristocracy of Europe. Here they lived a typical English country house lifestyle, with tea drinking and fox hunting. The latter pursuit can hardly have been to Axel's taste, but everything else accorded with his ideals. Hilda was not only good and clever and pretty, she was also English, and through her upbringing and her travels she had cultivated an interest in art and culture that he valued highly. However, Hilda's father was not enthusiastic about the relationship. Her mother too did what she could to prevent the marriage, which led Hilda to call her a 'stupid undeveloped woman' in a letter to Axel. Whether it was the difference in their ages or Axel's reputation as a lady-killer that made them uneasy, or both things together, Hilda's parents did all they could to make their daughter change her mind.

All their efforts were in vain. Hilda was determined to unite her life with Axel's. The wedding took place on 16 May 1907 in the little parish church near Hyde Park Terrace, where Hilda's uncle lived. But it was no splendid society wedding of the kind one might have expected, given the social status of the couple. When Axel wrote to Baroness Åkerhielm saying that no one knew about this change in his life, he was speaking the truth. It is not known when the Crown princess was informed about the marriage, but it only became official two months after the wedding, on 17 July, when it was announced in a small classified advertisement in *The Times*. 'Everything is "mysterious" and "secretive", of course,' was the sour comment of the Crown princess's chamberlain.

The wedding itself was a quick and unglamorous affair. According to his own account, Axel arrived in London from the continent at 10 in the morning and travelled back alone later the same day. This is an astonishing piece of information, even considering Axel's known egocentricity, but there is an explanation for it. The wedding took place while Victoria was seriously ill, and as her personal physician Axel could not leave Baden for more than a few days at most. As the Crown princess's lady-in-waiting noted, he was true to his vocation, and he suffered.

His behaviour was dubious from a romantic perspective but the more praiseworthy from a professional point of view. In so far as Hilda had views on the matter, his priorities ought to have raised him in her eyes rather than the other way round. Axel's strikingly passive attitude ('I was married in London a month ago') stands in stark contrast to Hilda's adoration of the person who had now become her husband – and to her respect for his need of freedom. In a long letter, written before their marriage and shot through with admiration and self-effacing love, she lays down the rules of play for their marriage:

I love you darling, I want to be near you, to see you – even for a small tiny bit each day I would be grateful – and now I smile as I remember once you said to me that if you had me with you for always that I must not think you would stay with me to go about with me all day. I laughed then too for I had thought of that often before and planned how I must keep out of your way often and never let you feel that because of me you were less full, or had to take me with you, or anything, save only when you wished and when it suited you. [. . .] Some days when I feel happier, when for a few minutes I allow myself to draw pictures in my thoughts – I think and almost cannot believe I should ever be good enough for God to let me be with you, living in your home, and able to do those humble services a woman can – that I might see you a little each day, save when you travelled for I don't think we should ever be rich enough for me to go a long distance too, but I should be quite happy at home waiting till you came back and taking care of it for you, and I could not cost much so long as I did not travel.

Axel must take care of himself and think of his health, Hilda is frightened that he is so thin and eats so little for someone of his size. He is only skin and bone, it feels as if he is about to disappear. 'Does it all come from insomnia – indeed it would be cause enough – and nervousness? Or do you think your food does not digest rightly and does you no good?' Hilda is not only a loving woman but also a Sister of Mercy. Axel was too good and his life too precious to waste – he was, she explained later, 'like Jesus Christ'.

As we have seen, Axel had received many proposals of marriage but had turned them all down. He was now almost 50, blind in one eye and in need of someone who could help him with the practicalities of life. Yet, according to his own words, he was not an easily captured prize – it was only 'after long hesitation' that he accepted her offer. Hilda had already shown what she was capable of before they married. For Axel's sake, she learned Swedish from the Swedish nurse who took care of her father during his last few years. And it was she who taught Axel how to use a typewriter.

As soon as Axel could arrange some free time, around midsummer, he took Hilda on a honeymoon trip to Scandinavia. He met her in Copenhagen, but Hilda was not impressed by the Danish capital. It was otherwise with Stockholm – 'most beautiful, islands with trees and wide roads of water, magnificent streets all so broad', she wrote to her mother. On 2 July the newly weds continued on to Dalarna. Like the wedding itself, the honeymoon was conducted at lightning speed: 'Axel has kept me going so fast that I had no time from ½ to 7 when I began my day until after 11 when I ended it.' The picture postcard that Hilda sent to her parents shows Leksand Church, girls in local dress and log cabins. She was delighted with the pretty folk costumes and by the little children who looked like 'small old pictures in wide yellow pleated skirts and lace fichews'. When Axel wanted to show Hilda Sweden, he chose the region he loved the best.

Axel and Hilda's first home was at 31 St James's Place, Piccadilly, in a house which belonged to Hilda's aunt. We do not know how long Axel stayed there, nor do we know how much time in general he spent with his new wife, in London or elsewhere. According to Carl Bildt, Axel had made clear to Hilda that he wished them to spend only half the year together, on Capri or in London. That Axel should have made such a condition sounds plausible, and there is no evidence that Hilda had any objection to make. On the contrary, it fits in with the spiritual and geographical freedom that she had promised him in the letter quoted above. When he now specified the conditions for their life together, it was not because he wanted to exploit Hilda's weak psychological position, but because he was that kind of person. Just as he seldom travelled in Ultima's company, so it was to be with Hilda.

The Malt House and Stengården

Quite apart from Axel's tendency to travel alone, Hilda was soon enough bound to the house for natural reasons. Exactly nine months after the trip to Dalarna, on 3 April 1908, the couple's first child was born: a boy who was christened John Axel Viking, but who was to be known as Peter. 'The boy is uncommonly big and lively, and – I am afraid – very like his daddy,' Axel reported to his cousin Ludvig: 'He would have done better to have taken after his mummy, who is more harmonious and calm and tranquil.' Two years later when Hilda gave birth to another boy, Axel wrote that same day, 30 January 1910, to Anna, asking her to send an almanac with 'old Swedish names'. This Anna did, and the baby was given the names Ludvig Malcolm Grane Martin. He was called Malcolm or Grane – the latter being the name of Sigurd Fafnisbani's mount in the Icelandic saga (and of Siegfried's in Wagner's *Twilight of the Gods*). Victoria could not have borne Axel any children, but now when he had children by another woman, she became their godmother.

Through his marriage to Hilda, and the fact that he had two children with British citizenship, Axel's ties to England were strengthened. His first contacts had been through the 'misses from Medstugan' and through Georg Sibbern and his English wife, and thanks to the English colony in Rome he had acquired countless patients in Great Britain. In 1901 he was elected a member of St James's Club in London. Among other members were the fifth Earl of Carnarvon, Axel's old acquaintance General Calthorpe, the sculptor Waldo Story, Cecil Rhodes, and – from 1903 – Carl Bildt (who for a few years was Swedish minister to Great Britain). The person who recommended Axel for membership was James Rennell Rodd, who between 1901 and 1904 was a counsellor at the British embassy in Rome and by the time of Axel's marriage had been promoted to His Majesty's envoy in Stockholm.

The boys were born in London. But the Munthes also had another home in England, The Malt House in the village of Broadway in the Cotswolds. Thus Axel and Hilda commuted between London, Broadway, Anacapri, Biarritz and Sweden.

The Crown princess had been spending the winter on Capri ever since Axel left his practice in Rome and had become deeply attached to the island. However, she could not always rely on getting the Hotel Paradiso to herself, and therefore she asked Axel to help her buy a house and refurbish it according to her needs. As Axel now lived in Torre di Materita she chose a house in the village of Caprile, only a quarter of an hour's walk from Axel's tower. Casa Caprile, as the house was called, was officially owned by Axel but was used by Victoria. While Axel was at it, he bought himself a house right next-door, the Villa Sole.

As soon as Axel started spending less time at San Michele, he started thinking about renting out or disposing of the villa, which was expensive to maintain. He was thinking so loudly that in October 1904 Elsie Carnarvon, widow of the fourth Earl of Carnarvon, enquired about the price. Axel initiated Hilda into his plans and she replied:

I have thought of your plan about San Michele again, and I know it is *right*, though it hurts to think that it would no longer be yours – that living house made from your heart and all you, with your true thoughts, made lovely and white and pure; but then dearest I too feel less the need of possessions one can touch, I realise how we should work *for the work*; and if the *end*, the *result*, is great then in addition to the work – one has left something beautiful to help and teach others, and you have done this so San Michele may pass from your hands without our regret. It made you happy to create it, and you did it nobly and well, now it shall stand as a living thing of beauty and you can pass on doing other things.

It was important to Hilda that Axel should not wear himself out again as he had done during the years in Rome. The money he received for San Michele would make him financially independent.

Axel did not sell the villa, choosing instead to rent it out. The first tenant was one of his American patients, Mrs Bodine, who from 1904 onwards rented La Foresteria and from 1905 San Michele too. The combined annual rent was 16,000 lire, which corresponds to £640 or around £32,000 in today's values. It was not small change. If Mrs Bodine had chosen to live for a year with full board at the Hotel Paradiso, she would have spent only a third as much.

Axel owned houses and homes everywhere except in Sweden. He was a manic builder but was home so seldom that he clearly felt he did not need a house of his own there. Now that Victoria was queen and Axel had been appointed her personal physician, he had to spend more time in Sweden than previously. In addition, he was married and one way to acquaint his wife with his homeland was to acquire an address there. Axel's gaze turned towards Dalarna, his favourite part of Sweden.

Dalarna was the focus of the strong National Romantic currents during the second half of the nineteenth century and the region came to be seen as the quintessence of pre-industrial, unspoilt Sweden. Here could be found genuine, industrious country people of a kind that had already disappeared in other parts of the country.

Axel, Hilda, their son Peter and their servants spent the late summer of 1909 in Leksand, one of the most picturesque towns in Dalarna, in order to negotiate taking over the lease of a building plot, and in September the parish council agreed 'that physician-in-ordinary A. Munthe could lease a site belonging to the church for 50 years'.

Building work began in March 1910. The house in Leksand was a stone manor house in partly Danish style. If Axel had designed – or at least conceived – San Michele himself, this time he relied on a well-known architect, Torben Grut, whom he had got to know during the building of Solliden. The house was ready by the end of 1911. When the courtyard was paved at the beginning of the 1920, the house, which hitherto had mostly been called 'Munthe's', was given the name 'Stengården' (The Stone Yard).

MESSINA

In December 1909, Axel published his first book in Swedish since 1888. It was called *Bref och skisser. Gammalt och nytt av Puck Munthe* (Letters and Sketches. Old and New from Puck Munthe). It contained nothing new, with one exception: the sketch 'Messina', which was the first new piece that Axel had published in twenty years. The event that released his creative powers was a catastrophe that occurred at the end of 1908: the earthquake at Messina in Sicily and at Reggio di Calabria on the other side of the strait. The area had been hit many times before, but the earthquake which devastated Messina and Reggio on the morning of 28 December 1908 was the worst ever. Over 70,000 people were killed and towns and villages lay in ash and ruins.

Axel, who happened to be in Capri, immediately rushed to the scene, driven by the twin forces that always drew him to disaster areas: the desire to help and his curiosity about death.

On 11 January he wrote from Catania in Sicily to Karl Warburg:

> I came here yesterday evening from Messina where it is not worth the trouble of staying any longer – nevertheless, *yesterday* (11 days under the ruins!) I saw a man + a woman who had been buried alive – the man surprisingly well, the woman looking as if she might die – many died just as they were being dug out. I have experienced things compared with which the cholera in Naples was child's play. Messina was dreadful, but Calabria (Reggio and the villages up as far as Palmi) *even worse!*'

He wanted to write about the catastrophe, but three days later when he was in Naples he told Warburg:

> I am just beginning to feel the effects of the dreadful events I have experienced and I have not yet regained sufficient coolness of mind to be able to compress the unspeakable things I have lived through into article-form. I am well aware that the newspaper would like to have such a contribution *immediately*. But I cannot. Moreover, I fear I will soon have to travel to meet the queen. I am currently in a very unsuitable mood for practising at court and shall try to postpone this business for as long as possible.

Nevertheless, he had committed to paper some 'first impressions'; 'As you can see I am still an idealist down here – *vis à vis the people*. The behaviour of the authorities has been deplorable and the muddle is still unbelievable and the official reports untrue.'

The 27 January 1909 saw the publication of the article 'From the Land of Natural Catastrophes and Scenes of Horror. The Impressions of a Swedish Reader and Doctor', with an editorial commentary informing readers that the letter had been sent in by 'the well-known physician and author Dr Axel Munthe (pen-name Puck)'. Chamberlain Carl Ossbahr was critical about what he saw as a 'sentimental and disingenuous' account of events: 'All that he denies was true; it was the people themselves who were the wild animals let loose. When M. arrived, this was perhaps no longer obvious, but from his letter one would almost believe that he was there from the start. The troops have, as always here, been best, although of course people abused them [. . .].'

Bref och skisser was greeted enthusiastically in the Swedish press. Munthe's old admirers were joined now by the influential literary critic Klara Johansson, who said she was 'blushing at having for decades ignored one of the finest and most individual prose lyricists writing in Swedish'.

In June 1910 the president of Italy's council of ministers presented Axel with the Messina medal for his contribution after the earthquake disaster. He accepted it, but undoubtedly with mixed feelings. What had he done apart from paying off another instalment of his moral debt? Messina and Calabria had meant experiences of a kind that no honours could undo. Axel returned to the disaster in *The Story of San Michele*, the illustrated edition of which (London, 1936) contained no fewer than twelve photographs of the victims of the earthquake.

THE QUEEN

May God reward you for all you have done for me.
Princess Marie to Axel Munthe

L ESS THAN A month after Victoria became Queen of Sweden she headed south again. On 4 January 1908 she travelled to Baden, where she took to her bed for almost the entire month. At the beginning of April she made her usual trip to Venice, where she remained for three weeks.

We do not know if Munthe was with the queen in Venice. Perhaps he was in London, where his son Peter was born on 3 April. But he was present during the state visits that took place after Victoria had become queen. The first began in Berlin on 31 May 1908. On the same day Kaiser Wilhelm made Munthe a Knight of the Royal Prussian Order of the Crown, second class. But for Munthe, the visit to Berlin was memorable for quite another reason. One of Wilhelm II's closest associates was the diplomat and statesman Prince Philipp zu Eulenburg (1847–1921), a politician of liberal views and a multi-talented person who wrote poetry and stories and composed *lieder*. During the Kaiser's visit to Tullgarn in 1893 he had entertained the royal couple with his music and his dazzling conversation. Victoria had known Eulenburg since his time as Prussian minister in Karlsruhe and had a high opinion of him. Just as had been the case with Munthe, it was music that united them.

When Victoria came to Berlin in 1908, the influential courtier was in disgrace. In his newspaper *Die Zukunft*, the social-democratic journalist Maximilian Harden had accused the father of six of homosexual debauchery and of abusing the Kaiser's trust in him. The attacks were inspired by Eulenburg's political enemies, who wished to neutralise his political influence. For those in the know, the details of the prince's sexual excesses came as no surprise. Chamberlain Carl Anton Ossbahr, for example, could tell stories about Eulenburg's 'repulsive acts', some of which he had even witnessed himself during the latter's time as German attaché in Sweden. According to Ossbahr, Eulenburg's sexual behaviour was 'linked to a kind of mysticism which is supposed to have fascinated the Kaiser'.

Despite what had happened, Victoria refused to shun her old friend. If her 'intimacy' with Eulenburg caused Ossbahr 'endless discomfort', it was otherwise with Munthe, who took himself off to the prison hospital on the queen's account to deliver a letter from her. Eulenburg later told some friends how important the visit had been for him. If the queen found the situation delicate there can be no doubt that Munthe found the task a stimulating one. It satisfied his natural desire to provoke. Kaiser Wilhelm was less amused by the queen's and her doctor's initiative, something that hardly bothered Munthe, who had had been keeping an eye on the Kaiser since his visit to San Michele four years earlier.

Maria Pavlovna

Victoria's custom was to travel south at the beginning of the year, but her winter holiday of 1913 began as early as November 1912, when her poor health forced her to leave Sweden. To prevent the queen from feeling lonely, the king asked Prince Wilhelm's wife Princess Maria to keep her company during the Christmas holiday. The princess had lived in Sweden since 1908, but it was on Capri that she first met Munthe, whom she described as 'a rather elderly man with a little pointed beard', whose tinted glasses did not quite succeed in hiding his piercing gaze, which was 'keen as a blade and shone with intelligence'. Munthe was living as usual in his tower but he visited the queen each afternoon, and on these occasions they would make music together. The queen played the piano and the doctor and the princess sang.

The queen was too weak to spend much time outdoors but Princess Maria and Munthe went on long walks and excursions, and he showed her all the sights of the island, 'for which he had a real passion'. Maria had never before met anyone who talked to her like Axel did. He was a man with a 'rich talent', he had 'profound knowledge of the human heart' and his conversation was always extremely interesting. 'The lonely life he had led for years had taught him a great deal', remembered Princess Maria, 'and he talked to me about both books and history, about nature and human beings'. She called on him in Torre di Materita, where he lived like 'a hermit, sunk in thought and in contemplation of the silent world that surrounded him'.

The princess very soon grew to trust Munthe, and opened her heart to him. She told him about her childhood and upbringing, about her marriage and the 'disappointments' life had brought her. Her marriage to Wilhelm was unhappy and she did not feel at home at the stiff Swedish court. In actual fact Princess Maria was in roughly the same situation and state of mind as Crown Princess Victoria when she had contacted Munthe twenty years previously: her marriage was in a bad way, and here was a sympathetic person who was willing to listen to her problems. She complained about her 'spiritual loneliness' and talked about her physical health, which was suffering from all her troubles. Munthe conscientiously noted down all she said and came to the conclusion that she was probably suffering from a kidney disease. When Maria returned to Stockholm it was with the certain conviction, she wrote, 'that I had acquired a new friend and perhaps a very powerful ally'.

Maria left Capri on 28 December 1912 and was back in Stockholm in early January. As soon as she got home she wrote a letter to Munthe, enclosing two photographs, of which he preferred 'the girlish looking one in the white frock'. It was clear from her letter that she was as depressed as before: it had, he replied, a 'sad note of loneliness', and it was a bitter feeling that he could not help her. But he had an idea:

> Already in the autumn I insisted to the king upon the necessity to find somebody later on to come here to keep the queen company, as it would be far too long a time to be here with me as almost sole companion. I knew already then that she would hardly speak to her suite, what in fact she has hardly done since you left. I insisted upon the fact that this long isolation would be unhealthy if prolungated [sic] almost one half of a year. We all agreed. So does her mother. [. . .].

After much thought, Munthe had found a suitable person whom he would ask to come down at Easter, as soon as he was convinced that she was willing to come 'to our rescue'. He therefore wrote to Princess Maria to ask her to investigate the matter. It is clear from the letter that Munthe had fallen for the princess's charm just as much as she had for his:

> This person is young and bright as we want her to be and she has on a previous occasion shown great tact and kindness in dealing with my patient. She is buoyant and full of untamed strength like a caucasian pony and can brush away depression and morbid thoughts from a tired brain like a fresh gush of wind from the sea brushes asunder some old cobweb from a dusk corner in my tower. She sings and whizzles like a bird the whole day and there is a vague parfum of Rose-Mary about her – God knows from where it comes! She loves chocolate and brown bread – alas! she loves flirting also, but when there is no victim at hand she is just as jolly for all that and quite satisfied to put this eminent quality of hers to a well-earned rest contenting herself with occasionally turning upside down a guileless chamberlain to Her Majesty the queen of Sweden or a sulky old pilot in a watchtower. She has green eyes, at least she says so – well, I will tell you more about those eyes of hers when we meet, if you

promise me not to repeat it to her. But will she accept to come if the queen asks her, or is the hand that holds her in Sweden strong enough to keep her back from her evident duty as well-educated daughter-in-law?

'She' was of course Maria herself. Axel advised her to travel down to Capri, taking full responsibility himself. In a complex metaphor he saw her as a ship that had strayed onto the wrong course, and he offered himself as her pilot:

The ship is sound, I know, for I have a keen eye for all that belongs to the sea. A fine ship, graceful and strong, capsizable maybe, but unsinkable I believe. Even the rudder may not be broken, maybe it is only the compass that is out of order. If so she needs a pilot for there are rocks ahead and plenty of hidden reefs where the finest ship may founder. I happen to belong to the finest sailing club in the world as far as seamanship goes, I have steered many a boat through worse weather than the ship is facing now. Will she not take me as a pilot for a while until she is safe in port? Nelson, England's finest sailor, had only one eye and only one arm and I have two arms and pretty strong ones too, my words are somewhat rough and my hand somewhat hard but my head is clear and my heart is in the right place, she has heard it beat and she knows it is so.

Maria was overjoyed by Munthe's initiative, assuring him how 'delighted' and 'thankful' she was that he was helping her. And the king was, she wrote, 'secretly delighted that he will not be obliged to be alone with your patient during his stay on the island' – another confirmation of the total estrangement that existed between the royal spouses. She herself would be happy to 'get away from Stockholm and all the horrid people' – she was in bad shape mentally, and Munthe must promise to be very kind to her as she would be very lonely: 'I want the old tower to hide my sad eyes and help me on. Oh, how lovely to see all that fairy tale again, I hope the moon and the stars will be kind to me this time also. Dear Anacapri, I will see it all very soon now again.'

On 15 March Maria came with the king to Capri. Gustaf, who did not want to spend too long in his wife's company, stayed for only one week before travelling on to Rome and Nice.

The habits they had adopted during the Christmas visit were resumed: Munthe and the princess sang, accompanied by the queen, they went on long walks and they continued to converse. But according to Maria, there had been 'a small change' in 'Doctor Munthe's manner'. His earlier mildness and friendliness had been replaced by a noticeable sternness. He rebuked her for superficiality and thoughtlessness and reproached her for living a life lacking in spirituality, in other words, the same reproaches that he used to direct against all women from the higher social classes. But Maria did not complain, she found it quite natural that he talked like this to her and 'honestly hoped to find in his advice help and guidance for the future'.

According to Munthe, the princess suffered from 'intense headaches, nausea, fits of retching, great weakness and anxiety, poor sleep, powerful itching all over her body, lack of sensation in her fingers (doigt mort), shortness of breath, pain around her backbone [. . .], cramp in her calves and vertigo'. In his opinion, these ailments were symptoms of a 'mild renal poisoning'. The princess's temporary loss of sight pointed in the same direction, he wrote in a report to the king.

In mid-May the queen and the princess left Capri and travelled to Rome and Karlsruhe, where Maria was examined by Munthe and a German professor who confirmed Munthe's diagnosis. 'Now my fate hung in the balance,' the princess wrote in her memoirs, published seventeen years later: 'In future I would be obliged to leave my family and my home, to live for more than half the year abroad and be regarded as ill.'

It sounds plausible: the authoritative and authoritarian doctor who diagnoses his patient as ill in order to get her in his power. This would also agree well with the picture of Munthe as he emerges from the pages of this book – a man with a boundless need to give orders and be obeyed. But was this really the case? The correspondence between the princess and Munthe tells a different story.

On 3 June Maria, her husband Crown Prince Wilhelm and the 4-year-old Prince Lennart travelled to Moscow to take part in the tercentenary celebrations of the Romanov dynasty. 'When I returned unwillingly and with anxiety in my heart to Sweden, I found that plans for the winter had now been definitely laid down,' Maria wrote in her memoirs, as if she had had something against these plans. But the letters she wrote after her homecoming to Munthe, who also happened to be in Sweden, give another picture both of the travel plans and of her relationship to her doctor:

> I have been counting the hours till I will see you again, I am thinking of you the [w]hole time, always. How delightful it will be to see you[,] to talk to you, why did you not decide this before. I would have certainly not gone to Russia, it will be so short only to see you the day. [. . .] I have just had my dinner all alone in the big dining room and am delighted to be alone. You will only come the day after tomorrow, but I love to sit here and talk to you in my thoughts even if I will see you only a few hours after you read this.
>
> I have been in very low spirits all these days and come more and more to the conviction that I will never be able to get well in this place [. . .] I long for you the [w]hole time. You are the only friend of this now tired, sad, lonely thing which I have become and you are the only person I

want painfully to see. I am longing for you. [. . .] will you come and have breakfast with us at 9? The motor will fetch you. *Do* come as quick as you can. Will you be with me the [w]hole day, please do, dear. Love from Rosemary.

On 13 October 1913 one could read in a bulletin from the court that two days later Maria would travel to southern Italy, as she had been ordered to spend the winter in a more southerly climate on account of 'a kidney complaint acquired during the past winter'. 'Thus,' chamberlain Jean Jacques De Geer wrote to Munthe, 'if you hear nothing further, the Princess's first lunch at San Michele will be on Monday the 2th of this month.'

There was no lunch at San Michele. Maria was met in Berlin by her brother Dmitri, who took her to Paris, where her father and stepmother were waiting. On 21 October Maria's father, Grand Duke Pavel Alexandrovitch, sent a letter to his nephew Nikolai, the Russian tsar, describing the princess's wretched state of health on arrival in Paris: 'She was fainting every minute, she was white as a sheet, she could not eat or sleep, she was coughing dreadfully, and she still complains about her kidneys.' It was, he continued, 'unthinkable that she should return to Sweden, and I beg your permission for us to begin negotiating a divorce. At any rate, it is better than her life there and the harassment of the impudent old mesmerizer Munthe.'

Maria had left Wilhelm and Sweden for good. The marriage had never been harmonious and after the birth of their son Lennart in 1909 the couple had drifted apart more and more. The divorce came through the following year.

IN SAVINSKY'S CLAWS?

At first, Princess Maria had seen in Munthe someone who would 'solve all difficulties' and give her life 'a new meaning', but after living with him for ten months, she wrote in her memoirs, she was 'even more irresolute than before'. Moreover, Munthe had wanted to transform her into an invalid. Against the background of the letters quoted, this looks like a rationalisation. Besides, to classify his patients as ill was not part of Munthe's method of treatment. On the contrary, his method was to employ suggestion in order to make them well again.

Maria was emotionally suggestible at this time and it is clear that the 22-year-old princess saw something of a father figure in Munthe, who was nearly twice her age. That he in his turn found her fascinating emerges clearly from his letters to her, which in tone and language are at the limits of what could be regarded as permissible in exchanges between a doctor and his patient.

It is, however, clear that Maria's view of Munthe changed radically after the break-up with Sweden and her husband. This can be seen, for example, in a letter to her lady-in-waiting, dated 1 December 1913: 'My God, if only people knew what a dangerous man Munthe is, if only the Queen would wake up and see him as he is, then perhaps all my dreadful experiences would have served some purpose. Yes, I wish him nothing good.'

According to the princess, there were two circumstances that precipitated her decision to leave Sweden: her unhappy marriage to Wilhelm, and her fear of becoming all too dependent on Munthe. That Maria left Wilhelm was not too surprising; the marriage was a disaster. But how could her profound trust in Munthe change into its opposite in such a short time? After all, as late as the end of July she had thanked him for all the good he had done her and said that she was longing to come to Capri.

One reason for her sudden change of attitude may have been the visit that Munthe (for once accompanied by Hilda) made to Russia at the end of September and which Maria saw as an attempt to win over her aunt 'totally for his plans regarding my future'. But this suspicion can hardly have sufficed to awaken the hatred of Munthe that in such a short time wiped out her earlier feelings for him. Were there other factors that could have contributed to her sudden change of attitude?

There were indeed. In the autumn of 1913 a serious diplomatic drama was played out in total secrecy between Sweden and Russia. A Swedish officer was accused of having passed on important information to a foreign power, and the Russian military attaché was asked to leave the country. The Russians refused to accept the grounds for his dismissal and asked the Swedish government to present further proof, which they declined to do. Why? Rumour had it that the government could not lay all their cards on the table as a high-born lady of royal blood was involved.

The rumours were further fed by the fact that the Ministry of Foreign Affairs, at a confidential meeting, asked the Swedish newspapers to keep quiet about Russian involvement in the affair, an appeal that was respected. However, in the Scandinavian and European press it was reported that the princess had had intimate dealings with the Russian minister in Sweden, Alexander Savinsky. When Savinsky as well as Princess Maria suddenly left Sweden, it was taken as proof of her involvement. It was even rumoured that King Gustaf had ordered her to travel abroad and to stay away for as long as the spy affair continued.

According to Carl Bildt in Rome, there was some substance in the claim that the princess was involved with Savinsky in one way or another. Building on confidential information from the Ministry of Foreign Affairs, the envoy reported that she was 'in Savinsky's claws' and feared 'being blackmailed by him, as he has in his possession several letters which could possibly be compromising'.

It is presumably to this affair, with its classic ingredients of love and espionage, that we should look for an explanation of Maria's sudden change of attitude to Munthe. Was it actually Savinsky and a potential blackmail attempt that she feared and fled from? Perhaps Munthe, who was always the subject of rumours, was a convenient scapegoat in a situation where other more compromising circumstances had to be concealed? If it could be proved that a Swedish princess had engaged in such a superficial erotic or political flirtation with the ambassador of her former homeland, the consequences could be catastrophic.

IN THE FINNISH ARCHIPELAGO

Grand Duke Pavel Alexandrovitch's description of Munthe as 'the impudent old mesmerizer' indicates that Axel was well known at the Russian court. And so he was. As a result of Wilhelm's marriage to Maria, the Russian imperial house and the Swedish royal house had been linked more closely to each other, and members of the Romanov family often visited Sweden. In June 1909 the Russian imperial family paid a visit to Sweden and three years later Gustaf and Victoria made a return visit. In 1912 defence was the pressing issue of the day, the Swedish people contributed 17 million kronor towards the building of an armoured cruiser, and the famous explorer Sven Hedin wrote a fervent appeal – *A Word of Warning* – about the threat from Russia. In July the Swedish and Russian royal couples met on their respective vessels *Oscar II* and *Standard* in the Finnish archipelago. The meeting was planned as a family get-together, but took on a political dimension. The foreign ministries had talks on board and the official press emphasised that the meeting was a 'new proof of the growing friendship between the two countries'.

Munthe was included in the queen's suite. In connection with the state visit of 1909 he had been awarded the Order of Stanislaus, second class, and this time he received a present from the imperial couple. Munthe had several private conversations with the Russian imperial couple, and on one occasion the Empress Alexandra asked if he would not consider becoming her physician, given that he had done so much to make 'Vicky' well.

Munthe's trip to Russia at the end of September 1913 may well have been connected with the empress's offer, even if Princess Maria put a different construction on it. Whatever the truth of the matter, Munthe met the tsar's family and received from the tsarina the gift of a silver box bearing a representation of St Michael. It was supposed to have belonged originally to Peter the Great. The tsarina never became Munthe's patient; perhaps it was simply that the war intervened. But the thought is mind-boggling – Rasputin and Munthe at the same court!

EVERY APPEARANCE OF A WILD MAN

However one interprets the business with Princess Maria, it is clear that Munthe was to some extent a different person now from what he had been fifteen or twenty years earlier. Certain aspects of his personality had become accentuated. If almost all earlier testimony had been unanimously positive and had asserted his kindness, goodness and 'sympathetic nature', now, more and more often, it was the negative aspects of his character that were commented on: his need to give orders and be obeyed, his need to be in control, his irritability and irascible moods.

No doubt certain inherent tendencies became more pronounced over the years. But if we want to understand Munthe's character we must also take account of his great handicap: the deterioration of his sight. Since losing the sight in one eye in 1904 he was constantly afraid for the other one, in which he also had poor vision. As a result, he seldom spent time outdoors during the day. Munthe's fear was justified: the vision in his left eye was gradually getting worse and by the end of the 1920s he would become almost totally blind.

In addition to the deterioration of his eyesight, he suffered from insomnia, an inheritance from his father who 'went to pieces from the same evil'. Munthe was therefore forced to take medication to help him sleep: at this time, usually veronal, earlier, morphine, the nineteenth century's universal cure for anxiety and insomnia. These two afflictions in combination contributed to his recurrent depression and to the irritability and impatience to which he himself and others bore witness and which increased with the years. 'Insomnia does not kill its man unless he kills himself,' he wrote in *The Story of San Michele*. 'But it kills his joie de vivre, it saps his strength, it sucks the blood from his brain and from his heart like a vampire.'

To free herself from Munthe's influence, Princess Maria was forced to turn against him. But not everyone reacted in this way; many women who found themselves under his spell dealt with the 'problem' in less dramatic fashion. One of them was Clare Frewen (1885–1970), who belonged to a famous English-American family. Her maternal aunt Jennie was married to Lord Randolph Churchill, making Clare herself a cousin of Winston. She was encouraged to become an author by Henry James and Rudyard Kipling, who was a near neighbour when she was growing up. Clare Frewen was a self-taught sculptor who spent some time in the Soviet Union in the 1920s and made portraits of some of the country's leaders, including Lenin and Trotsky. Her best friend Margaret Connaught became Crown Princess of Sweden and in September 1909 she and the Crown princess received an invitation from Queen Victoria to visit Solliden. In her memoir *Nuda veritas* (1928) she draws a brilliant portrait of Munthe that shows him in all his majestic contrariness: cultivated, charming, captivating, good with the poor, but at the same time brusque, impatient, demanding, domineering. First, on a visit to Solliden:

> He seemed strangely out of place, a courtier neither in manner nor appearance, he wore rough clothes, ran long knotted fingers through his hair till it stood on end, paced the drawing-room back and forth as if he wanted to get out, drummed impatiently on tables and window panes, emitted grunts instead of answers – and had, in fact, every appearance of a wild man; he was not young and he wore black glasses. [. . .]
>
> The things that people say are never worth repeating, but Munthe was an endless theme of discussion and of conjecture, of love and hate. Remembering the things I had heard I was much interested at meeting him. We used to go for long long walks – he said I was young and needed exercise. He made me get up at seven in the morning and walk with him for an hour before breakfast. He suffered, he said, from insomnia, and liked to begin his day at dawn. He had a disease of the eyes and had lost the sight of one, the other was threatened. Sunlight hurt him, he preferred the day before the light grew strong. [. . .]
>
> Perhaps it was Munthe's presence that was responsible for the absence of ceremony in the Queen's household. One felt she might be ceremonious, and that she would enjoy pomp; but Munthe would, I think, have left the house. He was dreadfully impatient.

Munthe invited Clare Frewin to come and visit him on Capri, where she could stay in Torre della Guardia. She travelled there the following spring together with her mother.

> I remember how preciously he guarded 'Guardia', that none except a few peasants living near, might know of it. Even the postman was not allowed to bring me letters, but had to deposit them at 'Materita'. [. . .]
>
> [The tower] consisted of a sitting-room, full of books and flowers and old Italian furniture, from which a ladder led up through a hole in the ceiling to my bedroom. It was domed and had white tiles on the floors, a coloured porcelain Madonna over the bed and whitewashed walls. In the face of one window the sun did rise and in the face of the other it did set. There was a delicious Spartan simplicity as of a convent. [. . .]

During the ensuing weeks, Munthe ruled me with a rod of iron. He was by nature domineering and dictatorial; he set himself to enforce all kinds of rules, with which, however, I was in such complete accord that conforming made me appear docile. For instance, I must never go for long walks alone. This I had no need to do, for he was always ready to accompany me and a pleasanter companion could not have been chosen.

I must never, he said, go down to Capri, which was a foul place full of tourists. I had no desire whatever to go down to Capri!

I must remain, he said, awfully secluded and hidden and quiet, whether I liked it or not. I liked it!

I must live simply, not in the lavish worldly way in which I was accustomed. I never had lived in any but a simple way.

I must try to cast out the Americanism that was in me. I must forget the crowds and the amusements and the garishness of my habitual life, and try to appreciate the stillness, the peace, the grandeur of nature, the atmosphere of the gods that reigned on my mountain cliff. And I laughed and danced for joy because I had found the realization of my dreams. [. . .]

He had the qualities and faults of Tiberius; his tyranny and kindliness, and his vanity also. He might have been, and I believed he was, a reincarnation of the Imperator, drawn back to the scene of his past and doomed in this life to pay back an overburdened Karma. [. . .]

Every morning before the light was strong, Tiberio and I met somewhere outside my gate and went for a long walk. I was never sure where he would be. Sometimes I was impelled thoughtlessly to start off in a quite unusual direction, and sure enough, it always led me to him.

During the glare of the day which obliged him to remain in his cool darkened house, I sat in the olive groves sketching. All day and every day I sketched. Everywhere there was a background of vivid blue, either sea or sky, and the fantastic silhouettes of twisted thousand-year-old stems. Munthe's garden, too, was an endless delight, full of orange trees and terraces, pergolas where geraniums grew like weeds, and shady paths bordered with acanthus. His house had Greek carved marble doorways and the windows were inset with twisted marble columns. [. . .]

Only once did I ever see him without his black glasses. He took them off deliberately and looked at me. The sensation was indescribable. I cried out as if hurt, and turned away, but without knowing the reason why. I always wished that I could face his eyes again, the second time I should have been prepared. [. . .]

When the glare of the day was over he went to see the Queen, who, I may add, was extremely displeased with him for bringing me to Anacapri. Sometimes, from my look-out post, I saw her familiar figure in a tight tailor-made, surmounted by a man's hard straw hat, walking down the stony track that led to the lighthouse, followed by her suite, dressed in imitation of herself – a comically sedate procession. Fortunately I lived in the back of beyond, and never crossed her path.

I find myself still wondering to what extent Munthe influenced her life and character, for influence he must have had. No one could live in the shadow of his company and not be affected. Although he was by no means infallible, his opinions carried conviction. They were carefully and seriously thought out. He was able to dominate one with his knowledge; he had read everything that was worthwhile in English, French, German and Italian without the meagre mediumship of translation.

His tastes and talents were wide and varied: he knew about music, and one could listen for hours while he played the piano. He was a connoisseur of Greek sculpture. Periodically he would produce some marvellous Greek fragment and explain he had fished it up from the sea. His house was like a museum. Above all he was a student of Nature. He loved animals and knew about flowers and trees and birds with the instinct of an elemental. The great tragedy of his life was his affliction of the eyes, which cruelly divorced him from his two greatest loves – the sun and the sea.

Whatever effect he may have had on others in his environment I do not know. Perhaps he 'treated' each in an individual way. In me he sowed the first seeds of Bolshevism! The word was then unknown. Call it what you will, Munthe's teaching where I was concerned, fell on fertile soil. He upheld the simple life, and the sharing of whatever one possessed. When my father sent me a present of a hundred dollars, Munthe made me give twenty-five dollars to my maid. He said I had no right to keep it all for myself. His strictures concerning food were equally emphatic. No one required the varieties of food that are served habitually in 'courses'. One might eat plenty; there was no virtue in going hungry, but one needed only one course. At his table one ate a peasant dish piled high with rice and vegetables, etc., and perfectly excellent, as Italian peasant food knows how to be.

Before they parted, Munthe told Clare that she should get married. Shortly afterwards she married Wilfred Sheridan, whom she had known for some time. They spent their honeymoon in Italy. Mr Sheridan had no desire to meet Munthe, but Clare wanted to show him Munthe's collection of antiquities and the mountain top where she had lived. They met, and Munthe showed them the Villa San Michele, which happened to be unoccupied. They stayed in the villa, and Wilfred Sheridan noted in his diary:

I rather like Munthe, only one must not be civil to him or expect civility. Manners are not in his line. He eats like a wolf, snapping his teeth. Did one not know that he knew most of the personalities in Europe, one would put him down as an ill-tempered hermit. He is a bully and has no respect for women, a fault which he is never tired of exhibiting. And yet he is a genius undoubtedly. He is kind and more than kind to all the poor people at Capri, most of whom adore him and all fear him. He is simple and direct with them and almost affectionate. I walked with him down to Capri and through Capri up to Lady Algy Lennox's villa; the whole way people genuflected, salaamed and welcomed him . . .

Red Cross & Iron Cross

I thought so far that that slow death from cholera was the worst sight a man could ever witness but this is a charitable death compared to the agony invented by the germans with their gas.

Axel Munthe to Esme Howard, 1916

O N 1 August 1914 Germany issued a declaration of war against Russia and two days later against France. Next day, 4 August, Great Britain responded by declaring war on Germany. A world war had broken out, in which Germany and Austria–Hungary stood on one side and the so-called Entente, consisting of Britain, France and Russia, on the other. Italy declared itself neutral until further notice.

The war was to bring big changes to Munthe's life, as to everyone else's. The queen was German, while Munthe had always been strongly anti-German. His old love of England had deepened with the passing of the years through contacts and bonds of friendship with Englishmen, and his marriage to Hilda had bound him even more closely to this country. His children were British citizens.

Axel reacted to the outbreak of war with the same dismay as he had to the disasters in Naples and Messina. But this time it was not only the tragedy in itself that roused his emotions and made him despair. The whole thing was complicated by the fact that his attitude to the warring sides differed so radically from the mood that dominated at court. Sweden was neutral but opinion was strongly pro-German, not least within the army and court circles. For many, their position was dictated by fear of the Russians. Germany was seen as a spearhead in the struggle against Asiatic Russia. Munthe was also anti-Russian, but he saw no problem in combining that position with support for Britain and France.

Two weeks after the outbreak of war he wrote an excited letter from Stockholm to Hilda, who was in Leksand with the boys. He believed that they would have to remain in Sweden for quite some time and asked her to 'cut short all luxuries in the way of food'. People were hoarding, and there were shortages of flour, bread and potatoes. Munthe had managed to lay his hands on fifty kilos of wheat flour but was worried about heating. The greater part of the letter, however, was about the war and his increasingly untenable position at court:

> The shameful lies the Germans tell and they all believe here as the origin of the war makes my blood boil. My position is most difficult – not one person has a word of pity for France or sympathy for England. The worse is that I am unable though I try to keep my thoughts back and they all look upon me as a traitor.

Munthe had not met a single person at the court who shared his views. The Swedish newspapers were overtly pro-German and he had not seen an English newspaper since 1 August. He got his information from the British ambassador in Stockholm, Esme Howard (whose sister Elsie, Lady Carnarvon, had enquired ten years previously about the possibility of buying San Michele), but even he had difficulty in ascertaining the facts. Axel was resigned and on the point of giving up:

> As long as I feel I am of some use I can hold out but when I see I can do nothing except for my patient I must go. I have never been in such strain – much worse than Messina. When the agony begins I cannot s[t]ay here. She knows my opinions and so does the king and all. I have now ceased to speak with her about the war news but she tries to say she is sorry for the others. Nobody else seems to be so. The king au fond likes to hear me say what nobody else says and it is probable, in fact I know it[,] that he secretly is not as German as he has to pretend.

Axel was worried about the queen, who had an 'uncanny, "starry" expression in her eye and may she only not get fits'. But not even concern for her could keep him in Sweden. On 20 August the German army marched into Brussels. The German advance was fast and effective and could only on occasions be halted. On the three days from 20 to 22 August, tens of thousands of Allied soldiers were killed. Munthe's patience was at an end, he had lost his nerve, and on 24 August he and Hilda collected Swedish passports for a trip to England and France. By the beginning of September they were in London.

This behaviour is astonishing, since Munthe thereby also left his post as the queen's physician. His official motivation for the decision is unknown, but the political differences between himself and the court were irreconcilable. According to his own account he and Victoria quarrelled and he handed in his resignation, which, however, was not accepted. Victoria may have respected Munthe's political arguments, but for her his decision was catastrophic for quite different reasons: how long would the estrangement last, how long would she be compelled to live with Gustaf, closer now than ever, without the calming influence of Munthe's presence? For Munthe too the step must have been incredibly hard to take – after all he knew how dependent Victoria was on him.

Having left his family in London, Munthe rushed over to Paris where he witnessed a German aeroplane dropping bombs over the city. From Paris he went to the front north-east of the capital where he worked with an ambulance as an anaesthetist. After the battle of Marne between 5 and 12 September, when the German offensive was stopped, Munthe returned to London where he wrote a letter to the British foreign secretary – and ornithologist! – Sir Edward Grey, to whom he had been introduced during the Swedish royal couple's visit to Windsor in 1908. He informed Grey that the Swedish newspapers were so pro-German that Crown Princess Margaret had stopped reading all of them except for 'the much despised Socialist paper, which formed the only honourable exception to this rule'. To counteract this tendency, Munthe suggested that Britain dispatch a competent journalist to Sweden, one who could, day by day, contradict the lies of the German news agencies: 'I do not know how much importance you may attach to the state of public feeling in Sweden, but I who since my boyhood have learnt to love and honour England above all am too grieved and ashamed at the way the Press of my country has been led astray to watch this deplorable spectacle in silence.'

Munthe's choice to turn directly to Sir Edward says a great deal about his self-confidence but even more about the genuine despair he felt about the situation in Sweden, which forced him to take the drastic decision to leave his country and his queen.

Britannia

The winter of 1914–15 was spent in Anacapri. Axel stayed as usual in Torre di Materita and Hilda and the boys in the Villa San Michele. Materita was poorly fitted out for small children and Axel preferred to live alone.

On 22 December Munthe was made an honorary citizen of Anacapri because of his work for the poor. His mind was wholly taken up with the war and Sweden's pro-German stance, and during the winter he began to incubate a radical idea: to renounce his Swedish citizenship. Ever since the outbreak of the war, Munthe had feared that Sweden would give up its neutrality and join in the war on Germany's side. So far the king had not wished to allow Sweden to join the German side without external provocation. Nor had there been overwhelming enthusiasm from the Kaiser's side, despite Victoria's lobbying. But in the spring of 1915 the

German armies had had great successes on the eastern front and Sweden was seen as a potential means of applying pressure in the struggle against Russia. A Swedish intervention on the German side would tie up large Russian forces and open the way to Petrograd. In these endeavours the queen made use of her cousin Max, who tried to persuade Gustaf and the government of the appropriateness of such a step.

The government did not give way, but Munthe was well aware of what was happening behind the scenes and he was worried that the sensible souls who were still in the government would be forced to yield. In May 1915 he wrote to Carl Bildt that if the queen's new country joined in on her old country's side, he would immediately apply for British citizenship. But he asked Bildt not to publicise the matter as it would make Victoria even more bitter, and she was already 'very sad about my siding heart and soul with her enemy'.

In the foreword to *The Story of San Michele* Munthe claims that Henry James promised to be one of his 'sponsors' if he, like James, chose to seek naturalisation in England. The claim is correct. James, an American who was as incensed by the USA's neutrality as Axel was about Sweden's pro-German stance, was naturalised in July 1915, and his name is one of several on a list of referees that has been preserved among Munthe's papers. Others include the British diplomat Louis Mallet and Axel's publisher John Murray. In his efforts to achieve naturalisation Axel also drew on two former British ambassadors in Stockholm and one current one – Rennell Rodd, Cecil Spring-Rice and Esme Howard. He repeated to Howard what he had said to Bildt, that he was 'determined [. . .] to apply for naturalization in your country rather than to be on the German side', adding that he was doing this as much for his wife and their sons, who had been born in England and were to receive their education there. 'The rest of my life will be spent in England and Italy and very little in Sweden,' he added, 'my official position there I neither can nor will hold on to and have given my demission more than once.'

However, Sweden remained neutral and Munthe never needed to make use of the letters of recommendation that Howard and others provided. Instead, he found an outlet for his despair and aggression by enrolling in the French Red Cross as a field doctor. In 1915 and 1916 he served for a total of nine months at the front, and was present at the battles of Verdun, the Somme and Arras. But service at the front told on his eyes and by the summer of 1916 he could bear it no longer. Instead he worked in a hospital for nervous diseases in London and in August/September he visited the British field hospitals in France.

'It grieves me that Axel is working in France,' commented his sister Anna, who was not wholly in favour of Axel's political stance, feeling that 'it would have been better if he had stayed "neutral".' But Axel loathed Germany and was in many ways more English than the English. His 'admiration for the english officers + men is *boundless* – they stand anything, never complain and the way they bear pain is amazing', he wrote to Esme Howard.

Munthe's admiration for Britain and the British contribution to the war was so 'boundless' that it inspired him to start writing again, for the first time in many years. Just like in 1908, it was a catastrophe that set his pen in motion.

In November 1915 Munthe returned to Capri with severe sciatica. He was supposed to return to the front in January 1916 but the pain forced him to postpone the journey until the worst of the winter cold was over. On 9 March he returned to Paris and immediately went to a field hospital. He had made good use of the winter months, and during a lightning visit to Paris in April he sent off a manuscript to John Murray. Needless to say he himself had no desire to see it published, it was his 'old friend' Sir Rennell Rodd who had talked him into it:

> If it is half as good as he says, you will be pleased to publish the book. [. . .] I do not wish to have my name on the book – I have tried my best to hide myself as much [as] possible – so much that I have even committed suicide in the Preface. I have also tried for the same reason to shape the narrative into the form of fiction, but God knows there is enough of reality in it, reality in all its horror.

Murray replied by return of post that he would very much like to publish the book. Munthe had suggested that it be published under the name of 'A Doctor in France' but Murray preferred him to do it under his own name, 'as this would undoubtedly help the book much'. He also wanted Munthe to add a few pieces about 'Tommy', as the book 'could well bear a little expansion'. Munthe's answer is lengthy and firm. As regards 'Tommy', he was too worn-out to write anything else just now but he aimed to write a separate book about him on a later occasion. And as for the author's name, he refused to adopt a different standpoint, largely out of consideration for the queen:

> Those who know will tell you that I have played a very important role in her life during over twenty years, and so I have. She is grateful to me and she looks upon me and treats me as a friend, notwithstanding our estrangement since the war broke out when we quarrelled. She is in a very shaky condition and has just been sent abroad to her mother. She is the granddaughter of the old Emperor and everything connected with her country is sacred to her. Not only would she never forgive me for putting my name under a book so damning to her people as long as my name

is still somewhat associated with her – I might after all face that – but it would without any exaggeration make her *positively ill,* and the business to put her on her feet again would fall on me. I intend to tell her all about it in due time, but it cannot be done now, I must see her first.

Murray accepted Munthe's conditions and *Red Cross & Iron Cross* came out in London at the beginning of June 1916. It took the form of a report from Dr Martin of the Red Cross, that is Doctor Munthe (whose middle name was Martin). The book was a success and went through five editions in as many months. Every penny of the author's fee went to the French Red Cross.

The action takes place during three days and nights in a little village church on the French eastern front. A hundred soldiers are lying on the floor, most of them mortally wounded. Savage attacks on 'the Boches' are put in the mouths of the book's two leading characters: the narrator and the main protagonist. The argument derives extra weight from the fact that the Red Cross doctor is neither British nor French. His nationality emerges only indirectly: he says that he was born in a country that claims to be able to preserve the peace without losing its honour. But he himself is at war, and for the individual 'there is no neutrality between right and wrong'.

The Germans are led by a cold-blooded, Iron Cross-decorated officer called Graf Adalbert von und zu Schönbein und Rumpelmayer, whereas the British are portrayed without exception as noble and brave. When Dr Martin is shown a soldier with a gunshot wound in the back, he reacts with the words: 'Rather an unusual place for an Englishman to be hit in' – an English soldier does not flee! And indeed the soldier turns out to be a German spy. The British soldiers love their officers while the Germans fear and loathe theirs. The Germans are Huns and barbarians and worse than that: they are 'cool-headed, scientific criminals, guilty of horrors which have not as yet got a name in our language'.

There is only one German in the book who wins the doctor's sympathy. He is a Bavarian and a Socialist and he curses the war and Kaiser Wilhelm, 'the greatest destroyer of happiness the world has ever known'. The man dies of his wounds and the doctor comments: 'I am sorry that this man is dead, I wish he had been spared to his country, a dozen Socialists as far gone as he are worth a whole brigade for breaking down the stronghold of Prussian militarism.'

Munthe was obsessed both by the war itself and by the Germans' war crimes, and he read copious amounts of war literature. *Red Cross & Iron Cross* was one of many propaganda pieces published in these years, but it also relates to earlier books by Munthe, not least the 'Letters from Naples'. This applies both to the presentation of the main character – a doctor who is assisted by some self-sacrificing women, one of whom is a nun, sœur Martha – and the medico-philosophical and religious argumentation. As in other texts of Munthe's, the reader is struck by the author's fascination with death, which is depicted in such graphic detail that the publisher felt obliged to ask if the book was 'accurate throughout'. Munthe answered with the same argument he once used to explain the 'Letters from Naples', namely that it was not a question of 'a historical document but a *human* document' with a certain value 'to the student of life as well as to the student of death'. The book describes, for example, a soldier who in the moment of death develops 'tetanus', tonic spasms, and whose face stiffens in a fearful laugh, *risus sardonicus*. Murray found the scene 'too startling to be true'. Axel replied:

> If I had not known it since long, this war would have taught me that life itself is infinitely more startling than fiction, and that invention is a very tame business compared to reality. What would you have said, for instance, if I had written down all that happened in that charnel house? Not only did the man curse the officer at his side but he wanted to *strangle* him, he was of course semi-delirious, he said the officer was laughing at him – and laughing he was with that terrible 'risus sardonicus' which is not rare in Tetanus cases and is indeed a terrible sight. Not only did the dead officer lay there with his laughing muscles stiffened in a last cramp, but the man also died with the same 'risus sardonicus' on his face and they lay there both dead grinning at each other and they were grinning still when they were carried to the grave. Is this startling enough for you?

There is also room in the book for Axel's medico-ethical hobbyhorse. There are no medical supplies in the village, neither bandages nor iodine. But most of all Dr Martin lacks morphine, this 'priceless and mysterious gift from benevolent Mother Earth, giving power to the physician to bring relief to those the surgeon cannot help, to those who lie waiting for the other, the Great Physician who goes from bed to bed with his one remedy, his everlasting sleeping-draught'. If the doctor cannot help the patient to live, he should at least help him to die – we recognise the thought from the Naples letters. In the absence of morphine Axel puts the soldiers to sleep with the help of hypnosis. When the nun asks him how he can make them sleep so peacefully he answers that he has no more idea than she has, but he knows that he has the power.

Faced with the horrors of war, Dr Martin is preoccupied with thoughts of God, but not the God to whom tribute was paid in the letter to Violet Bentinck (see page 175). The war has made the doctor abandon his earlier almost pacifist stance: 'I used not to believe in any other God than the God of Mercy. How could I believe in the God of Wrath – I, who have been forgiven so much and so often? Now I have lived to learn to believe that there is and must be a God of Vengeance as well.' To Sister Martha's question as to whether he is a Protestant, he answers: 'Dear Sister, I do not know what I am, [. . .] I only know that I believe in the same God as you, and that I love your Madonna.' The name of the doctor talking here is not Martin but Munthe.

The book's dramatic climax comes when the doctor stops at a house where five German officers are sitting drinking toasts and carousing. Only an hour before, one of them has ordered a young boy to be shot. The doctor has five shots in the revolver in his pocket. He fights against his instinct to finish them off and finally pulls his hand out of his pocket and rushes away from the window. Then suddenly he hears a rich and tuneful voice taking up Schubert's 'Ständchen':

> Leise flehen meine Lieder
> Durch die Nacht zu dir;
> In den stillen Hain hernieder,
> Liebchen, komm' zu mir!
> Flüsternd schlanke Wipfel rauschen
> In des Mondes Licht, in des Mondes Licht.

Later, when the doctor reports where he has been, he says: 'I have been in hell.' Schubert and the officers represented two extremes in the German 'national character', and in order to describe the outrage perpetrated on the composer whom he esteemed above all others Munthe did not hesitate which words to use.

Murray also found this scene too strong for his stomach, but Axel maintained that he had not written anything that he had not witnessed himself:

> Would you have believed me capable of firing at some Germans through a window? I who would not kill a stag if you offered me thousand pounds and who disgusted my comrades by objecting to the poisoned cheese put out to kill the rats infesting the wretched hole we were sleeping in! Well, I very nearly did it. The scene is not described 'accurate throughout', for it was not in the least the horror of the crime that stopped me but simply my fear of what would have been our fate had I missed the mark.

Red Cross & Iron Cross was hailed throughout the British Empire – from London to the Transvaal and Melbourne – for its unadorned depiction of the war, and was said to be 'one of the most fearful and poignant indictments of German militarism that has ever been uttered by word or pen' (*Pall Mall Gazette*, 17 July 1916). It ran to six English editions in total and in the autumn of 1918 an Italian translation, *Croce Rossa e Croce di Ferro*, was published with financial assistance from the 'British Mission of Allied Propaganda'.

GERMANIA

Red Cross & Iron Cross was the furious culmination of the anti-Germanism that Munthe had been incubating since his young days and which now broke through all barriers. Where previously he had made fun of the Germans for their vulgarity and loud tastelessness, he now saw them as the incarnation of evil. The book, wrote the *Daily Mail*, was 'packed with incidents which throw a searchlight on the ways and manners of the Prussian in his most arrogant mood' (24 June 1916). But Munthe did not content himself with writing an anti-German lampoon; he took an even more drastic step – sending back his German decorations to Kaiser Wilhelm. 'The All-Highest himself has always been supposed to have a certain liking for me,' Axel wrote to Lord Northcliffe, 'but I fancy he has cooled down somewhat after my decidedly insulting letter returning his decorations [. . .].'

Munthe's view of Germany and all things German undoubtedly contains a paradox. At the same time as the country represented much of what he most hated, all of his idols were German: in the field of poetry, Heine; in philosophy, Schopenhauer; in music, Schubert, Schumann, Wagner, Hugo Wolff. When asked about his attitude, he stressed that it was Prussianism, not Germany itself, that he was against.

Another part of the paradox was that his royal patient was German. However, the political differences between the queen and Munthe did not mean that contact between them was broken off completely. They exchanged letters and presents, mainly via the Swedish legation in Rome. The queen sent Munthe a silver tankard and he bought her rope sandals on Capri. In the summer of 1916 Munthe planned to visit her in Germany, but the plans came to nothing.

AXEL UND MAX

The war meant that the old Europe went to its grave and many of its leading representatives with it. Munthe had known a few of them personally or at least met them. The Russian emperor Nicholas II was deposed in March 1917 and executed in the summer of 1918, and Kaiser Wilhelm II abdicated in the autumn of the same year. In Russia, a social and political experiment without parallel in the history of the world was embarked upon and in Germany the work of political reform almost led to the same catastrophic consequences. The attempt to democratise Germany was led by Prince Max, the queen's cousin, who made a considerable contribution during the war in the Red Cross's charitable work for prisoners of war. In October 1918 Max was appointed chancellor in a government with a distinct leftish tinge that agreed to US President Woodrow Wilson's fourteen-point peace programme, part of which involved German disarmament.

The prince's time as chancellor was to be short: five weeks. At the end of October 1918 a mutiny broke out in the German Baltic fleet and on 7 November there was revolution in Munich. When the uprising reached Berlin two days later, Max tried by different means to save the monarchy, but when on the same day the social democrat Philipp Scheidemann proclaimed the republic, he stepped down. Kaiser Wilhelm was forced to abdicate and fled to the Netherlands.

In the midst of this political chaos, Victoria travelled to Baden. Her mother's eightieth birthday was on 3 December. If she had hoped that her stay in the parental home would have a calming effect, she was wrong. The revolution had reached Karlsruhe and she and her family were forced to flee to Count Douglas's castle of Langenstein, where they remained until the summer of 1919. Munthe was on Capri planning to travel home to Sweden, where he claimed to be 'badly wanted' by his old patient. This would have been their first meeting for five years. But the trip did not come off as the queen was forced to remain in Germany.

Another person who was longing to meet Munthe was Prince Max, who had not seen him since the outbreak of war. Like his cousin, Max was a fervent German patriot with a quite different perception from Munthe's of the war and its causes. Where Munthe saw German militarism as the cause of the outbreak of war, for Max it was the contrary: it was the forty-five years of peace 'in which the German people worked hard and became thriving and rich' that made Britain 'anxious for its own supremacy in commercial questions' and eager to weaken Germany and clip its wings economically. Max's description of the behaviour of the German soldiers compared to that of the British and French also directly contradicted Munthe's account in *Red Cross & Iron Cross*.

The friendship between Munthe and the prince was so solidly established, however, that it cleared all hurdles. As Max put it, they could meet, despite everything, 'on the ground of purely human questions' and they exchanged their thoughts by letter throughout the war. 'I often long for a talk with you without bitterness, only sorrow over the immense tragedy which has turned us all into mourners as long [as] we live,' Munthe wrote to the prince in the summer of 1916. In a letter to Lord Northcliffe he apostrophised Max, as 'the most human' of all the more than a dozen German princes he knew.

THE WAR ON CAPRI

Munthe had left France and travelled to Capri at the end of September 1916 and since then he had kept to the island. The family stayed by turns on Capri and in Biarritz.

In the beginning, Capri was very little affected by the war as Italy was neutral until the spring of 1915. Any foreigner, irrespective of nationality, could visit the island just as before. Yet the situation for citizens of countries at war was naturally more complicated than previously, and when Italy joined in the war things became far worse for those Austrians and Germans who lived on the island. Some of them were even interned. Munthe avoided this because Sweden stayed neutral, but he suffered as a result of his involuntary passivity: 'I suffer more than ever to sit here in helpless inactivity but my eyes are now in such a state that I dare not even attempt to return to any work in France,' he wrote to his publisher Murray. As his contribution to the war effort, in the summer of 1917 he let San Michele to the British Red Cross. He also took to writing – among other things, the sketch 'Twilight of the Gods', a surrealist dream about the German Kaiser, which is preserved among his papers but seems never to have been published. At the same time as *Red Cross & Iron Cross* was emerging from the presses in London, in June 1916, Munthe wrote to Victoria that he was working on a book 'about the nervous disorders that this war has brought out and the mental aspects of these cases', and in a letter to Prince Max he announced that the book would be called 'Courage and Fear': 'The whole question as looked upon before must now be revised – fear is natural and a thing not to be ashamed of, a man may now become afraid *because* he is running away, *not* run away because he is afraid. I believe it has to do much with the effect of *sound* upon the central nervous system.'

When Spanish flu broke out on the island in 1917, Munthe found an outlet for his need to be active. This is how a young American woman on the island described him: 'It is thus, striding like an ancient, bearded Viking through the narrow streets of Capri, with women stretching out their hands to him in doorways, imploring his help, that I remember him, no longer the protagonist of his old legend, but truly the physician and healer.' Once again Axel tried to 'seek to serve, to the extent one's disposition and individuality show the way', as he wrote to Sibbern in 1888.

Gorky and several of the other Russians who had spent their political exile on Capri had gone home even before the war, after the amnesty proclaimed to mark the 300th anniversary of the Romanov dynasty in 1913. The vacuum left by Gorky was filled by another author, the Scot Edward Montague ('Monty') Compton Mackenzie, who came to Capri that same year with his wife Faith. They just had time to become acquainted with Gorky before he returned to Russia, and they took over his writing desk and enormous divan. Compton Mackenzie suffered from severe sciatica and his doctors had advised him to take himself off to a warmer climate. Besides, he was tempted to head south by Norman Douglas's recently published first book *Siren Land*. Mr and Mrs Compton Mackenzie immediately fell in love with Capri and decided to settle there. After only a year or so they rented a newly built house on the east side of Capri, La Solitaria, one of the most beautiful houses on the island, positioned on a hillside overlooking the Faraglioni cliffs. Compton Mackenzie later wrote a *roman-à-clef* about Capri – *Vestal Fire* (1927) – but is best known for his book *Whisky Galore*, written in 1947 and filmed two years later.

The fact that the Russian revolutionaries had left Capri did not mean that the island was emptied of Russians. Where Gorky and his friends had fled from the tsarist regime, the new Russians fled from the world war and revolution. During the war many rich Russians sent their daughters abroad. One who came to Capri was Princess Olga de Tschélischeff. At that time there were already people of Russian background on the island, such as, for example, Olympia ('Lica') Riola, who had an Italian father and a Russian mother. Her cousin Natasha Khaliutine, who came to Capri after the Bolshevik coup, would later become Munthe's secretary. Both were active in the Italian Red Cross on Capri.

Munthe knew most of the foreigners on the island. His blindness and 'apparent remoteness from the preoccupations of common humanity was deceptive', Faith Compton Mackenzie maintained, 'for no one had a livelier finger on the pulse of local gossip than he'. However, we know little about the company he kept. One of his close friends was Baroness Gudrun von Uexküll, who had inherited the Villa Discopoli from her maternal aunt and who will crop up in our narrative several times later on. But Munthe and Norman Douglas were not a good match. In his memoirs – which consist of visiting cards he saved and commented on – Douglas wrote in detail about his encounters with various people, but Axel, whom he had known for almost forty years, got only one line: 'We have known each other since 1897.' To Douglas, Munthe was a 'portentous fake', a characterisation that a person who knew both of them, Dr Elizabeth Moor, found utterly unjust. 'Norman liked only knowledge – Munthe's world was a little chimerical, and Norman despised this. He felt only contempt for the "afterlife" to which Munthe paid such great attention.'

If Munthe and Douglas shunned each other, the Mackenzies saw all the more of Axel, who, according to Faith, was 'the most remarkable and exciting figure on an island that was full of personalities'.

PEACE AND WAR

The old friendship is strong & will last till I shut my eyes for the last sleep!

Queen Victoria of Sweden to Axel Munthe, 1921

THE WAR HAD brought sweeping changes to Europe. In the autumn of 1917 the Bolsheviks took power in Russia, in 1918 revolution broke out in several German and Austrian cities, Finland became independant and new republics were founded along the Baltic coast. In January 1918 US President Woodrow Wilson set out a fourteen-point programme that, in the words of the historian R.R. Palmer, aimed at 'the fruition of the democratic, liberal, progressive, and nationalist movements of the century past'. America's intervention in the war had been decisive and Wilson enjoyed a unique popularity in Europe, where he was seen as a guarantor that the world would move into a new and more peaceful phase of development.

The former college professor was an idealist with a poor knowledge of conditions in Europe, which meant that the peace process dragged on. Axel was sceptical and saw him as a 'missionary', one of a 'sort of people' he had never liked nor trusted. But the peace treaty was finally accepted by Germany and signed in June 1919 at Versailles.

During the war years Hilda and Axel had spent more time together than ever before. During the summer months of 1915 and 1916 Axel was to be found at various sectors of the French front, but true to his custom of over twenty years he spent the winters on Capri. Unlike in the pre-war years, he now had the company of Hilda and the boys. The war made it more difficult to move freely between countries but the Munthe family nevertheless did a fair amount of travelling. They visited England and Biarritz, and Hilda and the children spent the summer of 1918 in St Gervais-les-Bains in Savoie. In October they returned to Capri.

The winter of 1918–19 would be the last that Hilda and Axel spent together. Europe was heading towards peace, but in the Munthe family war was raging and in February 1919 Hilda left her husband for good. There were several reasons for the separation. Axel and Hilda often seem to have quarrelled, and about most things. 'I am insisting that the boys should go to their school in England,' Axel wrote to an acquaintance, 'but as usual my wife and I do not agree, and I am rather angry about it all.' After Hilda left him and went to Biarritz with the boys at the end of February 1919, he gave more general reasons for the break-up. One was that Hilda was 'a better mother than he was a father, so he had left her to bring up their sons'. Another was that he did not want to expose the family to the depression that followed in the footsteps of his blindness: 'My family is at Biarritz and better so as I bear my cross somewhat easier when I am alone.' These 'official versions' were not untrue, but they were Axel's versions and they were not exhaustive. Moreover, they indicate that the decision to part was his. Such was not the case. We do not know Hilda's version; or, more accurately, we know it through Axel, who in a long letter to Hilda's friend Cathérine Solal de Céligny in February 1919 explained the incident that was the last straw – for Hilda.

Axel's physical relations with Hilda had ceased long ago, he wrote. In actual fact he had not had sexual intercourse with any woman since the outbreak of war and then he saw a red mist for two days afterwards and feared for the sight in his remaining eye. The family conflict had begun in 1910, a few days before their son Malcolm was born, when Hilda claimed to have seen her husband kiss a young woman in her aunt's home in London. She immediately declared that their 'marriage was broken and could never be mended'. Although the girl wrote a letter affirming that this was not true, Hilda refused to withdraw her accusation. 'Since then or probably even before,' Axel wrote, 'every woman of whatever social standing she may be that I have approached has according to Hilda been more or less my mistress.'

Axel acknowledged that Hilda was right in *one case* but did not find this particularly strange since Hilda had announced that their marriage was over. As long as they lived as man and wife, he had no lovers. He was now 62 years old and, thank God, had 'not the slightest need or wish' for sex. The girl in question was his maid Maria Viva, 'an insignificant and not even good looking servant', but 'most intelligent and capable and almost indispensable' to him. She read the newspaper and even books to him. It was the second volume of *Don Quixote*, Axel wrote, that brought him bad luck:

> Since my insomnia has been almost unbearable of late she often reads me
> to sleep while I lay in bed, it is in fact the best sleep I get. Since I started
> her having lessons in french from a starving half crazy russian lady, who

is a spiritist and a medium, Hilda's suspicions, always ready to exert themselves, grew stronger. The russian lady who has more or less lived on me since over a year and who used to send me 'des vibrations de son âme à travers le cosmos', to quote one of her letters I once sent to Hilda, has rewarded me in truly russian fashion by telling Hilda that she saw in a dream the girl in bed with me. The same evening Hilda had been down here where I live alone [= Materita] and hidden in the dark under my bedroom window she 'saw' the same sight. In her first version she writes she saw me in bed with her, in her second version she writes she saw the girl going to bed in my bed, and then saw me come in and 'prepare to go to bed'.

Axel claimed that, from her vantage point, Hilda could not possibly have seen more than the girl coming into his bedroom and Axel following immediately afterwards. Hilda maintained that she had climbed up, grabbed hold of the iron grating on the window and seen everything. Axel then asked two men accustomed to picking olives to repeat the feat, promising them 20 lire if they managed it. They failed, and Axel explained in detail why:

The height from the soft soil to the window sill is two metres and 38 cent. The width of the window sill is nineteen cent. which adds at least twenty cent. to the height from the soil where the iron bars could be got hold of. The solid wire net before the window makes it impossible to get a grip on the iron bars even if a person could jump so high what is excluded except for a professional acrobat.

According to Axel, Hilda could never be persuaded to give up an opinion once she had formed it. In reality the whole thing was a mishmash concocted by the Russian lady, a full-blooded hysteric ('hystérique pur sang') who had twice been an inpatient in a clinic for nervous diseases. Hilda herself explained that the Russian spiritualist's dream was the result of a telepathic communication between them: 'Admitting the possibility of such a transmission between two such brains as I have to deal with here, the question is who influenced the other?' Axel wrote to Catherine, adding: 'If Hilda's "seeing" me in bed is not an autosuggestion or a waked dream like the one she had in London, it is an invention to catch me into confessing what she believed was the truth.'

Axel's reason for telling Catherine all this was that there was 'a considerable psychological interest attached to this lamentable affair'. Hilda's apparently calm exterior concealed a complicated nervous system and, moreover, she had a hereditary taint: 'I know of not less than four cases of madness among her near relations and there are probably more.'

Now that the decision had been taken he declared himself content to be left in peace and to leave Hilda in peace. But his attitude to the boys, with its hard-won rationalism, reveals a deep bitterness:

> She is an excellent mother and as the boys are far better off under her care than mine and I have always acted according to this belief, I shall not interfere with them either. I have long since kept aloof from them in order not to become too fond of them and have only to stick to it. They do not care the very least for me so they will not mind in the least.

Hilda and Axel decided not to institute divorce proceedings. Instead, the great bone of contention was the house in Leksand, which Hilda wanted to take over in exchange for war bonds. Axel, however, refused to accept any compensation. Instead, he wanted to buy another building plot in Leksand to build a house for himself, which led Hilda to protest. This would be as 'distasteful' as if she had bought a property on Capri or in any other way interfered in his life there. She therefore asked Axel to instruct a lawyer to draw up a deed that 'transfers the Leksand property in its entirety' to her, so that she will be '*alone* responsible for it' and free to act as she wishes. Axel's reply was as follows:

> You may consider the Leksand property as yours. But I am too fond of this place which I have created not to want to see it once more before leaving it for good. As soon as I can get to Sweden – I hope in April or May – I shall go up there for a couple of days to say goodbye to the house and to old Gorm [the dog], and to remove some of my belongings I wish to keep and give away some others, never to return to this house anymore. According to your wish I shall not interfer [sic] in any way neither with the land nor anything else concerning the house. [. . .]
>
> This is my final word as to the Leksand house and I shall not return to any further discussion on this question. You have had your way.

THE MARRIAGE COUNSELLOR

Munthe had been unlucky with both his first and his second marriage. Obviously his psychological insights were of little help in his own relationships. But he was skilful at analysing those of other people.

In the winter of 1917–18 the Compton Mackenzies were able to benefit from Munthe's analytical skill. Monty was several years younger than Faith, who had shelved her acting and piano playing to support her husband in his writing career. His rapid success meant that he did not need her as much as before. While Monty was absent from Capri during the war, Faith fell in love with a young artist. She was almost 40 and Nino Caracciolo had just turned 22. When Monty returned to Capri in the autumn of 1917 Faith explained to her young lover that the relationship had to end. He was heartbroken, developed rheumatic fever and died. He had a congenital heart condition, but Faith assumed the blame for his death and fell ill herself. Monty outwardly pooh-poohed the love affair, but their marriage had taken a knock.

Enter 'that remarkable man' Dr Munthe, who gives a 'remarkably accurate appreciation of the state of affairs'. For two hours he and Monty discussed what had happened and what could be done. Munthe's diagnosis was sharp as a knife:

> There are three courses open to you. You can both of you pretend to yourselves that last summer never existed and go on as a conventional marriage. In that event I will prophesy that sooner or later you will find yourselves involved in divorce. Now, I know you well enough to be sure that such a divorce will make you feel guilty because, even if you no longer feel an emotional responsibility for your wife, you will feel that she once gave you a great deal and that without her you might never have reached the position you have. Will you be able to leave her in her mid-forties to make a life for herself and start trying to fulfil the aspirations she once had to be a creative artist herself?
>
> Your second course is to break up your marriage now. But will you excuse yourself to yourself, or for that matter to others, if after apparently letting everybody suppose that you didn't believe it was a serious love-affair you make it an occasion for a divorce?
>
> But there is a third course. Why don't you both admit that marriage in the conventional sense is no longer possible? Why don't you give freedom to each of you to live his or her own life and yet agree to live together in friendship as man and wife? You have no children. Neither of you is handicapped by any responsibility except to the other.

'Dr. Munthe's friendly visits were consoling,' remembered Faith, who joined with Monty in choosing the third way: 'He has a healing presence and his blunt manner conceals what we all know is a very soft heart.'

La Solitaria, the villa where the Mackenzies stayed, had been designed by Edwin Cerio, a multi-talented man who belonged to one of the old Capri families and had great influence on the island. His father, Ignazio Cerio, was a doctor, as was his brother Giorgio. He was himself Capri's mayor from 1920 to 1923. Another villa he designed, Il Rosajo in Anacapri, received its first tenants in 1919: the 35-year-old English doctor and author Francis Brett Young and his wife Jessica, a professional singer who among other things had appeared with Henry Wood's Promenade Orchestra. During the war Brett Young had served as a doctor in East Africa, and his experiences there he committed to paper in the novels he wrote in the 1920s on Capri. For this couple, too, Munthe came to play the role of marriage counsellor.

A close friendship soon sprang up between Munthe and the Brett Youngs, not least through music. 'I do not ask many people to live on the island,' he said to them, 'but I think you two should remain.' Yet he warned Francis to look after his wife, although he thought 'she is sound'. What he feared was that an attractive woman like Jessica would end up in the claws of the island's lesbians, led by the notorious Mimì Franchetti. Jessica in turn drew the following quick sketch of Munthe: 'He could be kind with his right hand and yet so cruel with his left. He would lend his houses to his friends, but if they became ill they had to leave at once; ill people were not wanted.' The information that Munthe was terrified of sick people in his houses is interesting and is confirmed by other sources as well. 'Women fell for him and were under his spell,' Jessica Brett Young continued, naming the example of Lady M. (perhaps Lady Morrell?), who confided to Jessica that Munthe had destroyed ten of the best years of her life, 'but it was worth it'.

Munthe was delighted with the Brett Youngs and when in the autumn of 1920 their marriage cracked at the seams he intervened with authority and genuine concern. The crisis was possibly caused by an erotic escapade on Jessica's side (even if she herself gave another explanation). On Christmas Day the Brett Youngs received a package from Munthe. It contained a geranium-red *scolastica*, an academic gown that used to decorate the back of a chair in Materita and glow in the evening sun, and which Jessica had admired. The package was accompanied by a letter:

You have to thank your devoted husband and not me for this Christmas gift, for it was his assurance last night that except for your tommy [sic] your inside and outside had at last returned to its normal condition of unselfish understanding and loving harmony – with or without the accompagniment [sic] of the piano – I say it was this assurance of his that makes me part with the 'scolastica' since many years much coveted by innumerable *femmine* of various sexes and nationalities. Much to your displeasure I stick to my diagnosis that your irritation – for irritated you were, say what you like – was principally du [sic] to the old worm all women bear in their inside, and I am also willing to grant you attenuating [sic] circumstances du [sic] to bad irish whisky. Luckily for us I saw with my one remaining eye that the worm was expelled with its head – your husband will tell you the importance of this observation – so we have every reason to believe that there never will be a return of the symptoms which made you so sick and miserable. Now listen to my words. If ever again this false note in the old love song you sang so well resounds in my ears – and beware! I know more of good music than you think and notwithstanding the mental falling off du [sic] to old age my hearing is still good – I shall mercilessly strip you of your beloved scolastica. [. .] You have had exceptionally good luck in the selection of a husband and you must never forget this for a single instant of your daily life even if by some oversight of the devil the old worm should attempt once more to bite your inside. I speak with a certain auctority [sic] on this subject and I am even more competent to classify a husband than to classify a worm for so far I have never had a worm of my own but I have always been a bad husband. Now good luck to you both young people and NEVER AGAIN!

'This was Munthe at his best,' commented Jessica. Munthe was famous for his diagnostic acuity, but in this letter it is not primarily the professional psychologist who is speaking but the husband who was himself abandoned by his wife. The admonition NEVER AGAIN! resounds with self-experienced pain: not yet another wrecked marriage!

La Casati

Whenever Munthe wanted to break out of his isolation he had, as we have seen, access to stimulating intellectual company. English writers in the post-war years included Hugh Walpole, D.H. Lawrence and Somerset Maugham, but it is unclear whether or not Lawrence and Maugham socialised with Munthe. He had a complicated relationship with the island's own man of letters, Edwin Cerio – or rather it should be the other way round: Cerio found Munthe puffed-up and pathetic, bordering on comic, and thought that his collection of antiquities was all a bluff.* Whatever one thinks of Cerio's view of Munthe as a ridiculous poseur, he was not alone in thinking so. When Compton Mackenzie was working on his *roman-à-clef* about Capri, *Vestal Fire*, his wife made him promise not to write about Munthe as she was frightened that he would portray him as a comic figure.

As before, Munthe had guests staying in his various houses. In 1919, Torre della Guardia was lent to a Russian lady, 'penniless and homeless with two children one of which is born blind and paralyzed and a complete idiot' – the same lady who claimed to have telepathic contact with Hilda. She was supposed to stay for a couple of months but stayed for a whole year; although Munthe offered to rent her a little house she refused to move.

---

* After Munthe's death Cerio drew a devastating portrait of him as a vain poseur in his book *L'ora di Capri* (1950).

At the same time as Munthe was trying to get rid of his Russian lodger he was saddled with an importunate tenant: Marchesa Luisa Casati, one of the most extravagant individuals ever to set foot on Capri. The marchesa was the lover of the Italian author and aesthete Gabriele D'Annunzio (otherwise best known for his stormy romance with Eleonora Duse), she was enormously rich and enormously eccentric – a performance artist who saw her life and her personality as one great work of art. Her appearance was striking: her face was covered in white powder, her enormous green eyes were ringed with coal-black circles, her eyelids were painted with India ink and her lips were cinnabar red. The whole effect was crowned with a firestorm of henna.

One of Luisa Casati's homes was the Palazzo Venier dei Leoni by the Grand Canal in Venice (later acquired by Peggy Guggenheim and now a museum). She transformed the palace into a decadent amusement park: mechanical birds sang in golden cages, at night torches burned in the orchard and in the trees sat the marchesa's albino blackbirds, which she used to colour according to her whim. The classical statues were covered in gold leaf and there was a servant whose sole task was to feed one of the marchesa's white peacocks so that it sat still on its windowsill where it made an attractive silhouette. During her nightly promenades in St Mark's Square a black footman bore great torches to illuminate the marchesa, who was stark naked under a voluminous fur-coat, and her two hunting leopards. Known for having more perfume than clothes on her body, nakedness was an important part of her image.

It was this 39-year-old one-woman-show who in the summer of 1920 turned up on Capri with her black footman, two hunting leopards, two greyhounds, two gilded gazelles, a couple of parrots, a boa constrictor, an owl and an innumerable number of trunks, to take possession of the Villa San Michele. How the whole thing came off is unclear. Munthe had met the marchesa earlier, in Paris or perhaps at one of Rennell Rodd's receptions in Rome, where she once appeared as a sun goddess, clad in gold and followed by gilded servants and a peacock on a lead. According to Munthe, she announced without further ado that she was coming to Capri to live at San Michele. He seems to have agreed to this but when she actually appeared he regretted his decision. As Munthe was staying at Materita she forced her way into the villa without much trouble. When he tried to get her out, she asked if he was not aware of the law? Did he not know that she had the right to remain there once he had given his permission? She had already contacted her lawyers about drawing up a contract.

The marchesa did indeed have the law on her side. Soon, the whole interior fittings of the Villa San Michele were changed. Black velvet draperies and curtains of gold lace were hung up, black mats and animal heads were laid over the marble floor and Munthe's antiquities were cleared away to make room for the marchesa's ebony furniture. French proverbs were painted in black on the white walls and one of the rooms was filled with black magic paraphernalia. Only two objects were left in peace: the Medusa head and the Egyptian Sphinx. When D'Annunzio came on a visit the whole garden was filled with glass flowers specially ordered from Murano.

The marchesa herself went around dressed entirely in black, while her black footman was gilded from top to toe like the gazelles that guarded the entrance. The footman was a considerable nuisance as he had to be fed on two chickens per day, which Munthe was supposed to supply him with. When he complained to Compton Mackenzie, the latter replied: 'He'll probably eat the Marchesa's parrot if you don't keep him in fowls.'

The Mackenzies saw a lot of *la Casati*, and Monty described one of his visits to San Michele:

> Sure enough a gilded gazelle was standing on either side of the heavy front door, which was opened by the Negro servant, dressed now in a blue plush tailcoat and breeches. [. . .] The *cicisbeo* was fluttering about in the entrance hall to say the Marchesa was waiting to receive me; presently we would be taking tea in the pergola. I passed on to the *salone* and went in. Surprise scarcely expresses what I felt when I saw my hostess lying on the big black bearskin in front of the huge fireplace [. . .] with absolutely nothing on.

Munthe did everything he could to get rid of the pushy incomer. 'Munthe and the Casatis are involved in a cross-fire of law-suits,' wrote Francis Brett Young in August 1920, but according to Munthe 'this new absurd law' made it unsure whether he could win: 'She is one of the lowest type[s] of women I ever came across.' During the autumn, however, he could live in the villa for a week, although Casati had not formally left it: 'Although I have suceeded to tame my turbulent tenant into a sort of temporary submission, the future outlook remains very uncertain and my desire to seize her by her red perruque and scalp her and fling her degenerated carcass over the precipice is stronger than ever.'

The fact that Munthe rented out San Michele indicates that he was in need of money. In the autumn of 1924 he invited the Mackenzies to rent the villa for £200 per annum with the right to sub-let it and to acquire it themselves if they wanted to. 'Unfortunately the days of past splendour, when I could afford the luxury of lending San Michele to friends instead of letting it, are past and my financial situation is such that I am obliged to let it.' The Scot Mackenzie would, according to Munthe, be capable of appreciating 'the incomparable beauty and romance of San Michele and Barbarossa' and be the right man to put the garden in order after Casati's departure. But Compton Mackenzie left Capri for good and Faith rented a *villino*, La Carmela, for herself.

In actual fact the eccentric marchesa and her gilded menagerie controlled San Michele throughout the 1920s, despite all the rows about her rent. 'He is always saying how poor he is but now he has rented out S. Michele for 70,000 lire per annum to the same Marchesa that he took to court to get rid of once her contract ran out,' wrote Wivica Ankarcrona, exclaiming: 'Can you make him out!' Despite the high annual rent, *la Casati* stayed for only a few autumn weeks at San Michele. When she finally left the villa Munthe returned it to its original condition, with one exception: the motto *Oser. Vouloir. Savoir. Se taire* – 'Dare. Wish. Know. Keep silent' – which the marchesa had had painted on the wall in the 'French saloon'.

After Seven Long Years

After many years of involuntary isolation on Capri, Munthe was eager to travel again, but it was complicated while the peace treaty was not signed. As soon as Germany signed, Munthe tried to get out, but his sight was poor, worse than before the war, and he found it difficult to manage on his own. This can be seen, for instance, in his typewritten letters, which become more and more difficult to read. He tried to persuade an English acquaintance in Rome to accompany him – to Sweden, Greece or Cairo, whose museums tempted him. Also in Cairo was Rennell Rodd, who in the autumn of 1919 left his ambassador's post in Rome to join the British delegation working on the report that led to Egypt's attaining independence. However, neither the Greek trip nor the trip to Cairo came off.

Munthe did not see his queen again until the summer of 1921. On 15 May Victoria wrote a letter to him that shows that Axel had doubts as to whether he would actually be welcome – after all, they had parted in dramatic circumstances:

> Let me begin with the most important answer to your questions & that is about your coming to Sweden. No, it is not so that I don't want you to come, on the contrary, I want us to meet again – you know what I am afraid of, i.e. controversies in political questions concerning these last terrible years. You know full well that I could not stand to hear unkind things about my beloved country, therefore let us agree beforehand not to enter into conversations on these painful topics where our opinions alas! always will go in different directions. If we succeed to avoid them it will only be pleasure and satisfaction in meeting again, & God knows we have much to speak about. I look forward to seeing both friend & medical

adviser again & I need both. So there is my answer to your question & it is truly meant!

There was, however, one complication, Victoria continued. Since she did not believe that Axel would want to come when *the Sposo* was there, they ought to make sure that they meet when he was elsewhere. Axel's room was waiting for him and after reading this letter he would know that he would find his old friend 'unaltered in her heart'. 'The rest', she wrote, 'you must decide for yourself.'

When Axel visited Solliden in September 1921 it was the first time he had set foot on Swedish soil for seven years. It is not hard to imagine the tension that filled the air. That many at court regarded Munthe's self-imposed exile as treachery goes without saying. As for the queen, she and Munthe had had more or less continuous contact by letter during their estrangement – however, it was not only time and space that separated them but also a war about which they had quite different perceptions.

Could their relationship be resumed after so many years? Their reunion was to be a confirmation of the strength that was still left in it. Axel spent two weeks at Solliden. After his departure Victoria sent him an alarm clock that struck the hours, quarters and minutes and which she hoped would be of some comfort to him when he could not sleep. In the brief accompanying letter she wrote: 'Pray accept this tiny clock in remembrance of our meeting after 7 long years which seem a whole life-time. I look back upon these weeks with gratefulness. The old friendship is strong & will last till I shut my eyes for the last sleep!' Three sentences, but they say it all.

If the queen had not seen her doctor for seven years, it took all of ten before she came back to Capri: it was only in March 1923 that the 68-year-old queen took possession of the Casa Caprile again. But the stay was short: her mother, the Dowager Duchess Luise, died at the end of April and Victoria and Munthe had to hurry off to Baden. 'I am now enjoying my solitude after a long and disturbing visit here of my old patient the queen of Sweden,' Munthe wrote to a friend after his return to Capri: 'The sudden death of her old mother last week cut short of her stay but the end was dreadful for I had to rush north with her at a few hours notice and I am just back in the old tower since three days.'

The queen rejoiced at being able to stay on Capri again and with Axel nearby, but he seemed to be as uninterested and bothered as before. Did the old agreement still hold good, that they should pretend to be indifferent to each other in order to conceal their true feelings? Or was the relationship different now, after so many years? Of course it was: Victoria was queen, Axel was married and had children, both of them were over 60. Their love had turned into friendship and fondness, feelings that Victoria had had confirmed during their meeting at Solliden in 1921. But why was Axel still so nonchalant when he talked about the queen? The answer is that his relationship to Victoria was marked by the same duplicity as his relationship to other patients. His willingness and need to help were matched by an equally genuine need to be solitary. He liked being by himself and if the isolation was to be broken it had to be on his terms, when he himself wished so.

EGYPT-MANIA

Because of his poor eyesight Axel was finding it harder and harder to manage. Above all, he found it difficult to travel on his own. His increasingly poor vision was exacerbated by severe pains in the eye that had suffered a detached retina in 1904. In the autumn of 1922 he had it removed in Karlsruhe. The operation, he wrote, was 'dreadful without anesthetics'. The optician who created an enamel eye for him claimed never before to have seen such deep-blue eyes and had to visit Axel three times in order to determine the exact hue. The operation stopped the pain, and Axel suffered less from the sunlight. He could now travel in southern climes again.

The beginning of the 1920s saw one of the biggest finds in archaeological history. After searching for several years, in November 1922 Howard Carter discovered the pharaoh Tutankhamun's grave in the Valley of the Kings near Luxor. In February 1923 the burial chamber was opened. Egypt-mania swept over Europe and America, reminiscent of the similar phenomenon at the beginning of the nineteenth century when Napoleon's campaign in Egypt led to a colossal interest in Egyptian history and culture. Newspapers and journals were filled with reports of the astonishing discoveries, and copies of the objects found – including Queen Nefertiti's bust – spread all over the world. Even fashion was Egyptianised: women's coats were immediately decorated with hieroglyphs and Egyptian patterns.

Munthe had wished to visit Egypt right after the war, when Rodd was stationed there. But his trip did not come off and Rodd left Cairo. Carter's work was financed by the fifth Earl of Carnarvon, who had obtained the concession to dig in the Valley of the Kings in 1914. Munthe knew Carnarvon, who was a member of St James's Club, but he did not manage to meet him in Egypt as Carnavon died as early as April 1923. The insect bite that propelled the noble lord into his grave was seen by some as the pharaoh's revenge for not allowing him to rest in peace.

At the end of November 1923 Munthe finally made it to Luxor. Anyone wishing to view the grave had to go through Carter, who at this time was particularly harassed by visitors, ranging from the Queen of Belgium to the usual ancient history enthusiasts. Munthe knew it was not easy even for a Swedish court physician to gain access to the burial chamber. Besides, Carter was well known to be an awkward customer. Munthe had therefore come armed with two letters of recommendation that Carter could not disregard. One of them, from Sir Edmund Allenby, high commissioner for Egypt, described Munthe as 'a very distinguished Swedish archaeologist, who is deeply interested in Egyptian art' and an old friend of Carnarvon's. The other letter was written by Rennell Rodd, who informed Carter that Munthe had, in his home on Capri, 'some interesting Egyptian things' that Carter ought to know about. 'He is one of the most interesting of my many interesting friends,' Rodd wrote, adding, just in case: 'Though he is a Swede his books have been written in English by himself.'

Once installed in the Luxor Hotel, on 23 November Munthe sent both letters of recommendation to Carter together with one of his own in which he wrote that he 'knew Lord Carnarvon well and had his promise to visit the tomb'. Carter received Munthe, who spent a day in the burial chamber. By way of thanks, Munthe gave him a copy of his *Memories & Vagaries*, published in 1908.

This visit, around the New Year of 1923–24, was the first of several that Munthe made to the Valley of the Kings. It is not known who accompanied him on the first trip. When he returned to Luxor in January 1925 it was with the Brett Youngs. Jessica remembered how on the train from Cairo Munthe frightened the life out of them by lighting a spirit stove so that the flames billowed around the inside of their jolting carriage – he was trying to boil water for his Earl Grey tea.

In October 1925 Tutankhamun's coffin was opened and Munthe made a third trip to Luxor. On 3 December he wrote from Anacapri to his brother:

> I'm taking the boat to Alexandria tomorrow to spend a month in Luxor with my good friend Carter, the discoverer of Tutankhamun's grave. There is so little I am interested in nowadays, but ancient Egyptian art is an exception, and I look forward to seeing wonderful things. You must have read about the opening of the coffin. Only a few people have seen it and I have my friendship with Carter to thank for what I have seen and am allowed to see.

The last sentence has been interpreted as meaning that Munthe was present at the opening of the coffin, but such was not the case. The examination of the mummy began several weeks before he arrived in Luxor. In his official report Carter enumerated those who were present: the company consisted exclusively of professional archaeologists and representatives of the Egyptian government – ten people in all.*

The examination of the mummy continued for eight months, until May 1926, so that Munthe had several opportunities to see the pharaoh in his coffin during his stay in Luxor. As a souvenir of his visit to the burial chamber, Carter presented Munthe with a signed photograph of Tutankhamun's mask, dated 25 December 1925, six days before Carter handed it over to the museum in Cairo. Another souvenir was a ring representing a three-headed cobra. This he had also received from Carter, who assured him that it had been found outside the grave. Munthe in turn gave Carter a silver beaker: 'You seemed to have divined my weaknesses,' replied Carter by way of thanks: 'old silver and carnations.'

By the following New Year Munthe was back in Luxor, where Carter, who quarrelled with everyone, was 'very kind and friendly' towards him. Over the years he and Carter seem to have developed a very close relationship that even included discussions of financial questions. Munthe also invited Carter to call on him in Anacapri, where he said he lived 'well protected against intruders by my dogs and by my reputation as a savage'. However, the visit never came off; Carter was too preoccupied by his grave. But in 1930 he carried out a lecture tour of Sweden, possibly on Munthe's initiative.

Carter was a complicated person who found it easy to make friends but difficult to keep them. As far as Munthe was concerned, the relationship was probably more one-sided than he himself believed or wished – Carter probably saw Axel as rather obtrusive in his enthusiasm. Carter's interest gradually cooled, for reasons that had little to do with archaeology. Munthe had once called on Carter in Qurna, where he had his permanent home in Egypt. But when he wished to see Carter in London in 1932, Carter refused to receive him. When an acquaintance of Carter's, the poet John Drinkwater, said that was a pity since his wife had been so captivated by Munthe, Carter exclaimed: 'Exactly!' Carter had thrown Munthe out of his house in Qurna precisely because of his own wife's interest in him.

---

* On a photograph of the opening of the tomb one can see a person resembling Munthe; it is, however, Professor Pierre Lacau, director general of Egypt's Antiquities Service.

VILLA SVEZIA

The patient was rather difficult to handle at first but ended up by obeying.

Axel Munthe on Queen Victoria of Sweden, 1927

A FTER THEIR SEPARATION in 1919 Hilda forced Axel to agree never to contact her again. But at Easter 1924 he broke the agreement and sent a long letter to his wife. He quite simply could not bear to live any longer in ignorance of his sons' fate. The letter led to a six-month correspondence between the spouses.

When Hilda and the boys left Capri, Axel wrote, he had not realised that it was for good. Had he known, he would have acted differently. He had accepted her demand that he should keep his distance from the children and only yielded to his desire to see them twice in all that time. His first request was turned down; his second proposal went unanswered. He did not know where they were, which school they were going to or what their prospects for the future were:

> After long hesitation I send you this letter to tell you that I am no longer willing to accept the position in which you have placed me. [. . .] If it is so that I have lost my wife and my children for ever, I wish to say so openly to those who ask me. To pretend that we are married when I am a dead man to you is undignified to us both and I think also to the children whom you have taught to think and to act [as] if they had no father – vengeance is mine said the Lord. And when my sons have grown to know what life is and not what it ought to be, and of what poor stuff man is made – there will then be another surprise in store for them, for they will behold nine out of ten of the average men around them, seated on the same bench of the accused by the side of their dead father.

One way of resolving the situation would be for Axel to disappear out of her life – and out of life generally – in the purely physical sense. But if suicide had once been an option, Axel had now reconsidered. Another way out would be to try to make up, to forgive and forget – for the children's sake. But he knew Hilda's 'hard and unforgiving nature' too well to suggest anything of the kind. Moreover, with only one half-blind eye left and the prospect of soon being unable to move without help, he had so little to offer her. A third solution would be 'to make an end to this mockery by dissolving the legal ties which still hold us together before society'. A divorce, Axel assured her, would not lead to any changes in his way of life: 'I am according to you a bad man, but I am not a fool. I am sixty six and thank god I have done with women.'

Hilda replied by return of post. According to her, Axel was being hypocritical: he knew very well that she and the boys had left for good. And even if many men were unfaithful, 'nine men out of ten' did not have lovers, 'nine men out of ten' did not, like Axel, find it possible to keep a lover in their own home, let her play with his children and associate with his wife ... To resume their relationship was therefore unthinkable, the words 'forget and forgive' had a hollow ring to her.

As regards the offer of a divorce, Hilda reacted furiously. She opposed the very idea, 'this contemptible thing!' But if Axel insisted, she could contemplate agreeing to the divorce – on one condition, that he would sign a legally binding paper in which he would promise that in no way, either morally or materially, would he interfere in her life or that of the children. Personally, however, she would prefer if they could stick to their old agreement and 'act as if nothing had taken place'.

If Hilda was rock-firm on the question of divorce, she was more conciliatory with regard to the boys. Axel really knew *nothing* about his sons and Hilda seems to have felt a sort of guilt. She devoted several pages of her letter to them, especially to Peter, who had been very ill in 1921. He had a disease of the hip which risked making him an invalid. He found it hard to walk but was able to ride, swim and row. The boys were attending King's College, a private school in Wimbledon, where they lived.

'At their home my aim has been to make it so bright and gay a place that they find their greatest amusement in it,' she wrote. 'People drop in, there are often parties, it is open house and the boys are thus accustomed to like society of their own class.' Their home was not, however, quiet enough for Axel, whose inevitable 'rows and upsets' might be damaging for Peter: 'I do not think it would be right [. . .] to consider you before the boys – at any rate not until Peter is well and has done growing.' But at the same time she thought she could detect 'a different spirit' in Axel's letter that made her believe that he has at last attained some sort of insight. He was therefore welcome to see the boys when it was convenient, 'if it can be of any pleasure or distraction' for him.

The double messages mirrored Hilda's ambiguity. Axel clutched at the proffered straw, but when he arrived in London in July, Hilda and the boys had already left for Leksand. The person who managed to see Peter and Malcolm that summer was not Axel but the boys' godmother Victoria, who spent 7 and 8 July in Dalarna with Gustaf. The king spent the night in his train compartment at the station in Leksand while the queen was Hilda's guest. Victoria gave Axel a report on the boys. 'I was glad to hear from the Queen that Peter, though pale, looked fairly well and fit,' he wrote to Hilda, adding sarcastically that he was 'sorry to hear he looked like his father'. Although he found it difficult to travel on his own he had thought about going up to Leksand – but to live at a hotel and meet the boys there would negate Hilda's efforts to keep up the marital pretence.

Once again Hilda replied by return of post. She was sorry that Axel had missed the boys in London but saw no reason why he should not come and live at Stengården: 'I can hardly suppose that with mutual courtesy there could be any great discomfort in two well-bred people spending some days together on neutral ground as this house is – being the boys'. For such it is and all that is in it.'

This was news to Axel! He had left Stengården to Hilda, but she refused to accept the property if she was not allowed to pay for it. However, the money that she believed to be at her disposal – some kind of rent for life – could not be touched, so she chose to pass Stengården on to the boys as a present from their father – 'they know well it is theirs and *who* gave it to them.' Hilda's theory 'of two well-bred people spending some days together on neutral ground' was never put to the test – Axel developed an inflammation in his good eye and stayed on in London.

Although Axel and Hilda did not meet, something had nevertheless happened in the relationship between them. The silence had been broken. They were in contact with each other again, Hilda found 'a different spirit' in Axel's letters and Axel for his part noted a 'somewhat changed tone' in hers. Hilda even offered, surely to Axel's surprise, to come to Capri and help him sometime in the future, when Peter no longer needed her so much. Yet the offer was not unconditional. It presupposed that he changed his life and got rid of his 'ugly and sordid entourage', consisting of so-called secretaries and maid valets. Hilda had in fact heard from someone who had spent the winter in Capri that 'The *situation* at Materita is unchanged though the subject is a different one.'

The 'subject' in question was Axel's new helper, the Russian Natasha Khaliutine, born in Moscow in 1890, who had come to Capri after the Bolshevik revolution of 1917. Natasha worked as his secretary and lived with Giovannina's sister Rosina, and Axel protested that she had not as much as had a meal with him. Natasha was both 'sexless and brainless', he wrote, and he ought to have got rid of her long ago, but she was utterly helpless and, despite her shaking hands, she was beginning to be good at plucking fleas out of the dogs' coats. 'Pity the Queen had not time to tell you about Natasha, she knows her well since she came almost every day to the Harem.'

As regards Hilda's immediate reason for leaving the island – the maid Maria – Axel informed her that she had been dismissed long ago and for good reasons, but this meant that nowadays, unfortunately, he was 'badly looked after': '[. . .] never in my life have my own belongings been in such helpless disorder and whenever I go down to Capri – not often – people generally begin to scratch away spots on my clothes and so they all did here when I came with my best clothes all worm-eaten and full of spots.' If Axel could get hold of the money owed to him by the Marchesa Casati, he was thinking of going to Egypt for the second year in succession to spend a week in the Cairo museum. If Hilda was coming to inspect his 'harem' might she perhaps like to come with him to Cairo?

The joint trip did not come off, despite Hilda's interest in Egypt. Yet she seems to have begun to feel some sympathy for her increasingly helpless spouse, and thought seriously about travelling down to Capri. But she did not intend to come unless Axel decided that this was what he really wanted: 'I would not come unless you decided that in spite of my many shortcomings you wanted me *instead* of your supernumerary. [. . .] I listen sadly to you say [sic] you are badly looked after, but if so it will be less difficult perhaps to "select" when the time comes.'

Up until now Axel and Hilda had signed their letters with both their first names and surnames, but this letter was rounded off with a warmer form of words: 'The boys send you their love with mine, Hilda.' Enclosed with the letter was a photograph of the boys. It was the first time in five years that Axel had seen a picture of his sons and he commented: 'Peter looks thin and his face is a very sensitive one, but intelligent. The two brothers belong to a different race, one is a specimen of the longheaded race, the other of the roundheaded. That Peter require[s] careful handling is certain. He is in good hands and I say nothing more.'

One senses in this brief comment a repressed pain, as if Axel had suddenly realised that the boys were no longer his. Even if he was allowed to meet them sometime in the future, they now belonged to a world outside his control. His psychological defence mechanism induced him to draw back and blame himself, just as he did in 1919:

Apart from moral unfitness – discovered by you – to associate with them my ever growing despondency and love of solitude is a sufficient reason for me to be the first to admit that I [am] no suitable companion for children – I had enough of that from my own father who threw a shadow over my whole childhood and youth. With my mother I had nothing to do and so much the worse for me.

THE BOYS

Axel's repression of his feelings did not have the hoped-for effect, and he continued to long for his boys. Having learned the lesson of the previous summer's fiasco, on 3 June 1925 he sent a letter to Hilda containing a single sentence: 'Dear Hilda. I beg you to inform me by a line at what date the boys are leaving England for Sweden. Their Father.' The letter was directed to London, but sent on to Leksand. Hilda and the boys had already left England. There was to be no meeting; according to Hilda, the boys expressed 'astonishment' at his suggestion.

In 1926 the queen had arrived in Capri by February. She remained there until the beginning of June and was accompanied on the homeward journey by Munthe. She fell ill on the way and when she got to Solliden in time for midsummer she was in such a bad way that she immediately had to take to her bed again. The queen was having severe coughing fits that could last for hours, and her heart was showing signs of strain. She also had a consistently high fever.

Her condition was life threatening and the king sent an urgent message to Munthe, who was in London. By the time he got to Sweden he was worn out from lack of sleep. His sister Anna, whom he had not seen for fourteen years, reported that during the hours they spent together in Malmö he sometimes had to lie down and shut his eyes: 'He was suffering pain and saw red flames.'

When Munthe arrived at Solliden he was told by the queen's two physicians that it was a miracle that she had survived the latest heart attack and that she would not survive the next one. He informed the king that he shared their opinion of the immediate danger but that he had a different perception of both the nature of her illness and the methods of treatment. Her heart problems, he believed, came not from the heart itself but from the severe cough. He seems to have been right. In actual fact the queen had a strong heart, as would emerge in the next few years.

In order to decide who was right, he or his two Swedish colleagues, Munthe asked for permission to send for Professor Krehl of Heidelberg, one of the world's leading heart specialists. 'It was so urgent', Axel wrote to Hilda,

> that I dared not even wait for his arrival and with the kings consent I changed the whole treatment. The Queen who could hardly speak was too ill to be told anything about all this. It was a very trying time for me who knew quite well that she might die at any moment. But I was lucky. After two days watching the case (by Krehl), the two attending doctors were called here again on sunday and in the presence of the king Krehl

declared that he shared entirely my opinion in everything. [. . .] The two leading doctors returned to Stockholm the same evening, you can imagine with what feelings of sympathy for me.

Just as the queen's illness was at crisis point, Axel told Hilda that he would very much like to see his sons. If she was agreeable, he promised not to stay in a hotel in Leksand but in a boarding house in the neighbouring town of Tällberg and to meet the boys there. If his offer should be greeted with the same 'astonishment' as on the previous occasion, he would of course withdraw it and never mention it again.

Axel did not need to withdraw his offer. Hilda answered with a letter that was unusually friendly and, for the first time, completely free of reproaches. He was very welcome to live at Stengården but would hardly find the house restful as they had two other children visiting and the boys, who had become accustomed to regard the house as theirs, were all over the place and very noisy:

But I daresay you will arm yourself with patience for the days you have to spare. The two rooms you had originally, downstairs, are empty: the Flygel [=wing] not so, for it has been the boys' workshop for years and a blessed safety-valve for all their inventions, modelling, paintings and mess of every description. I tell you this that you may not expect the quiet there cannot be. En revanche you will find the place as beautiful, or more so, perhaps, mellowed by time and the two boys unaccustomed to hear anything but good about you.

Munthe came up to Leksand around 6 September and stayed for three or four days. It was the first time he had visited his home in Dalarna for twelve years and the first time in seven years that he had seen his sons. Peter was now 18, Malcolm two years younger. Back in Stockholm he wrote a letter that showed that there had been a degree of reconciliation between himself and Hilda:

Dear Peter and Grane
I have sent c/o your mother a little present of 500 kronor [almost £1000 today] to be divided equally between you two and to be spent on whatever you may need in way of colour-boxes, brushes, palettes and different tools for your painting and your modelling. You have both of you been equipped by the grace of God with a fine and safe sense of beauty and with very remarkable artistic gifts. It is your duty to develop these gifts by hard and *serious* work, and it is the duty of your parents to try to help you in this by wise guidance and advice. More they cannot do – the rest remains with you. So far you owe to your mother what you are, and you owe her everything. What is to become of you in the future depends upon

yourself [sic]. Give my love to your mother and thank her for the happy days I spent with her and you.

When Axel left Leksand he took with him, from the Stengården library, a book about life in Dalarna – he was, he told Hilda, collecting 'impressions from Dalarna' for something he was writing when he was 'too low'.

The Patient Ended up by Obeying

On 15 September 1926 the queen spent a month or so at the Brenner sanatorium and then continued on to Rome, where she rented a villa over the winter. Once Victoria was settled in, Munthe carried on to Capri, completely exhausted after two months in the company of his ailing patient.

Victoria was not allowed to accompany him to Capri – she was too ill to manage and Axel could not help her as his sight had become much worse of late. In fact he had also opposed her stay in Rome, but she had turned a deaf ear – 'It is the first time she has disobeyed me and it will shorten her life a lot, she is too ill for Rome.' His decision to leave the queen in Rome was not popular, either with the king ('who dislikes much that I have declined to stay with her'), or with his son Malcolm, who complained to his mother: 'It is sad about Father, how silly of him to leave the Queen alone when he has taken her there, it will look bad.'

Munthe had hoped that the meeting with the boys in Leksand might mean the beginning of a new relationship. At the beginning of December, however, he declared that 'the door has closed again and once more I am left in the dark.' But he did not give up. His eye specialist had advised him to look for a drier climate and for the fourth year in a row he travelled to Luxor, where he also slept much better. Back in Leksand he had tried to talk Hilda and the boys into coming with him, but instead they chose to spend Christmas in Biarritz with Hilda's mother. On the eve of his trip to Egypt, to his great surprise, he received rent money to the tune of 10,000 lire from the Marchesa Casati, after he had threatened her with yet another writ: 'She is never there but refuses to leave San Michele and since there is no chance of finding another tenant I have to leave her there. The house is besides going rapidly to pieces from neglect [. . .].' He now offered this sum to his family so that they could pay him a 'flying visit' in Egypt. But Hilda and the boys turned down his invitation, and after the holiday they returned to London.

At the beginning of March 1927 Axel travelled up to Rome from Egypt. The queen had been afflicted by a severe bout of influenza with 'both lungs blocked by a colossal secretion of mucus, her nerves in a deplorable condition'. The king was in Monte Carlo playing at the tables and in his bulletins Munthe played down the seriousness of her condition so that he would not have to feel obliged to come to Rome, 'which the Queen only wanted him to do if she was going to die'.

During her stay in Rome the strong-willed Victoria was more stiff-necked than ever. In Munthe's absence she had begun to take morphine again, something that he had to put a stop to since otherwise she would have suffocated from the accumulation of mucus in her lungs. In a letter to marshal of the realm Otto Printzsköld he summed up the situation: 'The patient was rather difficult to handle at first but ended up by obeying.'

Munthe was sitting by Victoria's sick bed day and night, and once again he was worn out. The stock of good health he had built up in Egypt had been squandered and as he had travelled to Rome straight from Egypt, without passing through Capri, he was dressed in veritable rags. 'I know you have no pity on me,' he wrote to Hilda,

> but cannot you at least feel sorry that I have only two shirts and my underlinen, I think from you, is so torn that I have washed [it] myself for shame to give it to the laundry, my boots are leaking, I blow my nose in a newspaper, my one and only handkerchief I need to dry my only remaining eye which is running the whole time, again I cannot read, my room is icecold the rest of the house is like a furnace.

At the same time, Munthe continued to be plagued by problems with his houses. 'The terrible Casati' owed him 50,000 lire and a combination of worsening health and taxes made him think about selling Materita or San Michele, 'even at a low price'. Nothing came of these plans. On the other hand he disposed of the Malt House in Broadway, the first home that he and Hilda had shared. It had been rented out for many years. 'Personally I think it is a great mistake to possess so many places,' he wrote to Hilda in a moment of belated insight: 'I know it alas from personal experience.'

As if Munthe did not have enough problems, it fell to him to bring another housing project to fruition. After the queen's stay in Rome the previous winter it was decided that she should also spend the winter of 1928 there. To continue renting, however, was both impractical and expensive and therefore a house was bought in Via Aldobrandi 27: the Villa Svezia.

At the beginning of September, after a spell at Mainau (which since the death of Victoria's brother had come into her possession) and a week with Prince Max, Munthe travelled to Capri, accompanied by a servant put at his disposal by the prince. Some English friends came to call, which did not, however, put the more and more misanthropic Munthe in a better mood.

'The most tragic part of the situation is however that I am less miserable alone with the dogs than with any male or female.'

When at the end of the month Munthe received a visit from a 'female', the queen, it was against his will. After having tried unsuccessfully to oppose the visit, he complained to Hilda: 'I look forward with terror to the coming of the Queen after tomorrow. I am too ill for all the demands she makes on me and I shall also have her cousin on my shoulders this winter.' Munthe's misgivings were confirmed: Victoria took to her bed the minute she landed on the island.

At the end of November Munthe and Victoria returned to Rome, where the queen's house had to be put in order. But while the queen and her attendants pitched camp in the fashionable Palace Hotel, Munthe lived above the garage in the Villa Svezia. How he carried out the task of supervising work on the queen's villa is something of a mystery, given that he could hardly see. 'I do not remember having passed through such hardships and real privations in my whole life,' he told Hilda, 'all the finishing and installation fall on me who is totally unfit for this work.' According to the plans, the move was supposed to take place at the New Year, but the house was not ready until some time into 1928.

You Have Got the Children, What Have I Got?

The Munthe family were also on the move. In the autumn of 1928 Hilda and the boys moved to Stockholm, where Peter and Malcolm enrolled in the humanities faculty of Stockholm University. The move was connected with Hilda's desire to make the boys into Swedish citizens, like herself. Axel opposed both the decision to move to Sweden (among other things, because he feared the tax repercussions) and her ambition for the boys to become Swedes: 'I know that it is a great error of judgment, founded on insufficient knowledge of modern Sweden – had it been one generation past, it would have been the right solution.' Despite Axel's opposition, Hilda stood her ground in the citizenship question. The boys became Swedish subjects but, for some reason, applied for this to be overturned as early as 1929.

The last letter from Axel to Hilda that has been preserved, dated 10 January 1928, is resigned in tone. Perhaps Hilda's stubbornness about the boys' citizenship was the last straw. Every initiative, every attempt to reach a reconciliation had come from him, and perhaps he had had enough of what he saw as Hilda's indifference to his fate. Ever since she left him in 1919 he had been forced to endure many difficulties 'unaided by a single word or sign of the slightest sympathy or good wish' from her or the boys. His wish to be allowed to see the boys had been met with 'the expression of their surprise' and Hilda's 'reiterated disapproval and horror' about his 'immoral life in Materita'. His invitation to Egypt 'met with no luck' and he had been forced to turn to strangers 'for help and a comforting word'. He summed up their respective positions with the following words:

> Our mutual position will always remain the same, you the supreme and infallible judge, I the criminal. There is nothing to do, you thought it right to leave me and to take the children from me, I thought it wrong and still think so, but when you write about your ruined life, what about mine? You have got the children, what have I got?

This was Axel's view of the relationship. Hilda's letters to him, with the exception of those quoted above, have not been preserved. But there is another source of information about Hilda's view of the matter, namely the queen's letters to her. Over the years Victoria and Hilda had become close, and they often corresponded. The queen's letters to Hilda in the years 1928–29 are interesting for two reasons: first of all, they show the mutual lack of understanding between Axel and Hilda, and secondly they bear witness to the two women's obsession with a man whom they found attractive and repellent at the same time, but on whom all their thoughts were centred. It is a remarkable correspondence, which was carried on in the greatest secrecy, as it had to be kept from Munthe's knowledge or, God forbid, his eyes. 'I think it is safer you don't write to me just now, as he may be coming,' the queen warned Hilda once, words that were repeated in one form or another in several letters. For reasons of prudence Munthe was referred to in Victoria's letters as 'he' (often within inverted commas):

> 'He' is not nice about you, I am grieved to say so. Disapproves highly of your establishment in Sweden & says he has worries about taxes in consequence. How can I know if it is so? I cannot & will not have you discussed, I never say a word when he begins & try to change the theme of conversation as quickly as possible. I hope he does not worry you with nasty letters, dear friend. (16 November 1928)

> If he only could be sensible & ask you to come here & help him a little! but he alas! rather enjoys feeling a martyr. (19 January 1929)

> And to think he has such a touching dear wife who would do anything for him if he only let her! It makes me quite miserable & [I] am so helpless. (5 February 1929)

> 'He' had sent so many unkind messages through [chamberlain] De Geer to you. So unjust, so very nasty. I really do not understand him. There is

surely something wrong in his brain in connection with you & the boys. He does not see the truth. (22 April 1929)

After her first winter at the Villa Svezia, and despite her uncertain state of health, Victoria travelled to Stockholm to be with Gustaf for his seventieth birthday on 16 June. But she was so weak that she could not take part in any of the many events planned to mark the occasion. Axel accompanied her to Sweden. They must have made a pitiful spectacle, the ailing queen and her half-blind doctor, who allegedly looked so 'shabby' that he was stopped by the guards when he tried to enter the palace.

THE STORY OF SAN MICHELE

I am dictating with terrible difficulty a book – it helps me to forget my misery for a while.

Axel to Hilda, 1927

T HE DAY BEFORE Munthe left Sweden in August 1928, in company with the queen and prince Wilhelm, he sent a letter from Drottningholm Palace to his old publisher in London, John Murray. He hoped that Murray had not forgotten his 'humble existence', and continued:

I was to be in London in June but I have been kept here the whole summer by the severe illness of the Queen, and now I am obliged to go to Baden-Baden with very little hope of coming to England. It was my intention to ask you to have a look at a M.S. of mine before submitting it to anybody else. It may not be a very good book but it certainly is a curious book 'unlike anything else', according to my old friend Rennell Rodd who has read part of the M.S. and insists upon its publication.

By referring to Rennell Rodd – precisely as he had done in the case of *Red Cross & Iron Cross* – Munthe was guarding against a potential refusal. It was, after all, not his idea to offer the publisher his manuscript! Murray had no time to react before an impatient Munthe sent a new letter from Capri. Rodd, he wrote, 'excludes absolutely the possibility that it might *not* suit you to publish the book', and has asked him to find out when Murray is thinking of printing it. Rodd has in fact promised to read the proofs, as Munthe's sight is so poor: 'The book is called "The Story of San Michele", the name of my beautiful home here from where I have been driven away by the glare of the sun. Contrary to my first intention it has turned out to be the story of my own life but Rodd says it is better so.'

It is a remarkable way to behave. Just as with *Vagaries* and the new translation of *Letters from a Mourning City* thirty years earlier, Munthe was asking Murray to publish a manuscript he had not seen, let alone read. Not until a month later did he send off *The Story of San Michele*, which reached

Murray's desk on 15 October. 'I had originally intended to enclose in the book a psychological study of Tiberius,' Munthe told Murray, adding as an appetiser that he had 'decided to make this into a separate book to be submitted to you later on'.

John Murray read the manuscript and liked it, but suddenly fell ill and was unable to take the matter further. His son John Murray (V) explained to Munthe that he would be delighted to publish the book but did not dare print more than 1,000 copies. Given the author's fee of ten per cent, the publishing house would not get its money back even if the whole print run sold out. He therefore suggested that the book be set in a smaller print style so that the number of pages could be kept down. In addition, he asked Munthe to obtain a further recommendation that the manuscript be published, so that the firm could feel justified in printing a first edition of 1,500 copies.

Axel was conscious of the fact that the product he was offering for sale was better than anything else he had previously offered the firm: 'From a literary point of vue [sic] "The Story of San Michele" is a far better book than those you have published before by the same obscure author.' Accordingly, no further recommendations were required, but as he was anxious to have the book published he could envisage making certain financial concessions and offered to waive all royalties and, if necessary, cover the risk of printing a larger edition than 1,500 copies.

His willingness to compromise, however, had its limits, and did not extend to the book's appearance. In this, Munthe was as determined as ever. 'A greater type and a more open page would surely improve the appearance of the book, be it even fifty pages more. The book is full of Italy and animals – all English people like to read of such things – and I am not afraid they will complain of these fifty pages added to the book [. . .].' On 13 November Murray sent the manuscript to be typeset without waiting for any new recommendation.

As emerges from his letter to Murray, Munthe had been unable to come to London in June 1928 because of the queen's illness. A trip planned for August did not come off either. And at the beginning of September Munthe was forced to hurry from Rome to Capri, where his two dogs had been poisoned. The queen suspected it was intended as 'a vengeance on him', but said nothing about the motive. (In *The Story of San Michele* the episode is linked to Munthe's battle to stop the hunting of birds on Capri, which was true). To cheer him up, Victoria bought him two new dogs, which were waiting for him on his return to Rome in mid-October. 'Hope they will be a success!' she exclaimed anxiously in a letter to Hilda.

However upset Munthe was by the murder of his dogs, his thoughts at this time centred mostly round *The Story of San Michele*. He had been secretive about his projected book before, but now the queen became aware that something was brewing. In mid-November he finally got to London for a few days; officially, to call on John Murray, who was still unwell, but also 'on account of his famous book', as Victoria put it in a letter to Hilda, adding: 'The whole affair rather mystic, as usual!' On 15 November John Murray and Munthe agreed to print 1,500 copies of the book 'with good print and on good paper, bound in smooth blue cloth, with a frame and Sphinx on the front in gold'. If the book was a success the profit was to be shared between the publisher and the author.

When the project was no longer a secret, the queen asked Munthe to dedicate the book to her, but this he had no desire to do: 'Contrary to what most people would have done I have kept my many royal associations out of the book.' The proofs were sent out in batches at the beginning of December and Munthe travelled to Capri where he read them for himself before Rodd received them. When they were returned to the publisher at the end of December, there was an addition: a chapter about the earthquake in Messina, a translation of the article that appeared in *Stockholms Dagblad* in 1909.

It was not only Munthe who had suggestions for changes. John Murray, who obviously read the book first at the proof stage, found the chapter about the baby farmer ('sage-femme') Madame Réquin rather gory and asked the author to 'tone it down' out of consideration for his female readers. This Munthe did, just as he rewrote the kissing scene with the nun in cholera-stricken Naples – to spare Mr Farquharson, the production manager, from blushing, as he jokingly put it.

During the period leading up to publication day there was an intensive correspondence between the publishing house and Munthe, who had his own views on just about everything. Instead of the Sphinx, San Michele – the archangel Michael – was to grace the cover, and the picture was to be reproduced precisely according to Axel's wishes. Just as with *Red Cross & Iron Cross* he wanted a slip pasted into the book, on this occasion with the message 'The author's profits on the sale of this book will be handed over to the Naples Society for the Protection of Animals', of which he was a long-time member. (Two weeks later he tried to change it to 'The International Society for the Protection of Migratory Birds', but by then it was too late.)

He talked about which bookshops the book should be sent to and about potential reviewers. One possibility was Rebecca West, who had visited him on Capri and sent him one of her books – 'She would like to have mine I am sure and probably review it.' On the other hand, he did not wish any review copies to be sent to French newspapers:

My description of medical life in Paris is very severe and the French papers will tear both the book and myself to pieces if they get hold of it now. Better postpone my execution for a while until the book has had a good start. This also applies to the medical press in England [. . .]. *It is not a medical book* and I do believe that is good tactics to delay this onslaught for a while and let the literary papers have their say first. [. . .] Better to draw the attention of lovers of animals to the book and lovers of Italy.

The book was to be sent to Brentano's bookshop in Paris, Wilson's bookshop at the Piazza di Spagna and an English bookshop in Florence. Fritze's in Stockholm could also have a few copies 'though there is no hurry in this'. Munthe also asked Murray to help him subscribe to press cuttings ('I would like to read some of the abuse I expect to get'), but the firm promised to see to that. He showed a lively interest in how the book was to be distributed in the USA and was told that 365 copies had been ordered there, compared to only 236 in England.

All this activity demonstrates how eagerly and impatiently Munthe was waiting for his book to appear in print. The queen, he admitted, was still disappointed that he had not dedicated it to her, and to make up for this he asked the publisher to try to get a copy printed for Victoria Day, 12 March. Whether this request was an expression of his bad conscience or a tactical ploy to speed up the printing is hard to say.

It proved impossible to comply with his wishes, but one week after the queen's name day Mr Farquharson informed Munthe that the first copies had come off the presses and that he had sent one to Rome. On 24 March Munthe acknowledged receipt: 'The book looks attractive, the Michael is beautifully done.' After declaring that the book lived up to his expectations he asked the publishers to send it 'with the author's compliments' to the following people: Rennell Rodd, Mrs R. Crawshay, Her Majesty the Queen of Sweden, H.R.H. Prince Philip of Hesse, Baroness von Uexküll and Dr Max Dressler.

WITH THE AUTHOR'S COMPLIMENTS

Munthe had long been searching for someone to help him with the practicalities of life. In the autumn of 1928 Rosina's 16-year-old son Vittorio Massimino moved to Rome to work for him as a sort of factotum, or 'valet', as Munthe called him. The Russian Natasha Khaliutine had since 1923 fulfilled the function of secretary and reader – she took care of some of his correspondence and read aloud to him for several hours each day, also in Swedish. It was Natasha who had helped Munthe with the proofreading of *The Story of San Michele* in December, and now he wanted her to come to him in Rome. However, the suggestion aroused stiff-necked opposition from the queen, who loathed the Russian and could only talk of her in terms such as 'that odious Bolshevik'.

Whatever the queen thought of the matter, by the beginning of February Natasha was installed in Rome, where Munthe rented a room for her in a French convent not far from the Villa Svezia. The ardour with which the queen attacked the unfortunate Natasha in a letter to Hilda indicates that she actually saw her as a rival for 'his' attention:

> I have given strict orders to my own people to ignore her – the only possibility of accepting this new whim, which I find exceedingly tactless. Excuse the strong expression. Everything was so nice & peaceful before, he was in good spirits with all his good sides prevailing, now he is irritable & difficult to deal with. I think he must feel with his keen perception that I disapprove of the scheme. I assure you, I am convinced that there is nothing morally wrong about it, but the tactlessness remains. He praises her good qualities; before I knew she was really coming I told him I found her 'odious, filthy, dirty, impossible'. She reads *all* letters to him, as he says he can scarcely read anything any more - & that is the tragic side of the whole matter. What shall become of him if it grows still worse!

Despite the proximity of 'that odious Bolshevik', the queen's condition improved somewhat during the winter of 1929 and she was able to make excursions by carriage at the Villa Borghese. But after more than a year at the queen's side Munthe himself was so worn out that he sent to Baden for a locum, Dr Krieg, in order to get some rest. At the end of March he went to Capri for a month. When he returned to Rome on 2 May *The Story of San Michele* had come out and the queen had received her copy of the book.

It had come from the publisher's, 'with the author's compliments'. The way in which the book was delivered was so impersonal that the queen could not help remarking on it in a letter to Hilda. Why had Munthe not handed his life's work to her in person? Had he gone to Capri deliberately in order not to be in Rome when she took delivery of the book? Was he uneasy about her reaction to a work which she had hoped would be dedicated to her, but in which she was barely mentioned, despite the central role she had played in his life story? Or was it an expression of the doctor's habitual apparent indifference to his authorial self, a manifestation of the anguished attitude he had to his literary work? His speciality, after all, was writing out prescriptions . . .

In any case, it was the queen who produced the first 'review' of the book, in the course of several letters to Hilda; whether Axel was treated to the same version is unknown. On the positive side, she wrote, is the fact that it is 'charmingly written as all his books are', which is why the public will appreciate it. 'It is more des anecdotes de sa vie & lots about animals & most charming too.' On the negative side, Victoria noted 'a vein of conceitedness' which she disliked. The author, she wrote, is also too preoccupied with 'sexual problems': 'It is a mania of his right now, this topic.' The queen's reaction was thus a mixed one, but it is not impossible that she was keeping her potential enthusiasm in check out of consideration for Hilda, who had neither read the book nor could be expected to wish to hear it praised.

After a month in Rome Munthe left the queen at the end of May and travelled to London in company with Natasha, 'as I have nobody else who will help me & I am utterly alone', as he explained to the queen. The trip was, of course, a result of the book, which had already attracted a certain amount of attention. 'He is tremendously taken up by his book & all the praise & admiration he gets from all sides for it,' Victoria reported to Hilda after his departure. 'In fact, he is childishly happy about it, though he professes not to care. "Wherever I come I only hear about my book".'

That Munthe was a master of simulated modesty should hardly be a secret by this time. With the publication of *The Story of San Michele* all records in this genre were broken. One German professor of philosophy called the book 'eine liebenswürdige Selbstbespiegelung' – 'a lovable self-reflection' – and the queen agreed. How lovable the self-reflection was is debatable, but a self-reflection it certainly was. If narcissism was tangible in the pages of the text, it was even more conspicuous in Munthe's behaviour after the book's publication. When Rebecca West visited Capri she had shared his *maccaroni* and 'wept bitterly' into his best handkerchief, which he was still waiting to get back. Now he wrote to her and asked to be allowed to invite her to lunch in Soho in order to consult her about a question that was bewildering him:

> My friend Rennell Rodd, who persuaded me to publish this book for the sake of the donkeys and mules and horses in Naples, told me it was a 'very unusual book'. Old John Murray, who printed it, wrote me in one of the last letters he ever wrote that it was a 'very unusual book', and in less than a week his son has forwarded to me 3 letters from 3 unknown readers who tell me that it is a 'very unusual book'. But nobody has told me why. What is the matter with the book, why is it 'unusual'? If anybody can satisfy my curiosity to have an answer to this question it is you, will you tell me in return for the handkerchief at our dinner in the Soho? [. . .] Why do all these people say the book is 'unusual'? Is it me or the book that is unusual, or both?

Although many readers assured Munthe of the book's excellence, it took some time before it was noticed in the press. The official launch was on 17 April, but Munthe was snorting with impatience and complained after only a few weeks that the publishers were making a botched job of marketing it: 'Cannot you lay your hands upon a reviewer who likes dogs – it is probably our only chance to escape a premature burial. [. . .] Friends of mine are yelling for the book. They say there are no copies left in the English bookshops.'

The book had been mentioned briefly in *The Times* on 26 April, and had received a long and positive review in *The Times Literary Supplement* on 2 May, but otherwise had failed to attract much attention. 'Is there nothing in The Observer?' Munthe wondered at the end of May. Not yet – but a month later, on 23 June, the paper printed a notice by the well-known Scottish politician and writer Robert Cunninghame Graham, which would prove to be decisive in determining the book's fate: 'Seldom have I read anything more moving, tender or more full of "respect humain". [. . .] It has style, wit, humour, great knowledge of the world, mixed with that strange simplicity of mind that often is the attribute of genius.' After Cunninghame Graham's long and enthusiastic review it was not long before a second edition of the book was printed. Before the year's end, there were to be six printings in all.

In order to understand Munthe's childlike delight at the success of *The Story of San Michele*, one ought to consider that at the end of the 1920s he was no longer in the limelight in the same way he had been in the period before the First World War. In England he was 'quelqu'un', as Karl Warburg put it, thanks to his enormous social network. But he seldom visited his homeland and had had nothing published in Swedish since 1909. In the Swedish national encyclopedia, volume 18, 1913, Axel and Arnold received roughly the same amount of coverage – Arnold for his 'leading position among our maritime historians and biographers', Axel for his travel writing and sketches, 'universally admired for their sensitive realism and their delightful presentation'. In the supplementary volume, which appeared in 1926, however, not a single word was devoted to Axel, while Arnold was lauded in a big article. But Arnold died in December of the same year, during Axel's third sojourn in Egypt, and was unable to witness the success of *The Story of San Michele*, which would alter once and for all the balance of strength between the brothers.

THE STORY OF *THE STORY OF SAN MICHELE*

After a period of relative anonymity Axel Munthe had once again leapt into the spotlight – just as he had done forty years earlier when he had moved from Capri to Rome and in a short time become the leading society doctor. Now, in 1929, he found himself on a different level of society, but the circles he moved in were limited, and his blindness and service at court had isolated him from large sections of the world around him. *The Story of San Michele* turned his entire life upside down.

However, the most important explanation for the feeling of triumph Munthe experienced was different, and deeper. With the publication of *The Story of San Michele* a 30-year-old seed came to fruition. The book was a life's work, a revelation of the vision that had directed Axel's life: the dream of a home on Capri, the dream of San Michele. What was to be reviewed was not a book, but a life. The glow in which he now bathed was self-generated and not, as previously, reflected in a royal mirror. His joy was unbounded but he could only express it indirectly, by making light of it.

In the foreword to the book Munthe says that he began writing it during the final phase of the First World War. Compton Mackenzie states in his memoirs that it was written in 1918. But *The Story of San Michele* was not written in a single year – it grew over a long time and was not finished until the end of the 1920s. As a matter of fact, Munthe had been incubating the idea for thirty years, ever since the Villa San Michele was completed. In a letter to John Murray in 1898 he mentioned 'the book about Capri and Tiberius' which he had begun long since and a year later he was even more explicit: 'My house in Capri [. . .] is quite worth seeing and I have written a whole book about it called by its name San Michele.'

The statement that he had already written 'a whole book' should be taken with a pinch of salt. In *The Story of San Michele* Munthe declares that he takes responsibility only for those chapters he has written 'with my own hand', that is, before he started using a typewriter. His duel with the typewriter began around 1904. That some sections of the book were probably composed before then is borne out by drafts in Munthe's early notebooks. But even if some chapters had already been written or conceived by the turn of the century, the writing of *The Story of San Michele* in the version we know must be assigned to a ten-year period from 1917/18 onwards. The bulk of the work seems to have been done after 1926, when the first hints that a book is under way begin to surface. In June 1927 Axel confided to Hilda: 'I am dictating with terrible difficulty a book – it helps me to forget my misery for a while.'

In *The Story of San Michele* Munthe claims that it was Henry James, during his trip to Capri in June 1899, who encouraged him to write a book about the villa, but the letters to Murray show that the work had been started before James's visit. The last time they saw each other, in London during the First World War, James, according to Munthe, encouraged him yet again to write the book: 'There is nothing like writing a book if one wishes to forget one's own misery, there is nothing like writing a book if one cannot sleep.' Perhaps James served in the first place as a sort of alibi for Munthe, who was prone to defer to authority figures, but it is not inconceivable that he really did also supply the impetus. Both Henry James and his brother, the philosopher and spiritualist William James, belonged to Munthe's circle, and Henry James's high opinion of Munthe emerges from a letter to Compton Mackenzie in the spring of 1914:

> If my old admirable friend Axel Munthe is still at Capri (which I apprehend he may not be, however) I should like to ask you to beg him for me that he kindly let me know of his next whereabouts – and whenabouts – in England: so extremely would it interest me to see him again, after much too long an interval, so do I suffer from lack of knowledge of him. If you had been in his care, as I surmise, I rejoice in the conviction of your great profit of it.

That She is Going Downhill is Certain

Munthe had to deal with the proofreading of *The Story of San Michele* and the correspondence it generated in tandem with his daily attendance on the queen, who arrived in Rome in October 1928 and suffered from repeated attacks of cramp and subsequent breathing difficulties during the winter. 'To hint at these attacks in a bulletin is particularly difficult, and doing so would naturally give the King an excuse to pop over here immediately, which would quite certainly make her worse,' Axel reported to the marshal of the realm.

A precondition for the queen's welfare, according to Munthe, was that she be 'left in peace', even by her own family. When the king came to Rome in January 1929, Munthe asked the court to try to persuade him not to stay too long. If the queen's relations with her husband and children were strained, she was deeply grateful to have Munthe as her 'medical adviser'. He had difficulty controlling his temper, but in the autumn of 1928 he was 'more quiet and sensible than last winter': '"He" is now his own best self & looks after me with great care & understanding, as always in cases of emergency,' Victoria reported to Hilda.

As *The Story of San Michele* was making the first stage of its triumphant procession through the Anglo-Saxon world, the queen's condition worsened. On 18 December she gave Hilda an account of the atmosphere at the Villa Svezia:

> Over 6 months now that I have been more or less continually in my bed! [. . .] here things are not always easy. 'He' is wonderfully well, I think, & no one could believe that he is 72. The eyes are, of course, a heavy burden

to bear & I suppose that it is this heavy cross he has to carry which makes him very difficult for his surroundings. [. . .] The Bolshevik is everything now & he lets her read (and open!) all his letters & even the German doctors' letters to him about me are read out by this filthy, detestable beast, whom I loathe.

THE SWEDISH EDITION

Although Munthe showed his best side whenever the queen was ill, his growing vanity made her disillusioned and caused her distress. 'The conceitedness & self-satisfaction are alas! increasing more & more,' she had complained to Hilda the year before *The Story of San Michele* came out: 'Sad with such an eminently intelligent man, indeed a genius, but succumbing to small petty stuff.' Once his success was an established fact, the dam burst and the book became, according to Victoria 'the pivot around which everything moves inside & outside him, the emotive part of his life & all his thoughts move round it. [. . .] it is so childish & not worthy of him.'

The queen's reproaches were undoubtedly justified, but even a less vain person than Munthe would have found it difficult to deal with the fame that followed in the book's wake. Proofs of its success followed each other in rapid succession, and not only in the form of newspaper reviews. The future Nobel prizewinner John Galsworthy wrote to Munthe that the book was 'an amazing record – quite inspiring in many ways; and told with a jest and a candour that wins the heart'. Rudyard Kipling was less effusive, but thought that it was 'a good book, both artistically and in interest', which he enjoyed greatly.

If *The Story of San Michele* did well in England, its success was even greater in the USA. The number of advance orders was 365, but soon the book gathered momentum, and at the beginning of October the publisher, Dutton, announced that they wanted to print an edition of their own. The American edition was dedicated 'To my old friend Sir Esme Howard', Munthe's other British ambassadorial friend (who was now ambassador in Washington), and became an unprecedented success – the book topped the non-fiction bestseller list for 1930, occupied second place the following year and underwent over 100 reprints. The only fly in the ointment was that he was competing for first place with the memoirs of Princess Maria, a writer who, according to Munthe, was 'very given to lying when it suits her'.

The book caused a big stir beyond the confines of the English-speaking world. Publishers in Europe were queuing up to acquire the translation rights. In Sweden alone five publishers wanted to publish it. Bonnier's, who had lost out to Norstedts forty-five years previously over Munthe's first book, this time won the battle. On 20 August Karl Otto Bonnier telegraphed Munthe on Capri and declared himself willing to publish the book. The reply was vintage Munthe:

> My hope that The Story of San Michele should not reach Sweden has evidently been in vain. I had in fact prevented John Murray sending any copies to Swedish newspapers and bookshops. [. . .] Already before receiving your telegram I had received offers from four Swedish publishers and today I have had a telegraphic offer from a fifth. Still more surprising is the number of known and unknown readers who are writing to me, all full of praise of the book. Unfortunately for me I have no literary ambition and what vanity I may possess has already been amply satisfied by the astonishing reception the book has had in England. There is already a second edition and I am told more are soon to follow for all the leading critics are writing their appreciation in words enough to 'faire rougir un cuirassier' as they say in Paris. The American edition is doing very well and Murray has handed me offers from two French and three German editors which I have declined. That the book would have a very large sale in Sweden is certain for several reasons. But I am very reluctant to publish this book in Sweden. I dislike publicity and prefer to die in the obscurity I have lived in to the best of my ability. I only consented to the English edition after receiving the offer of a large sum of money for the protection of Animals – you will see from the slip inserted in the book that all the money goes to my friends the animals, not a penny to me. Owing to the small fees paid to authors in Sweden it would not be worth while [sic] to issue a Swedish edition. Anyhow I have been amusing myself by rewriting the book in my own Swedish chiefly in order not to forget writing in my own tongue, it is high time, I already write easier in English. Maybe you may publish it after my death. This being said I thank you for your offer.

The letter is a distillation of all the earlier letters Munthe wrote on the same theme. He did not wish the book to be published (but everyone else insisted); he 'only consented to the English edition after receiving the offer of a large sum of money' (in actual fact it was he who almost forced Murray to publish it); the book was not worth publishing in Swedish, but he had translated it anyway (but only so that he did not forget his mother tongue).

Although he maintained the opposite, Munthe was in other words desperate to see the book appear in Swedish. This is borne out by the mass of correspondence that was exchanged between himself and Bonnier's during the autumn of 1929. He negotiated with Bonnier for months, but in actual fact he had already made up his mind, having been prevailed upon by the queen:

To the many people who are urging me to forego my reluctance has now been added my patient who has in effect forced me to promise her not only that the book shall be published in Sweden but that it shall be dedicated to her. [. . .] The Queen loves the book and all the animals in it, she is a great lover of animals and it was at her request I even included one of her own beloved dogs in it.

On 27 February 1930 Munthe informed the publisher that the translation was finished. He had made significant alterations to the translator's text, of which not much was said to remain. But even if the book was now available in a Swedish version, no contract had yet been signed. If Bonnier's wished to acquire the Swedish rights, they would have to satisfy his conditions. Munthe had opinions and demands to the very last, and he had nothing against presenting them in the queen's name:

1) No omission or alteration of any sort.
2) I wish to see the last proofs by instalments to be returned rapidly.
3) As the Queen insists more than ever to have her name on the front page with a short dedication, the book must appear in a dignified form in good print and paper etc., approved by us. I warn you she is rather particular in this respect much more so than I but she is so ill that I do not feel like depriving her of the pleasure she takes in fussing about the Swedish book, in fact she takes more interest in its publication than the author. Even if she dies before the book is published she wishes to have her name on it anyhow with the same little dedication already written and much liked by her.

The dedication, which the queen was so fond of, read:

To
THE QUEEN
Protector of oppressed animals
Friend of all dogs

Since July 1929 the queen's state of health had deteriorated ever more rapidly, and during the winter months she became so weak that she was no longer able to write her letters herself. On 26 January 1930 King Gustaf came to Rome. 'Her physician takes a gloomy view of her condition,' it was reported on 18 February by Agnes Bergman, the queen's lady's maid, who at regular intervals kept Hilda informed of the queen's condition. Victoria had severe attacks of breathlessness. 'The situation is actually worsening week by week, and Her Majesty is finding it very hard and troublesome,' Mrs Bergman wrote: 'The phlegm in her lungs has increased and H.M. really needs a great deal of medication to ameliorate the cough and prevent severe attacks of breathlessness.' On 12 March, Victoria's Day, Alexandra Bildt noted in her diary: 'We did not dare believe that she would survive the day. Munthe now completely exhausted, having overstrained himself, called in to her several times a day. His presence calms the poor soul, she gets injections and he sits and holds her emaciated hand.'

As the queen was sinking, the publication date for the Swedish edition of *The Story of San Michele* drew ever closer. The queen wished to see it in print during her lifetime, and there now began a race against time. 'She took an almost morbid interest in the book and insisted trying to read the proofs up to the last when she could hardly hold the pages in her hands'; although Munthe tried to make her stop, 'a few sheets of the MS were lying on her bed the day she died.' During the queen's last week of life there ensued an intensive exchange of letters between Munthe and Karl Otto Bonnier, in which the author tried to speed up publication – at the same time as he himself was slowing it down with his detailed demands regarding the book's appearance.

On 28 March Munthe wrote to Bonnier that the queen was 'most eager' to know when the firm was thinking of publishing the book. But she was now too weak to help with the proofreading, a task that her son had taken over: 'Please let me know about the publication date. If the proofs come soon Prince William who is with us here has offered to read them, myself I cannot do it.' As regards the fee, it was not to be sent to Rome as the money was presumably to be used for the acquisition of an island in Sweden for seabirds. Enclosed with the letter was the signed contract for the book, which Munthe said he had mislaid but now found again.

On 31 March the king left Rome and travelled to the Bay of Naples. Victoria had actually wished to die on Capri, but 'that would have been difficult', according to Munthe. Yet she wanted to die in peace and quiet and it was for that reason that she saw to it that the king left. 'She insisted on sending away both the king and her son, the one to Naples the other to the Riviera when she had only a couple of days to live, she said she wanted to die in peace. I stopped his son going at the last moment but had to let the king go [. . .].'

While the king amused himself in the Bay of Naples (where among other things he spent a day on Capri) Munthe continued to correspond with Bonnier. On 1 April he returned the first sections of the proofs. He said he had 'little time for the book', his time and thoughts being wholly occupied by his dying patient, who like him was insisting that the text be more spaced out. The queen also wished to know when the book would appear, 'she says she must live till then, even if she does not, what is very uncertain, she insists upon the dedication to her.'

Although Munthe claimed to have 'little time for the book', he sent yet another letter to Bonnier the very next day, this time with even more specific demands:

> Both my patient and myself were struck by the crammed appearance of the pages compared to the English book and I hope you will by reducing the number of lines make it look a little better and less commercial. I was also struck by the many alterations in way of spelling especially the foreign words. I repeat again that I do not accept any alterations whatsoever in the MS and if this is not adhered to I shall insist upon having the proofs returned here once more. [. . .] I beg you to see to [it] that this does not continue or as I said before I shall not godkänna [approve] the proofs as ready for print.

The king's stay in the Bay of Naples was to be short: on 3 April Munthe recalled him to Rome. At 7.40 p.m. the following day he issued the following medical bulletin: 'The queen died quietly and peacefully of heart-failure this evening at 7 o'clock. A. Munthe, senior physician-in-ordinary, doctor to H.M. the Queen.'

COME SOON

During her last few weeks the queen had suffered unbearable torments, and Munthe declared that he 'helped her to die without further suffering': 'The greatest service I have ever done to her during these thirty seven years was when I helped her to die according to my promise,' he confided to Cunninghame Graham. What he was referring to was pain relief, perhaps in the form of morphine, a method that he had employed throughout his medical career and which he had extolled in private letters as well as in publications.* Whether this method should be described as pain relief or euthanasia is a question of the strength of the dosage.

Everything points to the fact that the queen did indeed wish for a death 'in peace and quiet', without visits even from her nearest family. Her decision to send her husband away when she believed she was about to die speaks for itself. According to Munthe, during the last weeks she met her relatives for only a few minutes each day, and that 'unwillingly'. When Munthe described the family's reaction to the queen's death he did not mince his words: 'The family is delighted she is dead and takes very little

---

* In a letter to William Blackwood from 1894 he writes that unfortunately he was not able to help Mr Story's wife to live but that he helped her to die, 'which is quite as important'.

trouble to conceal it,' he confided to his son Peter, adding: 'All this is of course private, the legend must be allowed to go on.'

Munthe had a weakness for drama and drastic turns of phrase, but his comments about the tense relationship between the queen and her intimate circle were not exaggerated. They are supported by Alexandra Bildt's diary, according to which the queen allowed no one to enter her room during the last few weeks. 'The only [visitor] has been Munthe, her devoted friend, who till the bitter end had the ability to calm her by sitting beside her and holding her hand. Everyone else tired her – however dear they were to her [. . .].'

The particulars Munthe gives of relationships within the royal family are borne out by one conspicuous absence at the queen's deathbed: that of the Crown prince. Where was Gustaf Adolf, her eldest son and the heir to the Swedish throne? He was not in the Villa Svezia; he was not even in Rome. The explanation is given in a letter from Munthe to the Swedish archbishop Nathan Söderblom:

> We will talk about the Queen you and I one day, it was a stately ship, but she was a poor human being in many ways, she belonged besides to another century than we do. She was wrongly judged both by her admirers and her enemies, friends she had none according to her own saying to me the day before she died. She was a very bad judge of men and women and kept aloof from those who might have helped her to see clear, the only one of her own family for whom she felt some affection [= Wilhelm] is the least satisfactory of them. The best of them, her eldest son, remained a total stranger to her heart and mind til the last. In vain did I try all these last years to open her eyes and make her understand what a fine fellow he is. Our last quarrel, and we had many, was when she opposed with her last strength my suggestion to make him come here when the end was approaching.

Relations between Queen Victoria and her eldest son had been strained for a long time. Since his young days – and not least since his marriage to Margaret of Connaught – the Crown prince had been strongly pro-British and was regarded by many people, not only by his mother, as a political radical. His pro-British stance was strengthened when in 1923 he married his second wife, Louise Mountbatten.

Four people were present at the queen's death-bed: the king, prince Wilhelm, Munthe and Agnes Bergman. 'The last words she spoke she whispered them to me, and strange words they were,' Munthe confided to his son Peter: 'Soon after I put her to sleep.'

What were those 'strange words' that the queen of Sweden addressed to Axel Munthe before she closed her eyes? There is no reply in the letter to his son Peter. But seven years later, in a conversation with his English publisher, Munthe felt prompted to reveal the secret. He related how he and the king had stood on either side of the queen's sick bed, holding her hands. The last words the queen uttered, turning to Munthe, were: 'Come soon.'

THE LAST RITES

According to a newspaper report, the queen was embalmed by Dr Munthe early on the morning of 6 April. What the newspaper did not reveal was that it was Victoria's 'express wish' that Axel should embalm her. It was her way of extending their relationship beyond death and assuring herself that the last person to see her before her coffin was closed would be her beloved; a last expression of the intimacy that had distinguished their relationship from the outset. For all his professionalism, it cannot have been an easy task for Axel to perform. What did he think and feel, 'half dead from fatigue', carrying out that last rite on a body which had in more than one respect been his for almost four decades?

Three days later Victoria's remains, encased in a lead-lined coffin, were transported by train and boat to Stockholm. Axel stayed in Rome: 'I am so tired out that I have declined to go home on Wednesday with the king but will remain here for the present to break up Villa Svezia and arrange about sending home all the things.' Hilda, who lived in Stockholm, was not only present at the interment in Riddarholm Church on 12 April but was also invited to have a chat with King Gustaf.

The quotation above is taken from a letter to Karl Otto Bonnier, written on 5 April, the day after the queen's death. A telegram from Bonnier had caused Munthe some anxiety about whether or not the publisher had received the instructions about chapter headings. The queen was dead, but Munthe continued to agonise over the appearance of the book, on behalf of himself, the queen and Prince Wilhelm:

> Prince William was horrified at the sight of the proofs and insists with me that the pages must have less lines and more space between the lines and that your intended cramming together of the book into about four hundred pages will ruin its appearance and cannot be accepted by us. The Queen herself repeated the thing even the day before she died.

When the book came out at the beginning of May, Munthe's typographical demands had been satisfied in full measure and the dedication to the queen closed with the following postscript:

The day before her death
the Queen made me promise
that this dedication
would remain unaltered
in the book

A LIFELONG RELATIONSHIP

During Victoria's long struggle for life, Munthe revealed his unique qualities as a doctor. He had once committed himself to the 'saving of this poor lady', in Prince Max's words, and in the last months of her life he came into his own – just as he did on the earlier occasions when she was near death, in 1907 and 1926.

A lifelong relationship had come to an end. During the thirty-seven years that Victoria and Munthe had known each other, they had been infinitely closer to each other than the queen had been to her lawfully wedded husband. A simple mathematical calculation demonstrates that, from 1893 until her death, Victoria met her doctor significantly more often than her husband; on the contrary, she went out of her way to see as little of him as possible.

In point of fact, Victoria lived two parallel lives, an official one with her husband, and a secret one, which she chose for herself, with her beloved doctor, whom she adored. Axel Munthe was the man in her life, it was he who made life worth living for her. But it is equally true to say that no other woman occupied such a large place in Munthe's life as Victoria. He often complained about all the trouble that his position as Victoria's doctor brought in its wake, but that was partly – and especially in the beginning – a way of concealing the nature of the relationship, partly an expression of a genuine need for solitude. It was also a convenient argument to resort to when he wanted to avoid other commitments, something Victoria was well aware of: 'It is, of course, so convenient to say such a thing & to get out of all other obligations in that way.'

Yet there can be no doubt that Victoria was more dependent on Munthe, both intellectually and emotionally, than he on her. In this respect their relationship was no different from the general pattern of Munthe's relationships with other people, men as well as women. He was happy to associate with people whom he regarded as stimulating or agreeable company, but seems not to have had a deeper need of them. As far as Victoria was concerned, it is obvious that Munthe was truly devoted to her, but after the passion of the early years the relationship, on his side, seems to have been characterised mostly by loyalty and sympathy. 'The only people I really liked', wrote Munthe with great self-knowledge in *The Story of San Michele*, 'were those I felt sorry for.' Fellow-feeling was in fact a precondition for successful treatment: 'You cannot be a good doctor without pity.' Whatever form Axel's relationship to Victoria took over the years, compassion was a basic constituent.

Munthe's sway over Victoria was multi-faceted, ranging from medical interventions to a strong ideological influence. With the passing of the years Victoria came to be deeply influenced by his opinions, not least in the field of animal protection. And it is not difficult to see Munthe's ideas behind the queen's charitable work among the Lapps and other forerunners of the 'people of the wasteland' in the northern parts of Sweden.

His influence over the queen made him highly controversial. Right from the very beginning he was regarded with scepticism, envy and pure loathing by medical colleagues as well as courtiers. According to a person with a good insight into court life, there emerged, with the passing of the years, 'a party within the inner circle which wanted to distance the doctor from his patient', but the way in which Munthe handled Victoria's health crisis in the summer of 1926 meant that the attempt failed. Even if Munthe had his intimates, the court set took every opportunity to slander him behind his back. During his stay at Drottningholm Palace in the summer of 1928, Munthe, according to Victoria, was 'very good & patient the whole time', although he was so uncomfortable:

> It must have been such an ordeal for him remaining so long & in surroundings which he disliked thoroughly. Luckily he did not seem to realise *how* they dislike him. He has scarcely a friend, they all abuse him, behind his back, of course, & play then amiable with him & flatter through making him convey things to me which they want me to know. And he is so naïf that he accepts it all.

As far as Gustaf, the third factor in the equation, was concerned, most of the evidence points to his having found the triangular relationship of practical benefit. He could hardly avoid noticing what a positive influence Munthe had on Victoria in general and during her periods of acute illness in particular.

Munthe was, in fact, the price Gustaf had to pay for his freedom and for preserving the royal marriage and the myth surrounding it. The price was high but the arrangement kept all the parties concerned happy. Perhaps this arrangement evolved naturally, perhaps at some particular point in time an agreement was reached whereby the rules of the game were laid down.

There was nothing Gustaf could do about his spouse's feelings for Munthe, but propriety, as well as pride, made its demands. He could not, for example, approve of her making decisions about her life and travels totally on her own, and on Capri it was rumoured at least on one occasion that Gustaf wanted to stop Victoria visiting the island: '[. . .] she is coming down here quite soon,' wrote Wivica Ankarcrona in the winter of 1926: 'So it was a lie that the King forbade her to set foot in Italy because of Dr. M., as people have been saying here – for there is a fair amount of talk about those two here, unfortunately.'

The fact that Gustaf's attitude to Munthe varied from time to time is natural. It must have hurt to see Victoria so openly preferring another man's company and advice. Yet he was king, and she was queen, he was her superior and entitled to make decisions for her. Victoria also knew her place in the hierarchy. That she associated unwillingly with her husband is one thing – when he entered the room, she invariably rose to her feet.

But it was to Axel that she whispered her last words.

Death

1930–1949

THE BESTSELLER

Physician, metaphysician & genius.
James Rennell Rodd on Axel Munthe

IN A LETTER to Karl Otto Bonnier, Munthe declared that he lacked literary ambition, that the fate of the Swedish edition was a matter of indifference to him, that he belonged to a past generation and therefore did not expect much respect from 'all your great modern writers and critics', in his self-deprecating formulation.

As we have seen, Munthe did not present a copy of the English edition to the queen in person, but sent her a copy by way of the publisher 'with the author's compliments' – probably because he was unsure what her reaction would be. When the Swedish translation came out there were further evasions, this time in relation to Gustaf V, who did not receive a book until he asked for one himself. 'The King told me in the telefon [sic] that he was very offended I had not given him a copy, so he better get one,' Munthe wrote nonchalantly to his publisher, asking him to send a copy with greetings from the author. Thus neither the king nor the queen received a signed copy from Munthe.

What the king thought of the book is not recorded, but Munthe's anxiety about the reaction of the press was unfounded, as usual. Although some reviewers pointed out that certain parts of the book were written in an old-fashioned style, by and large the reviews were glowing.

If there was one notice that Munthe probably read with a degree of apprehension, it was the one signed Tor Hedberg. The review was essentially positive about the book and its author, who was said to be 'a splendid, extremely entertaining storyteller of the pronounced English masculine type, whose grim, drastic or humorous images drawn from a more than usually varied life entertain and captivate and burn themselves into the memory'. But the events at Högsjö manor forty-five years earlier lived on in the mind of the 78-year-old Hedberg – now a member of the Swedish Academy – and can be glimpsed in phrases whose autobiographical background were obvious to the initiated:

A book which is largely about Italy, written in English by a Swedish doctor, then translated into Swedish by another hand, is already a rather unusual phenomenon by its very nature, yet it is not too surprising to one who on his journey through life has come across and kept company with its author. For – and partly at his own instigation – his life has turned out to be an exception, a vagabond existence outside the usual parameters, a quirky, ostensibly chance scaling of the heights of society. With remarkable consistency he has been a man who does whatever occurs to him, and he has had an unusual talent for winning over people by neglecting them.

One of the few people – perhaps the only one – who knew how to interpret this text was Munthe himself: 'The sarcastic article by Tor Hedberg in *Dagens Nyheter* was exactly what I had expected and I am sure more in that style will follow,' he wrote in a form of words which he varied in other letters.

But that was as autobiographical as Hedberg got, although he could hardly have failed to see the episode with Baroness von Mecklenburg reflected in the chapter 'Château Rameaux', in which the author seduces a young countess behind her substantially older husband's back. Munthe could not resist portraying the great love of his younger days but chose to transpose the action to France.

Munthe's letters and conversations during these years centred round a single topic – the book and its improbable success in different countries. An eyewitness to a lunch in London, where not all the guests had heard of Munthe, remembered how he 'immediately started by complaining in a loud voice about how onerous life was when one had become a "best-seller", how he was never left in peace, how people rang him up from all over the world asking for a contract to translate his book into this language or that, etc.'. A letter to John Böttiger, senior curator at the Royal Palace, will serve to illustrate the mixture of self-publicising and unreflecting boastfulness that coloured Munthe's attitude:

The danish edition is having an even greater success than in Sweden, according to the amazing press-cuttings from danish and norwegian papers I have just received. The incomprehensible finnish edition is surprisingly smart in appearance to such a small public. The english has reached seventeen editions and in America it was a month ago in its fortieth edition, the publisher expects it to have sold one hundred thousand copies at the end of the year. Five other translations are going on, but what pleases me most is that the National Library for the blind in London is editing the book in Braille, the biggest book ever done, next to the Bible.

When Munthe's old acquaintance from Capri, Helena Nyblom's daughter Ellen, interviewed him for a newspaper, he once again posed the question:

> Tell me, I want to know, *why* has my book become such a success? From a purely psychological standpoint, I would be grateful to know the truth, for it is really a mystery to me. I am not an outstanding human being. It is no masterpiece. And yet people still seem to be crazy about it. [. . .] *What is the reason?*

On the Borderline
Between the Real and the Unreal

However aware he was of his worth as an author, Axel was undoubtedly astonished by the enormous sales of his book. So astonished, in fact, that he felt compelled to supplement the book with three new forewords: one to the Swedish edition, which in turn formed part of the basis for the foreword to the twelfth English edition (autumn 1930), and one to the illustrated edition (1936).*

In the first two forewords, Munthe addressed the question of the book's genre. Some reviewers had called it 'An autobiography', but it is not, he wrote: 'I never meant to write a book about myself; it was, on the contrary, my constant preoccupation the whole time to try to shake off this vague personality,' he explained, with a telling insight into his own character. To call the book 'The Memoirs of a Doctor' seemed to the author even more inappropriate. A doctor was entitled to laugh, like everyone else, but he was not entitled to laugh at his patients, let alone to cry with them, 'a whimpering doctor is a bad doctor': 'An old physician should [. . .] think twice before sitting down in his arm-chair to write his memoirs. Better to keep what he has seen of Life and Death. Better write no memoirs at all, and leave the dead in peace and living to their illusions.'

The Story of San Michele had also been called 'a story of Death', an interpretation Munthe could accept as death was seldom absent from his thoughts. (This was something the Czech translator latched onto when he gave the book the title *Kniha o živote a smrti*, 'A Book of Life and Death'.) Here, he further teased out a thread from the 'Letters from Naples', about authors who (subtext: as opposed to himself) preferred to write 'short sensational stories' sitting in a comfortable armchair rather than to 'toil

---

* The twelfth English edition also included a new section, about the maid Anna who sells photographs of Munthe's famous patients (in the chapter 'Miss Hall').

through life to collect the material for them, to describe diseases and Death [rather] than to fight them'.

No, *The Story of San Michele* was a book about Life. About Life, which is 'untouched by time and fate, indifferent to mankind's sorrows and joys, full of mystery and unfathomable as the Sphinx'. Life itself is 'the greatest writer'. 'But is Life always true?' Munthe wonders, with a formulation that leads us directly to that question which has preoccupied readers and critics ever since the book came out: how much of what is depicted is true? This question is never put to fiction writers, who after all are usually judged by their ability to use their imagination. That it was posed in Munthe's case is due to the fact that the author appears under his own name and that most of the other persons – and places – in the book are either named or possible to identify. At the same time, the stories have obvious fictional traits. The answer that Munthe gave was as follows:

> I am aware that some of the scenes in this book are laid on the ill-defined borderland between the real and the unreal, the dangerous No Man's Land between fact and fancy where so many writers of memoirs have come to grief. It would be a great relief to me if the reader without further ado would consign these episodes to the peaceful realm of poetry. I have tried my best by means of a few well-known technical tricks to make at least some of these episodes pass off as 'short sensational stories'. After all, it is only a question of form. It will be a great relief to me if I have succeeded, I do not ask for better than not to be believed.

It is an evasive answer, but one that contains an important fact: that the author has availed himself of 'some technical tricks' to avoid confusion with reality. At the same time, we remember Munthe declaring, more than forty years earlier, that he never invented anything but 'wrote only *historically*'. The author's 'tricks' took many different forms, but several episodes in *The Story of San Michele* reflect genuine events in Munthe's life. That they were refracted through Munthe's clouded and fantasy-filled prism is another story.

This is true not only of the accounts of major events such as his work in Naples during the cholera epidemic or the mountain-climbing accident in the Alps, but also of biographical details. That Munthe chose *colitis* as his medical hobbyhorse undoubtedly arose from the fact that he himself suffered for lengthy periods from an irritable colon. At the same time there are decisive differences between the Munthe of the book and the Munthe of reality. One is that Victoria is not named in the book. Another is that Munthe is a bachelor. As we saw, this led to the flight from Paris in 1887 being ascribed to a conflict with Charcot, whereas the real reason was the divorce from Ultima.

Munthe's portrayal of Charcot is a good example of his tendency to upgrade his relationship with other people and thereby also his own importance. Like all egocentrics, he had a tendency to describe acquaintances as 'friends' and to imply an intimacy that was by no means always perceived as mutual. For instance, Munthe's flattery of Rennell Rodd and Esme Howard is out of all proportion to the amount of space he occupies in their memoirs, where he is allotted only a few lines. In Munthe's shadow, people as well as events grew to supernatural proportions.

Munthe writes several pages about his acquaintance with Maupassant, but we do not know how well the two men knew each other. However, the fact that we lack documentation to back up his assertions does not necessarily mean that they were pulled out of thin air. Most of Munthe's tales contain a kernel of truth, and even if it is often difficult to judge the size of the kernel, we would do well to take seriously Munthe's claim that he always wrote 'historically'. A case in point is that of Frederick Myers, founder of the Society for Psychical Research. Myers was convinced that he would survive death and, according to Munthe, his expression was 'calm and clear' when he realised that his hour had come. Myers had come to an agreement with William James, brother of the author, that whichever of them died first would send a message from the other side. In *The Story of San Michele* Munthe tells us that he and James found themselves at the Hotel Primavera in Rome on the day that Myers died: Munthe being there in his capacity as Myers's doctor. When Myers died James sat ready to note down the message, but nothing came.

Munthe's depiction of Myers's stoical attitude towards death corresponds with James's description in a letter to his brother Henry, written the same day: 'His intense assurance of a future life gives him, and through his example has given the family, a curious serenity and superiority to the accidents of his illness which seems to have struck immensely both Baldwin and Munthe who has been in consultation.' So Munthe was there, but was the course of events exactly as he described it in the book? The reservation about 'No Man's Land' tells us not to ask that question.

Another example of Munthe's way of writing 'historically' is the portrayal of his Swedish medical colleague Gustaf Norström, who also has the role of soothsayer and is therefore to some extent Munthe's alter ego. Norström is not a fictional character, but a doctor who practised in Paris for several decades. But when Munthe claims that it was he who discovered Norström's talent as a masseur and that they wrote a handbook together about Swedish massage, he is playing fast and loose with the truth. Norström was a well-known masseur and the author of several comprehensive books on the subject, none of them written in collaboration with Munthe.

Some of his 'tricks' were of a geographical nature. 'The chronology rather puzzles me in places,' John Murray wrote to Munthe. 'However I daresay you purposely leave chronology vague.' This was true; Munthe took both geographical and chronological liberties. To give only one example, he transposes to Paris events that happened in Rome or Sweden. His conflict with the Italian medical establishment is said to have taken place in the French capital, and the love story involving the countess at the Château Rameaux is obviously a veiled account of the passionate affair at the Högsjö manor. The sailing enthusiast Lord Dufferin figures in connection with the Villa San Michele although the ambassador left Italy long before the house was built – a chronological shift that makes it possible for the author to unite two passions, Capri and sailing, in one narrative unit. A similar act of compression, for reasons of narrative technique, is performed in relation to the Lapland journey, which took place in 1885 – not in 1884 as asserted in the book. This apparently innocuous chronological inexactitude is there in order to enable him to dramatise the journey to Naples, which happened in 1884. The distance from Lapland to Naples is greater than that between Högsjö and Naples and the wild nature of Lapland is more exotic than a manor in southern Sweden. At the same time, Munthe could not resist hinting that his walking tour of Lapland had a certain English connection. The misses from Medstugan are not mentioned, but it is from the English newspaper *The Times* that Munthe learns of the cholera epidemic!

'The Corpse-Conductor' is an example of a quite different sort of trick. The short story describes how Munthe brings the body of a young student who had died in Heidelberg home to Sweden. During the journey the coffin is mistaken for another that holds the remains of a Russian general. The whole thing finishes with the latter being buried in Uppsala while the young Swede is interred in Russia to the accompaniment of fanfares from the general's regiment. It is one of the best and most skilfully narrated episodes in the book, but it was not based on personal experience. Instead, it seems to have been inspired by a notice in Munthe's own newspaper, *Stockholms Dagblad*, which in 1885 reported exactly the same story, with the role of the Swedish student played by 'a woman from Berlin'.

'I think that "Der Leichenbegleiter" is good writing,' Munthe wrote to Esme Howard, adding slyly: 'God knows where it came from!'

This Vague Personality

The Story of San Michele is a blend of fiction and philosophy, of melodramatic cock-and-bull stories with varying degrees of verisimilitude and gobbets of philosophy that bring together the leitmotifs of Munthe's life and ideology. Munthe suggested to Murray that the book would sell well as it contained so much about animals, and the queen shared that analysis. They were right, as it turned out. Untold numbers of animal rights activists and ordinary readers wrote to the author to thank him for his battle on behalf of the rights of dogs and birds. The book's success meant in turn that Munthe could make some concrete contributions in that field; for instance, by initiating a ban on bird hunting on Capri (see page 300).

Alongside St Roch, patron saint of dogs, it was St Francis, the friend of birds and of the poor, who was Munthe's favourite among the saints. Since the last time he had apostrophised Francis, in 'My Thoughts Fly' (1885), the doctor and *Il Poverello* had found something else that united them: blindness. St Francis was Munthe's real hero, 'the frail dreamer' with his 'wonderful eyes' which 'neither God nor man could meet with anger in theirs', the bearer of Christ's message of love. Who shall fear Jehovah if the din of His wrath's thunder can be drowned out by the twittering of birds? The God of Wrath, whose voice rang out so powerfully in *Red Cross & Iron Cross*, had receded and, at the end of his life, Munthe had returned to Christ and Tolstoy. It is on holy Francis's shoulders that Munthe falls asleep in the closing lines of the book.

Munthe's love of animals contributed to both his own and the book's popularity, but not everyone appreciated it. On the contrary, there were many who criticised him for his misanthropy, for so openly preferring dogs and birds to human beings. One acquaintance, for example, spoke of Munthe's divided self as a 'deeply *tragic*' but 'indescribably moving dualism', 'not least because when the author with the most touching attentiveness listens to and empathises with "the sighing of dumb beasts", he does not have much left over for his fellow travellers in this wonderful world apart from the most bitter contempt – and yet as a doctor he has been sacrificing himself for their welfare throughout his life.'

Despite his ambition to get rid of his 'vague personality', Munthe devoted several pages of the book to a diagnosis of his 'dualism'. The *doppelgänger* motif that appeared in the early sketches returns in *The Story of San Michele* in a more developed form. Munthe made no secret of what both he himself and others perceived as contradictory in his personality. In the chapter 'Insomnia' he confides in Dr Norström that he is tired of artificial city life, of all the 'rich Americans and silly neurotic females'. He longed for 'a simple life amongst simple, unsophisticated people':

> All I needed was a white-washed room with a hard bed, a deal table, a couple of chairs and a piano. The twitter of birds outside my open window and the sound of the sea from afar. All the things I really cared for could

be got for very little money, I should be quite happy in the humblest surroundings as long as I had nothing ugly around me.

When Norström's gaze begins to wander scornfully over the valuable paintings, vases and tapestries in the room, Munthe retaliates by telling him about a conversation he has recently had with himself, or more accurately with his *doppelgänger*. As they walk along the elegant shopping streets of London, Munthe asks his *doppelgänger* to scrutinise each object in the shop windows. They pass shops selling Renaissance paintings, a Cromwell clock and expensive clothes. But the *doppelgänger* explains that he is more comfortable in old clothes than new ones, and more interested in the dogs strutting after their masters on the street.

Once back in Paris, Munthe tells us, the *doppelgänger* behaves like a caged animal. He hangs around the waiting room in the Avenue de Villiers and forces his way in to see the doctor in front of the rich Americans. During lunch he sits and stares at Munthe, his brain is tired and he has no appetite, and at night he leans over Munthe's pillow and implores him 'for God's sake to take him away', he can't stand it much longer. Neither can Norström, who asks Munthe to tell his *doppelgänger* that he is a humbug: 'I bet you anything you like that he will soon pick up another Bukhara rug to spread under your deal table, a Siennese Madonna and a Flemish gobelin to hang on the walls of your white-washed room, a Cinquecento Gubbio plate for eating your macaroni, and an old Venetian glass for drinking your Capri Bianco!' In the next chapter Munthe is on Capri, far from the city of ostentation.

What is interesting about this self-analysis is that it shows how conscious Munthe was of the split in his own character. He was a recluse who also moved in the *grand monde* and enjoyed his influence over those who had been born to a position that he himself had had to struggle to attain. He treated poor patients for nothing and donated substantial sums for charitable purposes while at the same time collecting expensive antiques. He was simultaneously an ascetic and an aesthete. He preferred simple food but liked to eat it off a *cinquecento* dish. 'Full of inconsistencies, yet simple as home-made bread', was his son Malcolm's accurate description of his father.

That the *doppelgänger* theme was central to Munthe emerges from his obsession with the figure of Faust. The historical Doctor Faust, who lived in Germany at the beginning of the sixteenth century, played a prominent role as an astrologer at the royal court despite his reputation as a charlatan. He made his way by means of all kinds of tricks and by his boastful bearing, but at the same time he was a Renaissance man thirsting for knowledge. He was generally regarded as being a black magician in league with the Devil.

Goethe's drama *Faust* to a large extent mirrors the author's own anguish and divided personality. Goethe too saw himself as a 'double nature' who had sold himself to the court and the aristocracy, the 'proud and dissatisfied', as he called them. It was not difficult for Munthe to see a parallel here with his own career. But his identification went deeper than that, as we see from *The Story of San Michele*, which is constructed as a Faustian drama with Munthe himself in the leading role.

In Goethe's play the knowledge-hungry doctor makes a pact with Mephistopheles to 'act unceasingly' without being fettered by human laws, and to gain access to secret knowledge. But the price is high; he must surrender his soul. In *The Story of San Michele* Mephistopheles makes several appearances: just like the other *doppelgängers*, always in the capacity of soothsayer and debunker of Munthe the fraud. In the first chapter Munthe describes how, during his first visit to Capri, he becomes lost in dreams of a future there. Then a 'tall figure wrapped in a rich mantle' appears who tells him about the tribute he has exacted two thousand years earlier from the Emperor Tiberius so that he could find peace on the island: that his name should be dishonoured for eternity.

When Munthe asks what price he will have to pay for the realisation of his dreams, for his striving, the answer is that he must give up his future and become 'an unfulfilled promise, a Might-Have-Been'. The expression is borrowed from the poem 'Superscription' by Dante Gabriel Rossetti:

> Look in my face; my name is Might-have-been;
> I am also called No-more, Too-late, Farewell.

The lines can be found inscribed in one of Munthe's early commonplace books, and the fact that he chose them to describe himself forty-five years later shows how important they were to him. Talk of a 'Might-Have-Been' can be seen as an expression of coquettishness. Instead, it bears witness to self-knowledge and resignation. If Munthe had not wasted his talent he could perhaps have been the leading researcher that not only he himself but others too saw in embryonic form during his years of study. But he had sacrificed that opportunity for the more attainable triumph of becoming a 'fashionable doctor' – just like Faust long ago.

As if this was not enough, before Munthe dies Mephistopheles will demand an even higher price from him: he 'will have watched for many years from this place the sun set over cloudless days of happiness and the moon rise over starlit nights of dreams'. Like Faust, he was robbed of his sight.

Munthe's identification with the German black magician was not a literary construction; he clearly believed himself to possess superhuman powers. What kind of 'mysterious power' was it that emanated from his hand and made the rich and powerful of the world obey him and the Lapps to believe that he was a healer? Where did it come from? Was he, as the Lappish people believed, in league with the 'little people'?

> I, of all people, am anxious to know it, because ever since I was a boy, I have been aware that I myself possessed this power, whatever name is given to it, in an exceptional degree. Most of my patients, young and old, men and women, seemed to find it out sooner or later and often spoke to me about it. My comrades in the hospital wards all knew about it. [. . .] All the keepers in the Jardin Zoologique and Ménagerie Pezon knew about it. It was a familiar trick of mine to put their snakes, lizards, tortoises, parrots, owls, bears and big cats into a state of lethargy [. . .] Still it is obviously impossible to speak of mental suggestion here. There must be some other power at work, I ask again and in vain, what is this power?

Yes, what sort of power was it that Munthe had known himself to possess ever since childhood? A power which made the superman Doctor Faust as obvious a figure to identify with as *Il Poverello* and Tiberius. Did Munthe also possess skills that, at least metaphorically, could be seen as the result of a pact with the Prince of Darkness?

A Genealogical Digression

One question that is raised in coded form in *The Story of San Michele* is the author's biological background. His father declared that Axel 'had not been begotten by him but by the devil himself', and his mother is said not to have understood 'that she could have given birth to such a monster', whom moreover she did not suckle. Did Munthe wish to say something with this? The question is worth a digression.

The whole thing could be dismissed as fiction – were it not for the stubborn rumours that give substance to the claim that Munthe was in some way related to the Swedish royal family. This kinship would explain his rapid advancement as a physician, not least within the court. But on the other hand it could have been his rapid ascent that gave rise to the rumour. Wherever it stems from, it is of long standing.

Among other things, people have pointed to the outward resemblance between Munthe and Gustaf V. According to this rumour, Munthe was the king's half-brother, the fruit of an illegitimate relationship between Crown Prince Oscar (the future King Oscar II) and Axel's mother. 'Here [on Capri] he is generally regarded as King Oscar's son,' Wivica Ankarcrona wrote to her sister-in-law in 1925:

Do they say that in Sweden too, he has become remarkably like him in recent years [. . .] There is certainly a lot of evidence for this, his feeling for music and love of art & then how he laughs at how unlike he & his brother are, which they certainly are to a marked degree. His need to give orders & and feel superior to everyone may also come from there.

There is no evidence that the rumour had any basis in reality. In the first place, there are no indications that Prince Oscar and the God-fearing Aurora Munthe ever met. In the second place, Anna and Axel were incredibly like each other. If Axel was Oscar's child, then so must Anna have been. This is implausible for several reasons, not least when we consider that Anna was conceived on the Munthe's wedding night. Arnold, on the other hand, was less like his siblings, something that Munthe himself, as we have seen, used to laugh at.

The Munthe family has always been preoccupied with genealogy. On a family tree preserved in the Swedish National Archives, Axel's son Malcolm has made the following note: 'Aurora's mother Johanna Fredrika Meurling was a famous beauty and often in the Crown Prince's company.' He cites a letter from Ludvig Munthe, which is obviously the source for this, but when the letter was written, and to whom, is not mentioned.

Nevertheless it is an interesting piece of information, especially when taken together with another document preserved among Axel Munthe's papers in the National Archives: a postcard signed with the initial A and bearing the stamp *H.M. the Queen's lady-in-waiting*. The card was written around the turn of the last century, before Crown Prince Gustaf became king in 1907. Whether the message on it was written by one of the ladies-in-waiting or whether someone else used the card is, of course, impossible to say. The paragraph in question reads as follows: 'The Queen herself has now told everyone about your dear Mama – both H.R.H. [Victoria] and the Prince [Gustaf] now know the whole story – you need not deny it.'

Read against the background of the rumours of a relationship, these lines take on a special significance. After all, why should Queen Sophia know a 'story' about the daughter of an attorney in provincial Sweden unless the issue involved the royal family? What kind of knowledge about Aurora Munthe did the Queen of Sweden and Norway possess, which Axel denied but whose accuracy Sophia now saw fit to confirm?

If we add this detail to Malcolm Munthe's note about Aurora's mother, the trail leads in the direction of Oscar II's father, the future Oscar I. If the judgement about her beauty is correct, and if it is true that she moved in the same circles as Crown Prince Oscar, then it is here that we should look for any possible relationship between Axel Munthe and the royal family.

Aurora Munthe's mother Fredrika Meurling was born in 1789 and in 1814 she married the attorney Carl August Ugarph. Aurora was born on 16 March 1819, the third child in her family. Were there any circumstances under which the 29-year-old Fredrika Ugarph and the Crown Prince of Sweden–Norway, the 19-year-old Oscar, could meet?

As chance would have it, in this particular case it is actually possible to establish where the Crown prince was exactly nine months before Aurora was born. On 11 June 1818 Oscar succeeded his father King Carl XIV Johan as chancellor of Uppsala University. Four days later there was a ball at Uppsala Castle. So if the Crown prince slept with mother-of-two Fredrika Ugarph, it must have happened at Uppsala on one of those days.

The time and the place are thus established: Uppsala in the middle of June 1818. Is there any chance that Aurora's mother could have been there? There is. Two of her brothers were studying at Uppsala and were childhood friends and fellow students of a senior assistant at the royal library, situated in the royal castle. There were, in other words, contacts with the Swedish Establishment. It is therefore not impossible that Fredrika was in Uppsala in connection with the celebrations in June 1818. But this line of reasoning depends on Malcolm (and Ludvig) Munthe's information being correct – and of this we cannot be sure.

What we do know is that Queen Sophia was aware of a 'story' about Axel's mother. If it is true that Aurora was sired by Oscar, it would make Axel a half-cousin to Gustaf V. Whatever the truth of the matter, it obviously had significance for Axel's perception of himself. Perhaps it was this putative relationship he was hinting at when, in the course of a conversation with Edith Balfour in 1885, he maintained that he came from a very fine family. Whether or not he was kin to the royal family is one thing; another thing, and one which is perhaps at least as important, is that he may have lived with that illusion.

CHARCOT FILS

The Story of San Michele was constantly being reprinted in both English and Swedish, and Munthe made no secret of how impressed he was by the large print runs. But the number of impressions is not an absolute measure of success. In England, at least, Munthe personally saw to it that the number of impressions increased at the cost of the size of the print run. In November 1930, when the book was into its seventeenth edition, he told Murray it was his 'ambition to arrive to a twentieth edition, the sooner the better': 'I therefore beg you [. . .] to reduce the number of copies for the next three impressions to one thousand each, in order to arrive while I am still on my legs, to a twentieth impression, for which I promise to write you a nice preface.' The publisher agreed to Munthe's suggestion and the twentieth edition came off the presses on 1 January 1931, though without a new preface.

At the same time, the book had made its triumphal progress around the world. In 1930 it came out in Danish, in 1931 in Dutch, Norwegian, Finnish and German, in 1932 in Italian, in 1933 in Icelandic, Polish, Serbo-Croat and Hungarian, in 1934 in Bulgarian, French, Slovene, Czech and Romanian, in 1935 in Hebrew, Latvian, Portuguese, Spanish, Turkish and Esperanto. It sold well in every country and Munthe's income from royalties was significant.

The Story of San Michele and its author were greeted enthusiastically by readers around the world. But in two countries, France and Germany, Munthe was sharply criticised from a professional standpoint. Even before the book came out in French, he aired his worst fears to John Murray: 'I am certain I am going to be fiercely attacked by the French for my outspoken criticism on [sic] their hero Charcot. It has besides already begun.' What Munthe was referring to was a letter in the *New York Times Book Review* of 18 January 1931, written by Jean Charcot, son of Jean Martin Charcot. The article was a furious attack on Munthe's depiction of his father and of his studies at La Salpêtrière:

Without contesting the literary and imaginative qualities of Dr Munthe I can certify that Dr Munthe never was trained by my father, Professor Charcot, and most likely not by Pasteur. He may, during his stay in Paris, where he was never known as a distinguished specialist in the treatment of nervous diseases, have followed, as hundreds of others, some courses of Charcot, incidentally, but he was not trained by him and certainly never had the intimacy of which he boasts. Dr Munthe is unlucky in the date he chose. I was, myself, a student at the Salpêtrière then, and can certify that he was not one of his students and that my father never knew him. All he says concerning Professor Charcot is false or literally translated from a mendacious book written by a French author who was incapable of passing his examinations. The same concerning his stay in the wards of Dr Tillaux, when he described himself as having played a prominent part during the memorable visit of our great Pasteur to the twelve (and not six) Russian peasants bitten by mad wolves. I was assistant to Dr Tillaux, and the scene Dr Munthe describes when he offered a cup of milk to one of the Russian peasants was not played by him but by myself, with a cigarette. [. . .] He shows [my father] as a hard man; in truth the prominent features of his character were an unlimited kindness, a nearly pathologic sensibility and an unbounded pity, not only for the sufferings of mankind but also for those of the animals.

Munthe did not respond to the attack until it was reported in the Swedish press three months later:

> That professor Charcot's son has not succeeded in identifying my humble self among the 100s of students and doctors who studied nervous diseases at his celebrated father's clinic half a century ago is something I can readily pardon him for. As far as I know, I never saw the son during those years when I was attending lectures and ward-rounds at the Salpêtrière [. . .]. In his blind fury, the author of the article forgets that I am by no means the only person who dared to condemn his great father's theatrical lectures on the phenomenon of hypnosis before *tout Paris* at the Salpêtrière. And a celebrated French author who studied at the hospital at the same time [. . .] has given a strikingly identical description of these sessions in his memoirs, which incidentally I had not read when I wrote my book.

That Munthe exaggerated the significance of his contacts with Charcot is obvious. This is shown by the episode with Geneviève, which probably never happened, however frenetically the author himself asserted the opposite (see the chapter 'A Semblance of Married Life', see page 85 above). That he attended Charcot's lectures, however, is beyond any doubt; to do that, he did not even need to be Charcot's student. As regards the treatment of the Russian peasants, Charcot junior and Munthe are equally mistaken as to their number: there were neither six nor twelve, but twenty-one. Yet this story too seems to take place on 'the ill-defined borderline between the real and the unreal', where Munthe was so much at home. Several years later Dr Adrien Loir, Pasteur's nephew and his assistant while he worked with the rabies-smitten peasants, claimed that he had never come across Munthe in that context.

The 'mendacious book' that Jean Charcot refers to was Léon Daudet's *Les Morticoles*, published in 1894, the year after Charcot's death. Léon Daudet was the son of the writer Alphonse Daudet and he knew Charcot from his parents' home. When he was not accepted as a medical student neither in 1889 nor in 1890, he responded by writing a *roman-à-clef* with Charcot (under the name of Foutange) and other famous Parisian doctors like the surgeon Jules-Emile Péan (Malasvon) in the leading roles. The book was hailed by the critics and by the turn of the century it had sold more than 20,000 copies. It was seen as a brilliant attack on modern science, 'this mania which has invaded the world in the course of this century and has brought in its wake nothing but doubt, anguish, suffering and misery'. To what extent Munthe took his inspiration from Daudet's book is hard to say, but it is unlikely that he would not have read it.

Charcot's criticism led French publishers to hesitate to bring out Munthe's book. In the end, however, Albin Michel decided to have it translated.

Munthe's exchange of letters with the translator shows how tortuous the road to publication was. In August 1932 the translator informed Munthe that he had decided to delete the chapter about La Salpêtrière and hypnotism and most other references to Charcot. The reason was the opposition from Charcot's family. Munthe accepted the cuts, and when the book came out in the autumn of 1934, it was in a heavily censored form. The complete text has not been published in French to this day.

On the Dunghill!

Why did Munthe demonstrate such willingness to compromise in the case of the French translation? Financial considerations are out of the question; the book sold so well in other countries that income from a French edition was of marginal importance. Ever since his debut as a writer Munthe had made far-reaching demands on publishing firms and newspaper editors. Not so much as a comma might be altered, let alone content. But his uncompromising stance applied first and foremost to his original texts; as far as other languages were concerned, his principles were often subjected to his vanity. The first example of this was Munthe's willingness to delete the most anti-German passages in 'Political Agitations in Capri' when it was printed in *Blackwood's Magazine* in 1889.

Moreover, the French edition was probably of particular importance to him. It was in Paris that he got his doctor's degree, it was there that he had started practising as a doctor, it was there that he began his adult life. But Paris was also the city he had fled from with his tail between his legs forty-five years earlier. The publication of *Le livre de San Michele* meant a triumphant return, especially as the book contained an introduction by a member of the Académie Française, Pierre Benoit.

The manner in which he handled the conflict with Jean Charcot was not the only example of Munthe's willingness to compromise. At the same time as he was negotiating the details of the French translation, he was involved in another dispute, in another country, about another of his books.

Munthe made a lot of money from *The Story of San Michele*, but he was also a golden goose for the publishers. They now turned eagerly to his earlier books, which by this juncture had been forgotten. In October 1930 Murray published *Red Cross & Iron Cross* again. It was the seventh edition and the first since 1916. It sold out within fourteen days and a new edition was printed the same month. A ninth edition never appeared, nor was it published in any other language.

When *Das Buch von San Michele* was published in Germany in the autumn of 1931 it caused a great stir in German medical circles. One doctor,

Paul Phillips, became so interested that he decided to examine the book more closely. Comparing it with the original, he discovered that the section describing Munthe's stand during the war had been deleted in the German translation: from commercial motives, he suspected. When he looked more closely at Munthe's attitude to Germany and the Germans he discovered that, in *Memories & Vagaries*, the author had found German toys to be inferior to their French counterparts. Worst of all, however, was *Red Cross & Iron Cross*, which according to Dr Phillips was 'the meanest and most mendacious insult to the German army and the German people that has ever been published'. In his article 'Gegen Dr Axel Munthe!' (Against Dr Axel Munthe!), he exhorted the German public not to buy *Das Buch von San Michele* until Munthe had withdrawn *Red Cross & Iron Cross*. Dr Phillips's criticism was published in a medical journal but was given greater currency in the National Socialist newspaper *Völkischer Beobachter*, which on 23 December 1932 published an article under the title 'Dr Axel Munthe, the Wretch from San Michele':

> All of us who still have a spark of feeling for Germany left in us demand that the books by the Swedish physician Dr Axel Munthe be thrown on a dunghill and that not another pfennig be spent on this fellow, who is so shameless as to insult us in such an infamous way, us, whose wine he has drunk, according to his own account, and at the same time to demand that we should buy and read his other books. As the only feeling that this slanderer possesses resides in his purse, we must hit him where he is most vulnerable. Out of Germany with Munthe and his books!

Munthe's reaction to these attacks was somewhat unexpected. He responded to Dr Phillips with a letter regretting that he had written *Red Cross & Iron Cross* and promising to do all that was in his power to have it withdrawn from circulation.

In actual fact this retreat had been prepared in the new foreword, where Munthe writes that only after 'some hesitation' had he agreed to a new edition of the book, which had been written 'in difficult circumstances and in a frame of mind not suitable for literary effort'. He cannot forget what he has written in this 'terrible book', if he is honest with himself, because he has written the truth as he experienced it then, 'with flaming eyes and bleeding heart'. Today, however, he would not be able to write anything of the kind. The foreword ends with the conciliatory words: 'Now, when at last the curtain has gone down over the titanic tragedy, all that remains in the onlooker's mind is awe and pity.'

The campaign went on for two months and only ceased when Munthe instructed Murray to destroy the remainder of the edition. 'Now, with Hitler at the helm it will probably be a tremendous affair unless we stop the sale of the book, what is the wisest course to take,' he advised Murray at the beginning of February 1933. On 15 February 1933 John Murray informed the Paul List Verlag in Leipzig that all 805 remaining copies of the war book had been destroyed and that no new edition would be printed.* Thus the first book-burning of the century took place in London – three months before Nazi students all over Germany threw books that threatened 'the very roots of German-ness' onto bonfires.

If Munthe was prepared to compromise about the French translation of *The Story of San Michele* because he wanted the book to appear in French, his decision to withdraw the English edition of *Red Cross & Iron Cross* and to stop all the other ones seems to have been influenced by the insight that his depiction of German officers and their atrocities was really exaggerated. If he had a generally split attitude towards his authorship, that was particularly true of this book.

Just as part of the proceeds from *The Story of San Michele* went to animal protection, a share of the royalties from *Das Buch von San Michele* – 10,000 marks – went to German soldiers who had lost their sight in the First World War. It was Munthe's way of making up for those exaggerations he felt he had been guilty of in his book about the war. 'I feel a sort of war guilt in common with you for having reprinted my terrible little Red Cross and Iron Cross,' he admitted to John Murray: 'I have tried to atone for my sins by handing over ten thousand marks to the blinded german soldiers from the german San Michele book.'†

That someone like Munthe was giving money to German soldiers was of course hard to digest for nationalistically minded sections of the German medical profession. But those who supported the boycott against *Das Buch von San Michele* faced a moral dilemma since the contribution to the visually impaired soldiers decreased with every unsold copy. The German doctors therefore arranged their own collection so that the organisation for those blinded in the war would be able to return Munthe's money to him. Their collection raised 13,000 marks but Munthe's donation was not returned. The blind soldiers thus received money from two sources.

Munthe did not want to see the value of his gift diminished either. Even if by the New Year of 1933 *Das Buch von San Michele* had sold over 140,000 copies, it is likely that consideration for the wounded veterans would have weighed heavily with him when he chose to sound the retreat. He also

---

* The Paul List Verlag even published a couple of brochures containing materials about the conflict, 'Im Sachen Axel Munthes' (About the Axel Munthe Affair), which were distributed to German booksellers.

† The blind American author Helen Keller also gave her royalty fees to blind German soldiers. Was it Munthe who inspired her, or the other way around?

had Gudrun von Uexküll to care for. As she had lost her assets during the First World War and was in dire need of money, Munthe had made over the German rights to her. 'Personally I do not care a rap if San Michele is boycotted in Germany,' he wrote to Murray, 'but I am sorry for Baroness Uexküll, who has translated also "Memories and Vagaries" and was to make some money out of it, but if this continues, this book will not be published.'

It was *Memories & Vagaries* that the publishers' interest centred on after the success of *The Story of San Michele*. In the autumn of 1930 Murray published a new edition of the book from 1908, with a dedication to Robert Cunninghame Graham from 'his friend and admirer'. This too soon appeared in a number of languages. The German version, *Ein altes Buch von Menschen und Tieren* came out in 1934, with the anti-German sketches deleted. The French translation, *Hommes et bêtes*, followed only in 1937.

A SANCTUARY FOR BIRDS

The conflicts with Jean Charcot and the German doctors showed that, when necessary, Munthe could display a significant talent for diplomacy. While he could be principled and unwilling to compromise – as when he left the Swedish court during the First World War – he permitted himself a striking degree of flexibility when he wanted to achieve a goal that he saw as of prime importance.

Such a goal was the protection of birds on Capri, which he had fought for ever since settling on the island. He had been a *socio benemerito* – distinguished member – of the Società Napoletana per la Protezione degli Animali since at least 1901, and after buying Mount Barbarossa in 1904 he was able to protect migratory birds on that part of the island. But he was more ambitious than that: he wanted to forbid the hunting of birds on the whole of Capri.

In *The Story of San Michele* Munthe pleaded his case so eloquently that it came to the ears of Mussolini. 'I have to give it to Mussolini who has begged me for it, he has read it and says he has never read such a book, he reads English well though he does not speak it fluently. I hope to induce him to do something for the birds.'

To further his purpose, Munthe took refuge in his favourite literary device. The Italian translation of *The Story of San Michele*, which came out in 1932, was provided with a new preface, written with the avowed aim of 'influencing public opinion against the mass murder of migratory birds, which is inflicted on them during their journey between Africa and Northern Europe'. *La Storia di San Michele* was dedicated to the Italian princess Mafalda, daughter of King Vittorio Emanuele III and wife of Prince Philip of Hesse.

Spoilt by 'so many of heaven and earth's wondrous works and with so many powerful saints and patron saints within earshot', the Italians are inclined to 'take each day as it comes', in the certainty that the wonder will take place when necessary. But now 'the miracle has occurred once again', 'the great wizard', in other words Mussolini, has made the blood surge in Italian veins again, and Munthe wonders expectantly:

> Will that day come when it will be granted to the terrified migratory birds which fly for their lives through Italy each year to rest their tired wings for a while in the homeland of St Francis, before they resume the long journey to bring summer to the North? Shall that day come, when Assisi's bells and the trill of the skylark are heard among the jubilant fanfares in the Fascist hymn 'La Giovinezza'?

Well aware that his flattering tone could be misinterpreted, Munthe explained that it was a question of simple tactics: 'The flattery about the new miracle is meant to prepare the way for getting the authorities interested in the matter. I am told the book can be of some use in this direction.'

His efforts paid off. On 12 November 1932, a decree was passed according to which 'the hunting of birds is forbidden on the island of Capri in all forms and at all times, until further notice.' Mussolini had visited Capri in the spring of 1925, been captivated by the island's beauty and had decided to make it a showcase for Fascism. Large sums of money were allotted for public works, the harbour was extended and the roads improved. That Il Duce reacted so quickly and decisively to Munthe's initiative was in large part because it fitted so well into this scheme. Capri was to become a model island.

The people of Capri protested loudly against the decree, and the anger of the hunters against Munthe was so great that some of them even wanted to use violence against him. But around Europe Mussolini's decision was greeted enthusiastically. 'Bird lovers the world over', wrote *The Times* on 14 December 1932, 'will give thanks to Signor Mussolini, who, there is every reason to believe, has taken a personal interest in the question, and who by this measure will save every year the lives of many thousands of song birds.'

A lifelong struggle had ended in victory, and Munthe was jubilant: 'I now feel that my mission in life is over', he wrote to Cunninghame Graham, 'and that it is time to emigrate to another planet of which I know nothing except that there are plenty of singing birds.' Naturally enough he attached no weight to the proviso in the text of the decree: 'until further notice'. That notice came as soon as Mussolini was deposed, when this decree, like so many others issued by the Fascist regime, was abolished.

Munthe also thanked Mussolini personally, saying that he 'could not have entrusted to more eloquent collaborators than these thousands and thousands missionaries of the sky the propaganda abroad for the sacred cause he personifies'. The words grate on our ears now, but the flattery was hardly meant in earnest and was rather a further example of how Munthe could suppress a conviction in order to achieve an important goal. One must also remember that although in 1932 Mussolini was a dictator, he was not yet allied to Hitler and was in fact supporting Austria in its struggle against German plans to take it over. Mussolini's siding with Hitler and the alliance between Italy and Germany only took place at the end of the 1930s. It is hard to believe that Munthe did not perceive Mussolini as the clown he was, and if he had wanted to justify his 'flattery' it would have sufficed to point to, for example, Winston Churchill, who saw Mussolini as an important counterweight to Hitler and maintained that in Italy he would himself have been a Fascist. Moreover, Britain's Royal Society for the Prevention of Cruelty to Animals (RSPCA) awarded their highest distinction to the Italian agriculture minister Acerbo for the Capri decree.

Munthe did what he could to give the decree international currency. Esme Howard wrote a letter to *The Times* on the basis of a communication from Munthe and the *New York Times* carried a leader paying tribute to the author of *The Story of San Michele* for inspiring Mussolini's decision. On 27 January 1933 Munthe himself had an article published in the same newspaper with the title 'To Those who Love Birds'. At the same time, the fact that it was he who had brought about a ban on hunting inspired a degree of jealousy among other inhabitants of Capri, including Blanche Gordon-Lennox, who in a letter to *The Times* pointed out that both she and the Cerio family had fought the same battle as Munthe.

The campaign was carried further in England, where Esme Howard, with Munthe's willing support, attempted to force through a ban on the trade in migratory birds; however, this did not meet with success. Munthe's status in animal protection circles was immense, and whenever he made a public appearance – which he rarely did – it was reported in the press. At a lunch arranged by the Royal Society for the Protection of Birds, with over 1,000 guests, Munthe gave a short talk and was greeted by George Bernard Shaw as one of the few people 'who had made themselves speak for the conscience of mankind'. At the same time Shaw regretted that there was no sanctuary for people like the one for birds, continuing: 'Although there are arrangements for shooting them, nobody has started any protection-for-humans sanctuary where they cannot be shot. I am not at all sure that this cult of making a sport of bird slaughter has not a lot to do with the sport of kings – the slaughter of men.' One can see Munthe nodding his approval.

In the King's Trusty Hands

Munthe wanted to create a sanctuary for birds in Sweden too. He wrote to Bonnier's on numerous occasions pointing out that the royalties from *The Story of San Michele* should 'go to the animals in Sweden', 'probably to buy an island for the seabirds'. In May 1931 a piece of land north of Solliden was acquired and turned into a bird reserve.

The 10,000 kronor that Munthe set aside for the purchase of the sanctuary was only a fraction of the money that he donated for various charitable purposes during the 1930s. At Christmas 1932 he made a donation of 100,000 kronor (almost £200,000 in today's money) to the memory of Queen Victoria of Sweden. The money was to be divided equally between the blind, the Lapps and animals. 'The Lapps are happiest among their own kind and know how to live and die in pleasure and need without our help, however well-meaning our intervention may be,' Munthe explained: 'But when Lapps become old and incapable we must look after them.' As for 'the animals' money', Munthe handed it over 'without hesitation into the King's hands', but not without a good-natured reservation: 'despite his long catalogue of sins in his hunting bag'.

Munthe's letter, which was published on 23 December 1932, ended with the words:

Opinion and taste change as quick as the wind, no-one knows from which direction it will blow the next day, following wind or contrary. No-one is a prophet in his own country, but forecasters in sixteen other countries forecast that the following wind will continue, that *The Story of San Michele* will survive its author. If their prophecy comes true, the sum of 100,000 crowns which today I deliver into the King's trusty hands will increase over the years, and I will be in touch again, alive or dead.

The forecasters were right; the wind remained favourable. Three years later it was time for the next gift. It was for the same sum as before and was delivered precisely as before into the king's trusty hands.

THE MISSING CHAPTERS

Is there not going to be a new book from Dr Munthe?
Karl Otto Bonnier to Axel Munthe, 1932

MUNTHE HAD PROMISED the queen that the dedication to her would remain in *The Story of San Michele* even if she died before the book came out. He kept this promise. But he had also made her another promise, which for different reasons was more difficult to fulfil, namely, to write a book about her. In a letter to Sven Hedin, Munthe claimed that the king was 'very anxious' for him to write a book about the queen, but that it was a very difficult task 'and nobody will understand this better than you, who knew her well and also her surroundings'. Karl Otto Bonnier was enticed with the following words:

> I have more or less promised my dead patient to write a book about her. She always said I was the only one who knew her and she is not far from the truth there. A psychological study of this lady would surprise most people[,] even the few who believed they knew her. She had very few friends and hardly any intimates, she lived and died a stranger to most people in Sweden. I had ample opportunity to know her – thirty seven years, and not only as her doctor.

As always, Munthe included a few reservations. One prerequisite, he wrote, was that he continued to sleep badly, since 'insomnia and its sequel depression is apt to drive me to write'. But in another letter, written at almost the same time, he knocked the legs from under that argument by maintaining the opposite: 'I might try it when I have got a little sleep.' Wanting to keep all his exit options open, he ignored the fact that one argument contradicted the other.

Against the background of the fantastic success of his book, the prospect of Axel Munthe writing a book about Sweden's queen was irresistibly tempting to publishing firms. To crown it all, in the course of 1931 Munthe attached two at least equally attractive projects to the bait: a sequel to *The*

Story of San Michele, 'The Missing Chapters of San Michele', and a book with the working title 'Death and the Doctor'. The latter was based on Munthe's conviction that it was a doctor's duty to help his patient to die when he could no longer help him to live. The difficulty lies in deciding 'how' and 'when', he declared in an interview for a Norwegian newspaper – as well as with overcoming opposition from the medical profession, not least in the Catholic world.

All three books were offered jointly to Bonnier's and Murray's. But time passed and nothing arrived. Karl Otto Bonnier wrote to Munthe: 'As I have not heard anything from you for several weeks, may I repeat my question, whether you can give an answer, not only to Sweden but to the whole world, to the question which is now heard on all sides: "Is there not going to be a new book from Dr Munthe?"' Bonnier did not receive a reply to his question, but several weeks later Munthe gave a situation report to A.D. Peters, an English literary agent who cultivated contacts with film companies. It was going to take longer than he had thought, 'as the book is turning out a much bigger book than I anticipated at first, maybe it may even have to be split into two books. I believe it contains far better stuff for a film than the San Michele [book].'

Munthe played hide-and-seek with his publishers. In August 1931 he told Bonnier that 'Death and the Doctor' was finished but that he was not sure he wanted to publish it, at least in Swedish: 'It is a strange book and perhaps a good book.'

Considering the loose structure of *The Story of San Michele*, it is not difficult to imagine a sequel with short and tall stories of a similar character. Both Bonnier and Murray tried at regular intervals to tease the manuscript out of him, but Munthe emphasised that the new book was different in kind and more personal than the previous one, and it was this that was holding him back: 'I am still reluctant to allow this all too personal MS to be printed before my death,' he wrote to Bonnier in March 1936.

Was there a manuscript with the title 'The Missing Chapters of San Michele'? Or one about the queen? Or about 'Death and the Doctor'? Vittorio Massimino, who saw Munthe almost daily throughout the 1930s, laughed and shook his head when the question was put to him a few years ago – according to him, none of these manuscripts ever existed.*

In actual fact Munthe does not seem to have written anything new after *The Story of San Michele*, apart from an address to Gustaf V on his seventy-fifth birthday in 1933, and an article that he sent to *The Times* two years

---

* In an interview with the author. When John Murray, after Munthe's death, asked his son Malcolm to search for manuscripts, the latter answered that he had found no traces of any finished manuscripts.

later. 'The Problem of Vivisection' was a development and clarification of the argument in the chapter 'Patients' in *The Story of San Michele*. There were many arguments against vivisection, Munthe wrote – but it ought to be allowed in the name of science so that cures for ailments could be found, but only 'under most rigorous control in a few State laboratories, entrusted solely to men of the highest scientific standard'.

Contrary to Munthe's fears, the editor of *The Times*, Geoffrey Dawson, did not find his views particularly shocking and thought moreover that no one was better suited than Munthe to address the subject. But for the present vivisection was 'a dead subject' in England and he therefore asked if he might put the article aside until 'a more opportune moment presents itself'. It obviously never did, as the article remained unpublished.

On the Recommendation of Douglas Fairbanks

It was not only book publishers who were after Munthe. A British playwright, C.B. Fernald, wanted to write a play based on *The Story of San Michele* but the project came to nothing. Hollywood film studios had also picked up the scent. According to his own account, Munthe had never seen a film, but he had met Chaplin once and 'liked him very much'. Paramount Pictures – so Axel told a reporter in April 1931 – were so keen to obtain the film rights that they sent a representative to Capri with a ready-made contract in his pocket. But he claimed to have driven the American out.

In actual fact, genuine negotiations only got under way in the summer of that year. On the recommendation of Douglas Fairbanks, whom he had met in Italy, Munthe demanded $200,000 for the film rights – an amount that according to Paramount was pure fantasy: 'It is absolutely useless to talk about figures which are at least five times the value of the property from a picture standpoint.' When they came back with an alternative offer of $50,000, itself a significant sum (in today's money, $1,500,000), Munthe declined and instructed his agent A.D. Peters to contact other American film studios. His attempts led nowhere, and Peters advised Munthe to accept the offer from Paramount, but Munthe referred him yet again to Douglas Fairbanks, who advised him to 'lay low' – in time he would definitely get the sum he was demanding.

It took only three days for Munthe to change his mind. According to what he told Peters, he had just found out that he would have to come up with £10,000 before 1 January 1932 if he wanted to realise his plan 'to buy land for the bird sanctuary' in Sweden. This was a pure deception: the bird reserve on Öland had already been bought. Something or someone had quite simply convinced him that it would be best if he accepted Paramount's offer – which he now did, with the condition that the amount was not to be mentioned in the press and that the chapters about Charcot and hypnotism were not to be used in the film as he had condemned public demonstrations of hypnotism in his book – which was, as we have seen, not the real reason for this demand.

When Munthe's American publisher, Dutton, claimed a share of the proceeds from the sale of the film rights, Munthe refused, offering them instead the rights to his next book, on condition that the publisher understood that he 'cannot be subjected to any pressure to hurry up the delivery of the manuscript': 'All I can say is that I will finish the book as soon as I can, to my own satisfaction.' That was equivalent to promising nothing.

By the time Munthe had come to an agreement with Dutton, it was already too late; Paramount had decided to withdraw their offer. 'The reason they gave me', Peters wrote to Munthe, 'was that they had been waiting for some time to complete the film deal, and had kept various actors unemployed in readiness for it. Owing to the deal they had to let these people go and cut their losses. I have no doubt that the general depression in Hollywood is also partly responsible.' The leading role, it would appear, had been reserved for one of the fixed stars in the 1930s firmament, John Barrymore. Munthe responded resignedly:

> After the withdrawal of the Paramount, I have abandoned the idea of filming the book. I wish to close as soon as possible this unpleasant chapter of The Story of San Michele, this sordid business has been irritating my nerves far too long. It is high time to put an end to it. I wish to concentrate all my thoughts on my new book.

Munthe was undoubtedly genuinely divided in his attitude to the filming of his book. Yet it was only a few months before he was describing Paramount's decision as 'lamentable' and asking Mr Peters to recommence negotiations with the film studio. But Paramount were no longer interested; by this time Peters had begun to tire of Munthe and his inability to make up his mind. 'I do not think he is allowing any other agent to handle it but one cannot be sure,' he wrote to his partner in New York, 'In fact one cannot be sure about anything with him, and I expect that he would accept an offer from any source if it seemed good enough.'

One source that Munthe possibly might have accepted was the star producer Alexander Korda, 'a man full of understanding & poesy, altogether different to any of the usual type of bumptuous arrogant producers', as he was described by Baroness Emmuska Orczy in a letter to Munthe. Korda, the producer of the film The Scarlet Pimpernel, based on the baroness's novel, loved Munthe's book, and according to Orczy it was 'the dream of his career to make a really beautiful picture of it, never losing its spirit & its sentiment.'

The dreams of Korda and the baroness were never realised. When it was rumoured in 1934 that Munthe had finished 'The Missing Chapters' it was Warner Brothers instead who expressed an interest; a new book by Munthe, so the thinking went, would tempt the public to see the film. But now it was no longer a question of $50,000 but rather $10,000 to $20,000. The disillusioned Peters replied that there was nothing more he could do in the Munthe case: 'Nobody knows when the book is going to appear, and it is extremely doubtful whether he will ever finish it. [. . .] And I am quite sure the old man would not accept anything like $20,000 for the film rights.'

How much Warner Brothers bid is unclear, but the contract was drawn up in August 1936. 'I have at last consented to the filming of my book, on certain conditions,' Munthe wrote to Lady Rothenstein:

> The same people who have done the Pasteur film are going to do it. I do not suppose much will be left of the book, all I want is to be excluded myself as much as possible and that the scenario shall become a sort of propaganda for the animals. They even want me to come to Hollywood to superintend the scenario, but I have refused.

Apparently Paul Muni, who had starred in the film about Pasteur, was to play Munthe. But by the end of 1937 there had still been no screenwriter assigned to the job, and the project was postponed.*

Munthe's behaviour towards the film studios followed the same pattern as his discussions with newspaper editors and publishers. Ever since his debut in the 1880s he had maintained that he abhorred being in the spotlight and that he would only reluctantly publicise his thoughts. 'The idea is hateful to me,' he commented on several occasions with regard to the rumours of a film. 'Only after long hesitation did I agree to their publication in book form,' he wrote about the *Letters from a Mourning City*. Of *Små skizzer* he said 'the appropriateness of publishing these small articles in book form has long seemed to their author rather doubtful'; and 'After nine months' deliberation I have reluctantly agreed to the publication of a Swedish edition of *The Story of San Michele*. Moreover, it took me almost as long to agree to the publication of the original English edition.' 'The idea is hateful to me,' he commented on several occasions with regard to the rumours of a film.

---

* Several years later, in 1962, a very mediocre German film was made: *Axel Munthe, der Arzt von San Michele* (Axel Munthe, the Doctor from San Michele).

Munthe's correspondence with publishers and film studios shows that in actual fact the exact opposite was the case. Munthe wanted nothing better than to see his books in print or *The Story of San Michele* on the film screen. He forced his books on publishers and insisted that they should accept them before they had even read the manuscripts. If there was anyone who 'reluctantly agreed' it was the publishers, not Munthe! It was Munthe who, through his agent, kept up the pressure on the Hollywood film studios. So when he maintained the opposite in newspaper interviews, he was lying.

The question is whether he was aware that he was lying. For it was not lying in the usual sense of the word: something one does in order to hide something. His behaviour was a constituent part of his way of being, of his personality. It is easy to interpret his way of dealing with publishers as an expression of effrontery and arrogance. Instead, it was a sign of an almost neurotic lack of confidence, which at the other end of the publishing process came out as feigned indifference (or aggressiveness) towards the judgements of critics and readers. The fact that Munthe did not wish to be present when Victoria received a copy of the book was an expression of the same neurosis.

His lack of confidence also manifested itself in the way that he almost always acted in someone else's name. When he 'consented' to the publication of *Letters from a Mourning City* it was because Maude Valerie White wanted to see her translation in print. When he offered *Red Cross & Iron Cross* and *The Story of San Michele* to John Murray it was because Rennell Rodd asked him to do so. When he asked for $200,000 for the film rights he did it with the support of Douglas Fairbanks. When he then agreed to a lower figure he did it for the animals' sake. The decision and the responsibility were never his own.

New Human Discoveries

In the 1930s Munthe was also a frequent quarry of the press. Journalists wanted to interview 'the old doctor' and the reading public wanted to see pictures of his home, which was now renowned throughout the world. But the interviews can be counted on the fingers of one hand. Munthe had an in-built aversion to talking to journalists and moreover had had his fingers burnt more than once. On one occasion, to avoid being misquoted, he interviewed himself.

Munthe was equally careful when it came to allowing photographers into his life. Yet he made a few exceptions. In December 1933–January 1934 the magazine *Country Life* published three photo-reportages from the

Villa San Michele, Torre di Materita and Mount Barbarossa – but Munthe allowed no photographs of himself to be taken. Two years later he gave permission for the preparation of an illustrated edition of *The Story of San Michele* which contained seventy-five photographs, some of them taken by himself. Despite his shyness he made an appearance for the BBC in a short television programme ('Picture Page', 16 June 1937) – one of the first in the history of television – and a radio programme ('Retrospect', 20 July 1937). In both instances the theme was 'a better understanding between man and the animals'. Munthe informed his 'famiglia' in Anacapri with touching pride that the programme would be broadcast 'all over the British Empire', but he was unsure if they would be able to hear it in Anacapri.*

The excitement over *The Story of San Michele* was so great that there was even talk of a Nobel Prize for Literature, at least Munthe thought so. 'In Sweden they are talking a lot about the Nobel prize[,] also in America,' Munthe wrote to Murray in the autumn of 1930, 'but this is absolutely excluded because the eighteen members of the [Swedish] Academy who are to give the prize are nearly all futurists and besides green with envy and they cannot forgive a Swede for having written in English.' One can only fantasise about the conservative academicians' reaction to Munthe's characterisation of them as 'futurists'.

Two years later Munthe was actually nominated for the prize. The Academy's expert witness, the literature professor Olle Holmberg, wrote in his report that although he certainly had a high regard for Munthe's 'narrative gifts', the suggestion that he be awarded the prize 'cannot be supported from a more strictly literary standpoint'. Munthe was not of course a serious candidate for the Nobel Prize, but it is worth noting that Alfred Nobel was acquainted with his earlier writings.

During the 1930s Munthe spent some time in the Villa Svezia, but Rome had changed. Within the space of two years several of the people who had been intimately bound up with his life in Italy had died: in 1929, Prince Max of Baden, in 1930, Claes Lagergren and the queen, and the following year Carl Bildt. With their deaths a whole epoch came to an end; Rome had had its day in Munthe's life. His social life in the 1930s centred more and more on England and London, where he often stayed with Mrs Mary Crawshay, the daughter of Lady Constance Leslie, renowned, like her mother, for her quick wit. She owned a large and handsome house in Upper Berkeley Street. If he put up at a hotel, his preference was for the Prince Court or the De Vere. He had his mail sent to the St James's Club, where he often arranged to meet people.

---

* The TV programme has not been preserved, but the radio broadcast has. This was also published in *The Listener*, 28 July 1937, with the title 'In the Isle of Capri'.

Munthe was a celebrity but no social lion. He seldom appeared in public and was an infrequent guest in the larger world of society, even if he enjoyed visiting Covent Garden to listen to music. Yet his status as a bestseller led inevitably to new acquaintances – and to the rekindling of old ones. He met George Bernard Shaw – and his wife, who had bombarded Munthe with her emotions forty years earlier. He spent time with Ottoline Morrell and Lady Oxford (Margot Tennant), whom he had also known for forty years, as well as Lady Oxford's step-daughter Violet Bonham-Carter, the liberal politician and journalist. He had frequent contacts with Esme Howard, who in 1930 was elevated to Lord Howard of Penrith, as well as with Rennell Rodd (from 1933, Lord Rennell of Rodd). According to Gudrun von Uexküll, Munthe also used to return from London each year with a couple of new human 'discoveries'. One was Cunninghame Graham, whose review of *The Story of San Michele* had helped to turn it into a bestseller, another was the poet John Masefield, a third was Margaret, Ranee of Sarawak, the widow of Charles Brooke, Rajah of Sarawak, an independent kingdom in Borneo that had been founded by his father and then become a British colony. Such life stories intrigued Munthe and stirred his imagination.

Back in Dalarna

Following Victoria's death Munthe was to visit Sweden more often than he had done before. He spent the winter months as usual in the tower in Anacapri and the early part of the summer and the occasional autumn month in London, but from 1931 onwards he spent a month of each summer at Solliden as a guest of Gustaf V. There was something paradoxical about this: Solliden was the creation of Axel and Victoria and to begin with Gustaf had disapproved of the place. Now, the king and Axel met there every summer, played croquet and talked. On his seventy-fifth birthday in 1933 the king demonstrated his regard for Munthe by awarding him the Grand Cross of a Commander of the Order of the Pole Star.

The honour came forty years after Munthe had been appointed a knight of the same order by Gustaf's father and forty years after they first met. On several occasions Munthe had made disparaging remarks about Gustaf and for obvious reasons relations between them had been strained. But despite his close relationship with Victoria, he was well aware that the history of the royal marriage could also be seen from another perspective. As he wrote in the festschrift for Gustaf's seventy-fifth birthday, the king's life was 'a page of Sweden's history, an open book, accessible to all, where each and every one can read of his continuing achievements in the strong light of day'. But he himself had read another book about the king, 'a closed book, which it is given to few to read':

> I have read it in the subdued light of the lamp by a sickbed, I have read it with emotion and admiration. A gripping human document which has never been put into words, a reserved man's unwritten diary, page by page. Year after year of bitter trials and sorrows, frustrated hopes and vain struggle against suffering and death. [. . .] Long, oppressive winters with continual bad news and new disappointments, new misgivings. Ever shorter summers with the joy of reunions more and more overshadowed by new menacing warnings that all was in vain.

The fact that the book began with Munthe's tribute underlines his unique position with regard to the royal family. What did he and the king talk about during the summers at Solliden? Naturally they talked about the woman who had been in their joint care. They were both over 70 years old, they had common memories going back to the 1890s and they were complicit in a dreadful secret that could not be revealed at any price: that for thirty-seven years Victoria had led a double life, one as Sweden's queen and Gustaf's wife, and another together with Munthe. It was this knowledge that united them. It was only with each other that they could speak – or keep silent – about their lives. Munthe gave out that the king wanted him to write a book about Victoria. Was this really true? What would it look like when he could not write the truth about her wrecked marriage and her love for him? The book was never written.

Hilda and the boys spent the summers as usual in Leksand. But although Munthe visited Sweden every summer during the 1930s, the time spent with his family was limited and his relationship with Hilda continued to be extremely strained. The temperature of their relationship can be gauged from a letter that Axel wrote to Karl Otto Bonnier after Bonnier had asked Hilda for a photograph of Munthe to use for publicity purposes. He referred to his 'terror of being photographed and exposed publically' and continued with a furious attack on Hilda: 'My wife with whom I have little in common but the name had no right whatsoever to give you this photo and she will bitterly regret it.'

Hilda for her part did all she could to minimise the boys' contact with their father, just as she had done before. How they reacted to *The Story of San Michele* is also unknown, but that it did not grace the bedside table is clear from a letter Axel wrote to Peter after the Swedish translation came out: 'I wonder how the book reads in swedish, maybe your mother will allow you to read the swedish preface [. . .].'

Munthe had a certain amount of contact with the family by letter, but whenever he wanted to meet the boys, the old game of hide-and-seek began. He longed for Leksand, but when he hinted that he could come up there, Hilda began packing their bags:

> Why are you leaving Leksand and why so soon? I had still hoped to face the torture of the long railway journey and come up to Leksand once more. But if you are breaking up the house and on your way to Stockholm I well know that I would be less welcome than ever and only an additional burden to your mother.

In the autumn of 1931 Hilda and Peter left Stockholm and returned to London. Malcolm had already gone back in May of the previous year. When the boys met their father in London in May 1932 they reported anxiously to their mother in Stockholm:

> Father seems on the verge of starting for Sweden and wants to know when you are coming back, so far we have seemed vague but do tell us what we are to tell. Any way if you want us to say or not say anything special you can telegraph. He will probably hear from the King that you have been there.

Although the boys were by this stage 24 and 22 years old respectively, they could not see their father without discussing the form with their mother!

In the late summer of 1933 Axel finally made it to Leksand for a few days. The event was of such moment that it was reported in the weekly press, which declared reverentially that 'among the celebrities who have domiciliary rights in Leksand [. . .] none attracts more attention than Doctor Munthe.' Only a very few people knew he was coming, the paper wrote:

> A car turned into the lonely road, the double gates opened wide and the old man climbed out. The gates closed again with fearful precision. In the house they were walking on tiptoe and speaking in whispers to each other. And throughout the village the rumour spread that the doctor from Capri had at last come back. That rumour spread only every tenth year.

As a matter of fact it was Munthe's first visit to Stengården since 1926.

There are no witnesses as to how the visit went, but as Munthe also returned to Leksand the two following summers, his contacts with the family must have been relatively free of friction.

THE BELLS OF ASSISI

During his stay in Leksand in 1935 Munthe could make out the details of his house for the first time in several decades. At the beginning of October

1934 he had undergone an operation for a cataract on his remaining eye. The operation was performed by Dr Vogt of the eye-clinic in Zürich, the same doctor who a few years earlier had operated on James Joyce. Munthe regained his sight. With the help of spectacles he could now read for the first time in ten years, and he began writing letters by hand again. 'I can see quite well and even read, may it only last,' he wrote to Esme Howard, adding: 'I receive letters by *hundreds* from almost every country, indeed people are kind to me!' It was no exaggeration – the successful operation was reported in all the world's press and Munthe thanked his correspondents in a letter to *The Times* and several other newspapers:

Ever since the day your great paper thought it worth while to tell its readers that I had undergone a successful operation in Zürich and had regained my sight, I have been receiving by every mail a large number of signed and unsigned letters of congratulation from your country. Since it is wholly impossible for me to answer personally all these letters, I venture to ask leave to trespass on your columns with these lines to express my deep gratitude for so much kindness. I did not know I had so many friends in England. I am under no illusion as to whom I have to thank for this friendship. I owe it all to our mutual friends the birds, so near the heart of every English man and woman, and so near my own. As I am writing these lines after weeks of anxious suspense, I begin to ask myself whether my indebtedness to our winged friends is not even far greater.

The night after my operation was full of torment. I had been operated on by a master hand, but my fate was uncertain. My head was exhausted by insomnia, and my courage was beginning to flag, for man gets his courage during his sleep. My thoughts were as dark as the night around me; the night I well knew might never come to an end. Suddenly a ray of light flashed from my tired brain down to my very heart. I remembered all at once that it was the *giorno santo*, the anniversary of St Francis of Assisi, the life-long friend who had never forsaken me in the hour of need. The day of St Francis! I heard the fluttering of wings over my head and far, far away the soft, silvery chime of the bells I knew so well. The pale Umbrian saint, the friend of all forlorn creatures on this earth, stood by my side in his torn cassock, just as I had so often seen him on the frescoed walls of his dim chapel when my eyes could see. Swift-winged birds fluttered and sang around his head, others fed from his outstretched hands, others nestled fearlessly among the folds of his cassock.

The fear that had haunted me so long left my tormented brain, and a wonderful stillness and peace fell over me. I knew I was safe. I knew that the Giver of light was having mercy on me and would let me see again His beautiful world.

'The day is breaking', whispered the nurse.

When the *New York Times* commented on *The Times* letter in a leader, it was in almost sacred terms: 'The story of Munthe's waiting for the light after the operation upon his eyes presents what Chesterton would call one of the masterpieces of the art of life.'

According to Munthe, the best thing about the operation was that he could see the stars again. On the other hand, he was not convinced that the sight of his fellow men added much to his existence. 'I still see pretty well both the flowers and the stars and it seems to me that I even see too much when I look into the faces of my fellow men,' he wrote to William Rothenstein, who had drawn his portrait for his book *Contemporaries*. By that time, in the autumn of 1937, Munthe's sight had deteriorated again and there was talk of a further operation. However, he decided at the last moment to postpone it until he had nothing to lose; it was never carried out.

THE DOCTOR AND DEATH

If you can make me believe what you believe I will give you my remaining eye with gladness.

Axel Munthe to the Swedish Archbishop Nathan Söderblom, 1931

MUNTHE'S CORRESPONDENCE DURING the 1930s was dominated by his literary successes. But introspection and the need for acknowledgement were only some of the facets of Munthe's richly cut personality. For just as often as he asked himself and others why the book had been such a success, in letter after letter he would be posing questions about death and what came after it. His fascination with death went back a long way. This was what had enticed him to Naples and Messina and to the frontline during the First World War. It was this that had precipitated him into life-threatening Alpine adventures. It was this that had made him decorate a wall in the Villa San Michele with a mosaic depicting a skeleton with a wine-jug in its hands. It was this that had made him furnish the Villa San Michele with genuine children's skeletons – a form of decor perceived as decidedly odd even in a period more accustomed to symbols of vanity than our own. Death interested him, he admitted, long after he had ceased to be interested in life.

'Strangest of all, the further we advance towards our graves, the further does Death recede from our thoughts,' Munthe wrote in *The Story of San Michele*. It was not true. The nearer Munthe came to his own death, the more preoccupied he became by the question of what comes next. His musings about death originated in his religious doubts; he had lost his Christian ideals, his childhood faith. His relative Gustaf Munthe wrote that he was 'an unhappy man who never completely succeeded in harnessing his conflicting powers and hitching his brilliant chariot to one great star'. In a letter to the Swedish archbishop Nathan Söderblom Axel wrote:

> I well know that many pages in this hastily written book must have irritated you and I almost feel as if I wanted to beg your pardon for many flippant jokes and silly tournures de phrases on what is sacred to you and,

you may believe it or not, also sacred to me. The altar to the Unknown God still stands erect among the ruins of my orthodox faith. If you can make me believe what you believe I will give you my remaining eye with gladness.

The question of immortality was central to Munthe. There were many books on this theme in his library. By 'immortality' he did not mean a general merging with the cosmos but 'a life in which his own personality could carry on as a recognizable, separate unity'. The idea was rejected by Tolstoy, who pointed out in *What I Believe* that Jesus 'never said a word that would bear out [the idea of] personal resurrection and immortality beyond the grave'; as we saw previously, Munthe read this book with close attention. But he never ceased to be tormented by the issue and even promised Torre di Materita to anyone who could convince him that the individual human being could survive death.

The pressing doubts that beset Munthe simultaneously formed the basis for his qualities as a curer of souls. His tussles with death had taught him that 'there is no drug as powerful as hope' and that 'the slightest sign of pessimism in the face or words of a doctor can cost his patient his life.' Hence his positive attitude towards the nuns and their crucifix. If he thought he had deceived his patients when they were relatively healthy, he was unfailingly self-sacrificing in the hour of death. If the pain was too unbearable he injected morphine. In other cases he filled the dying person with hope. One example can suffice: Edwin Cerio's father Ignazio, one of Munthe's medical colleagues on Capri, was a skilled conservator who repaired several of Munthe's antique vases. When in 1921 he was on his deathbed, Munthe asked what he could do for him. 'Do you have another vase that needs repairing?' Cerio wondered. 'Certainly,' replied Munthe. There was no broken vase, but in order to give Don Ignazio hope, Munthe broke one that was whole.

Munthe had a soulmate in the author Stefan Zweig, who fled to England in the 1930s to escape the Nazis. In his book *Die Heilung durch den Geist* – where among other things he wrote about Mesmer and Freud – he dealt with questions that were of the greatest interest to Munthe. One can easily imagine with what interest Zweig read *The Story of San Michele*. Sometime at the end of the 1930s (perhaps in 1939, when he was suffering from severe depression) Zweig rang Munthe from Naples and insisted on coming to call on him. 'He was in Anacapri for exactly three hours,' Munthe remembered. 'During and after lunch he questioned me in detail about different methods of committing suicide – which of them were painless and why. I have never met anyone who was so obsessed with death.' A few years later Zweig and his wife took their own lives.

CRIMINALS AND GANGSTERS

Munthe's pessimism deepened during the 1930s, not only from thoughts of his own imminent departure but also because of the increasingly grim world situation. After the First World War tourists had begun to return to Capri and life had returned to normal. Almost. Italy was no longer the same: 1919 saw the founding of the Fascist Party, which in 1922 was behind the great march on Rome; in that same year the Fascists came to Capri. Local self-government came to an end and the inhabitants were no longer allowed to elect the *sindaco*. As part of the reforms Capri and Anacapri were amalgamated into one municipality.

After his visit to Capri in the spring of 1925 Mussolini declared that it was *un'isola che si non scorda mai*, 'an island one can never forget', and large amounts of money were set aside to regenerate the island economically. Mussolini's idea was that important foreign guests could be invited to Capri to enjoy its natural advantages and to be impressed by the improvements brought by Fascism. In 1933, for example, the British foreign minister Lord Simon was invited for a holiday.

Mussolini's Capri project involved the cleaning-up not only of the road network but also of morals. The methods used were not quite as primitive as on the mainland, where the Fascists sometimes filled their opponents with castor oil to cleanse them of anti-government opinions. But some of the most active homosexuals were ordered off the island; others thought it best to take themselves off. But not even the Fascists could overcome Capri's libertine traditions and the moral cleansing campaign eventually petered out.

Despite the fact that Fascism on Capri was less brutal than elsewhere in Italy, many people joined the party out of sheer self-preservation, in order to be left in peace. This included several of Munthe's medical colleagues, among them Dr Cuomo, and his lawyer, the highly respected Roberta Serena.

Munthe himself was on his guard against the totalitarian movements in both Italy and Germany from an early stage. In May 1933, after the Reichstag fire in Berlin and the subsequent restrictions on democracy, he put together a letter to Karl Otto Bonnier that shows that at this time he was more clear-sighted than most people: 'I hope that recent events have at last opened the eyes of the Swedes and made them realize what a set of barbarians these people are and have always been. England knows it now and so does the whole civilized world except your Swedish newspapers, at least some of them.'

To Munthe, developments in Germany simply confirmed that his ancient scepticism regarding everything German was justified, and the German doctors' campaign against him had been grist to his mill. The day after the remaining stock of *Red Cross & Iron Cross* was destroyed, John Murray was treated to the following prophetic words of warning: 'I have had enough of your friends the Boches. Your country, always the first to be deceived, will soon find out that they remain exactly the same people who invaded belgium [sic] and shot miss cavel* [sic] and they mean to do it again as soon as they have succeeded to blindfold you.'

To Speak Out Means Deportation

'If only Heine had been alive now, how quickly he would have put an end to the Hitler business,' Munthe commented to his English publisher in September 1936. Yet at this time, in the mid-1930s, it was Mussolini who worried Munthe the most. As part of Il Duce's ambition to re-create the greatness of the Roman Empire, in the autumn of 1935 Italian forces invaded Abyssinia, the only independent country in Africa. The war was waged with great brutality, the primitively equipped Abyssinian troops being bombarded from the air, as were Red Cross ambulances.

Britain and France did not want to offend Italy, which they saw as an ally in the struggle against Hitler's Germany. Even Winston Churchill accepted the government's conclusion that no vital British interests were at risk in Abyssinia. The League of Nations forced through sanctions against Italy, the first ever against a nation waging war. But the sanctions were not military ones, being instead confined to toothless and ineffective punishments 'to deprive Italy of everything the country can do without', as Lloyd George tellingly put it. The import ban included mules and camels, but not lorries and motorcars.

By May 1936 Italy had crushed all resistance. Munthe was 'so upset by the political situation' that he could think of nothing else. 'I cannot sleep for anxiety and grief over what is going on here,' he wrote to Märta Lindqvist, a Swedish journalist: 'If I was young I know very well where I would go. I am very pessimistic about the outcome. If this infamous aerial war is allowed to go on, the outcome can only be destruction. The atmosphere here is unbearable and I find it extremely difficult to be silent, but to speak out means deportation.'

Munthe was so outspoken in his criticism of Mussolini's war policies that he risked being sent to Lipari, one of the islands to which Mussolini deported politically inconvenient people. 'I am coming to England next

---

* Miss Edith Cavell was a British nurse who was executed by the Germans in Brussels in October 1916.

month for a "change of air" as it is getting more and more difficult to hold one's tongue,' he wrote to the editor-in-chief of *The Times*, adding: 'I need not tell you that this letter is strictly private. I am too old and too ill to end my days on the island of Lipari.' He depicted himself as more anglophile than the British diplomats in Italy, who according to Munthe had not the faintest understanding of the Italian mentality.

Munthe managed to escape Lipari, but his anxiety was not unfounded. He was in fact under surveillance by Mussolini's *polizia politica*, who had been gathering intelligence about him since 1935. It had probably amused him to know that he was described by police headquarters in Naples as 'Prof. Muncht, di origine germanica', of German origin, and the author of the book 'Monte San Michele'. He was suspected of spying for Sweden and was said to have obtained intelligence about Italian troop and weapon transports at Naples docks. In January 1936 the Interior Ministry reported that Munthe, who previously hardly ever left Capri, had made repeated visits to Naples and Rome, where he met with representatives from the Swedish legation. As he was of German origin it was also suspected that he was supplying Germany with secret information about Italy.*

That Munthe should devote himself to active espionage was not of course very likely, given his age. Presumably there was someone who wished to cast him in that light and provided the police with false information. Only a month or so later the Naples police reported, quite rightly, that there were no grounds for the assertions about his military espionage. Munthe, it was claimed in the report, had never during all his years on Capri given cause for suspicion about his behaviour; he was old, sick and blind, he lived unobtrusively, was popular with the local people (except for the bird hunters) and did not associate with suspect persons. It was also noted that he had gifted 80,000 lire to the municipality for care of the poor and the sick (something, incidentally, that he had been doing for many years).

Despite this it was decided to keep him under continuing surveillance and to introduce 'a discreet check' on his correspondence. This however produced no results, and in April 1938 the Interior Ministry declared that the four letters they had opened since the previous summer could not justify their continued interest in Munthe's correspondence.

Munthe wrote letters strongly critical of Mussolini during the Abyssinian war, but it was not until after it that the police began opening his mail. The fact that they were only able to lay their hands on four letters suggests either incompetence, or that Munthe was not seen as sufficiently important, or both. In any event the intercepted letters were politically

---

* The material about Munthe collected by the secret police can be found in the archives of the Interior Ministry in the Italian State Archive.

innocuous. To take one example, there was the letter in which Munthe asked John Murray to send a copy of the illustrated edition of *The Story of San Michele* to Mussolini's daughter, Edda, who was married to Galeazzo Ciano, Italy's foreign minister since 1936. The Cianos had a villa on Capri, which according to Munthe was 'a monument to bad taste and money'. Edda sometimes came to see him in his tower, but he was not particularly pleased by her visits as he did not think they had much to say to each other. However there was one thing they had in common, and that was 'a loathing for Ciano'. Edda had her reasons: her husband was an insufferable playboy who preferred to take his amusement elsewhere; Munthe had his reasons, which were political.

One example of how negligent the police were is that in the summer of 1937 they let through a letter to the Swedish explorer Sven Hedin in which Munthe claimed that the English 'are all hypnotized by fear of Germany and unable to understand that Mussolini is by far more dangerous to peace than Hitler'. On the other hand, they stopped a letter to Munthe's French publisher Albin Michel, in which Mussolini is depicted as 'un cas de "folie de grandeur" où tout est possible' ('a case of megalomania where everything is possible'). Thus the Naples prefecture were justified in refusing to accept the exemption warrant that the Interior Ministry gave Munthe and to continue to read his mail.

During the course of 1938 Germany annexed Austria and the Sudetenland and in September Britain and France were panicked into signing the Munich Agreement, according to which the western powers recognised these annexations in return for a German promise not to expand any further. The British prime minister returned in triumph to London in hopes of having saved Europe from a major war.

Munthe was dismayed by Britain's compliancy and from the autumn of 1938 his letters gave the Italian censors rather more to chew on. In the course of a few months, from October 1938 to January 1939, he criticised Britain in letter after letter for its political naivety and vented his spleen on Hitler and Mussolini. While most of his letters in English failed to reach their addressees, having been stopped by the censors, his letters to Sweden seem to have slipped through. After the Kristallnacht in October 1938 Munthe wrote to Bonnier, who was Jewish, that he was following 'with shame and sorrow' 'the infamous war of extermination against your brave people and I am ashamed to be a human being': 'How is it possible that there are still educated individuals in Sweden who sympathise with modern Germany? If there is a God of Vengeance it is certainly time for him to wake up from his hibernation.' From 1938 onwards, Frau Gleitzmann, an elderly Jewish lady who had fled from Germany, was his guest in the Villa Sole in Anacapri.

According to Munthe the sabre rattling was 'an enormous bluff' staged by the 'two dictators', who had never intended to go to war. Neville Chamberlain was certainly an honourable man but like Don Quixote he lived 'in the firm conviction that his windmills really were magnificent and his house [. . .] a fortress'. It would therefore not be long before the western powers were forced into yet another 'gentleman's agreement' (a reference to a treaty between Great Britain and Italy in 1937 intended to regularise relations after the Abyssinian war), from which they would wake up to a 'new deception, a new defeat, a new humiliation'.

'Is your country still desirous to shake hands with murder, what more do you want to realize that you are dealing with criminals and gangsters and not with your equals?' Munthe asked Esme Howard on 19 November 1939, adding: 'I suppose the next step will be an offer for 25 years peace from the 2 dictators which will silence all opposition, *but leave you in their mercy.*' His hopes lay with America, he wrote the same day to his English friend Bella Middleton; France was too weak. Munthe was so incensed by the British stance that he cancelled his subscription to the pro-government *Times* and changed to the ever more popular *New Statesman*.

HERMANN GOERING

Against the background of Munthe's anti-Nazism and general anti-Germanism, his negotiations with Hermann Goering about the sale of San Michele appear strange in the extreme. On 21 January 1937 the following notice could be read in the Swedish press: 'On Wednesday Prussian Prime Minister Goering and his wife visited Dr Axel Munthe in the Villa San Michele on Capri.'

In January 1937 Hermann Goering was in Italy to meet Mussolini, to discuss, among other things, German plans for the annexation of Austria. Between rounds of negotiations he and his wife Emmy travelled to Capri for a few days. Goering had visited Mussolini's model island at least once before, in 1933, when the people he met included Prince Philip of Hesse. The Prince of Hesse and his consort Princess Mafalda were enchanted by Capri and were looking for a house there. Munthe had invited them to buy the Casa Caprile, but instead the royal couple acquired the Villa Mura down in Capri. It was in all probability Prince Philip who now introduced Goering to Munthe.

Goering was curious about San Michele and Munthe showed him the villa and his art collection. 'It gave him pleasure to show off his house, and when he noticed how genuinely delighted we were by the many treasures in his home, this shy, almost bashful man was transformed,' Emmy Goering remembered. Their visit made a deep impression not only on Goering but also on Munthe, who six months later reported to Sven Hedin:

> I had a most unexpected long visit from Goring [sic] who made a far better impression on me than I had expected. To my amazement he said he wanted to write a preface to the popular german edition of my book, one hundred thousand copies. Luckily it was too late, the book was already in the presse [sic]. He came twice to see me during his two days stay in Capri and now he has asked via Prince Philip of Hesse if I am willing to sell San Michele to him.

On his second visit Goering wrote in San Michele's visitors' book: 'Once again in your wonderful San Michele'. He made so bold as to ask Munthe if he would sell San Michele to him because it was well known that he wanted to get rid of the villa, which had been rented out for over thirty years and was more of a monument to its founder than a home. Since 1934 it had been open to the public for four hours a day. The price of admission was five lire, which went to the poor of the island. In the first year the villa received 500 visitors, but the amount of wear and tear was considerable and artefacts were stolen. Apart from San Michele Munthe still owned Torre di Materita, Torre della Guardia, Torre Damecuta and the Villa Sole. But age was beginning to take its toll. In 1937 Munthe was 80 and no longer as able as he had been. Moreover, he was once again experiencing poor vision in his remaining eye. As one strand in the dismantling of his Capri empire, and to show his gratitude for the decree to forbid the hunting of birds, Munthe in the mid-1930s gifted the Torre Damecuta and surrounding land to the Italian state.

Goering was not the first to try to buy the villa. Munthe had had many offers over the years but had turned down all of them. Now, though, he was mentally prepared to dispose of it. Just before Goering arrived with his enquiry, Munthe had been discussing a possible sale with Alice Garrett, wife of John Garrett, the American ambassador to Rome from 1929 to 1933. The Garretts had rented San Michele several times during the 1930s and on at least one occasion, in the summer of 1930, they had brought with them a string quartet from Baltimore, which played in the chapel every day.

Mrs Garrett became so fond of the villa that she asked if she could buy it. On 21 February 1937 – one month after Goering's visit – Munthe told her his conditions. The amount to be paid must cover the donations he had made in his will to animals, the Lapps, the blind and some private individuals, which came to £10,000. He needed as much again for the protection of birds in Italy and Sweden. If he managed to get two million lire for his artworks – the same sum he had been offered twenty years earlier – he was prepared to hand over San Michele as a present to Mrs Garrett. He also hinted that after her death the villa ought to be gifted as a summer residence to the American embassy or the American Academy in Rome. The offer was hedged around with so many specific conditions that one cannot help wondering if Munthe really wanted to sell. Sure enough, the response to his letter was a polite rebuff.

When Munthe's contacts with Goering became known, Munthe denied that he had received the Nazi leader voluntarily, saying to a French journalist:

> That dreadful Goering, remembering that I had received the German emperor before the war, pursued me, when I was staying there recently, right into the old tower. My caretaker, impressed by his authority, having allowed him to climb the ramparts, I barely had time to go in search of my Légion d'honneur rosette and fasten it to my chest before receiving him face to face.

Munthe's condescending remarks about Goering were reported in several German newspapers, which made him assure both the List Verlag and Goering himself that he had said nothing of the kind; in actual fact, he said, having learned from experience, he had given no interviews for two years.

Of course Munthe had said what he was reported as saying – no interviewer could have put such words in his mouth. Moreover, his utterance was wholly in keeping with his views on the Nazis and Germans in general. But this was not the only time he denied statements made in the context of an interview.

However painful the revelation of Goering's interest in the villa may have been for the anglophile Munthe, he did not break off discussions with the Nazi leader. Instead he wrote to Goering, hoping that he would honour him with yet another visit to Capri, where he wanted to show him his other tower as well as the Barbarossa fortress. As far as the Villa San Michele was concerned, he would gladly *lend* it out if Goering could ever tear himself away from his 'tremendous work' 'for a well-earned rest'.

Goering's answer has not been preserved. On 25 October of the same year Munthe wrote to him again and three weeks later he sent another letter, in reply to a telegram from Goering. The letters are similar in tone. Munthe now tells Goering that he has decided to *sell* San Michele on condition that he can find the right man. 'I would rather hand over my beloved old home to you than to one of these american millionaires with no other qualifications to own this unique place than their money,' he writes in the later letter, continuing:

i do not want any money for myself, i have enough to live on til i die, and i have no wish to possess anything that can be bought with money. The entire sum will go the same way as all my earnings from my book to the poor of this island and of Sweden, not the least to my special friends the Laps and for the welfare of the animals. During the thirty years of my life as a doctor, i have spent all my earnings on making San Michele what it is today, regardless of expenses and often, no doubt, in a very reckless way. After endless difficulties i bought nearly forty years ago Castello Barbarossa and spent very large sums on restoring its crumbling walls and building a small hermitage where i used to live for months in complete solitude, perhaps the happiest days of my laborious life.

i possess no detailed accounts of what S. Michele and Barbarossa have cost me during all these years of almost uninterrupted work, but it is certain that it cannot be less than five hundred thousand Swedish kronor, most probably a much larger sum. if you can see your way to re-pay me this money i have spent, i am willing to hand over to you my beloved old home as it stands today with all its antiquities and works of art and furniture, much of which cannot be bought with money at any price. The actual house is no doubt too small for you – it was built by me on the principle that *the soul needs more room than the body*. But there is ample room for enlarging the villa. The large terrasse on the top of the garden where i intended to build an open greek theatre is a wonderful emplacement for a guesthouse and there is the whole mountain of Barbarossa behind to enlarge the property if need be. It might interest you to know that Prof. Maiuri, the Director of the Scavi di Pompeji, has in a recent publication confirmed the belief expressed by me in my book, that the two small roman rooms discovered by me under the chapel formed a part of a villa of Augustus and not of Tiberius as was formerly believed.

Goering replied that he was very 'moved by the prospect of owning this magnificent piece of ground', but that the economic situation in Germany could make it difficult for him to finance the purchase. But he promised to get in touch again as soon as he found a solution. 'I often long to return to that wonderful island,' he wrote, 'and it is not only the situation of San Michele that is so tempting; even more than that, it is the interior of the house, the whole atmosphere that emanates from it and everything about the unique way in which you have built San Michele.'

The correspondence ends here. The sale did not come off. Goering's talk of financial difficulties was, of course, only a pretext. As the man responsible for the German economy he had access to all the resources he could have wanted. The real reason was almost certainly that the villa was too small and would need a good deal of rebuilding and extending. In contrast to Munthe, Goering also knew that Germany's policy of expansion would soon create a situation in Europe that would afford little scope for such activities.

That Goering backed out is therefore understandable. What is harder to explain is why Munthe was prepared to sell the villa to a leading Nazi, the founder of the Gestapo and head of the Luftwaffe. Germany in 1937 was a state in which all democratic rights had been suspended and Jews and other undesirable persons were being sent to concentration camps – a dictatorship. Goering was the second-in-command in Hitler's Germany. Yet one must not make the mistake of looking at him with post-war hindsight. Goering in 1937 was not Goering in 1940 or 1945; Germany had not yet annexed or attacked her neighbours; the Kristallnacht had not yet taken place. At this period many European politicians saw Goering as a civilised alternative to Hitler. He was regarded as ridiculous and pompous, but also as a person who was charming, intelligent and interested in art. One British politician after another (apart from Churchill) visited Germany and was impressed by Goering, and the British ambassador to Berlin, Arthur Henderson, described him as quick-witted, disarmingly candid and possessing an irresistible sense of humour. This very year of 1937 also saw a period of political calm after the Berlin Olympiad.

However one views the matter, the equation does not add up. It is out of the question that Munthe would have been driven by political or personal sympathies for Goering or Nazism. One possible explanation is that, just as with the question of the bird-hunting ban of 1932, he chose to ignore his political convictions in order to achieve a goal that he saw as more important: to dispose of the villa, which he was no longer able to take care of. In this case it would be yet another example of the pragmatic turn of mind that Munthe could demonstrate when needed. But perhaps it was not pragmatism that governed his conduct in this case, but vanity. Perhaps he was flattered that it was one of the mighty ones of the earth who wanted to buy the villa. If so, his behaviour demonstrates a profound lack of judgement, and provides yet another example of how his constant need for acknowledgement triumphed at the cost of his common sense.

Perhaps it was precisely a question of *level*. At the same time as Munthe was negotiating with Goering, he was using the latter's interest in buying the villa to bring pressure to bear on the Swedish state. This emerges from a letter to Sweden's minister in Rome, Baron Beck-Friis:

> I am sending you one of Göring's letters in order to sharpen the Legation's appetite vis-à-vis S. Michele. Several letters & telegrams since this. Give me Göring's letter back when we meet again. Sorry to give you all this trouble already while I am still alive – take comfort from the fact that it will be even worse when I die.

Munthe had several balls in the air at the same time, just as when he was negotiating with his publisher. In the end it was the kingdom of Sweden that took over the property, of which more in the following chapter.

THE WAR

I do not see why I should not be able to postpone my death until after the war.

Axel Munthe, 1941

TRUE TO HIS habit Munthe spent the late summer of 1939 at Solliden and in Stockholm. With him in Sweden was a young New Zealander, Dorothy Johnstone, whom he had got to know on the boat from Naples to London in the spring of that year. Miss Johnstone had been captivated by *The Story of San Michele* and was equally enthusiastic about meeting the book's author. Munthe, for his part, needed company on the voyage and secretarial help, and he took her with him to London and Sweden. Vittorio could be helpful in practical matters but not with more demanding tasks, even if, over the years, he had learnt both English and Swedish.

In actual fact Miss Johnstone had fallen in love with Munthe, who was sixty years her senior, which shows that his attractiveness to the other sex was undiminished. 'She is not a flirt', was Munthe's diagnosis, 'but, unfortunately for her, she is attractive to men and far too confident both in them and in herself.' She had a tendency to depression and her letters to Munthe are carbon copies of those that admiring and needy women always sent him. In other words, she was a classic Munthe patient. She wrote that she found it difficult to live without his 'physical presence', she could laugh and have fun with other people, but 'something deep and dark' within her belonged to him, she had no control over it 'and whenever you call from this earth or beyond it, I must come'.

Miss Johnstone looked to Munthe as a father, she cut his hair and his beard and wondered in a letter who was doing this in her absence. Munthe for his part was grateful for her attention and helped her financially, for instance by persuading Murray's firm to employ her, if necessary at his expense. But her presence was sometimes so obtrusive that he was forced to employ drastic measures to avoid her. Once when he was about to set off for St James's Club and Dorothy wanted to come with him, he put her to sleep by laying his hand on her forehead and whispering some calming words.

He needed her help in Sweden, however, and explained to the king that she must be allowed to accompany him to Solliden, which was duly arranged. Not only that: she was given a room in the castle itself, where not even members of the court were allowed to stay, and she got to have lunch with the king. 'There has been absolutely no precedent,' she reported to John Murray, 'I am stepping not only into another world but into another age, about the etiquette of which I know nothing, and for the very reason that the king is so untraditional there will be greater need for care.'

After his summer visit to Solliden Munthe planned to travel back to London on 2 September and from there to continue by boat to Naples. But he did not want Miss Johnstone to come to Capri with him; the responsibility was too great. She was 'nice but very naïve', and if there was going to be a war she would be better staying in England, he wrote to Vittorio in a letter that finished with the words: 'I do not believe in an *all-out war* but everyone here believes it is inevitable.'

Events moved rapidly, however, and already on the following day, 28 August, Munthe was writing a further letter to Vittorio. The Naples boat had been cancelled – a 'bad sign' – and connections between Sweden and London were as good as broken off. As he could not take the train through Germany because of the summer heat, he would remain in Sweden at least until the middle of September. He still did not believe there would be war.

There were more 'bad signs' apart from the cancellation of the London–Naples boat. As early as March, Hitler had demanded that Danzig (Gdansk) in Poland be incorporated into Germany, and on 23 August Germany and the Soviet Union had signed a non-aggression pact. This time Munthe was let down by his normally reliable political intuition. Backed by the treaty with the Soviet Union, Germany invaded Poland on 1 September 1939, and Britain and France declared war on Germany.

When Munthe travelled to England at the end of September he was forced to go via Norway. 'I have arrived here via Norway–Newcastle with german aeroplanes circling over the ship, but no harm done,' he told Hugh Walpole. A month later he wrote to Vittorio that he hoped to be able to come home soon but could not say when. The boat he had been thinking of travelling on at the end of November had been sunk by a German mine.

Instead, Munthe remained in London throughout the winter, of which we know nothing except that he suffered from his sense of powerlessness. He was deeply concerned about Sweden's fate, and after the Soviet Union's attack on Finland on 30 November he wrote to William Rothenstein: 'I am in despair about brave Finland and the fate of my own country and if it comes to the worse I shall go there.' This was of course wishful thinking: Munthe was 82 years old, but, given his earlier contributions in emergencies, there is no reason to doubt the honesty of his ambition. The letters to Vittorio in the winter of 1939–40 show that war and suffering mobilised the very best in him, just as it had done many times before. Here it was once again the caring and endlessly generous Munthe who acted, the fellow human being with responsibility for his 'famiglia' and the poor on Capri, not the bestselling author and lord of San Michele. *Ce n'est rien donner aux hommes que de ne pas se donner soi-même*, was the motto of *The Story of San Michele* – 'Not to give people oneself is to give them nothing'.

He asked Vittorio to let the refugee Frau Gleitzmann know that if she needed money, he would transfer the required amount from Stockholm. He sent 10,000 lire to the mayor for the 'winter kitchen' in Anacapri and Vittorio received 3,000 lire to distribute among the poor of Anacapri at Christmas. The family at Materita also received Christmas money. Baroness von Uexküll had recently lost her estate in Estonia and Munthe instructed his lawyer to give her money if she should return to Capri before him.

During his seven months in London, Munthe seems to have had a certain amount of contact with his family, at least with the boys. In a letter to Vittorio he announced that Malcolm was to accompany him to Capri if he could get leave. Malcolm had volunteered for the army and been assigned to the Gordon Highlanders as early as the spring of 1939. When his call-up came he was in Sweden. During the autumn and winter of 1939–40 he underwent officer training, partly on the English Channel coast, so he and his father can hardly have seen each other very often. 'Grane is soon to be an Officer now,' Hilda proudly informed Emma Zorn – 'He is like himself in his endless good humour; be it long marches, or endless drilling, or a week of 'service' such as washing up from 7 a.m. till late at night, he seems to be able to find a joke in it.' As Malcolm spoke Swedish he was sent in the spring of 1940 to run Special Operations Executive activities in Scandinavia (his war-time adventures are described in his book *Sweet is War*, 1954). Not much is known of Peter's activities during the war. His health was poor and he suffered from not being able to contribute to the war effort in the same way as his brother. However, he served in the Royal Navy; towards the end of the war he became ill with malaria.

Munthe's eyesight had now worsened again. Just as before his operation in 1934, he needed someone who would be on hand the whole time, but Dorothy Johnstone was not the ideal option. During the early part of the 1930s Munthe had had secretarial help from a Swedish woman, Elsa Svensson, who was fluent in English and was also a practising pianist. Munthe had great confidence in her and he had barely returned to Capri before he contacted her again:

I am ill and exhausted by anxiety and insomnia and I can no longer look after myself without help. I must pension off Natasha who drinks and cannot stay with me. Rosina is also poorly and Vittorio has been called up for war service and cannot leave Italy. I am writing this letter with great difficulty to ask if you are willing to come to Materita to help me. [. . .] I do not believe that Italy will be dragged into the war, at least not in the immediate future. In any case I intend to travel to Switzerland and Zürich as soon as I have seen to Materita and from there I will return to London where I have rented a flat and I will stay there for the duration of the war. [. . .] I am relying on you to help me one more time.

Munthe received a negative answer to his request, and had to put up with the thirsty Russian, Natasha Khaliutine; nor did he make it to London. On 10 June 1940 Italy entered the war on Germany's side, making it impossible for Munthe to travel to England.

The First Last Will

Giving the prevailing conditions, Munthe's stay in Italy was not uncontroversial. The political police had long memories, and on 6 November 1940 the chief of police sent a memo to Mussolini saying that Munthe, whose state of health was very precarious, had expressed a desire to be allowed to return to Italy to die. Munthe had taken an outspokenly anti-Fascist stance, the police chief stated, especially during the period of sanctions, but he had only expressed this in letter form and in a purely ideological way (i.e. he was not an activist), and moreover as he was very famous, very old and very popular on Capri, the political police had no objection to his returning. Mussolini's authorisation is dated 7 November.

The memo was based on a misunderstanding as Munthe had been in Italy since May. But it was true that he was ill. His heart was giving him trouble and at the end of August 1940 the problems became acute. He could 'certainly live for a while yet but also die of heart failure at any moment', he wrote to Mrs Wallbom at the Swedish Legation in Rome. The king, he said, had telegraphed again, asking him to come home and had even wanted to send someone to fetch him, which was 'out of the question' in his present condition. Instead he wrote another letter to Elsa Svensson, asking her to come down and be his nurse.

Munthe did not manage to get to Sweden, nor Elsa Svensson to Capri. Instead he decided to draw up his will. For safety's sake he wrote two, one in Italian and one in Swedish, both of which were deposited with the Swedish Legation in Rome.

It was the Swedish will that was the important one. According to this one, Stengården was to go to Hilda, the Villa San Michele to Peter and Torre di Materita to Malcolm. His sons were also to receive £5,000 each. Gudrun von Uexküll received the Villa Sole, £1,000 and the rights to all Munthe's books in all languages. His 'faithful servant' Rosina and her family were given 100,000 lire and the right to stay on at Materita for the remainder of their lives. Natasha Khaliutine also received 100,000, 'if possible invested as a life rent', and the right to remain at Materita together with 300 lire a month, 'paid to Rosina for her food' (the proviso was probably motivated by Natasha's drinking habits). The poor of Capri would receive the remainder of Munthe's loan of 100,000 lire to the municipality in Anacapri.

As the boys were British citizens no provisions would be made regarding the real estate until the war was over. The hope was that in this way legal conflicts with the Italian authorities could be avoided. Munthe's properties on Capri would be administered until further notice by Baroness von Uexküll, at whose disposal he placed 25,000 lire in the Banco di Napoli. His remaining financial resources were donated to the Royal Swedish Academy of Sciences 'to set up a fund for the protection of Sweden's fauna'. If he died in Sweden, he wanted to be buried in Leksand churchyard 'without any funeral monument or inscription whatsoever'. If he died abroad, he wished to be cremated and his ashes 'thrown in the sea'.

This will was to be kept secret. The official will, written in Italian, was very concise and dealt only with the real estate:

I, Munthe Axel Martin Fredrik, son of the late Fredrik Munthe, hereby declare that I have given the whole of my fixed and moveable estate in the municipality of Anacapri, viz. the Villa S. Michele, Foresteria, Torre Materita and Villa Sole, together with inventories of their contents, to His Majesty the King of Sweden to dispose of as he sees fit.

The gift to the king was a pure *pro-forma* precaution against the houses being confiscated by the Italian authorities. The idea was that the king would turn them over to his heirs as soon as the war was over. On 4 October Munthe explained his intentions to his son Malcolm, c/o British Legation, Stockholm:

Jag är illa sjuk [I am seriously ill], heart failure, very uncertain if I will live for long, probably not, and shall probably never see you again. My will is with the Swedish Legation in Rome. I have already written to you that in order to avoid sequestration of my Capri property (as you all 3 are english) I have on lawyers advice in my will given S. Michele + Materita to the King of Sweden who will of course hand it over to you after peace.

If I die during the war *they will take it at once* as they have already done in another case.

The letter to the king is interesting, not least because it is here that Munthe for the first time floats the idea that San Michele might one day pass to the Swedish state:

Your Majesty!
[. . .] I do not believe that my wife wishes to live on Capri and if this should be the case my request is that Y.M. should donate S. Michele to the Swedish Legation in Rome as a summer residence and Materita to the poor in Anacapri and the furniture and artworks it contains to Baroness Uexküll on condition that the donations made in my will to my servants and to the persons named by me continue to be paid. [. . .] S. Michele, which with its contents is worth one million kronor, would be extremely suitable as a donation by the King for the Swedish Legation's summer residence. [. . .] With humble greetings and respectful thanks for half a century.

Axel Munthe

P.S. As my family have extremely poor prospects of inheriting the property on Capri – their prospects are de facto non-existent – they ought to receive from Y.M. the monies deposited by me in the Enskilda Banken and the house in Leksand. [. . .] The idea of giving S.M. to the Swedish state (or the legation) is a good one and I am sure that my family will agree to it in exchange for money in Sweden.

The king did not fall in with Munthe's suggestion, despite the 'half a century' they had known each other; there seem to have been legal obstacles. Munthe was therefore forced to think again, and in a will dated 20 November 1940 he transferred the properties to Hilda, who was a Swedish citizen (something he seems to have forgotten or suppressed earlier). It was not an ideal option, but it was the least bad one.

The will made Gudrun von Uexküll (1878–1969) not only a beneficiary and administrator of the properties on Capri, but also an executor. The baroness had lived on Capri ever since 1908, when she inherited the Villa Discopoli and she arrived at about the same time as Munthe in the spring of 1940 with her husband, the leading zoologist Jakob von Uexküll, born in 1864, who died on Capri in 1944. The baroness had translated both of Munthe's books into German and negotiated with German film studios about the film rights. Munthe did not believe that any of his heirs wanted to take over his 'Capri-possessions', whereas the baroness had been 'a good friend of the queen and also best suited to take care of her villa'.

The many wills and rough drafts of wills show that Munthe was extremely ambivalent about the posthumous fate of his life's work. In a letter to Mrs Wallbom he writes that he wants to donate the Villa San Michele to the Italian state for the benefit of the poor in Capri and Anacapri, but this is scored out. Then he wants the baroness to have Materita with all its effects, also scored out; after this, that the baroness should be allowed to stay in either San Michele or Materita until her death, after which it should go to the poor in Anacapri. In any event, Munthe's generosity to Gudrun von Uexküll testifies that in many ways he felt closer to her than to his own family.

MALCOLM AND THE RED HORSE

The will did not have to be executed. Munthe recovered; although he still suffered from asthma, especially at night, his heart worked satisfactorily and he walked around among the olive trees at Materita for at least two hours a day. 'I do not now believe there is any hurry,' he wrote to Baron Beck-Friis in Rome, 'and I do not see why I should not be able to postpone my death until after the war, which would make everything so much simpler.'

In the same letter, Munthe mentioned that Capri was 'empty and gloomy'. In May and June of 1940 Denmark, Norway, Belgium and France had capitulated and in June, as we have seen, Italy joined in the war. The English church was confiscated as 'enemy property', which confirms that Munthe's misgivings regarding his houses were justified. The winter of 1941 saw the first garrison set up since Napoleon's day, and Torre della Guardia was taken over by the Italian air defence forces. The waters around Capri were mined. The first German soldiers came to the island and were greeted enthusiastically by the island's traders, who were suffering from the absence of tourists. A Wehrmacht band sometimes played in the piazza in Capri and the soldiers spent freely in cafés and nightclubs.

Given Munthe's detestation of German tourists, it is easy to imagine his reaction to the presence of German soldiers on Capri, but Italy was at war and it was difficult to get away. One of the few possible travel destinations was Sweden, which was neutral. Previously, Munthe had always travelled via England, but that alternative was out of the question now. Instead he took the train from Rome to Berlin, from where he flew to Stockholm, where he arrived on 7 July 1941.

The letters that Munthe wrote to his son in the autumn of 1940 about the disposition of his estate were addressed to the British Legation in Stockholm. After his mission in Finland, Malcolm had moved on via England to Norway to support the British invasion forces (which never came). When the Germans invaded Norway on 9 April he stayed on in the country but managed to get to Sweden with the help of a Swedish passport issued in the name of Axel Axelsson. On 20 or 21 May he managed to cross to Sweden in a rowing boat.* On his arrival in Stockholm he was taken on at the British Legation as an assistant military attaché and promoted from captain to major.

In Stockholm Malcolm continued to plan acts of sabotage to be carried out in Norway. He tested time bombs in the Stockholm archipelago and founded the 'Red Horse' group, which sent Resistance men into Norway. This activity was of course incompatible with his status as a diplomat, and was severely frowned on in a country that was formally neutral but which allowed German military transports to pass through it. On 24 April 1941 a high official at the foreign ministry sent the Swedish Legation in London a 'strictly confidential' handwritten letter in which he wrote that 'Major Munthe's activities in Stockholm have long been a cause for concern, as we have clear proof that from here he has organised an intelligence service pertaining to Norway, by sending Norwegians and Swedes with specialised skills there.' The cabinet secretary had therefore informed Louis Mallet, the British minister in Stockholm, that Sweden could not tolerate such activity being conducted from Sweden and that those 'on the Swedish side [. . .] must regard Munthe as persona non grata'.

Even if Axel was not informed of Malcolm's activities in detail, he knew of course what his son was up to. During the twelve days of June when they were both in Stockholm they had a certain amount of contact by telephone. The listener who intercepted conversations between the British Legation and Stockholm Palace has disclosed that Malcolm's cover name was Stig. Axel, with his Anglomania, was enormously proud of his son's service in the British army and his contributions to the Norwegian Resistance. 'My son has done excellent work in Norway and here, is now a major in Gordon Scottish,' he wrote to John Murray on 15 July, three days before the ministry of foreign affairs informed the Swedish Legation in Berlin that 'Assistant military attaché Munthe at the British mission will be leaving for London any day now, not to return, and not a day too soon.'

On the following day, 19 July, Malcolm received permission to visit his father at the palace. They met in the king's study. The king clapped him on the head and Axel kissed him on the forehead without saying a word. Then he was driven out to the airport and a British courier plane that took him to London.

---

* His depiction of the events in *Sweet is War* is a dramatised version of the much more sober report he gave to the Swedish secret police during an interrogation on 20 June, 1940.

Things are Very Strict Here Now

Axel's stay in Sweden in the summer of 1941 was a dramatic one. He met his son for the first time in several years, and he saw him expelled from the country. If he had mixed feelings about this, he could at least comfort himself with the fact that his heart showed no changes since his examinations in 1934 and 1939. 'By and large an excellent constitution,' his cardiologist wrote in his report: 'ECG occasionally shows numerous extra systoles but otherwise normal for his age or rather better than normal conditions.' 'I am on the whole better and I hope and believe I shall see you again,' Munthe wrote to John Murray shortly before flying back to Berlin on 12 September on his way to Capri.

'Things are very strict here now, only the Germans are allowed to come and to do as they please,' Munthe reported to minister Beck-Friis in the spring of 1942. The island's isolation was almost total, it was hard to get information about the progress of the war and Munthe asked the legation in Rome to tell him how to pick up Swedish radio broadcasts. 'I hate it here and would never come here again if I were fit to be anywhere else,' he complained.

The situation on Capri as regards provisions had begun to be critical and Munthe received food parcels from the king and court. But deliveries were unsatisfactory: 'Nothing has been heard of the food box,' he complained to Beck-Friis, 'I have managed to get hold of a kilo of butter and otherwise am living on vegetables and fruit and I have enough crispbread to keep me going until I leave.'

The letter was written two weeks before Munthe commenced his summer trip to Sweden, again via the train to Berlin and a flight to Stockholm, where he landed on 16 June, Gustaf's eighty-fourth birthday. He stayed in the Royal Palace and only left Sweden three months later. It was Munthe's longest stay in his homeland for many years. As always when he was away for a long time he kept in touch with the family in Anacapri by way of letters, which testify to both his thoughtfulness and his excessive need to control:

Dear Vittorio
    Tell the colonel [Walton] who is looking after the olive grove at Fraita that the property will probably be sold and therefore I will not be able to allow him to stay on. But it is also possible that he will be able to stay – I will let him know when I come back, hopefully in September. Hope all is well at Materita. Let me know how Rosina's cheek is. I believe a new treatment is only necessary if it has got worse. Look after Lupa [the dog]. It is very cold here. [. . .] Don't forget the crop and the honey. Perhaps

tiles could be laid with cement on at least parts of the colonel's roof as we did above my room? Greetings to all at Materita, Villa Sole and to the Baroness [von Uexküll] and yourself.

On 10 December 1942 Munthe received by special courier a copy of Prince Eugen's memoirs with the dedication: 'To Axel Munthe with thanks for his good advice and for all the years of friendship, from Eugen'. In his thank-you letter Munthe praised the prince for his literary talent and at the same time lifted the veil from his own authorial laboratory:

It is a great joy to form thoughts into words, even for me it was a great help to write my book – praise certainly tastes fine in the mouth yet it is the actual work and not least the purely mechanical work that yields the greatest satisfaction, the power of the word is perhaps as great as that of the idea – 'vis superba formæ'. Do not think for too long in advance, it will come by itself in the course of working. I have little faith in Flaubert's 'jouir les délices de l'inédit', in any case he in no way applied this to himself. Waste no precious time on the *beginning*, as a rule one is well advised to *put it off* till the end of the book. Read the MS aloud in the morning and delete without hesitation everything you do not feel to be faultless and *good* and rely on your own judgement at least as much as that of others. One does not need to drink a whole bottle of wine to judge its quality – a couple of pages are as a rule enough for one to make up one's mind whether a person can write or not. Your Royal Highness *can* write and that is the main thing.

But the letter also bears witness to Munthe's homesickness:

For perhaps the first time in my life, I long to go home – is it because my country is perhaps in danger or because I myself am in danger of going under? Probably the latter – a man approaching death longs to go home. Anyway I am not happy here any more. Mussolini's Italy is no longer *our* Italy. The Florentine lily has been replaced by the Swastika, Botticelli's Primavera by Frau Göring, who travels around with special trains and drums and trumpets and buys up forged antiquities all over the country. Mussolini is in Hitler's power, Italy is not Germany's partner but its obedient *servant*, ill-treated and poorly paid. *Everyone* here, high and low, would like nothing better than to 'clear out' just as in the last war, but a separate peace is out of the question until the mighty colossus begins to totter – and unfortunately that is a long way off.

If it was not for my fear of the snow-light on my weak eye I would leave it all behind me and come home, but I dare not travel north until the early spring. Capri is like a fortress, no-one can either come here or get out. The island is full of Germans just like Naples and it is not certain that I will be able to stay here. All food goes to the Germans and the military,

I often go hungry to bed, my brain is sluggish from lack of sleep and my thoughts are gloomy. I have no doubt about the outcome but it will be a long-drawn-out war of attrition, not a war of conquest. My respectful greetings to the King, whom I often think of.*

By spring the fortunes of war had changed and the Italian army was in retreat. The last stronghold in Libya had fallen in January and on 13 May the last Axis forces in North Africa had surrendered. Mussolini changed his tactics and busied himself trying to prevent an invasion by Allied troops. 'We are having a rather lively time here, so far only the windows have been smashed in S. Michele but worse is to come, I fear,' Munthe wrote to John Murray in the spring of 1943. 'If the island is bombarded in earnest I feel as if I ought to remain here for the sake of good example but on the other hand I would not survive the heat of the summer here.'

In early June Munthe left Capri. The Allied bombing of southern Italy had already begun and the Naples boat with Munthe on board was fired on by American planes, but not hit. In the harbour he was met by a German colonel who had been delegated to help him in Naples. Munthe wanted to board the Rome train immediately, but as the station had been bombed several times in the last few days the colonel invited him instead to accompany him to the hotel where the German officers were quartered. In a report to British intelligence Munthe described his stay in Naples; like all his tales, it was filled with drama:

> Dr Munthe warned the German that he himself was anti-Nazi and did not wish to be under any particular obligation to the Germans, but the Colonel was most courteous and said he quite understood. He even referred quite politely to 'San Michele'. [. . .] He showed him some small pocket editions

---

* In his book *Kaputt* (1944), the Italian journalist Curzio Malaparte writes about his visit to Prince Eugen in the autumn of 1942, when he passed Stockholm on his way to Finland. From their long conversation about Munthe one gets the impression that Malaparte knew him well, but this was not the case. Malaparte also had a house on Capri, but had not yet met Munthe. When Malaparte returned to Capri in November 1942, Eddie Bismarck, the chancellor's grandson, who lived on Capri, wrote to Munthe: '[Malaparte] is an interesting person. Why don't you tell him to come and see you? I know he would love to come, but is afraid of disturbing you. He has been to Finland and his views on everything that is going on are interesting because he sees so many people. I am sure you would not be bored.' Thus Munthe and Malaparte got to know each other only in the winter of 1942–43. When, in April 1943, Malaparte went to Sweden, Munthe provided him with a letter of recommendation to the folklorist Ernst Mancker where he wrote that Malaparte is 'a highly intelligent person' and a 'great friend of the Lapps'. What made Munthe three months later characterise Malaparte, in a report to British Intelligence, as 'one of the worst rogues of his times even for an Italian' is unclear. But Munthe and Malaparte were both pronounced egocentrics, which paved the way for conflicts.

in German of the book, specially printed for the German army recreation centres. Dr Munthe was then driven in a very comfortable German car to the hotel, where he had a conversation with about 30 German officers, most of whom, like his host, Colonel Rutt, were medical officers, who were running the various hospitals in which 3,000 German wounded were being cared for in Naples. These officers admitted quite frankly that Germany had lost the war. [. . .] There seemed to be general agreement upon this defeatist attitude. The Colonel sent two orderlies to the station to reserve a seat for Dr Munthe. Half an hour before the train was due to leave, Dr Munthe left for the station in the German car, but half way there a new air-raid occurred, and a bomb dropped in the middle of the street, just in front of the car, so that they had to turn back and return to the hotel. After some more hours, they drove again to the station, and Dr Munthe was put into the train, where a seat had been kept for him. A fat woman came and sat on his knee with a baby. The train was terribly crowded with all kinds of refugees trying to get out of Naples [. . .]. At the last minute it turned out that this was the wrong train and it was going to Calabria instead of Rome. Finally Dr Munthe managed to get a seat in the right train, again fearfully crowded and several hours late. Just as the train was due to leave a fresh air-raid occurred but eventually the train managed to set off.*

One October morning in 1876 the youthful, weak-chested Axel Munthe had boarded the train in Stockholm on his way to the Mediterranean to try to regain his health. Now, sixty-seven years later, he was making the return journey – destined never again to see the region that, in his own words, had once reawoken him from the dead.

---

* On this report to the British Embassy in Stockholm (6 June 1943) an official made the following note: 'This report is of some interest in view of the source (Dr Axel Munthe), who should, I imagine, be reliable.' However, one of his colleagues was of another opinion and commented: 'I am afraid he is not very reliable (or was not 3 years ago).'

NOSTALGIA

Only when I'm dead will I stop dying.

Axel Munthe

MUNTHE LANDED IN Stockholm on 8 June 1943. Around midsummer he met a representative of the British intelligence service in Stockholm and handed over to him a report on the political situation in Italy (in which among other things he foresaw that the King of Italy would be forced off the throne after the war). When a newspaper asked him how long he planned to stay in Sweden he answered jokingly: 'Until the autumn if the king does not chase me out before then [. . .]'. His intention was to spend the summer in Sweden as usual and to travel back to Capri sometime in September.

On the way home he would have liked to make a stop in London, to which he was drawn not least for reasons of political solidarity – 'My thoughts are constantly with your country,' as he assured John Murray on several occasions. But if he travelled to London, he was told by the British Legation, he would be forced to sign a paper promising not to return to Italy before the end of the war. This he could not do, as 'the situation in my island home is so serious that I may even be obliged to return there before I planned to do in Sept.' Another problem was that the aeroplanes flew so high that his heart would not be able to cope.

During the summer Italy had been invaded by Allied forces. On 10 July the American 7th Army landed on the southern tip of Sicily and on 22 July Palermo was occupied. The Italian troops on Sicily offered only feeble resistance but the German units on the island fought all the harder, so that it was not until 17 August that the invading army reached Messina. Meanwhile, Mussolini's position had begun to waver and on 16 July Churchill exhorted the Italians to topple him. Rome was bombed by Allied planes, and foreign minister Ciano and others wanted an immediate end to the war; on 25 July Mussolini was captured and Marshal Badoglio set up a government. On 3 September Italy surrendered.

Munthe asked Murray several times for help in getting news about Malcolm, but without success. 'I do not know where my son Malcolm is and I am told not to write to him,' he wrote at the end of August. Malcolm, it turned out, was in southern Italy.* On 12 September General Eisenhower landed on Capri to take control of the island, and the following day the British Rear-Admiral Sir Anthony Morse arrived to take over as governor. Malcolm was with the British contingent who came ashore and on 13 September he visited San Michele along with British and American officers – a fact Axel heard about only several months later through an article in a Canadian newspaper, which informed its readers that they 'found all in order and that they took possession of Edda Ciano's villa [. . .]'. They all wrote their names in San Michele's guestbook, Munthe noted proudly. Ciano's villa was immediately converted into a headquarters for Governor Morse.

Travelling to Italy under these conditions was of course out of the question. Axel remained in Sweden, although he hated the cold and the dark and feared he would not survive the winter. The king put three rooms in the Royal Palace at his disposal; symbolically, they lay under Victoria's former apartment. Although the rooms were small, he found place for a little piano, as in all of his other homes.

'I have survived this winter but that is all I have to say about it,' Munthe reported to John Murray in the summer of 1944: 'My heart is worn out and I suffer much from cruel insomnia.' In actual fact there was more to say about the winter of 1943–44, which had been full of drama on both the political and the personal fronts. On 8 January 1944 Mussolini had his son-in-law Galeazzo Ciano put to death for his part in the coup against him. His daughter's plea for mercy for her husband was never delivered; she herself managed to flee to Switzerland. Princess Mafalda, to whom Munthe had dedicated the Italian edition of *The Story of San Michele*, had been arrested by the Germans in September 1943 and taken to Buchenwald (where she died during the Allied bombing raids in August 1944). Malcolm had been severely wounded during the fierce fighting around Monte Cassino in February, and had lain unconscious for five days.

The British governed Capri for only three weeks, after which control passed to the Americans. Rear-Admiral Morse moved to Naples and his place was taken by an American colonel who turned Capri into a rest camp for American fighter pilots. Unlike many other villas and hotels San Michele was not requisitioned, but Munthe was more than happy for the soldiers

---

* In connection with the liberation of Naples on 1 October, Malcolm helped to move the aged philosopher and anti-Fascist Benedetto Croce and his family to Capri; the action was urgent since Mussolini had meanwhile been freed from his prison by Hitler's army.

to be shown round the villa. In letter after letter Munthe exhorted Vittorio to maintain good relations with the Allied officers. 'Let the American + English soldiers visit also Materita if they come and always S. Michele without *paying any tickets*.' Munthe was now as proud to show off both his homes on Capri to representatives of the victors of the Second World War as he had been about the British Red Cross flag flying over San Michele during the First. His generosity paid off, in the form of appreciative letters about his life's work: 'The whole island of Capri has been turned into a "Rest camp" for american pilots, the commanding officer has written a most flattering letter to me about their love for S. Michele and the book.'

ADDIO CARA ROSINA

Just as before, the success of *The Story of San Michele* helped to lighten the physical and mental darkness enveloping Munthe. In his letters, anxiety about the state of the world and Malcolm's fate alternate with happiness and pride over the continued interest in the book. 'I am amazed to hear from the american minister here of the popularity of the book in America,' he wrote to Murray, 'I wish I could persuade myself to finish the new one, "The Missing Chapters".' This kind of wishful thinking was not unfamiliar to Murray. One may also note that, according to Munthe, the book was selling better than ever in Germany, where they had even printed a field edition for the army. 'Here people are always yelling for the english edition in vain,' he wrote to Murray in the winter of 1944, and when the following year a Swedish publisher brought out the book in English he was overjoyed. An edition of *Red Cross & Iron Cross* was brought out in Italian in 1945, for the first time since 1918.

The book was one of the few things that gave Munthe pleasure. He had little or no contact with Hilda, or at least no letters have survived. The same is true of his son Peter, who was also serving with the British military. That his relationship with his wife was glacial emerges from her letter to John Murray, inspired by the article about Axel in *Who's Who*:

> Certainly it will please my husband to have the boys mentioned as serving in the British Army, and it is right to do so for it is quite unfair that he should be thought to be pro-Italian, he is absolutely whole-heartedly on our side. But you little know Axel if you think it will amuse him to be branded a married man! I laugh as I write, but it is wonderful how unchanged he is and the zest he still has in life, and that any beautiful new lady he may meet should think of him as married would seem dull and prosaic. Things may have been difficult long ago, but I have long ceased to take Axel quite seriously [. . .].

Munthe continued to complain that he could not get away to England or
Italy, and every autumn he expressed his fear that he would not survive the
winter. 'I suffer terribly here from the *darkness* and the cold and think *with
terror* of the long winter,' he wrote to John Murray in December 1944 with
a form of words that was repeated the following autumn: 'I shall never
survive this winter and I shall never see Capri again.'

Despite his fears, Munthe survived both winters, but he felt lonely
and isolated. He lived a modest existence in the palace, exactly as he had
done in his tower in Anacapri. Every Friday he had lunch with the king. It
was boring, he admitted, but on the other hand they enjoyed being bored
together. However, Munthe did not enjoy all the talk of hunting. Asked
what the subject of conversation was during a palace dinner, he replied:
'Eh, they only talk about old roe deer they shot long ago.'

He received a few visitors, but seldom went out, even if he occasionally
made an unexpected appearance at some official event. He could 'at the same
time be a misanthrope and hungry for company, but he wanted to decide
himself whom he would meet and when and how this would happen.' All
his life Munthe had gone on long rambles; he looked on walking as a virtue
and liked to quote the words of Montaigne: 'My thoughts stand still if my
legs are not moving.' Even at the age of 87, a contemporary remembered,
he moved very easily and took hour-long walks. During the last years of
his life, however, he mostly walked around Stockholm's Old Town and
the palace courtyard, often accompanied by some younger person. The
summers were spent at Solliden, as usual.

When peace made it possible to travel in Europe again, Munthe made
renewed attempts to get to Capri. He contacted a travel company in
Stockholm, and pestered its employees with constant questions about
flight connections with Italy. He was extremely thorough in his planning
but could not make up his mind about his mode of travel. As before, he
did not like the idea of flying as he was afraid that his heart would not
cope with the high altitudes. He therefore considered chartering a plane
of his own so that he could fly at a height of his own choosing and make a
stop where he wanted. He weighed the pros and cons of driving through
Germany and then selling the car in Rome. For a while he was tempted
by the possibility of taking one of Lloyd's Swedish cargo boats and went
down to the quay to inspect them. 'He was a bit of a terror to the travel-
companies,' remembered Gustaf Munthe. He ordered tickets and reserved
seats but always cancelled his reservation. He could never make up his
mind. 'I don't know if he was like that when he was younger,' Gustaf wrote,
'but in his old age he was hopeless in that respect. A constant longing, and
a constant fear of fulfilling his plans!'

Munthe did not get to Capri. He was old and sick, and in his heart he knew that he would never again see his beloved island. His situation was hopeless. He did not like being in Sweden, and, as before, he was on bad terms with his family in London. In the summer of 1945 he wanted to travel to England, but whereabouts? 'My wife writes that I cannot come to her house,' he complained to John Murray.

'A man approaching death longs to go home,' he had written to Prince Eugen. But what was 'home' after sixty-seven years in Italy? On 5 November 1945 he wrote to 'Jock' Murray (John Murray VI):

> I am stupefied by insomnia and drugs and the thought that I shall die here in darkness and cold fills me with terror. I cannot fly and 4 nights in the train via Paris to Rome is not possible for me. I shall never survive this winter and I shall never see Capri again. I did not know it was so difficult to die and die alone. I suffer cruelly from insomnia and heart astma [sic] and *despair* and I have lost all hope of getting away and these last 2 winters here have made me 10 years older and taken away all my courage. [. . .] I have trouble with my one remaining eye and have nobody to read to me. [. . .] If I survive these winter months I shall come to England with a boat but it is most unlikely. My 'family' does not take the slightest interest in whether I am dead or alive – yes, perhaps Malcolm – Major of the Gordon Highlanders, he has a job at the War Office. Greetings to your uncle and feel sorry for me!

At the same time as he was penning these despairing lines, he was writing a tender letter to Rosina on Capri, which shows that it was there he had his home and his family (this time described without quotation marks): 'Dear Rosina, I think about you all the time and am quite unhappy to be so far from you all. [. . .] Good-bye, dear Rosina, and the whole family at Materita.'

Death Himself Like a Skeleton Sits on a Chair by my Bed

Axel survived the winter of 1945–46 too but found it ever more difficult to manage on his own. Throughout the war he had shown a touching concern for Dorothy Johnstone's welfare and at regular intervals he had sent her money. But when on one occasion she hinted that she would like to come to Stockholm, he was appalled and urged Murray to prevent this at all costs as 'she would only add to my worries'.

Instead he summoned Vittorio to Stockholm in 1946. Vittorio lived with Munthe at the Royal Palace, which they jokingly referred to as

'Långholmen', Stockholm's central prison. To look after Munthe constantly, day and night, afflicted as he was by asthma and ever-increasing anxiety, was no easy task. All his life he had been plagued by insomnia and now he was sleeping worse than ever. He often sat propped up on his pillows for whole nights at a time, tormented by shortness of breath, and thinking of death. During particularly difficult nights he saw 'the whole room fill up with skeletons and death's heads' and 'Death himself like a skeleton' sitting on a chair by his bed. 'He was not one to suffer his fate with equanimity,' remembered Gustaf Munthe. 'He complained the whole time about all the repellent aspects, especially the ailments which afflicted him, the asthma, the troublesome allergic nasal catarrh, the sleeplessness, his bad leg and much more besides.'

Thoughts of death, which had tormented and haunted Munthe throughout his life, now became an obsession. He had always maintained with Heinrich Heine that the worst thing was not death but dying. But it was not true. In his articles about the cholera outbreak in Naples in 1884 he had claimed that he did not fear death, but in *The Story of San Michele* he admitted he had lied:

> I had the cheek to put in writing that I was not afraid of the cholera, not afraid of Death. I told a lie. I was horribly afraid of both from the first till the last. I described in the first letter how, half-faint from the stench of carbolic acid in the empty train I stepped out on the deserted Piazza late in the evening, how I passed in the streets long convoys of carts and omnibuses filled with corpses on the way to the cholera cemetery, how I spent the whole night amongst the dying in the wretched fondaci of the slums. But there is no description of how a couple of hours after my arrival I was back once more in the station eagerly inquiring for the first train for Rome, for Calabria, for the Abruzzi, for anywhere, the further the better, only to get out of the hell. Had there been a train there would have been no 'Letters from a Mourning City'. As it was, there was no train till noon the next day, the communications with the infected city having been almost cut off.

All his life Munthe had helped people to die and made no secret of that. On the contrary, he saw it as the doctor's right and duty to hasten death for incurably ill patients. Stefan Zweig had interrogated him about different ways of committing suicide and now that he was severely ill himself he pondered how he could alleviate his agonies. To be sure, he had rejected suicide ('I much doubt I shall ever feel inclined to take my own life,' he wrote to Hilda in 1924), but during the last years of his life, Gustaf Munthe tells us, 'he enjoyed playing with the idea and wanted access to medicines in order to feel that he had mastery over his own life'. The child of Axel's cousin knew what he was talking about. When he visited Anacapri in October 1948 he was equipped with a letter in which Axel urged Vittorio to give Gustaf his Browning revolver to take with him to Stockholm. He also kept some poison (allegedly for his sick dogs in Capri) in a little cabinet next to his bed.

A Magnificent Donation

Munthe had made his last big donation, of 100,000 kronor, in 1935. During the war he resumed his charitable work in Sweden. In February 1944 the Committee for the Relief of Finnish Children received 5,000 kronor (80,000 in today's money), 'to be used for the relief of distressed Finnish refugees, people and animals', and in December he gave the same sum to Estonian Swedes who had moved to Sweden. So in the course of 1944 he gave away a good million kronor, or £750,000 in today's money. When it came to the Finnish refugees, this was not without a few flourishes: 'Charity and Vanity are twins with such a family likeness that short-sighted people often cannot tell them apart,' he declared, adding that he was 'grateful and glad to have got rid of my money in an honourable way'. Munthe's modesty was perhaps not entirely convincing, but his personal needs were genuinely few. For instance, he withdrew only 500 kronor a month from his bank for his personal needs. And Munthe's donations over the years show that in his case it is more important to look at the facts than at his words.

Gustaf Munthe thought that 'the key to Munthe's whole personality' was 'his warm heart': 'It was perhaps not always so easy to discover. He himself did all he could to hide it as thoroughly as possible under his usual mask of a cynic and poseur.' The fact that the poseur's mask concealed someone who throughout his life had paid instalments of his 'existential debt' is shown by all the more or less anonymous gifts of money that Munthe made during these years. He gave 10,000 kronor 'to German children'; he donated 5,000 kronor to pay off the 1944 dog licence fees for 'impoverished elderly people resident in Stockholm'; the Royal Veterinary College received 449 kronor for the upkeep of two Estonian dogs; old Lapps in homes for the elderly were given 250 kronor worth of tobacco and snuff every Christmas; and the organisation Europe's Children received 1,000 kronor. A more original work of charity was the tradition of treating the tramps in Stockholm's Old Town to a beer every Christmas.

Relatives and friends also received financial help. Both his sister Anna and Arnold's widow Edith got large sums on several occasions. In 1934 Malcolm got 5,000 kronor (125,000 in today's money) and £10,500 in 1945 (£260,000 in today's money). The cheques were sent anonymously but it is hard to believe that Malcolm would have had a problem identifying the sender.

In the wills that Munthe had hurriedly drawn up during his health crisis in 1940, it was the fate of San Michele that most preoccupied him. Ever since the mid-1930s he had toyed with the idea that after his death the villa could be converted into a recreational institute or something of the kind. After his return to Sweden he discussed the question on several occasions with Crown Prince Gustaf Adolf, to whom he wrote that he fully supported 'the plan to use San Michele as a base for students, artists, researchers and journalists on scholarships, to the benefit of our ties with Italy'. He found it difficult to decide how the handover should take place, but finally decided it should happen after his death. However, the 'magnificent donation' – in the words of the Crown prince – was made public during his lifetime, on 25 November 1946.

We Know We Shall Die, But We Don't Believe It

Munthe retained to the last his intellectual capacities and his unique memory: 'He could come up with the most unexpected associations of ideas, and his memories, even of things which lay very far back in time, could have a wonderful clarity,' Gustaf Munthe remembered:

> His sense of humour was in no way mild and indulgent. It was peppered with a fair amount of wit. Occasionally it could be quite merciless. He found it amusing to fire arrows dipped in generous amounts of poison. Some people he thought well of, others he could not abide. That he found it most amusing to talk about the latter goes without saying.

Munthe also retained his physical capabilities for a very long time, and was quick on his feet up to an advanced age. In the autumn of 1948 he was still showing a respectable electrocardiogram reading for his age and taking his usual walk round the Old Town. But he could not manage by himself, and after Vittorio returned to Italy in the summer of 1947 he had to try to find another helper.

Fate sent sister Brita Elmgren, who took him in hand during his last years and became his own 'Sister Philomène'. She read aloud to him. Many people have borne witness to her devotion and patience, and Munthe repaid her richly. In 1947 and 1948 she received cheques for a total of 42,000 kronor, which corresponds to £50,000 today.

Every summer, when the staff took their holidays, Munthe had to leave his rooms in the palace for a month. As late as the summer of 1946 he had gone to Solliden, but that journey was now too much of a strain. In the summer of 1947 he stayed in a resort hotel outside Stockholm, although he only went there after stout opposition. 'From his windows he looked out over a summer-blue bay, over swaying white-stemmed birches and high murmuring pines,' Gustaf Munthe recalled. 'He could hear the birds singing and the waves beating against the shore, and yet he was utterly miserable.' He longed to get back to his rooms in the palace and was 'seldom so happy as when he could return there after the summer excursion'. When he wrote to Hilda the following spring that he would very much like to spend the summer in Dalarna, she replied that she could not put up 'an invalid' at Stengården due to a lack of servants and suggested he book into a boarding house. Munthe paid three months' rent in advance but never got there; instead it was to be the resort hotel for the second year in a row.

On his ninety-first birthday on 31 October 1948, his rooms were filled with flowers. At Christmas, a small fir tree was set up in the apartment and his nurse read old psalms aloud. When the candles were lit Munthe asked Brita to lead him to the tree. He took off his hat, which he also wore indoors to shield his eyes from all kinds of strong light, and looked at the fir, lost in thought.

It was his last Christmas. Immediately after New Year his asthmatic problems turned into pneumonia, he developed a high fever and Malcolm and Peter flew up from London. The pneumonia was cured with the help of a new medicine, penicillin, and after a few days Axel recovered, to the astonishment of his sons and his doctors. 'Peter and I then – much to father's amusement – used to carry him from his bed into the little drawing-room next door,' Malcolm reported to Murray, 'where he sat for a short while each day. On our last evening he joked with us and spoke in his ringing voice.' The following day Malcolm and Peter flew back to London.

Josef Oliv – the Swedish journalist mentioned in the first lines of this book – remembered that one day Munthe asked him in a whisper what date it was. On being told it was 17 January, he mumbled to himself: 'The fires! The fires!' It was the feast of Saint Antonio Abate – the patron saint of animals – the day on which the poor of Naples light fires on the streets to keep the cold away. In the cold rooms of the Royal Palace in Stockholm Munthe's thoughts strayed to the land that for seventy years had given him so much warmth.

Hilda was in Lausanne but received a report about Munthe's condition from the boys. At the end of January she wrote to him:

> Dear Axel, I was so glad to hear from the boys that you were better, and now you must only think of getting back your strength and not worrying about anything – above all not about past things, or having given me

'bekymmer' [trouble] as you said to the boys. I could not 'come back', but I only think of you gently, and with balance and proportion in all that happened in this wonderful adventure we call 'Life'.

Unlike Axel, Hilda was inspired by strong religious convictions and a belief that our earthly life is only provisional, a transitional stage; and she tried to comfort him:

For I don't believe it is Real life at all – but just the last stage in animal evolution, with a glint of light in our little brains which makes us now and then realise truth. What we are able to even dimly conceive in our minds can always eventually be realised. This is our 'certificate', the *proof* that we shall 'carry on' further, and with much more scope, unhampered by the disharmony of the animal body. Death, as we stupidly call the change, is a birthday into freedom. I hope you will live on since you do not want to die, but I know you are safe if you go.

With my love, Hilda

Miraculously enough, Axel regained the use of his legs again and took a last walk along the palace corridor, supported by his nurse and Josef Oliv, who remembered that he quoted, half to himself, the words of Anatole France: 'We know that we shall die, but we do not believe it.' Shortly afterwards he suffered a series of small brain haemorrhages and gradually sank into a coma. He died at three o'clock in the afternoon on 11 February 1949. Death, which he had feared so much, showed itself merciful: he was beyond consciousness when, to use Hilda's expression, he 'crossed the bridge'. But he died alone, without either wife or sons by his side.

GOD'S PEACE

Two days later Dean Olle Nystedt of Storkyrkan (Stockholm's cathedral) held a short service in Munthe's apartment in the palace in the presence of the Crown prince, Gustaf Munthe, Brita Elmgren and several friends and close acquaintances. After prayers and the reading of a psalm, the coffin was carried out through the arched doorway of the palace chapel, where the palace guard stood at attention.

The funeral took place on 17 February in the Chapel of the Holy Cross. The king, the Crown prince and Prince Wilhelm were present, as were Sven Hedin and Sister Brita Elmgren. Malcolm and Peter had flown up from London, but not Hilda. On the king's wreath could be read : 'To my friend Axel Munthe with profound gratitude from Gustaf.' On Malcolm's and Peter's wreaths: 'Father love'. One wreath was conspicuously absent: Hilda's.

In his address the dean pointed out all the things that life had given Axel Munthe: 'The friendship of kings and queens, praise and riches, a mysterious power over human beings and animals, eyes which took in all of life's beauty and energy, and a heart which could feel tenderness and burn with ardour for the little ones of the world, for poor people and defenceless animals.' However, the dean was clear-sighted enough to see the contradictions in Munthe's personality:

> He who provided a sanctuary for birds to rest in during their long migrations felt himself like a captive bird in a cage. He who had such a marvellous power to bring peace to oppressed minds found it hard to attain peace himself. He who said that he loved St Francis all his life had little about him that was reminiscent of God's blithe jester, joyful to his dying day. On the contrary, he liked to turn an austere and harsh face towards his fellow-man. But if one was allowed to look more closely, one could sense a soft heart which longed for love, light and peace – God's peace.

After the ceremony Malcolm and Peter went up to the king and thanked him for the honour he had shown their father by his presence at the funeral. 'The king spoke with them for a long time, in a low voice and with obvious emotion,' according to a newspaper report: 'He appeared tired and depressed when he finally left the chapel, supported by the Crown Prince.'

Thus was laid to rest the queen's physician-in-ordinary, the lord of San Michele, the animals' friend, Axel Martin Fredrik Munthe, Empewow of Sina, born in Oscarshamn on 31 October 1857, died 11 February 1949 in the Royal Palace in Stockholm.

Post Mortem

I always wonder when people say he was so 'complex' and impossible to understand. He was as simple as a wayward child in spite of his very complete intelligence.

Hilda Munthe to John Murray, 1949

I N HIS WILL Munthe asked to be 'cremated in the simplest way possible', and that his ashes should be scattered in the sea. Despite the fact that the king hinted that Axel perhaps ought to have 'some little stone' in his native land, his sons decided to act according to the will, although it was illegal to treat ashes in this way.

Two days after the funeral Malcolm and Peter sneaked out of the palace with the urn wrapped in a little parcel and boarded a train to the west coast, where a childhood friend with a boat had promised to help them. The letter that Malcolm wrote to Jock Murray shows that Axel's last trip was no less dramatic than his life's journey:

> Our friend took us out to a bleak rocky island where his boat lay. By then unfortunately a violent storm had blown up and wireless warned all shipping by the 'storm alarm'. Our open boat proved too small for the high seas – so we had to abandon it but by a wonderful fortune came upon an old seaman who was willing – asking no questions whatever – to take us out in a life-boat with a powerful motor in it. He was a shrewd and understanding old ruffian and had a charming face. We went out to near the Pater Noster lighthouse in the North sea and there gave the ashes to the sea. And unbeknown to Peter and I our friend unwrapped a cloth from which he strewed masses of grey, red and yellow and white roses that floated on the great rolling waves. When we had turned back and were leaving the open sea behind the small islands you could still see in the distance like a jewelled veil the flowers lying on the tempestuous green water.

The empty urn was placed under the altar in the private chapel at Stengården, where it has stood ever since.

THE LAST LAST WILL

In a letter in the summer of 1947 Munthe had hinted that he planned to leave most of his fortune to 'poor old people in Sweden'. This did not happen, but in his final will, dated 16 November 1948, animals and the poor in both Sweden and Italy got their due – even if his 'warm heart' had burnt a large hole in his pocket during the years in Sweden: in 1943 he had a fortune of 1,147, 582.73 kronor (£1,250,000 today), at his death it had gone down almost by half.

This is how it looked, the final instalment of that debt which Munthe had been paying off throughout his whole adult life:

1) To the Swedish state my property San Michele as it stands at present with the adjacent Foresteria to be occupied after my death and administered by the Swedish Institute in Rome;

2) To my son, Major Malcolm Munthe, Torre di Materita as it stands at present with furniture and art treasures to be occupied after my death and be an inheritance for his sons;

3) To my son Viking the Villa Sole in Anacapri as it stands at present reserving the right of Baroness Gudrun von Uexküll to have the use of it and to dwell in it in the event that her own villa is confiscated;

4) To Baroness Uexküll ten thousand (10,000) kronor and the literary rights to The Story of San Michele;

5) To Rosina Massimino five thousand (5,000) kronor with the right to live on at Materita until her death;

6) To Natasha Khaliutine three thousand (3,000) kronor;

7) To the poor old people in Anacapri to be administered by the municipality twenty thousand (20,000) kronor;

8) For Animal Protection in Sweden, especially for campaigning against menageries and for the protection of migratory birds to be administered by the Swedish National Association of Animal Protection Societies one hundred thousand (100,000) kronor;

9) To the poor old people in the Old Town to be administered by the Dean of Storkyrkan ten thousand (10,000) kronor;

10) To old Lapps herding reindeer ten thousand (10,000) kronor;

11) To Sister Brita Elmgren twenty-five thousand (25,000) kronor.

The remaining cash went to his sons. Hilda was not named in the will nor did she regard herself as 'entitled to any marital right to half the property or any part whatsoever of the personal estate'. She did not have nor did she wish to have any part in either his life or his death. In fact, there were not many who knew that Munthe was married: in the register of deaths and burials the column headed 'The deceased's marital status' contains a question mark.

SAN MICHELE

Since San Michele had not been maintained for years and was in need of comprehensive and expensive repairs, the government was dubious about the donation, which was, however, finally accepted. The state-run San Michele Foundation was set up on 16 June 1950 with the aim of promoting cultural ties between Sweden and Italy.

From the start the Villa San Michele fulfilled two roles – as a guesthouse for scholarship-holders and as a museum. The scholarship-holders stayed in the Foresteria, and, from the mid-1950s, in newly built apartments on the vine-covered hill behind. At the same time, after the war the stream of tourists became ever more copious. The people who had worked for Munthe earlier at San Michele were now employed by the foundation. As before, a certain proportion of the income from tickets went to the poor of the island.

Axel Munthe's remaining properties on Capri soon passed out of the family's possession. Peter sold the Villa Sole and Malcolm Torre di Materita, his father's actual home in Anacapri. When Materita was sold in the 1960s it was mainly because Hilda, whom Malcolm loved above all, did not want to live on Capri. Instead, Malcolm bought a large Renaissance palace, Castello Lunghezza, outside Rome, around which he wove a myth even more powerful than that which his father had created around San Michele. The kernel of this myth was that in the 1880s Axel had received Castello Lunghezza as a present from the childless Count Strozzi, so that he could look after his patients there. In reality, it was acquired long after his death.

Hilda had done all she could to protect her sons from Axel's influence, but Malcolm was more like his father than he believed or was willing to acknowledge, and he felt just as much at home in the no man's land between fact and fiction where Axel preferred to dwell.

As for Stengården, it was renamed Hildasholm after Hilda's death in 1967 and is now a museum.

ACKNOWLEDGEMENTS

A XEL MUNTHE IS a person who leaves no one indifferent even today; on the contrary, the mystique surrounding him seems to have grown ever denser with time. If this book can in any way contribute to dispelling this it is because of the positive reactions I have met from everyone whom I have been in contact with in the process of writing it.

Anyone who writes a book based on source material is indebted to many, not least to owners of private archives. First of all, I would like to mention the Munthe family's own archive, to which Axel Munthe's grandchildren Adam and Katriona Munthe have given me access without conditions or restrictions. The same generous attitudes have characterised keepers of other archives as well: John Murray, Albert Bonnier (publishers), Edward Cederlund, Carl and Nils Bildt, Henric and Anita Ankarcrona, Lars Erik Böttiger and Prins Bernhard of Baden. To them I wish to express my deep gratitude. I also want to thank H.M. King Carl XVI Gustaf for his accommodating attitude to my work, which deals so intimately with his great grandmother, Queen Victoria of Sweden.

During his long life Axel Munthe left traces all over Europe, and without the help of enthusiasts in various countries this book would have been thinner in all respects. Among those whom I wish to thank are: in Rome, Roberta Graziano, without whose energetic efforts the part about Mussolini's secret police could not have been written; in Anacapri, Vittorio Massimino, Axel Munthe's assistant, whom I have interviewed on several occasions; in London, John and Virginia Murray; in Paris, Véronique Leroux-Hugon at the Charcot Library; in Sweden, all those connected with Munthe's home town Vimmerby and with his house in Dalarna, now a museum, first and foremost Kersti Jobs and Sune Björklöf, Mats Persson, Anders Lindström, Pia Thunholm and Menard Karlsson, as well as Göran Samuelson and members of the von Mecklenburg family.

The following persons have been helpful in different ways during the work on the book: Hans Henrik Brummer, Princess Elizabeth of Bavaria, T.G.H. James, Ulf Linde, Gunnar Munthe, Henrik Munthe, Sten Åke Nilsson,

Wivi-Anne Nilsson, Jean Nicou, Thomas Steinfeld, Cecilia Svensson, Elisabeth Tarras-Wahlberg, Ewa von Uexküll, Anne-Marie Westrin and Karin Wiking.

A special word of thanks goes to Turi Munthe, Axel Munthe's great grandson, whose perspicacious commentaries contributed to making the book more readable for English readers; and to Harry D. Watson, who has translated it.

The Swedish version of the book, *En osalig ande* (Stockholm 2003), is more comprehensive than the one the reader is now holding, covering Axel Munthe's childhood and Paris years in much greater detail. It also contains foot-notes to all quotations.

Bengt Jangfeldt
31 October 2007

ABBREVIATIONS

AB	Albert Bonnier's (publishers) Archive
AF	Ankarcrona Family Archive
ArkM	Museum of Architecture, Stockholm
ATA	Antiquarian-Topographical Archives, Stockholm
B	University of Birmingham, The Library, Special Collections
BF	Böttiger Family Archive, Stockholm
BFA	Bernadotte Family Archive
BL	British Library, Manuscript Collections
Bodleian	University of Oxford, Bodleian Library
BSA	Bildt Family Archive
CC	Churchill College, Cambridge
CK	Christina Kihl's Archive
CS	Cecilia Svensson's Archive
CU	Cornell University Library
Cumbria	Cumbria Record Office, Carlisle
EC	Edward Cederlund's Archive
FC	Fredonia College, NY State
GUB	University Library, Gothenburg, manuscript section
H	Hildasholm Archive, Leksand
HH	Harvard University, Houghton Library
JM	John Murray, London
KA	Royal Academy of Fine Arts, Stockholm
KB	Royal Library, Stockholm, manuscript section
KBK	Royal Library, Copenhagen, manuscript section
KVA	Royal Academy of Sciences, Stockholm
LS	Linköping Municipal Library
LUB	University Library, Lund, manuscript section
LVA	County Archive, Varberg
M	Axel Munthe's Archive, The National Archives of Sweden
MB	S.K.H. Markgraf von Baden's Archive, Salem
MFA	Munthe family's private archive, London
MM	Metropolitan Museum of Art, New York, manuscript section
MS	Munthe Family archive, The National Archives of Sweden
NBO	National Library, Oslo, manuscript section
NLS	National Library of Scotland, Edinburgh

NM   National Museum, Stockholm, manuscript section
NoM   Nordic Museum, Stockholm
RA   The National Archives of Sweden
SA   Swedish Academy, Stockholm
SFM   Stockholm Industrial archive
SKP   Swedish Church in Paris
SM   Villa San Michele, Anacapri
SR   Swedish Institute in Rome
SS   Stockholm Municipal Archive
UA   University of Texas at Austin, Harry Ransom Humanities Research Center
UD   Swedish Foreign Ministry Archive, Foreign ministry
UD 1902   Swedish Foreign Ministry Archive, filing system of 1902, Swedish National Archive
ULA   County Archive, Uppsala
UUB   University Library, Uppsala, manuscript section
W   Prins Eugen's Waldemarsudde, Stockholm
VaLA   County Archive, Vadstena
YU   Yale University, Beinecke Rare Book and Manuscript Library
Z   Zorn collections, Mora

Unpublished Sources

Letters

Below are all senders and recipients of letters quoted in the book as well as some who do not feature. The archives are given in parentheses (see list of abbreviations above).

From Axel Munthe to

Adlersparre, Sophie (KB, I a 7a:2)
Åkerhielm, Ebba (private collection)
Arne, T.J. (ATA)
Asquith (Lady Oxford), Margot, née Tennant (Bodleian)
Balfour, Edith (married name: Lyttelton) (CC)
Beck-Friis, Augustin (SM; UD, Swedish legation in Rome, P50: Casa Caprile 1941–54)
Bentinck, Violet (SM E1:1)
Bildt, Carl (RA, Swedish legation in Rome, F2:52)
Bjørnson, Bjørnstjerne (NBO)
Blackwood, William (NLS)
Bonham-Carter, Violet (Bodleian)
Bonnier, Albert; Karl Otto; Bonniers, publishers (AB)
Böttiger, John (BF)
Brett Young, Francis and Jessica (B)
Cariello, L. (SM, not catalogued)
Carter, Howard (MM)
Cederström, Carola (NM, Axel Gauffin's collection)
Cederström, Gustaf (UUB; KB, C I k:5)
Céligny de Solal, Cathérine (SM)
Compton Mackenzie, Montague and Faith (UA)
Cunninghame Graham, Robert (NLS)
Curzon, Frederick (SM, E1:1)
Dawson, Geoffrey (SM)
Edgren, Anne Charlotte (née Leffler) (KB)

Pennington Mellor, Catherine (H; M, Add. 2000)
Persson, Daniel (RA, Daniel Persson's archive)
Peters, A.D. (MFA)
Peterson, S.A. (MS, Vol. 115)
Philip von Hessen, Prince (M, Vol. 5)
Printzsköld, Otto (KB, Printzsköld's autograph collection)
Retzius, Gustaf (KVA; Gustaf Retzius's and Anna Hierta-Retzius's collections)
Reventlow, Ferdinand (RA, Swedish legation in Rome, F2:50)
Reynolds, Richard (M, Vol. 1)
Rothenstein, William and lady (HH)
Shoobridge, Mr (SM)
Sibbern, Georg (NBO)
Snoilsky, Carl (KB, S 21, 25, 38, 39:12)
Söderblom, Nathan (UUB, Nathan Söderblom's archive)
Sophia, Drottning (BFA, Queen Sophia's archive, Vol. 10; SM)
Story, Maud (Broadwood) (UA)
Svensson, Elsa (SM, F3:2)
Trolle, Alice (KB, L 92:2)
Varlese, G. (M, Vol. 6)
Victoria, Crown Princess, Queen (M, Vol. 2; MB)
Vivian, lord (SM, E1:1)
Wahlman, Lars Israel (NM)
Wahlström, P.K. (SS)
Wallbom, Mrs (SM, F4:1)
Walpole, Hugh (UA)
Warburg, Karl (KB, V 27:17)
Warden, Miss (SM, E1:1)
West, Rebecca (YU)
Zweig, Stefan (FC)

To Axel Munthe from

Bentinck, Violet (M, Vol. 2)
Bildt, Carl (RA, Swedish legation in Rome, F2:52)
Birger, Matilde (MS, Add. 1998)
Bismarck, Eddie (M, Vol. 1)
Bjerlöv, H. (MS, Add. 1998)
Bonnier, Albert; Karl Otto, Bonniers, publishers (M, Vol. 3; AB)
Carnarvon, Elsie (M, Vol. 2)
Carter, Howard (M, Vol. 2)
Dawson, Geoffrey (M, Vol. 6)
De Geer, Jean Jacques (M, Vol. 2; H)
Dillon, E.J. (SM, E1:1)
Douglas-Pennant, Hilda (M, Vol. 2)
Falk, Johan (M, Vol. 6)

Farrar Smith, Stuart (M, Vol. 2)
Fernald, C.B. (M, Vol. 3)
Galsworthy, John (M, Vol. 2)
Grut, Torben (M, Vol. 2)
Gustaf V, King (UD, Swedish legation in Rome, P50: Casa Caprile 1941–54)
Gustaf Adolf, Crown Prince (MS, Add. 1998)
Hedin, Sven (M, Vol. 2)
Holm, G.B.A., Norstedts, publishers (SFM, BIA:16; BIA:18–20)
Howard, Esme (M, Vol. 2)
Johnstone, Dorothy ('David') (SM, E1:1; M, Add. 2000)
King, Arthur (M, Vol. 1)
Kipling, Rudyard (M, Vol. 2)
Lindqvist, Märta (KB, L 52:9)
Luise of Baden (SM)
MacVeagh, E. (M, Vol. 1)
MacVeagh, Margaretta (M, Vol. 2)
Manker, Ernst (NoM, Ernst Manker's collection)
Maria, Princess (M, Vol. 2)
Martin, Fredrik (M, Vol. 2)
Max von Baden, Prince (M, Add. 2000)
Montelius, Oscar (ATA, Oscar Montelius's archive, Corr., Vol. 25)
Morrell, Ottoline (M, Vol. 2)
Munthe, Arnold (H; SM, E1:1; MS, Vol. 114)
Munthe, Hilda (SM, E1:1)
Murray, John (M, Vol. 2, 3; JM)
Northcliffe, Lord (M, Vol. 1)
Orczy, Emmuska (M, Vol. 1)
Pagenstecher, Hermann (M, Vol. 2)
Peters, A.D. (MFA, M, Vol. 3)
Pinsent, Cecil (M, Vol. 1)
Redlich, Fr. B. (M, Vol. 2)
Reynolds, Richard (M, Vol. 1)
Rodocanachi, Paul (M, Vol. 2)
Scholander, Sven (KB, L14:16)
Sophia, Queen (SM, not catalogued)
Söderblom, Nathan (MS, Add. 1998; UUB, Nathan Söderblom's archive)
Stokowski, Leopold (SM)
Uexküll, Gudrun von (M, Vol. 2; SM, F4:1)
Victoria, Crown Princess, Queen (M, Vol. 2; MFA)

Correspondence Between Other People

Allenby, Edmund to Howard Carter (MM)
Ankarcrona, Wivica to Sten, Helena and Gaella Ankarcrona (AF)

Beck-Friis, Augustin to Otto Printzsköld (RA, Swedish legation in Rome, P50: Da)

Bergman, Agnes to Hilda Munthe (H)

Bildt, Carl to Harald Bildt (BSA), Magnus Brahe (RA, Swedish legation in Rome, F2:50), Albert Ehrensvärd (RA, Swedish legation in Rome, F2:52; UD 1902, Vol. 123, 2 E:31), Claes Lagergren (NoM), Carl Anton Ossbahr (BSA), Carl Rosenblad (RA, Swedish legation in Rome, F2:50), Erik Trolle (RA, Swedish legation in Rome, F2:50)

Birger, Hugo to Pontus Fürstenberg (GUB)

Björnberg, Tor to Josef Oliv (SM, E5:1)

Bjørnson, Bjørnstjerne to Bergliot Bjørnson (married name: Ibsen) and Bjørn Bjørnson (NBO), F.V. Hegel (KBK)

Brahe, Magnus to Carl Bildt (RA, Swedish legation in Rome, F2:50)

Brett Young, Francis to Jessica Brett Young, Charles Evans and Martin Secker (B)

Bruzelius, Ragnar to Oscar II (BFA, Oscar II's archive, Vol. 50)

Brändström, Edward to Albert Ehrensvärd (RA, UD 1902, Vol. 995, 16 L:38)

Cederlund, Mathilda to Edward Cederlund Jr. (EC)

Cerio, Edwin to Francis Brett Young (B)

De la Gardie, Casimir to Carl Bildt (RA, Swedish legation in Rome, F2:50)

Edgren (Leffler), A.C. to her family (KB, L4b:22), Adam Hauch (KB, L4b:19:2), Gösta Mittag-Leffler (KB, L4b:24)

Elkan, Sophie to her mother (KB, L 84:3–3)

Eugen, Prince to Helena Nyblom (W)

Graham, J.C. to A.D. Peters (MFA)

Hedberg, Tor to his sister and parents (SA)

Heidenstam, Verner von to Oscar Levertin (KB, dep. 12:2,4)

Hemsted, Edith to Dr. Savage (M, Vol. 2)

Johnstone, Dorothy to John Murray (JM)

Key, Ellen to Rainer Maria Rilke (KB, MfH 225:1–5)

Larsson, Carl to Georg Pauli (NM, Georg Pauli's correspondence)

Lovén, Christian to Gustaf Munthe (SM, E8:1)

Mallet, Louis to the British Red Cross (M, Vol. 6)

Massimino, Vittorio to Elsa Svensson (SM, F3)

Munthe (married name: Norstedt), Anna to her parents (MS, Vol. 114), Klara Johansson (KB, L2:7), Ellen Key (KB, L41:55), C.G. Laurin (SS), Ludvig W: son Munthe (MS, Vol. 33, 115)

Munthe, Arnold to his parents (MS, Vol. 114), Ludvig W:son Munthe (MS, Vol. 33)

Munthe, Aurora to her children (MS, Vol. 114; Add. 1998)

Munthe, Hilda to Gustaf Boëthius (GUB), her parents (H; M, Add. 2000), Axel Munthe (MFA), Ludvig W:son Munthe (MS, Vol. 33), John Murray (H), Emma Zorn (Z)

Munthe, Malcolm to Axel Boëthius (GUB), Hilda Munthe (H), John ('Jock') Murray (JM)

Munthe, Peter to Hilda Munthe (H)
Munthe, Ultima to Ludvig W:son Munthe (MS, Vol. 33)
Nyblom, Helena to Prince Eugen (W)
Ossbahr, Carl Anton to Carl Bildt (BSA), Fredrik Vult von Steijern (KB, dep. 50), Anders Zorn (Z)
Palmstierna, Carl Fredrik to Erik Berggren (SM, E6:1)
Peters, A.D. to Carol Hill (MFA),
Printzsköld, Otto to Stockholms Enskilda Bank (RA, Swedish legation in Rome, P50:Da)
Rennell Rodd, James to Howard Carter (MM), Hill (M, Vol. 1)
Rilke, Rainer Maria to Ellen Key (KB, L41:63:11)
Rosenblad, Carl to Carl Bildt (RA, Swedish legation in Rome, F2:50)
Snoilsky, Carl to A.C. Edgren (Leffler) (KB, L4b:10), Gustaf Retzius (KVA)
Snoilsky, Ebba to Anna Hierta-Retzius (KVA, Anna Hierta-Retzius's collection)
Victoria, Queen to Carl Bildt (RA, Swedish legation in Rome, F2:52; UD), Hilda Munthe (H), Max of Baden (MB)
White, Maude Valérie to Matthew Arnold (JM), Edith Balfour (CC), John Murray (JM)
Zorn, Anders to Emma Zorn (Z)
Zorn, Emma to her mother (Z)

AXEL MUNTHE'S MANUSCRIPTS

'Croix rouge et Croix de fer' (SM)
Notebooks, commonplace books, prescription books, address books (M, H, SM)
'Götterdämmerung' (MFA; M, Vol. 5)
'The Problem of Vivisection. Towards a Solution' (MS, Add.)
'The Story of San Michele' (MFA)

OTHER MANUSCRIPTS AND DOCUMENTS

British Foreign Office (FO 371/37263A). Public Records Office, London
Martin, Fredrik, Manuscript of a book about Axel Munthe, 1932 (ATA, T.J. Arne's archive, Vol. 63)
'Mathilda Cederlund's letters compiled by Christian Lovén'. Typescript (CS)
Munthe, Ludvig W:son, 'Memoirs' I–IV (MS, Vol. 90)
Murray, John (V), Note after a conversation with Axel Munthe, 15.11.28 (JM)
Murray, John (VI; 'Jock'), Notes after a conversation with Axel Munthe, September 1936 and June 1937 (JM)
Laurie, Jerry, 'A Faithful Likeness'. [About Maude Valérie White and Axel Munthe] (JM)

Polizia politica. Archivio centrale dello Stato, Roma. Fascicoli personali: Axel Munth [sic], busta 881

St James's Club (London Metropolitan Archives. St James's Club. Minute Book 1901–1905)

Swedish Church in Paris (SKP, a:1)

Tarras-Wahlberg (married name: O'Brien ffrench), Maud [Memories of Axel Munthe], 1957 (SM, Ö1:1)

Westling (née Lund), Sofia [Memories of Axel Munthe] (SM, F2:1)

DIARIES

Cederlund, Edward jr (EC)
Celsing, Ulla (W)
Keiller (Bildt), Alexandra (SR)
Kempe, Bertha (CK)
Norstedt, Reinhold (KA)
Sibbern, Georg (NBO)

OTHER SOURCES

Estate administrations: Fredrik Munthe 1878-III-42; Aurora Munthe 1880-IV-334 1/2 (SS)

Population registers (SS)

School catalogues from Vimmerby and Stockholm (VaLA, SS, AII:2)

SELECTED BIBLIOGRAPHY

With the exception of books pertaining directly to Axel Munthe's life and work, this bibliography contains no references to Swedish sources used in the book.

Amiel, Henri-Frédéric, *Fragments d'un journal intime*, I, Geneva 1885 (4th edn); II, Geneva 1884 (2nd edn) [Munthe's copy with underlinings]
Andrén, Arvid, *Capri from Stone Age to the Tourist Age*, Gothenberg 1980
Arnold, Tonni, *Balladen om Marie: En biografi över Marie Krøyer*, Stockholm 2000
Asquith, Margot, *Places & Persons*, London 1925
Babini, Valeria, *Una 'donna nuova'. Il femminismo scientifico di Maria Montessori*, Milan 2000
Bonde, Knut, *I skuggan av San Michele*, Stockholm 1946
Bonduelle, Michel, Gelfand, Toby and Goetz, Christopher G., *Charcot, un grand médecin dans son siècle*, Paris 1996
Bonduelle, Michel, 'Léon Daudet, mémorialiste de Charcot', *La Revue du Practicien* 1999:49
Brendon, Piers, *The Dark Valley: A Panorama of the 1930's*, London 2000
Bret Harte, Geoffrey, 'A Famous Italian Villa. San Michele, Capri. The Property of Dr. Axel Munthe', *Country Life* 16 December 1933
—— 'A Castle of Capri. Torre di Materita. The Residence of Dr. Axel Munthe', *Country Life* 23 December 1933
—— 'Barbarossa and the Birds. Axel Munthe's Sanctuary at Capri', *Country Life* 20 January 1934
Brett Young, Jessica, *Francis Brett Young: A Biography*, London 1962
Broche, François, *La IIIᵉ République 1870–1895: De Thiers à Casimir-Perier*, Paris 2001
Brummer, Hans Henrik, 'Villa San Michele', *Artes* 4, 1999
Burton, Robert, *The Anatomy of Melancholy*, London 1621 (reprinted 1932)
Cannadine, David, *The Decline and Fall of the British Aristocracy*, London 1990
Cerio, Edwin, *L'Aria di Capri*, Naples 1927
—— 'Voices from Capri', in *The Story of Axel Munthe, Capri and San Michele*, Malmö 1959
—— *La vita e la figura di un uomo*, Rome n.d.
Compton Mackenzie, Faith, *As Much as I Dare*, London 1938

Compton Mackenzie, Montague, *My Life and Times, Octave 4, 1807–1914,* London 1965; *Octave 5, 1915–1923,* London 1966

Douglas, Lord Alfred, *Without Apology,* London 1938

Douglas, Norman, *Looking Back: An Autobiographical Excursion,* London 1934

Dunbar, Janet, *Mrs. G.B.S.: A Biographical Portrait of Charlotte Shaw,* London 1963

Edel, Leon, *Henry James: The Treacherous Years 1895–1900,* London 1969

Emessen, T.T (ed.), *Aus Görings Schreibtisch: Ein Dokumentfund,* Berlin 1947

Ellman, Richard, *Oscar Wilde,* London 1987

Erdeös, Levente A.S., *Axel Munthe's Villa in the Capri Sun,* Anacapri 2006

Eulenburg, Philipp zu, *Mit dem Kaiser als Staatsmann und Freund auf Nordlandreisen,* I–II, Dresden 1931

Fiorani, Tito, *Le dimore del mito,* Capri 1996

Fuller, Sophie, 'Maude Valérie White', *The New Grove Dictionary of Music and Musicians,* XXVII, London 2001 (2nd edn)

Gelfand, Toby, 'Medical Nemesis, Paris, 1894: Léon Daudet's *Les Morticoles',* *Bulletin of the History of Medicine* 60, 1986

Göring, Emmy, *An der Seite meines Mannes,* Göttingen 1967

Gorkij, Maxim, 'Lenin', *Literaturnye portrety,* Moscow 1983

Graziano, Roberta, *Il passato ha l'ombra lunga,* Rome 2001

Greene, Graham (ed.), *An Impossible Woman: The Memories of Dottoressa Moor of Capri,* London 1975

Hallengren, Anders, *Campagna per la felicità: L'avventura Caprese e Napoletana di Anne Charlotte Leffler, duchessa di Caianello,* Stockholm 2001

Hellqvist, Per-Anders, *Där citroner blomma,* Värnamo 1990

Helwig, Werner, *Capri, magische Insel,* Frankfurt-am-Main 1979

Howard, Esme (Lord Howard of Penrith), *Theatre of Life,* I–II, London 1935–36

James, T.G.H., *Howard Carter: The Path to Tutankhamun,* London and New York 1992

Jangfeldt, Bengt, *Drömmen om San Michele,* Stockholm 2000 (with the photographer Ingalill Snitt)

—— *En osalig ande: Berättelsen om Axel Munthe,* Stockholm 2003

—— *Munthe's Capri,* Stockholm 2005

Jansson, Heribert, *Drottning Victoria,* Stockholm 1963

Johannisson, Karin, *Den mörka kontinenten,* Södertälje 1994

Kesel, Humbert, *Capri: Biographie einer Insel,* Munich 1971

Klercker, Cecilia af, *Förgången glans,* Stockholm 1944

Krupskelis, Ignas K. and Berkeley James, Elizabeth M. (eds), *The Correspondence of William James,* III, Charlotteville and London 1994

Leone De Andreis, Marcella, *Capri 1939,* Rome 2002

Leroux-Hugon, Véronique, 'L'évasion manquée de Geneviève, ou des aléas de la traduction', *Hist. Psychiat. Psychoanal,* 2:4, 1987

—— 'La laïcisation des hôpitaux de Paris et la création des écoles d'infirmières', in *De Bourneville à la sclérose tubéreuse,* Paris 1991

Lyttelton, Edith, *The Sinclair Family,* London 1925

Marie, Grand Duchess of Russia, *Education of a Princess: A Memoir*, New York 1930

Maylunas, Andrei and Mironenko, Sergei (eds), *A Lifelong Passion: Nicholas and Alexandra: Their Own Story*, New York 1997

Money, James, *Capri: Island of Pleasure*, London 1986

Morani-Helbig, Lili, *Jugend im Abendrot: Römische Erinnerungen*, Stuttgart 1953

Morrell, Ottoline, *The Early Memoirs of Lady Ottoline Morrell 1873–1915*, London 1963

M.T. [Margot Tennant], *A Little Journey in the Winter of 1891 and a Week in Glasgow July 1892*, privately printed 1892

Munthe, Axel, *Prophylaxie et traitement des hémorrhagies post-partum. Thèse pour le Doctorat en Médicine, presentée et soutenue le 2 août 1880*, Paris 1880

—— *Från Napoli. Resebref*, Stockholm 1885

—— *Letters from a Mourning City*, London 1887 (1899)

—— *Små skizzer*, Stockholm 1888

—— *Vagaries*, London 1898

—— *Memories & Vagaries*, London 1908

—— *Bref och skisser*, Stockholm 1909 (reprinted 1910)

—— *La città dolente. Lettere da Napoli*, Naples 1910

—— *Red Cross & Iron Cross*, London 1916 (under the pseudonym 'A Doctor in France'; in 1930 under his own name)

—— *The Story of San Michele*, London 1929

Munthe, Curt, *Munthe från Flandern: Släktens svenska öden*, Stockholm 1963

Munthe, Gustaf, *Axel Munthe*, Stockholm 1949

——— and Uexküll, Gudrun, *The Story of Axel Munthe*, London 1953

Munthe, Ludvig and Åke W:son, *Släkten Munthe i Sverige . . . Genealogiska och biografiska anteckningar*, Växjö 1931

Munthe, Malcolm, *Sweet is War*, London 1954 (reprinted 2000)

—— 'My father', in *The Story of Axel Munthe, Capri and San Michele*, Malmö 1959

Nouaille, Henri, *Considérations médicales sur la vie et l'œuvre du docteur Axel Munthe*, Toulouse 1950

Oliv, Josef, 'Axel Munthe's Life and Work', in *The Story of Axel Munthe, Capri and San Michele*, Malmö 1959

—— *Vägen till San Michele*, Stockholm 1972

Olsson, Bror, 'Axel Munthe as an Author', in *The Story of Axel Munthe, Capri and San Michele*, Malmö 1959

Origo, Iris, *Images and Shadows*, London 1998

Oxford (Asquith), Margot, *More Memories*, London 1933

Palmer, R.R., *A History of the Modern World*, New York 1951

Peyrefitte, Roger, *The Exile of Capri*, London 1961

Platen, Gustaf von, *Bakom den gyllne fasaden: Gustaf V och Victoria*, Uddevalla 2002

Rainer Maria Rilke – Ellen Key. Briefwechsel, Frankfurt-am-Main and Leipzig 1993

Ring, Jim, *How the English Made the Alps*, London 2000

Rodd, Rennell, *Social and Diplomatic Memories 1884–1893*, London 1922

Russell, Bertrand, *Autobiography*, I, London 1967

Ryersson, Scot D. and Orlando Vaccario, Michael, *Infinite Variety: The Life and Legend of the Marchesa Casati*, New York 1999

Salières, François, *Écrivains contre médecins*, Paris 1948

Seiler, Helena, *Axel Munthe und sein Werk 'Red Cross and Iron Cross': die Auseinandersetzung mit der deutschen Ärzteschaft 1932/33 um ein in Deutschland unbekanntes Buch*, Munich 1992

Seymour, Miranda, *Ottoline Morrell: Life on a Grand Scale*, London 1992

Sheridan, Clare, *Nuda Veritas*, London 1928

Snowden, Frank M., *Naples in the Time of Cholera 1884–1911*, Cambridge 1995

Steinfeld, Thomas, *Der Arzt von San Michele*, Munich 2007

Strada, Vittorio (ed.), *L'altra rivoluzione*, Capri 1994

Tjerneld, Staffan, *Den mystiske dr Munthe*, Stockholm 1973

Tolstoi, Leo, *What I Believe*, London 1885

Werner, Arthur (ed.), *Begegnung mit Stefan Zweig: Ein Buch der Erinnerung*, Vienna 1972

Wilde, Oscar, *The Complete Letters of Oscar Wilde*, London 2000

Vandyne, Mary E., 'Sketches of Capri', *Harper's New Monthly Magazine*, June 1888

White, Maude Valérie, *Friends and Memories*, London 1914

Wiking, Karin, *Memories of a Swedish War Nurse*, Maine 2002

Winstone, H.V.F., *Howard Carter and the Discovery of the Tomb of Tutankhamun*, London 1991

Index

PICTURE CREDITS